Traveling Beyond Her Sphere

Traveling Beyond Her Sphere:

American Women on the Grand Tour, 1814-1914

Bess Beatty

Washington DC

Copyright © 2016 by Bess Beatty

New Academia Publishing, 2016

All rights reserved. No part of this book may be reproduced or transmitted in any form or by any means, electronic or mechanical, including photocopying, recording, or by any information storage and retrieval system.

Printed in the United States of America

Library of Congress Control Number: 2016906821
ISBN 978-0-9974962-2-2 paperback (alk. paper)
ISBN 978-0-9974962-3-9 hardcover (alk. paper)

4401-A Connecticut Ave., NW #236 - Washington DC 20008
info@newacademia.com - www.newacademia.com

All photos and illustrations are reprinted with permission.

For Dieter Risch
Danke für Alles

Contents

Acknowledgments	ix
Preface: I Do Love Freedom So: Women and the Grand Tour	1
Chapter I: A Trip to Europe Became the Great Desire of My Heart: Imagining a Grand Tour	11
Chapter II: Prelude to the Unknown Joys of Europe: Across the Atlantic for a Grand Tour	33
Chapter III: Getting Along the Best We Could: Quotidian Demands of a Grand Tour	69
Chapter IV: My Dreams Were All of London, Paris, Rome: Itineraries of a Grand Tour	119
Chapter V: In the Land of Tell: Outdoor Adventures on a Grand Tour	179
Chapter VI: Wondering at Myself for Being Here: A Grand Tour Alone and Together	199
Chapter VII: How I Wish I Was Safely Out of This: The Titanic, the Great War and a New Grand Tour	231
Epilogue: Laying Up Stores of Knowledge and Experience: After a Grand Tour	243
Notes	245
Bibliography	293
Index	311

Acknowledgments

I was a member of the history department faculty of Oregon State University when I began this book. I thank colleagues there as well as those at the University of Oregon who offered me early encouragement and advice. An Oregon State Library Research Grant facilitated my first research and a Humanities Center Fellowship afforded me time to begin writing. Wendy Williams invited me to give a lecture in a series honoring her husband, William Appleman Williams; Julee Raiskin twice invited me to present my work-in-progress to classes at the University of Oregon. These talks were early opportunities to present my ideas publicly. Responses to papers I presented outside the United States gave me an international perspective. I especially thank my colleagues in the University of Zagreb's Department of English Studies where I was a Fulbright Scholar in 2005-2006 and apologize that I did not make reference to their wonderful city.

A number of friends and colleagues have offered me shelter which made it possible to extend the range of my research. Keith Crudgington and John McCole loaned their apartment near Harvard and Mary Stevenson welcomed me into her home in Brookline; their generosity made a lengthy research trip in the Boston area possible. Nell Cant's hospitality (along with that of KLJ, SLJ, SvC, WW and LL) facilitated research at Duke and UNC. Howard Brick and Debbie Swartz, Cynthia Brokaw and Carol Berkin have also housed me for short research trips in their hometowns.

Several colleagues read part or all of the manuscript. Marilyn Farwell read several chapters early on and offered a number of useful suggestions. Laura Ferguson took time from writing her dissertation to read a complete draft and generously shared her skills as a historian. I am particularly thankful for her advice about recent secondary sources I needed to consult. Carol Berkin has been reading bits and pieces for years and has offered sound advice as well as the encouragement that was necessary to see this project to completion. Susannah Delfino forgave my apostasy in leaving behind southern textile workers and read the entire manuscript. She saved me from several errors about Italy as did Dieter Risch about Germany. Jenna Johnson did a thorough edit of a draft and helped shape the final book. Donna Baker offered good advice on a variety of matters. It was my great good fortune that Brenda Turner agreed to edit the completed manuscript; she is not only an excellent editor, but also has a keen eye for historical detail and saved me from errors. Nell Cant (with input from SLJ) also read the final version and is also an excellent editor. More errors were averted.

The input of several traveling companions has been more indirect yet still meaningful. Bobbi Christie was my companion and guide on several early trips to Europe. My Mother, Eleanor Spratt Hacker, was my mentor on all things Guido Reni; I apologize that he is not as esteemed here as she would have wanted. My sister, Nell Cant, joins me in pursuit of all things Roman.

My grandmother, Nell Rankin Spratt, and my great aunt, Bess Rankin, who traveled to Europe through books, did not live to see this book begun, but their spirit is in it. My mother and my aunts, Frances Spratt and Elizabeth Spratt, did not live to see the book finished, but their many years of encouragement and support made it possible.

I have twice had the good fortune to sail around the world as a professor for Semester at Sea. Thanks to all of my mates on my voyages in the Spring of 2008 and the Spring of 2011 who joined my adventures as we traveled far beyond our accustomed spheres. I especially thank Dieter Risch who shared the first voyage and many travel adventures since. This book is dedicated to him.

Preface

I Do Love Freedom So: Women and the Grand Tour

After his nine-month-long visit to the United States in the 1830s, Frenchman Alexis de Tocqueville, whose keen-eyed observations were later published as *Democracy in America*, posited that "the inexorable opinion of the public carefully circumscribes women within the narrow circle of domestic interests and duties and forbids her to step beyond it."[1] The ideal of domesticity Tocqueville identified served to root American women to their homes, their narrow and proper sphere, well into the nineteenth century. Even well educated females were offered limited alternatives to adult lives centered on marriage and motherhood. To be sure, in recent decades Linda Kerber and other historians have problematized the Frenchman's simple dichotomy, pointing out that the lives of men and women were never as static as separate-sphere ideology would have it; male and female boundaries were crossed in countless ways all along.[2] The innumerable challenges to gendered social restrictions included the abundance of information available to women from childhood about faraway places, knowledge that inspired their dreams of traveling well beyond the appointed sphere.

Twenty-two-year-old Clara Mitchell, who traveled with the Campbell family in the summer of 1888, was amomg the thousands of American women in the nineteenth and early-twentieth centuries who stepped far outside their domestic sphere for a Grand Tour of Europe. Clara's emotions fluctuated from loneliness to euphoria to boredom. Initially she was plagued with homesickness and would only "sally forth" with at least the company of teenager Sally Campbell; in time, however, she grew emboldened—touring London "all alone by myself"—and came to relish her independence.

As her days in Europe neared an end, Clara questioned, "If I'll ever go to Scotland again—or to Italy[,] that center of beauty in the way of art! Or to the grand mountains of Switzerland and the dark old forests of Germany," and concluded, "Truly I hope so!" Wonder and regret were intermingled in her diary: "I can't help wishing I were a man," she anguished. "O what nice times I'd have travelling wherever I pleased[,] stopping when I chose, loitering around picturesque old ruins and wandering about those countries so full of romance, art and beauty. It's horrid to be a woman. They're not half so free as a man & I do love freedom so!"[3]

My book is a study of American women who, like Clara Mitchell, made a Grand Tour of Europe between 1814, when a long century of war neared its end, and 1914, the year war again engulfed the continent.[4] No other woman represented here recorded such an anguished plea to be free from the restraints imposed on her sex with Clara's passion, but most recorded experiences that took them far from the genteel domesticity mandated in their day.

Grand Tour is the iconic name inherited from the ritualized trips young British males made beginning in the mid-seventeenth century as an aristocratic rite of passage.[5] In the closing decades of the eighteenth century American men with the inclination and wherewithal emulated the British tour, but they redefined it as a quest for republican virtue rather than for aristocratic privilege. Most of their female counterparts had to be content with learning second hand about the places men visited until the early-nineteenth century when the image of a tourist in Europe began to switch from male to female. Harvey Levenstein, chronicler of Americans touring France, suggests that the 1840s witnessed the "feminization of American tourism" as "upper- and upper-middle-class women began challenging the purely domestic image that tied them to home and hearth."[6] By the twentieth century, Blanche McManus's published account of her travels abroad could state with credulity that "the American man rather regards the trip abroad, as he does religion and society, as the particular province of his womankind and is usually quite willing that she should lead the attacking force against the foreigner and his language."[7]

The year-by-year rise of consumer capitalism mandated that to join the middle class, men make their entry into adulthood by pursuing economic independence as soon as possible; while freer than women to travel within their own country, they became less free to take time from responsibilities and indulge in a Grand Tour. The dawn of the nineteenth century also experienced the transformation of a hierarchical family structure with men and women working together into one that divided men and women into the separate, albeit overlapping, spheres of work and home. Women took responsibility for the private home as men increasingly worked elsewhere. Historian Richard Bushman explains that in this new order women were given a special role in assuring the gentility of their families and that the mandate of gentility in the nineteenth century "both exalted and restricted" women.[8] The industrializing economy mandated new domestic responsibilities but also fueled greater educational opportunities and freed women from many traditional domestic tasks. Ironically, an industrializing society that first aspired to narrow their sphere also allowed women greater freedom to travel.

An ideal of genteel domesticity prevailed throughout the nineteenth century and into the next, but it was questioned and eroded across these years. The long-nineteenth century, the years from the French Revolution to the First World War, was one of enormous change for American women as almost every aspect of their lives was negotiated and adjusted. Inspired by Englishwoman Mary Wollstonecraft's *A Vindication of the Rights of Women*, published in the late-eighteenth century, American women, individually and, after the Seneca Falls Women's Rights Convention in 1848, collectively, demanded that their legal and social status be brought more in accord with the rights their republic granted men.

Greater freedom to travel contributed to and also benefitted from the women's movement as it spawned covert changes in social organization and expectation. Henry James thought of women who traveled to Europe when in the late-nineteenth century he popularized the epithet *The New Woman*; women who populate his novels expanded their world physically by going abroad and psychologically as they developed new conceptions about who they were and who they wanted to be. Their real-life counterparts struggled to follow suit.

An appealing image that emerged was that of traveler; across time women began joining and then dominating the American Grand Tour. Thousands of Americans—approximately forty thousand every year in the last decades of the nineteenth century— visited Europe and after mid-century possibly a majority of them were women.[9]

By mid-century it was acceptable for women from families with adequate means to step far from their sphere for a Grand Tour of Europe. Much like ornamental subjects such as French and music, time in Europe came to be defended as a finishing gloss of gentility for the matriarch or future matriarch of the home. But for many women it was much more. Inspired by a Europe-centered education, they traveled, as one woman explained concerning her sister, "to test by actual contact with European life the conceptions of her bookish education."[10]

Maria Bayard—her trip is the earliest represented here—was one of the few women who toured Europe in 1814, long before there was a perceived need to identify new women; Maria could not own property, attend college, practice a profession or vote. Alma Peterson joined thousands of women visiting Europe a century later; she knew college-educated and professional women, many of them property owners, and was just six years away from full voting equality.

Understanding the transformation of women's lives has been a central topic of American historians for decades. Scholars have told us a great deal about how the rise of consumer-based capitalism, the democratization of politics and religion, the expansion of free education and the modernization of medicine impacted the lives of women. Customs as well as laws were negotiated; changes in both the *de facto* and *de jure* restrictions women fought against went hand in hand. This study attempts to deepen our understanding of change by considering how traveling impacted women's sense of self and society's constructed image of ideal womanhood.

The popular version of nineteenth-century American women abroad has been too much drawn from true tales of rich women seeking titled husbands, stories of women like Consuelo Vanderbilt who became the Duchess of Marlborough and Jennie Jerome, who, once married, was Lady Churchill. Carol Berkin's recent study of Betsy Patterson Bonaparte profiles a woman who realized a preference for European ways at an early age, married Napoleon's younger brother and spent a lifetime trying to secure a place for her family in the Old World's aristocracy.[11] This image is also drawn from fictional American women abroad including Henry James's Isabel Archer and Daisy Miller and Edith Wharton's Udine Spragg; they may have been more interested in independence than titled husbands, but their stories also perpetuate the stereotype that only wealthy American women, those whose wealth exempted them from strict domesticity, ventured to Europe for the status it awarded. This impression is stubbornly persistent, but my research makes it abundantly clear that it is a distortion. Education inspired far more women to travel there than did acquiring status or the pursuit of marriages and titles. To be sure, a woman making a Grand Tour had to have considerably more than average wealth or to know someone willing to pay her way. One guidebook published in 1838 estimated it cost approximately $800 to travel through Europe for seven months and $300 for round-trip passage, more than most Americans made in a year. Only around the end of the nineteenth century did professional tour companies make Grand Tours considerably cheaper, allowing women of more modest means to afford a trip.[12]

Literary scholars, who have dominated the academic study of Americans abroad, have focused on published authors who were conscious that others would read their observations. My work is not literary analysis but social history. Most of the women I write about never intended to publish their letters and diaries, but wrote exclusively for themselves, their families and their friends. Accordingly, their work is a genre that should be analyzed as a record of a lived experience.

My composite picture of women touring Europe is based on the letters and diaries located in nearly fifty libraries and archives, of more than three hundred women who crossed the Atlantic between 1814 and 1914. I have used some books published after the fact, but have based my work primarily on the numerous unpublished accounts written first hand. I excluded the wives and daughters of the financial titans of the age; Rockefellers and Vanderbilts traveled with a retinue of servants so theirs is a different story. For much the same reason, I have not included women who were famous or accompanied famous men. I have only used those portions of the letters and diaries of women in Europe for some purpose other than tourism when they took time off to see the sights. Most of the women represented here are largely lost to the historical record but for the letters and diaries they wrote during a Grand Tour which they and their families so valued that they were saved and eventually deposited in libraries and archives.

These women are in many ways a homogeneous group with Western European roots; few women from racial or ethnic minorities had the financial means for tourist travel.[13] Almost all were Protestants although a small number of Catholics and Jews are represented. Financial tycoon Jay Gould's daughter is included as is a lady's companion.[14] Most female travelers represented here, however, were neither as rich nor as poor as these two extremes. Almost all had a solid secondary education and in the later decades a growing number were college educated. They all lived in the century of Romanticism and its literature inspired what they wanted to see and how they responded to it.[15]

However, these women also form a heterogeneous group in significant ways. They came from New England, the Mid-Atlantic, the South and the Midwest and several were from the West. Some lived in cities while others were from small towns or rural areas. An age range of more than sixty years separate a twelve-year-old girl from several women in their seventies. Women traveled with their husbands, children, parents, siblings, other relatives and friends; they hired escorts, joined large tour groups and even traveled alone. Some traveled with men, but at least as many did not. Trips ranged in length from a few weeks to a year and more. A Grand Tour was a once in a lifetime experience for most, but some women crossed the Atlantic multiple times.

This is not a representative sample of all women who traveled to Europe in these years, but rather a sample of those whose descriptions of their travels were deemed worthy of saving and were eventually deposited in research archives. Clearly some more closely match the stereotype of shallow Gilded Age females going to find titled husbands, to shop or to acquire the patina of status a Grand Tour afforded. Women less interested in learning Europe's lessons were those least likely to write the kinds of letters and diaries that they and their families would come to treasure and eventually bequeathed for the scrutiny of historians; they are accordingly represented primarily by their critics.

American men never abandoned the Grand Tour and deserve their own book. John Sears, author of a history of tourism, suggests that tourist attractions were "free of being identified as either male or female space."[16] Certainly, in important ways, travel did break down separate spheres and brought men and women together in common pursuits. Most male and female Americans touring Europe were Protestants from families with at least above-average income. Their secondary educations were similar; both sexes were offered a European-based curriculum and were well educated in European art, music, history, literature and languages. Girls and boys studied Latin, French and other European languages, read European literature and history and became familiar with European countries, cities and sites through geography classes. A common background inspired similar responses to cathedrals and mountains and many other things. My exclusive focus on women's experiences allows only a partial picture of what was distinctive about the female Grand Tour. A more thorough comparison of men and women touring Europe must await a parallel study of the many unpublished letters and diaries written by men.

At the Historical Society of Pennsylvania, I discovered an anonymous diary written in 1843. In the first paragraph the writer acknowledged fear of "the dreaded hour for farewell" and of crying for half an hour as the ship pulled away. This expression of fears and tears, along with a very neat handwriting, prompted my assumption that the writer was a woman. A few lines further down, however, I read: "I am sure I am a man now or ought to be at least." This man's diary underscores that the spheres of men and women, emotionally as well as physically, were never entirely separate.[17]

Studying women exclusively, however, allowed me to explore the ways that travel was clearly a gendered experience. Until recently, most historians of Americans traveling in Europe, while recognizing some individual women, have assumed that the experience was one for men.[18] As a result, many authors of nineteenth-century travel missed the fundamental reality of a feminized Grand Tour.

The explosion of female travel was simply historically unprecedented. It was, explains Mary Suzanne Schriber, editor of a volume on women's travels, the moment when women began "seizing for themselves the freedom of movement that has been the historical prerogative of the male."[19] What was appropriate in this expansion of women's sphere had to be negotiated at every turn. Women had to be concerned with their reputations in ways that men did not. They had greater concern over safety and they had to make decisions they were unaccustomed to making at home. Questions about finances, dress and grooming, interactions with strangers, dining out, time alone—a host of matters—were answered differently by men and women because both law and custom demanded it.

The book is organized topically rather than chronologically. The years from 1814 to 1914 were hardly static and I have attempted to recognize change across time throughout the narrative. Yet it is defensible to deal with Grand Tours as a common experience over this one-hundred-year period. As Foster Rhea Dulles pointed out in his history of Americans traveling in Europe, visitors there in the first half of the nineteenth century "set patterns that have remained remarkably unchanged through the years."[20]

Topical chapters are organized around differeent aspects of a Grand Tour. Ellen Walworth was typical in recalling that from a young age her studies of European history, mythology and geography created a longing to see the Old World, "that far away, enchanted region."[21] Chapter I explores the education that inspired Ellen and many other women to travel.

Women who dreamed of seeing an enchanted land may have experienced nightmares when contemplating the requisite ocean crossing. Late in the nineteenth century a veteran of several voyages advised her daughter, who was contemplating her own journey: "it is for you to determine whether you have become strong enough to encounter the contingencies of an ocean voyage with its not-over-delicate cuisine...."[22] Chapter II is about how women coped with the fatigue and discomforts as well as the novelty of an ocean voyage.

She also warned her daughter about "various annoyances and discomforts incident to travel and sojourns on the continent."

Chapter III discusses how women faced quotidian demands once they began their travels in Europe and how many became savvy travelers who were proud of coping with annoyances.[23]

One woman's recollection that from an early age she dreamed of seeing London, Paris and Rome held true for many others as well.[24] These cities dominated Grand Tour itineraries, much as they do today. Other parts of England, France and Italy as well as Scotland, Ireland, Germany, Austria, the Low Countries and Spain were also popular. Chapter IV examines how women experienced these iconic cities and other places in Western Europe and what meanings they took from them.

The Romantic Movement's embrace of the sublime inspired dreams of Switzerland and placed it squarely on the Grand Tour itinerary. Chapter V explores how women faced the physical demands necessary to see the Alps, made famous by stories of William Tell, and other popular outdoor sites.

Protocols of female chaperonage waned through the nineteenth century, but even into the twentieth century assumptions that some places were inappropriate or unsafe for women lingered. Women had to frequently negotiate and improvise travel arrangements, balancing mandates of propriety and safety with individual goals. Chapter VI looks at the relationships of travel and how women created balance and grew more independent and comfortable alone.

The last chapter focuses on the early-twentieth century when in 1912 the *Titanic* disaster left many women questioning the safety of crossing the ocean and then, two years later, the First World War brought an end to the traditional Grand Tour. When Europe suddenly erupted into war, Americans in its path found themselves transformed overnight from tourists into refugees trying to escape a war zone. Although initially overwhelmed with a profound sense of their vulnerability, many women depended on their own resourcefulness to find their way home.

The Epilogue surveys the meaning women across the decades took from their experience of Europe.

I

A Trip to Europe Became the Great Desire of My Heart: Imagining a Grand Tour

In 1844 North Carolina schoolgirl Bessie Lacy wrote her father from Edgeworth Academy that she was learning "the principal things of geography such as the bodies of water, the globe, the rivers, capes, mountains, islands, capitals, subdivisions and provinces." For Bessie, geography was much more than memorizing the names of principal things; she vividly imagined herself in the faraway places her books described. Six years later, as Bessie nervously contemplated marriage, she warned a suitor "there never was a poor child born with such a wandering spirit as I have and were I not a woman I believe this moment I'd be in Africa or Japan … in some almost inaccessible place."[1] At century's end another North Carolina woman likewise penned despair about a wandering spirit thwarted by the limits placed on her sex. A friend's description of travels in the North Carolina mountains prompted C.W.S.'s despair that "there is nothing I could have enjoyed more than to have been amidst these grand and sublime scenes." "I really believe," she continued, "if I were a man I would become a tramp … but such longing on my part is void of wisdom, of worldly wisdom[,] and I must as I have ever done cultivate that [which] I have no taste for."[2]

Neither of these women became a tramp who reached inaccessible places, but rather conformed the best she could to her mandated sphere. The kind of curiosity they embraced about the world, however, was an important step that in time would propel more and more women to venture to places once inaccessible to them; even when physically at home, their minds could be far away. Improvement in female education was critical in facilitating wonder about the world. Year by year more families, even those of modest means, were able and willing to educate their daughters. Young women could not attend college until the 1840s—and few did so until after the Civil War—but between 1790 and 1860 at least 350 schools and academies were opened for female students throughout the United States.[3] Historian Mary Kelley points out that in the best of these schools "the curricula were as complete, the demands as great, and the learning as substantive" as for boys.[4]

Boys and girls alike pursued an education centered on Europe, a place made familiar from early childhood. French, lingua franca of the western world into the twentieth century, was the language most frequently studied—one academy justified it as an "indispensable accomplishment in a well educated female"—but Latin and Greek were reputable and frequent choices for girls as well.[5] These classical languages, considered necessary to train the virtuous male citizens a republic required, may not have been as integral a part of many female curricula as they were in male academies and colleges, but it was not unusual for girls to study them. In the late 1820s, the Greenfield (MA) High School for Young Ladies offered Latin as necessary for "an easy and thorough acquisition of the modern languages of Europe."[6] Boston's Mount Vernon Female School required Latin and also offered Greek, Hebrew and French as electives.[7] Emma Willard's Troy (NY) Female Seminary, one of the most rigorous female schools in the nineteenth century, also required Latin; girls attending this prestigious school were expected to read Caesar's *Commentaries* as well as Virgil, Sallust and Cicero, all in their original language.[8] Historian Christie Anne Farnham posits that Latin classes were even more commonplace in southern female academies because men there had less anxiety about well educated women challenging their domination of the professions; accordingly, women's knowledge of the classics could more easily be viewed as "emblematic of high social status."[9] Southern father Drury Lacy, for example, concerned that Bessie's Latin studies were not rigorous enough, advised her to spend at least two years "reading Caesar & Sallust from 'lid to lid'."[10]

Female academies offered their students a solid grounding in the history, literature, music and art of Europe as well as its geography. Kelley points out that these schools established a classical curriculum, "a classicism that was dedicated to self-culture," and that geography was "one of the staples in a woman's course of study."[11] Sisters Catherine Beecher and Harriet Beecher Stowe were two of the female educators with a keen interest in geography; Harriet published a textbook for Catherine to use in her school.[12] Teaching about place served the nationalistic purpose of spreading familiarity with the United States, but more time was spent studying world geography, both ancient and modern.

The Concord (MA) Greenfield Academy's smorgasbord of geography instruction is one example of what girls studied. In 1881 thirteen-year-old Margaret Harding launched her first term as a day student by writing all she knew about Switzerland and Italy in her copybook. Lessons on Turkey and parts of Asia followed. When school was dismissed early one winter day, she was assigned the orators and philosophers of Athens to read about at home. Margaret spent another cold day at home working on a geography assignment, but "did not accomplish much." Africa was introduced later in the year. It seems Margaret preferred history; she received 95 percent on her spring exam in that subject, but only 59 percent for geography. In the summer she read about martyrs of Spain and the liberation of Holland. Back at school for the fall term, she enrolled in Latin and French classes, but after two months gave up French for music lessons. Margaret took no formal courses in geography in her second year, but during one six-week period attended an Italian scholar's lectures on St. Peter's, Vesuvius, pagan Rome, triumphal arches, the Coliseum and a concluding one on Roman chariots and gladiators.[13]

Margaret lived in an area especially rich in educational opportunity, but female academies were available almost any place commanding a sufficient population to support them. The curriculum of the Charleston (SC) Female Seminary, founded in 1870, serves as an example of a Europe-oriented education in the South and is typical of what many American girls were offered in the last half of the nineteenth century. The school was organized into kindergarten — taught entirely in French — primary, preparatory and academic departments. In the primary department basic skills in reading, writing and arithmetic were emphasized for two years. In the third year, geography was added and the next year students read *A Child's History of Rome*. French was continued all four years. First year in the preparatory department required *A Child's History of England* and Englishman Thomas Gray's *Elegy Written in a Country Church Yard*, his poem of death and remembrance. In the second year a two-year study of United States history and literature commenced. Second-year girls also read Sir Walter Scott's poem *Marmion*, set in England in the time of Henry VIII, and the next year took up his *Lady of the Lake*, a poem about King James V. In the fourth year they studied the history of Greece and read Scott's *Lay of Last Minstrel*, a poem chronicling a sixteenth century border feud between England and Scotland; the students also read seven British classics. Washington Irving's *Sketch Book* represented American literature. The preparatory pupils studied French all four years and began German their last year. The academic department offered first year students ancient history. They also read works by English poet and essayist Joseph Addison for their study of diction and in poetry class read Lord Byron's *Prisoner of Chillon*, the story of a monk imprisoned in the Swiss Chateau de Chillon in the sixteenth century. French and German were continued and Latin grammar added. Second-year preparatory students studied Francis Bacon's essays in their diction class along with a variety of poems; they read about the medieval history of England in English and about France's history in French. The academic pupils continued Latin grammar and also worked with a Latin reader. In the third year, modern European history and the history of English literature were offered. Latin studies focused on Julius Caesar; French class required reading French literature and writing compositions. Fourth year students read Virgil and Cicero in Latin and Corneille, La Fontaine, Racine and Moliere in French; they also had a class in German literature. In their last year, as they neared the end of their formal education, the girls undertook a critical study of classical authors and were introduced to the history of art. They also studied the United States Constitution; study of American history, literature and politics was woven throughout the curriculum, but received considerably less attention than European studies. Students attending the Charleston Seminary paid approximately $300 each year for room and board and tuition with an extra fee charged for Latin, music and painting. Instrumental music was offered "according to the German method" and singing "by the Italian method." Both were "taught by experienced New York and European teachers."[14]

This school was only one in Charleston that offered French; despite its decidedly British bent, the city was rich in opportunities for girls to expand their language skills beyond English. Caroline Pettigru (Carson), born in 1820, was especially close to her father who guided her early education. She studied French at the Misses Robertsons' school followed by a year in a New York City academy where all classes except English were taught in French. After returning to her hometown, Caroline studied Latin with a Catholic priest and mastered Italian well enough to produce skilled translations of Dante's sonnets.[15] Mary Boykin (Chesnut), famous for her Civil War diary, was twelve years old when she entered Madame Talvande's French School for Young Ladies in Charleston where she mastered fluency in French and studied German.[16] Elizabeth White (Nims Rankin), born in Fort Mill, South Carolina, in 1835, spent a year studying in Charleston which sparked a life-long interest in European literature. In the 1850s she moved to Mount Holly, North Carolina, a more friendly climate for her Massachusetts-native husband, but far removed from centers of learning; to compensate she accumulated a sizable library that included Burns, Byron, Carlyle, Coleridge, Goethe, Schiller and Scott, among others.[17] Elizabeth Sinkler (Coxe), born in South Carolina a decade later, spent her childhood moving from her family's plantations to Charleston and Philadelphia; largely taught by her mother, she mastered fluency in French and Italian and read German so well that according to a descendant she could read "with ease and pleasure most of Schiller's and Goethe's works."[18]

Academy students paid extra for music and painting, considered ornamentals. The sentiment "Why should girls be learn'd and wise? Books only serve to spoil their eyes," put to rhyme by John Trumbull in the late-eighteenth century, hardly survived into the nineteenth, but the debate as to whether female schools should emphasize these subjects or academic ones played on with proponents of the academic side increasingly more influential. Reformers determine to improve female academic education were especially successful in northern states because educated females were needed to teach in its pioneering public schools, but, as the Charleston Seminary curriculum makes clear, a rigorous education was available to many southern girls as well. By mid-century, academics were paramount in most schools although art and music were also popular. Farnham suggests that in southern female academies music, drawing and painting were the most popular ornamental subjects offered.[19] Most of the pictures produced were copies of European artists and most of the music performed was by European composers.

Female literacy in New England was close to universal by mid-century and in all parts of the country the literacy gap between white males and females had sharply declined.[20] Educated girls offered a feast of European studies in school were also likely to choose European topics to read about on their own. Historian Barbara Sicherman explains that many women "found in reading a way of apprehending the world that enabled them to overcome some of the confines of gender and class," that "the freedom of imagination women found in books encouraged new self-definition."[21] One of the new self-definitions encouraged was that of traveler, even if possible only through imagination. Hannah Adams, distant cousin of namesake presidents and one of the first American women to make her living by writing, never left her home country, but at the dawn of the nineteenth century, as she approached old age, she enthused, "I travel every day through the world of books … an inexhaustible fund to feast my mind."[22] Decades later, Emily Dickinson, who rarely ventured beyond her Amherst home, echoed Adams with poetry: "There is no frigate like a book. To take us lands away."[23] At the turn of the century, twenty-one-year-old Agnes Hamilton, from a Fort Wayne, Indiana, family Sicherman describes as "self-consciously literary," recorded that "I live in the world of novels all the time[.] Half the time I am in Europe[,] half in different parts of America."[24]

But not all educated American women were satisfied traveling to Europe through books and their imagination. Women's rights activist Margaret Fuller is the most famous example of antebellum females well educated in all manner of things European who resolved to actually see the places they studied. Timothy Fuller overcame any disappointment that his first child, born in 1810, was a girl and devoted himself to her education. By age seven Margaret could read Virgil, Horace and Ovid in Latin with ease, next tackled Greek and learned French, Italian and German sufficiently to read European authors in their original language. Her biography of Goethe was thoroughly researched although never finished. At the age of thirteen Margaret met an English woman who inspired her vow to see Europe for herself, a goal delayed by family responsibilities. For years she joined other young women who looked on with envy as their male counterparts set off to emulate the British Grand Tour. As an adult Margaret realized with regret that so much of her childhood had been devoted to books, but a biographer explains she "never ceased to cling to the dream that in Europe her life would flower."[25] In 1846 the generosity of friends finally allowed Margaret to realize her dream; her life did flower in Europe in unimagined ways. After months together, she parted company with her benefactors and remained in Italy four more years, a time of revolutionary turmoil throughout the peninsula. In the summer of 1850 Margaret was returning home with her Italian husband, an impoverished aristocrat she met in a chance encounter while visiting St. Peter's Basilica, along with their young son, when they all perished in a shipwreck off the coast of New York; her history of the Italian Revolution of 1848 was lost as well. When months later friends gathered to mourn the woman they now knew as Margaret Fuller Ossoli, Bronson Alcott (as paraphrased by Caroline Dall) said of her: "she was no New England woman—she might as well have been born in Greece or Rome. Greece & Rome were wherever she was."[26] The cenotaph her family erected to her memory in Boston's Mount Auburn Cemetery reads: "Born a child of New England, By adoption a citizen of Rome, By genius belonging to the world."[27]

Through the years that Europe was her elusive goal, Margaret Fuller brought together intellectually inclined young women to read about its art, literature and history. The three Peabody sisters, all older than Margaret, joined one of her groups. Elizabeth, Mary and Sophia Peabody were not typical schoolgirls, but their interests approximated those of other well-educated females in the early-nineteenth century. Elizabeth, born in 1804, first studied in her mother's small school for local girls. For a geography lesson, Eliza Peabody's pupils chose a country, studied it by reading gazetteers and guidebooks, and then penned letters as if they were in this faraway place. Mrs. Peabody also read to Elizabeth and her classmates from European literature including her favorite authors, the English trio of Spenser, Milton and Shakespeare. The essays of Madame de Stael, French writer and founder of a solon that included women's rights in its pantheon of liberal ideas, inspired Elizabeth's life-long conviction that women were the intellectual equals of men. Her father agreed at least that girls could learn Latin and taught it to his oldest daughter; his mandate that Mary was not strong enough to join the lessons may have emboldened her secret study in the family's garret. In time, Elizabeth persuaded Sophia to learn Latin as well as Greek on the grounds that "if it is best for the minds of boys—it is best also for the minds of girls." In the summer they were eleven and fourteen, the two youngest Peabody girls put chairs in a river near their home and studied their Latin *Liber Primus* while enjoying the cool water. In her late teens Elizabeth joined her mother teaching school and used Greek and Roman tales to enliven her classes. For Greek lessons she engaged Ralph Waldo Emerson, at nineteen only a year her senior, for what her biographer describes as "a series of awkward lessons." Two years later Elizabeth launched a study of German in order to read the German Romantics, introduced to her in French by the writings of Madame de Stael, in their original language. Liberal clergyman William Ellery Channing, especially important in Elizabeth's intellectual development, shared works by British Romantic poets he had met on a tour of Europe. In 1826 Mary reported that her sister "has been living this winter upon Coleridge, Wordsworth and Dr. Channing." Elizabeth was emboldened to write Wordsworth, but when he replied with an invitation to visit, she sadly responded, "I fear I shall never see Europe." Her fear was at long last put to rest when, at the age of sixty-three, she was invited to make a tour of kindergartens there. In contrast to her sisters, who traveled with their husbands, she joined the growing ranks of women who traveled exclusively with other women or entirely alone.[28]

Mary defied her father's skepticism by mastering languages more easily than her older sister yet she preferred reading fiction. She read Sir Walter Scott's popular novels as soon as she could acquire a copy, but her favorites were by his Scottish countrywomen, Mary Brunton and Susan Ferrier. In 1843 Mary became the first of the sisters to tour Europe, a trip with her husband, educator Horace Mann, cut short by her first pregnancy.[29]

Sophia joined her sisters in language study and was well read in European literature, but distinguished herself as the most artistic of the three. Many of her paintings were copies of European masters and scenes; she used travel books and her own imagination to paint places including Scott's Abbotsford Castle, famous buildings from ancient Rome and Italy's Lake Como and adorned her marital bed with scenes from Guido Reni's famous fresco *Aurora*.[30] Like Mary, Sophia traveled to Europe shortly after her marriage; she lived several years abroad with her husband, author Nathaniel Hawthorne.

Caroline Healey (Dall) was one of many Boston women influenced by Margaret Fuller and the Peabody sisters. Although forced to end her formal education when only fifteen, her city's intellectual vibrancy enabled her to continue informal study. Diary entries for March 1838 reveal that a year after leaving school she was reading Italian, Spanish and French authors; she recorded growing tired of Scottish poet James Macpherson, once a favorite, and taking up his fellow Scott, historian Alexander Fraser Tyler, whose *Elements of General History, Ancient and Modern* she was carefully studying. When she was eighteen Caroline met Elizabeth Peabody who, according to the editor of Caroline's diary, was "a godsend" for giving her "serious attention." Elizabeth introduced the younger woman to the writings of Coleridge and Goethe and Sophia's paintings introduced her to European art and mythology.[31] Caroline was among the majority of American women with a Europe-centered education who never traveled abroad, but expanded their domestic circle through the European books, art and music they consumed.

Women who lived far from urban areas without their abundance of intellectual opportunity followed suit the best they could. Augusta, Maine, native Charlotte Farnham could already read Latin, French and Italian when she agreed to a competition with visiting teacher Elizabeth Peabody as to who could learn German the fastest.[32] In a survey of female literary interests, prominent Unitarian minister Thomas Wentworth Higginson profiled a young New Hampshire woman who spent summers in the woods and fields, but in winter "dwells in Greece and Rome with Plutarch." Love of European classics also traveled west. Higginson discovered that in faraway places such as Wyoming and Oregon many small towns had "a Shakespeare Club, Dante Club, and a Browning Club" which were maintained through "inexhaustible feminine energy."[33]

Charleston, with a long-standing affinity for all things European, led in offering southern women many of the post-academy opportunities offered to those living in major northern cities. A study of Charlestonians traveling abroad in the years after the Revolution suggests, "Europe remained Charleston's cultural fountainhead, perhaps more than it did for any other American city."[34] In the 1820s Fanny Kemble, the English actress famed for chronicling her two years spent on a Georgia plantation, praised Charleston as the most aristocratic city in American where "in one street you seem to be in an old English town, and in another in some continental city of France or Italy."[35]

Libraries all over the country made books by Europeans and about Europe widely available outside academies. In urban areas women could borrow books from small free or subscription (social) libraries; traveling libraries made books accessible in more remote areas. In the late-nineteenth century philanthropists financed large public ones, notably those in New York City and Boston; Andrew Carnegie's largess allowed the proliferation of free libraries in smaller communities as well. Numerous bookshops also facilitated reading. Female literary societies, first established before the Revolution and maintained in small towns and major cities alike, offered women an opportunity to discuss what they read. Mary Kelley argues they are evidence that even eighteenth-century women were not strictly confined to household, that these societies "reinforced the formal instruction provided in the classrooms of female academies and seminaries" thus enriching the domestic sphere and connecting it to the larger world.[36]

Parents, preachers and teachers all tried to keep novels out of the hands of young women, although newspaper and magazine serials constantly undermined their efforts. A Massachusetts librarian condemned German and French translations as "per se of the evil one."[37] Female academies typically banned fiction deemed evil, especially the ubiquitous stories of innocent virgins tricked into sexual relations with devastating consequences; Farnham explains, "the sentimental novel was thought to arouse sexual feelings in young women."[38] St. Mary's Academy in North Carolina forbade its students to read novels "except on Saturday after the duties of the day are over, and then only those that are approved."[39] The admonitions of their elders, however, hardly dented the popularity of novels, especially with young females on the cusp of adulthood. Farnham points out that "students saw in these love stories lessons to be learned from the little-known world of men and pitfalls to be avoided in their own lives."[40] According to her biographers, during her years at boarding school Mary Boykin relished "novel-reading as a treasured secret diversion."[41] Further north, Massachusetts teenagers Rhoda and Lucy Stone locked themselves in a room to read a forbidden European romance; when their mother discovered her girls' secret, she admonished them for giving in to reading what she thought a silly book, yet allowed them to finish it.[42]

Many popular nineteenth-century novels, as well as shorter pieces published in magazines such as *Godey's Lady's Book*, were about Europe. Madame de Stael's *Corinne*, published in 1807, introduced readers to the landscapes and art of Venice, Naples and Rome while entertaining them with the tragic story of love between a brilliant Italian woman and a Scottish aristocrat. The editor of a twentieth-century edition finds it "almost startling to see how much influence Stael and her novel exercised in the United States."[43] Elizabeth Peabody dismissed *Corinne* as a "high wrought romance," but also defended it as the "best account of Italy extant."[44] Sixteen-year-old Margaret Fuller and her friend Lydia Maria Child, another future abolitionist and women's rights activist, on the other hand, read the novel together and both adopted the title character as a role model.[45] Englishwoman Anna Jameson's anonymously published *Diary of an Ennuyee*, available in the United States in 1833, was set in Italy's museums and churches where a young woman, scorned by her lover, sought solace; it complemented *Corinne* in preparing women for a trip to Italy.[46]

The most popular novel-cum-guide for Italy, however, was Nathaniel Hawthorne's *Marble Faun*, published in 1860 during his sojourn abroad with Sophia and their young children. This gothic tale of the evil threatening innocent American women in decadent Europe also contrasted young and practical America with older and more romantic Europe. One woman, who read the novel while traveling a decade after its publication, questioned "who can have anything more to say of Rome after Hawthorne[?]"[47] After its publication in 1878, Henry James's popular novella, *Daisy Miller*, the story of an American girl sojourning in Rome who paid with her life for innocent but inappropriate flirting with an Italian man, established an indelible and distorted impression of young American women abroad.

Some novels set in the United States also introduced readers to the merits of a Europe-centered education. The main character in Augusta Evans's *St. Elmo*, described by historian Frances Cogan as "frighteningly erudite," turns down three suitors while immersing herself in the European classics. Susan Warner's popular 1851 novel, *The Wide, Wide World*, centers on Little Ellen's rigorous education in Latin, French and other academic subjects which made her more attractive than "several vapid and poorly educated cousins."[48]

Travel narratives, less controversial than novels, were another popular means for young women to explore the world beyond their narrow circle. In the late 1840s close to fifteen percent of the books women borrowed from the New York Society Library were this genre.[49] Mary Kelley suggests that "in taking readers to distant lands, in introducing them to the dangers and delights of unknown peoples, and in transforming movement through space into an emotion-laden introduction to the sublime," travel narratives had an affect similar to novels.[50]

New Yorker Katherine Johnson, perhaps an unusually voracious reader, kept lists of the books she read for several years. Over a three-year period she recorded over one hundred books, most of them by Europeans and about Europe including approximately thirty in French and at least five in Italian. Katherine wrote of Alessandro Manzoni's *The Betrothed*: "the style of this novel and the description are certainly admirable and fully warrant its high reputation." She thought Hippolyte Taine's *Italy: Rome and Naples* "decidedly the best book on Italy that I ever have read," but offered no opinion about his *Italy: Florence and Venice*. Katherine was not as charitable toward Bayard Taylor, concluding of his *Byways of Europe* that "even the dullness of this author could not prevent one's [*sic*] being interested in the accounts of short visits to faraway and little visited places which fill this volume." She was more positive about a "delightfully interesting" two-volume guide to Paris.[51]

American women were exposed to European painting and music in a variety of venues outside of school and their appreciation of what they experienced motivated many Grand Tours. Women interested in art were especially drawn to Italy and France while those who favored music were most likely to dream of visiting Germany and Austria. By the early decades of the nineteenth century, exhibitions and small collections offered Americans opportunities to see original European paintings. In 1838 Caroline Healey sought a ticket to "the Exhibition of Italian paintings, which I am very desirous to see;" she may have assumed all art was Italian since these paintings, later bought by the Boston Athenaeum, were primarily by Dutch masters, including Rembrandt and Van Dyke.[52] The Athenaeum was one of several collections that merged to form the Boston Museum of Fine Arts in 1870, the same year the Metropolitan Museum was founded in New York City; they were two of the most outstanding of the many art museums that graced major cities during the Gilded Age. Middle- and upper-class families frequently decorated their homes with copies of the European masterpieces they saw in these museums or in books. Guido Reni's *Aurora*, a classical depiction of dawn which so pleased Sophia Peabody Hawthorne that she copied it on her marital bed, as well as his portrait of Beatrice Cenci, legendary symbol of resistance to aristocratic privilege, were two of the paintings most frequently reproduced. Seeing the original *Aurora* delighted Constance Harrison for igniting her memory that as newlyweds she and her husband bought a copy they could not afford to create "a little art centre [sic] in our lives."[53] Elizabeth White Nims Rankin, along with her daughters, Nell and Bess, decorated their Mount Holly, North Carolina, home with copies of both of these Guido paintings as well as one of Rome's Castle St. Angelo.[54]

By the dawn of the nineteenth century, Americans from urban areas could enjoy European operas and classical music. Germanic and Italian impresarios and immigrants brought the music of their homelands across the Atlantic and vied to popularize it in America. Germanic composers dominated the symphonic repertory. The New York Philharmonic, founded in 1843 as the country's first symphony orchestra, was unusual in first hiring an American-born conductor, but subsequently conformed to the practice of appointing Europeans, most of them German. Italian operas, works by Verdi, Rossini, Donizetti and Bellini, were favored until the late-nineteenth century when Richard Wagner challenged their ascendancy. In his study of Wagner in America, Joseph Horowitz suggests, "the cult of Wagner came to dominate America's musical high culture, and helped shape its intellectual life."[55]

Until the last decades of the nineteenth century, women had only limited opportunity to formally pursue their interest in European culture after their academy education was complete. Linda Kerber explains that until colleges admitted them, "most 'higher' education was necessarily self-education," that "women shaped their intellectual lives out of their own reading, their diary keeping and their letter writing."[56] Those not satisfied with self-education longed for the chance to attend college. Elizabeth Cady Stanton recalled years later "my vexation and mortification knew no bounds" when her father expressed only horror that she begged to follow her brother to Union College.[57] Caroline Healey, who poured much of her intellectual energy into her diary, spoke for other educated young women who deeply regretted their exclusion from colleges and universities, writing of her wish "that women might enjoy—the advantages—of college education, of the severe and studious training, which is lavished upon our young men.... At fifteen—a woman's education—in common parlance—is finished—at twenty-five—a man's just begun!—Heigho!"[58] Less than a decade after Caroline vented her frustration, Ohio's Oberlin College opened its doors to female as well as African-American students. However, Oberlin was unique until after the Civil War when the advantages of higher education were lavished on a growing number of women as female private and public colleges mushroomed and some institutions long exclusively for men redefined themselves as coeducational as well.[59]

M. Carey Thomas was only sixteen when she could brag of passing the entrance exams for admission into Cornell University's classical course, but she had to appendage her regret that "Father was terribly opposed." Parental opposition failed to dissuade Carey from enrolling although it possibly undermined her confidence. As she approached graduation, Carey worried that her mastery of Latin and Greek was wanting, yet also consoled herself that "I do see light somewhat." After graduating from Cornell she earned a Ph.D. from the University of Zurich, qualifying her to become the first president of Bryn Mawr College.[60] By 1920 women made up more than forty percent of the college population. Female college students often traveled in the summer months when school was not in session and swelled the ranks of the Grand Tour.

As the number of women considering a trip abroad rose, travel clubs to help them prepare for a journey proliferated in tandem. These clubs entertained armchair travelers, but also offering practical advice for those resolved to see for themselves. The Hyde Park Travel Club was founded in Chicago in 1891 to facilitate women's "study of the art, literature, architecture and history of various countries." Members agreed that France would be the focus for several years as "every one is interested in France, every one goes to France or expects to." In the nineteenth century's final year, club members paid a professor $400 for twenty classes because they wanted "to study, to be entertained and to be educated—to become cosmopolitan." A few years later Miss Ingersole was hired to give a variety of lectures; after one talk, the club secretary reported "we thoroughly enjoyed a trip among the high Alps without any of the harrowing inconveniences so vividly depicted by our lecturer." In a subsequent talk about Italy "we approached Rome from the Naples side. The magnificence of the road along which we passed leading from Naples cannot be surpassed."[61]

The Women's England Rest Tour Association (England was soon dropped from the title), also founded in 1891, was a different kind of travel club. The four original members concluded from their experiences abroad that women traveling without men needed special advice. Their exclusive club was restricted to members "of the best social and intellectual understanding." First president Julia Ward Howe, author of *Battle Hymn of the Republic,* stressed "the necessity for strictly supervising the membership and constantly weeding out undesirable applicants." Julia's candor offers insight into the stubbornly entrenched view that for a Grand Tour to endure as a mark of status, the masses should be excluded. In 1892 the club began publishing *Pilgrim Script* offering travel advice to women deemed desirable. The leadership recognized that not all of its privileged elite was well off so awarded "travelships" to young women unable to travel entirely on their own resources. The group so closely guarded its list of accredited accommodations in Europe that members pledged to share it with no one, not even their husbands, and to make arrangements for it to be returned to the association after their deaths.[62]

Most members of the Rest Tour Association traveled to learn although the group's exclusivity reveals that status was sometimes a motivation as well. Learning about Europe's civilization was intrinsically valuable; seeing it first hand also enhanced social status. Historian Frederic Jaher posits that acquiring culture "purified the privileged, fitting them to rule."[63] Surely many of the association's women felt privileged by their opportunity to travel to Europe, but most relished the experience more than the status it afforded. For a minority, a Grand Tour was a fashionable exercise in conspicuous consumption, even the consumption of European titles; their trip was an opportunity to display their father or husband's success or even to find a titled husband.[64] They crowd popular images of nineteenth- and early-twentieth-century American women in Europe, but in reality they played a minor role in the feminized Grand Tour.

Adventure joined self-improvement and status in inspiring travel. The exploits of Nellie Bly, who, her biographer claims, had no passion for learning, popularized the idea of female adventure travelers. In 1888 the New York *World* sent her around the globe to break the fictitious Phileas Fogg's record of eighty days. The story grew in popularity after the editor of *Cosmopolitan Magazine* sent Elizabeth Bisland in the opposite direction, making it a two-woman race as well as a race against time. The editor trumpeted increased sales of the *World* as proof that Nellie's adventure was invigorating interest in geography and that "everybody will be, to some extent, improved by the Nellie Bly tour." The paper even published a namesake game to help readers follow her itinerary. After beating the record and winning the race (which she never acknowledged) she was celebrated as a national heroine. When asked how she had achieved such a feat, Nellie replied, "It's not so much for a woman to do who has the pluck, energy and independence which characterize many women in this day of push and get-there."[65]

Emelie's trip was inspired not by pluck and energy but by despair. In December 1865 she posted a message to her erstwhile lover: "Sarcasm and indifference have driven me from you. I sail in the next steamer for Europe. Shall I purchase tickets for two, or do you prefer to remain to wound some other loving heart? Answer quick, or all is lost."[66] Emelie self prescribed a trip to Europe for her emotional distress. From the eighteenth century, American men had frequently justified their travels as beneficial for physical health; nineteenth-century doctors inherited the custom and sometimes ordered a trip abroad for their female patients as a palliative for a variety of ailments, both perceived and real, that in the late-nineteenth century were typically diagnosed as hysteria.[67] Emma Cordozzo's doctor suggested a trip to Europe, but he forbade long walks and visits to cold galleries and churches.[68] Elizabeth Nichols also traveled for her health even though it meant leaving her three young children behind; she was more fortunate in traveling with doctor's orders to walk and sightsee as she wished.[69] When Elizabeth Cabot was advised a trip to Europe would be beneficial, she wrestled with ambivalence for days since it would mean a long separation from her baby daughter; her parents' doubts compounded her anxiety and left her feeling "an hour one way, another the opposite way, and selfish & cruel both ways." Only after her mother finally sanctioned the trip did Elizabeth resolve to go.[70]

A spirit of adventure, Gilded-Age materialism, doctor's orders, thwarted romances and dreams of new ones were all inspiration for a Grand Tour; most inspiring, however, was a thirst for learning about the civilization they embraced as theirs. Most women, of course, could only dream about the places they discovered in books. In the 1830s a New Englander confided to relatives about to depart for the Old World: "What would I not give to be with you in your rambles, to see what you will see, to go where you will go, but as this cannot be, I am content to rest satisfied to hear, but you must let me hear all about every thing that interests you."[71] Another New England woman bid farewell to a friend going abroad with the bittersweet sendoff: "Oh but you are going to that land here my soul is vested."[72]

Those with means and resolve could follow their soul's longing. One who finally achieved her goal of a Grand Tour queried a cousin at home if she remembered, "when we were children together how we chatted about the European trip we intended to take when

Laura Libbey in 1898, six years after her trip to Europe.
Library of Congress

we were eighteen."[73] Educator Fanny Hall likewise recalled that "almost from the earliest period of my recollection, at least from the time when the tales of the nursery began to be superseded by the graver studies of history and geography, and my mind opened to the perception of the wonderful fact that beyond the broad seas there existed other lands not less fair and goodly than my own, I have felt the most ardent desire to visit those lands."[74] On one of several trips she made around the turn of the century, Henrietta Greenbaum Frank mused that "all our lives are preparation for what we see & hear ... I am glad that I have devoted so much time in the past to the history of the past; it was a preparation for this journey."[75] Once in Europe, Laura Libbey realized that "when one has longed for something from earliest childhood to middle age which was seemingly utterly out of reach, has thought of it, dreamed of it, built air castles about it, and then when suddenly the way seems opened for a realization of all these hopes it is hard to feel sure that it is actually ones self that is really doing in the flesh what up to this time has only been dreams and imaginings."[76]

Of course some women never longed for Europe at all, but went only reluctantly. Eliza Gardner, who traveled with her husband for fear of being left alone, despaired on departing "how desolate" she was, how "my heart died within me."[77] Conversely, Madge Preston decided once in Europe that it was "folly" to have left her husband and begged him to never let her do so again.[78] Susan Marsh Emerson, who traveled as a lady's companion, realized as her ship pulled away, "I do not enjoy the idea of leaving home & friends for foreign lands and consequently am much depressed in spirit." She tried rationalizing that "beggars can't be choosers," so "succumbed to fate." In her case, at least, initial reluctance proved ill founded as a few days in Paris convinced her "I was never so happy in my life."[79] Chicagoan Julia Newberry (possibly the model for Henry James's Daisy Miller, who did not want to go either) was never happy traveling with her parents in Europe. As one of several trips she made commenced she despaired "it nearly breaks my heart to think of leaving it all & going to Europe again." Chicago, she rejoined, was "worth all London & Paris & New York put together."[80]

Julia's sentiment would have gladdened the heart of American nationalists (except, perhaps, those from New York) who from their revolutionary rejection of European governance had promoted an ideal of American exceptionalism. George Washington's *Farewell Address* questioned if Americans should "entangle our peace and prosperity in the toils of European ambition, rivalship, interest, humor and caprice?" The next two presidents echoed his concern; although both John Adams and Thomas Jefferson spent considerable time in Europe, and Jefferson was an avowed Francophile, both warned that European travel could be detrimental, that, in the words of Adams, Americans should stay home "to cultivate the manners of your own country, not those of Europe."[81] Noah Webster, in the forefront of a post-revolutionary American nationalism, strove to thwart mimicking British English by publishing his famous dictionary of the American language. Charles Bulfinch, Webster's architectural counterpart, ordered images of corn, cotton and tobacco, three major indigenous American plants, carved on the new Capitol's Corinthian columns to Americanize the neo-classical building.[82] Daniel Rodgers suggests that when American nationalists like Webster and Bulfinch referred to the Old World they meant "the continent of decadence and decay;" their New World was "the continent of rebirth, site of a new dispensation." Indeed, American nationalism fed off negative impressions of Europe. According to Rodgers, "the republican understanding of America depended utterly on its contract with an imaged Europe."[83]

However, even as some Americans strove to shun a Europe imagined only in negative ways and to embrace their frontier as the core of national identity, the education they offered their children and much of the culture they embraced themselves remained decidedly European. Despite a few distinct words and varied spellings, their language remained solidly English; corncobs hardly camouflaged the fact that most important buildings followed European models, both ancient and modern. Scotsman Sir Walter Scott's medieval tragedies consistently bested James Fenimore Cooper's tales of the American frontier in popularity.

American children learned about Europe's vices, but they were also taught, even bombarded, with its virtues. The haphazard nature of nineteenth-century American education was made more cohesive by the centrality of Europe's history, geography, languages, literature, music and art; libraries, travel clubs, reading groups, theatres and museums reinforced lessons learned at school. An imagined Europe and contemporary Europe could be rejected, but the enormous richness of European civilization, something many Americans knew quite a lot about, could not. Embracing European civilization at home was the reality for most, but for some it was not enough. First mostly men and then men and women, those who could afford to bring their European-centered education to life, embarked on a Grand Tour to discover their civilization at its fountainhead.

Women resolute about going abroad had to first endure an experience few hearts desired. A long journey on a sailing ship or a steam ship, an extraordinary step from the narrow circle, was a prerequisite for an American Grand Tour.

II

Prelude to the Unknown Joys of Europe: Across the Atlantic for a Grand Tour

The day before she left Massachusetts for Europe early in 1864, Emily Eliot contemplated whether to consider it the "last comfort for many long weeks of seasickness & discomfort" or "a prelude to the unknown joys of Europe."[1] Women assured of adequate means might find the narrow circle Tocqueville imagined a fairly orderly and predictable place. Seeing the European treasures they had learned about and dreamed about for years, however, demanded stepping from their comfortable lives and enduring the sickness and discomfort of an ocean crossing. Historian Stephen Fox describes a nineteenth-century sea voyage as "a strange, disorienting stretch of time with few comforting similarities to any related experiences on land."[2] This strange time could be especially disorienting for women unaccustomed to adventuresome alternatives to the socially mandated routine of their lives.

A half-century after Emily sailed, thirteen-year-old Edith Rosenshine shared "an uncomfortable journey" with her mother from California to New York City where they waited for ten days before sailing to Europe. Edith cried as their ship passed the Statue of Liberty because "it was bad enough to leave San Francisco, but to leave the whole United States was terrible."[3] Most American travelers to Europe were spared an uncomfortable transcontinental journey followed by a lengthy hotel stay, but all had to face a long and often agonizingly uncomfortable ocean journey.

Women who crossed the ocean in the early-nineteenth century frequently had no female companions. Reminiscing decades later about sailing with her father in 1821, Eliza Smith explained, "in those days it was not so common for ladies to cross the ocean as at

A drawing of Cunard's *Oregon*
Library of Congress

present."[4] Most likely Eliza sailed on a mail packet which offered spare room to passengers. Until 1818, when the *James Monroe* began pioneering regularly scheduled service, ships sailed when the captain announced that the weather was agreeable and he was ready to depart.[5] Trips scheduled from New York to Liverpool, the most common point of entry in the nineteenth century, took on average seventeen days and the westerly return about three weeks, although bad weather or mechanical problems could result in a considerably longer voyage. Anne Eliza Rodman described her 1817 crossing as "a delightful voyage of thirty days," an unusually long time as well as an unusually positive memory of an antebellum voyage.[6] Her cheerful assessment is especially surprising given that in the first decades of the nineteenth century ship owners displayed little concern for passenger safety and comfort. An historian of early travel explains that in those years people sailed on ships designed to carry cargo "and passengers were often treated as such."[7] Since few women traveled, not much effort was made to accommodate those who did. The Black Ball Line, American leader of packet service, offered cabins with two bunks, a two-drawer chest, a washstand with a pitcher, a washbasin and a commode. Two hundred dollars assured passengers a berth as well as food and wine for the duration of the trip. Black Ball's *Canada*, launched in 1823, pioneered competition for passengers by offering at least a modicum of luxury; the women's cabins, for example, had fine blue silk curtains.[8]

In the 1840s steamships began offering a faster and safer voyage; it was, in turn, the decade that witnessed the feminization of European travel. Mary Suzanne Schriber explains "the advent of steam-powered ships and eventually of the 'steam palace' changed dramatically the conditions, speed, and practicality of travel and with it women's exposure to foreign lands."[9] The first steam ships were noisy, overcrowded and offered little improvement over sailing ships, but decade-by-decade passenger comfort was addressed.[10] Women were freer to cross the ocean for a Grand Tour if ships made some effort to approximate domestic space that allowed them a sense of propriety. The American Collins Line, which pioneered luxury ships, boasted its *Artic* had space for 200 first-class passengers. Collins designated "a gentlemen's smoking room and a gentlemen's barber shop," but offered no comparable facilities for women, signifying that it calculated most transatlantic voyagers would be men although the addition of five large bridal suites reveals they did anticipate at least a few female passengers would cross as well.[11] By the end of the century, when many and perhaps the majority of passengers were women, ships had become so luxurious that the finest were dubbed *floating palaces*.

Even later-day travelers presented with modern conveniences were familiar with the more ominous nautical depiction of *a watery grave*. When she crossed in mid-century, Florence Scofield recorded fear that the "disagreeable and dangerous" fog engulfing their ship would result in a collision, dooming her family of five to that dreaded fate.[12] Rare but deadly shipwrecks reminded that such fear was not unwarranted. News in 1850 that the freighter *Elizabeth* had crashed off the shore of Long Island with Margaret Fuller and her family among the casualties publicized the risk involved. Four years later the famed *Artic*, sailing from Liverpool with 281 passengers, collided with a smaller French steamship in heavy fog. Only twenty-three on board, all of them men and most of them crew members, survived; subsequent reports maintained that some of the survivors had forcefully prevented fellow passengers from boarding lifeboats. Stephen Fox conjectures that "in the history of transatlantic steam, no other event had such thudding, mournful impact in both America and Britain until fifty-eight years later the *Titanic* sank."[13] In the years between, accidents were rare enough that most Americans felt confident that they could cross the Atlantic and then re-cross it safely. That confidence was shattered on April 14, 1912, when the largest and most luxurious passenger ship ever built, one thought invincible, hit an iceberg and sank within three hours, killing over fifteen hundred of those on board. In contrast to the alleged brutality on the *Arctic*, an officer's gun mandated gallantry as the *Titanic* sank, preventing men from going first.[14]

No doubt upsetting news about the fate of the *Artic* and, a half-century later, even more devastating accounts of the *Titanic,* fueled by awareness of less publicized disasters, dissuaded some women from realizing trips dreamed of for years. Those who could stare down the possibility of a shipwreck still had to ponder their tolerance for the almost inevitable sickness suffered during long weeks at sea. Most women bold enough to sail, whether on antebellum packets or *fin de siècle* luxury liners, survived both crossings, but few escaped the agonies of seasickness. The afflicted sought humor in their plight by usurping phrases from French (*mal de mar*) or Italian (*mal di mare*) and by dignifying the inevitable vomiting as a tribute to Old Neptune or St. Ulrich. Neither foreign phrases nor the evocation of gods and saints, however, staved off the misery. Almost all letters and diaries written on board ship, as well as memoirs written years later, testify to intense suffering.

Those who sailed on antebellum sailing vessels offered the most pitiful accounts. Eliza Smith, one of thirteen passengers on a voyage from New York to Europe sailing in the 1820s, feared venturing on deck unless "clinging to the arm of a strong sailor." For three days she was too ill to open her trunk to change her wet dress or even comb her hair. Memory of her travails was so vivid thirty years later that she felt justified in claiming, "a sicker mortal was seldom seen." Searching for at least some humor of the absurd in her plight, Eliza remembered joining two other women in a small space with only a curtain separating them from the men, including a church bishop. "One morning," she recalled, "a very funny scene occurred. The ship was rocking tremendously; we girls attempted to dress but could not keep on our feet so we all took refuge on the floor with our basins in our laps when suddenly a fearful roll brought the poor bishop straight through the curtain in the midst of us all." A "ludicrous" scene followed when "basins flew and the night gowns all drenched."[15]

Likely Judith Page Rives found nothing humorous at all about days she was "reduced to helplessness" during her antebellum voyage. When her maid, the only other woman on board, fell ill, Judith lay unattended "motionless and almost senseless, with my hair disheveled over my pillow." Her suffering became so all consuming that she cast aside vanity and permitted it to be cut "as I would have clipped the superfluous shoots of my favorite multiflora." A flooded cabin compelled her to seek sanctuary in a room designated for male passengers and there she lay "stupid and motionless sometimes sleeping, utterly regardless of the presence of the Commandant of the Mediterranean squadron and other men." Judith thought they pitied her too much "to see any impropriety in the occasional visitation I was compelled to make to the common parlor."[16] Seasickness continued to undermine propriety well into the twentieth century.

Catherine Pritchard and her husband endured sailing for nearly two months from New Orleans to England. Catherine, the only woman on board, was well the first days although her husband quickly succumbed; as he recovered she took her turn among the afflicted. Without "the unremitted attentions of Mr. P.," she recalled, "I really believe I should have died."[17] Eliza Cox's family experienced storms that "rendered us exceedingly uncomfortable and myself sick from the time we parted until we came in sight of land." Day and night for nearly a month she sought sleep on a mattress on her cabin floor "tossing and tumbling until my brains were almost unsettled." The couple commenced their journey embracing the folk wisdom that only women suffered, but early on Mr. Cox confronted the sobering reality that he was not exempt. His wife reported that "poor hub, contrary to all expectation, was very sick for many days and squeamish the whole passage."[18] One antebellum woman was teased for her exemption as "it was so masculine—so unladylike—to feel perfectly well when all the other ladies on board are ill."[19] In reality, almost everyone suffered at times. Alicia Middleton's fifteen-year-old daughter resolved to disprove folk wisdom that seasickness was women's fate; unfortunately Alicia had to report on their first morning at sea that before the girl could dress, she "found her boastings vain, and the basin was in requisition." In days to come Alicia admitted that "every lady indeed every female not excepting the stewardess [was] sick, some most desperately." Her adult son Izard's suffering, however, was familial proof that men were not immune. On a day mother and daughter felt well enough to spend time on deck, Izard was unable to leave his bed or take anything but a little brandy and water; Alicia described him as "very miserable" and noted another man was "deplorably sick" as well.[20] Sarah Newberry found herself in the "unladylike" position of feeling well while her husband suffered. She read to him as a diversion as he was "a good deal distressed." One day he was so sick that she was left to spend hours alone battling her own malady of homesickness.[21]

A woman sailing in the 1830s despaired that life at sea was "indeed a dog's life," and questioned if she would have undertaken the trip if she had anticipated the misery. She joined fellow passengers feeling such relief on approaching land that "the ladies frolicked in their cabin until midnight" where "whiskey punch and the Saturday night toasts were drunk."[22] Frolics and toasts were among the ways antebellum passengers well enough sought to upgrade their experience to more than a dog's life. Sarah Tuckerman held long conversations—including a discussion of German authors—read Tocqueville's recently published *Democracy in America*, walked the deck and stared at the sea; even so, she confessed, "the truth is I am—sadly idle."[23] A few days on the ocean left Sarah Cleveland feeling no longer "an intelligent animal," but rather "a fit companion only for fish, sea-weed & sponges."[24] Anne Eliza Rodman, less critical of forced idleness, could enjoy "watching the glorious deep or walking the deck and conversing." She was amused by a fellow passenger's sage conclusion that "I must be <u>in love</u> because I am so fond of sitting alone upon the rail & gazing upon the ever changing world of waters about me." With books and backgammon to supplement an eye on the sea, time passed more pleasantly than she had anticipated.[25]

At mid-century, Charlotte Horlbeck's father mandated that his family cross in a sailing ship, assuring her place as one of the last women to travel this way. She first pitied the men who made do without cabins until she realized the "discomforts of this sea voyage are great & increasing every day," and decided it would be preferable to sleep on the floor as the men did "even if I had to do as Mr. Ford once did covering with a pair of shoes and 3 skeleton's tools." Instead she and her sister endured hours "stuffed in" with a stranger who was "sick & vomiting all the while" in a room so small she couldn't turn around, equipped with a basin of discolored water and a soiled towel. Stormy weather left Charlotte with little to do but study French, skim old novels, daydream and talk about where the ship was and when they would reach land. Four tedious weeks at sea at least inspired her opinion that one could not appreciate "the grand old ocean in any other manner half so well."[26]

Passengers on the Atlantic after mid-century may not have appreciated the grand ocean as much, but most embraced the comforts of steamships, including a shorter crossing and a greater variety of entertainment than books and backgammon. In the 1850s Britain's *Cunard*, mid-century's largest steamship line, adopted the motto "Speed, Comfort, and Safety," forcing its competitors to assure greater comfort as well. American companies aspired to compete until loss of the *Artic* and several other disastrous wrecks in the mid-fifties ended vital government subsidies. From the 1860s into the twentieth century the United States government focused on the railroads essential to western expansion. Challenges to British domination of the ship-building industry came primarily from Continental Europeans who competed for American passengers. John Maxtone-Graham, author of a history of passenger liners, suggests that European ship builders realized "the riches of the American traffic made innovation a realistic economic risk." He describes a symbiotic relationship that developed between European ship owners seeking American dollars and Americans eager to see familiar treasures of the Old World.[27]

From mid-century on a steadily increasing number of those wishing to have a look were women. Mary Suzanne Schriber explains, "as entrepreneurs seized financial opportunities in catering to women, so women seized ideological opportunities from the taste for profits that motivated the captains of industry."[28] This collusion of interest expanded narrow circles; as it became easier to reach Europe, it also became easier for women to imagine themselves on a Grand Tour.

Steamships became ever more luxurious every decade, but luxury did not alleviate all the travails of an ocean crossing. Although perhaps not as wrenching as those told by antebellum sufferers, most steam-age travelers had their own sad tales to tell. After "old Neptune exacted his tribute," Madge Preston succumbed to protracted seasickness that overwhelmed "all power of action, all thoughts, all thought of others, all desire, saving that one longing wish to die!"[29] One woman described feeling she "had swallowed red hot lead that will not digest" and another of imagining herself "a cat that has lost eight lives and is heading to the ninth."[30] Nineteen-year-old Catherine Van Rensselaer's suffering was exacerbated by her younger sister Eleanor's immunity. At first they enjoyed running together on the deck, but in short order Catherine felt "as if I would like to be thrown overboard." She retired to her berth while Eleanor spent the rest of the day making "ever so enduring friends among the gents." As their voyage ended, Catherine still complained of protracted suffering while "E. was as bright as if steamers were never invented."[31] M.E. Winslow likely articulated the sentiment of more than a few when bemoaning "what fools we were to come when we might have stayed at home just as well as not," because "no place is worth going to that is only attained by means of a 'sea ship'."[32]

Folk wisdom that alcohol could ease the agonies of seasickness may have transformed some inveterate teetotalers into ready imbibers. Despite ample warning, Mary Jane Blair ate a hearty meal her last night on land, rationalizing she "might as well die for a sheep as a lamb." As a result, on her first day at sea, "before I had gone half across the deck (how far it seemed) I gave two or three gulps in my handkerchief then made a desperate rush for the side of the boat where I paid my respects to St. Ulrich & threw my kerchief to the sharks." She began a morning ritual of whiskey and smelling salts, hoping the combination would preclude paying her respects again.[33] A glass of whiskey was not unusual, but champagne, described by one woman as "the finest support," was the favored alcoholic palliative and champagne punch was commonly available.[34] A variety of diets were recommended to stave off seasickness; one allowing only "lemons, sourballs, mint drops, gingernuts and apples" was surely more restrictive than most.[35]

Well into the twentieth century, medical science echoed folklore's diagnosis of seasickness as largely a female affliction. The assumption that *the weaker sex* was more likely to succumb was remarkably enduring and could become a self-fulfilling prophecy. Levenstein asserts "women could express fears of shipwreck, seasickness, and loneliness, but males had to repress them."[36] Indeed, *Baedeker's*, the most popular nineteenth-century guidebook, called on its presumably male readers "to fight manfully against sea sickness" when crossing the ocean. They tried.[37] Mrs. A.T. Bullard described her male companions as facing the seafaring malady with "resolution and defiance" while the women were "all passive, gentle and silent, if not amiable."[38] But some women, while perhaps giving lip service to the assumption that they were the more likely sufferers, were also quick to identify men who fell ill. Martha Griffis's report that "no ladies made their appearance at table except myself (and even then seven gentlemen were out)" is an example of how women covertly challenged this curiously gendered diagnosis.[39]

Those who recorded sympathy for men who fell ill sometimes spiced their concern with a dash of mirth. Once recovered from her own bout of misery, Mary Fraser confided disappointment that a male companion had not been sick at all.[40] Marion Burgess was "much amused" when a man who offered her assistance on deck was soon forced to make a hasty retreat so "not proof against [male] sea sickness after all."[41] Mary Jane Blair, proud of her alcohol-infused resilience, described a companion as "forlorn" and when he stayed in his berth an entire day, claiming to work on his accounts, quipped, "my private opinion is that the old sea god was too much for him."[42] Mary Gay recalled a morning when "after vain attempts to dress and avert the dreaded illness, we ladies were obliged to succumb while the gentleman [her husband] with a few others of his own sex only breakfasted in the deserted saloon and then mounted to the smoking room above where all the principal questions of the day were discussed and summarily settled." With barely veiled glee, she reported "his triumph, however, was comparatively short, as before he retired somewhat unsettled within and without, to his berth, unable to leave it the next day or the next."[43] Fannie Smith sketched her amusement watching three men struggle with this unmanly malady. In the first frame Jones says to Smith standing on the deck: "Of course you are never sea sick," and a chorus of three replies "Oh dear no—." In the second frame the three men lean overboard, repeating "Oh dear no." To one side of her drawing Fannie penned: "The dinner bell is ringing <u>amidst groans</u>," and "put them in their little beds."[44]

Even in the era of floating palaces women (and, of course, men as well) still had to give Old Neptune his due. Weather was the primary culprit causing bouts of seasickness to wax and wane. Adella Hughes and Jeanette Aglionby both sailed in the spring of 1890 on similar ships. Adella reached Europe pleasantly surprised that a calm ocean allowed "such a delightful voyage;" Jeanette had the more depressing postscript that her crossing had been "a tedious & trying one in the extreme," that "all were sick ... even the men couldn't keep on deck."[45]

In the 1840s Sarah Newberry boasted of being the only passenger fit to join the captain for an evening meal; when he fell sick she could further brag, "all acknowledge me the best sailor of all."[46] Boastings about being a good sailor, of having the reputation as "the best sailors of our party," of feeling "quite proud of my exemption," were more frequently penned later in the century when the athletic Gibson Girl model, while still emphasizing proper femininity, also inspired women to challenge an ideal of fragility.[47] Herma Clark felt "a bit giddy" but assured those at home "pride keeps me at table."[48]

Sarah was an exceptional sailor on deck but described her cabin as "purgatory."[49] Even accommodations on modern steamships could be especially hellish during rough seas. Reports of being tossed from berths spanned the century; one woman reported seven such mishaps in one night.[50] Another was so frightened by stormy weather that she spent a night in the music room wearing her life preserver.[51] Louise Kellner's vivid description of a storm at sea may have dissuaded friends at home from following her path.

"The last two nights have been a heavy strain on our nervous systems," she wrote, "for in the silence of darkness, with the angry sea dashing and crashing against our ship as if a thousand canons were fired off at one time, and trunks, valises, ladders, water-bottles, tin cans, and no end of crockery dancing to and fro—hail, rain and snow making their own mysterious noises against the windows, and a sick lady in the state room next to ours moaning and groaning—it was [uncanny?] enough to excite and unnerve the strongest of us for the time being."[52]

The greater comfort steamships offered did not necessarily eliminate morning toilets almost as comical as Eliza Smith's encounter with the bishop on her sailing vessel. Mary Jane Blair's description of her morning routine offered her family a glimpse and a laugh: "I had the lower berth & made mine (such as it was) first. I would crawl out, sit on the floor, put on my stockings, then after a short respite lean over to try the other then a gaiter, another, rest. Then in a fit of desperation on would go the other …. The worst part was putting on our garments for with them we were obliged to stand up & give ourselves an occasional shaking."[53]

Women had no choice but to sleep and dress in their cabins and remain there when captains mandated; some preferred the confined space most of the time. Jeanette Aglionby described her companions as "dragging about wretched" on deck, while she was convinced that "solitary confinement" was the lesser of two evils.[54] Louisa Stephens preferred being in her cabin after dark because its light gave her a sense of security. As a result she was often alone, left to confide in her diary "how I wish the family would come in off the deck."[55]

Her female relatives joined a number of women who preferred spending time in the open air. Mary Bradbury became better acquainted with the male passengers—she described them as "especially nice"— since few women joined her outside.[56] On one stormy night Eliza Gardner insisted on walking the deck despite the rush of women below; another day, as the ocean churned, she was again "the only lady who had ventured beyond the cabin."[57] Martha Griffis usually left her cabin soon after she awoke and walked for an hour or more until joined by her brother.[58] Isabel Rogers was awakened early "by heavy kettles and heavy stepping servants above my head getting ready to prepare breakfast," so was often the first person on deck where she resolved to stay until late at night to avoid "turning into my miserable stateroom."[59]

When not preoccupied with seasickness, passengers coped with many other inconveniences of life at sea. In the 1820s, the captain's wife and a female passenger led a promenade on a tilting deck; despite holding fast to the arms of their "squires," both women fell, one flying over the hen coop and the other sliding under it.[60] The hens and other live animals required to assure a continuous supply of meat fueled complaints that early ships were dirty.[61] A woman grappling with the common antebellum annoyance that there was nowhere to sit found it "amusing how wistfully we look one out of his seat."[62] Storms, the occasional snow day, mechanical problems, extended travel time, lost ground—these were among the grievances that left some questioning their decision to undertake a sea voyage.

Modern steam ships available from mid-century on had means of refrigeration that rendered floating chicken coops obsolete, were reasonably clean and provided comfortable deck chairs, yet their passengers continued to offer up a litany of complaints. One "elderly stout woman," as a fellow passenger described her, endured most of her voyage without false teeth that flew over the ship's rail when she hastened there to greet Old Neptune.[63] Frances Gaston reported to "land lubbers" at home that during a "first class storm at sea," her daughter tumbled against the ship railing with no one available to help her so "scuttled back like a crab." Frances was thrown across their cabin and skinned her nose "much to the amusement of the captain."[64] Harriet Trowbridge watched with amazement "at the green foam-crested waves, when suddenly there was a dash and a roar, and I found myself drenched by the very wave whose approach I had been breathlessly watching;" she was left to ponder "whether old ocean meant it as a baptism, or as a warning that henceforth his glories were to be looked upon from afar."[65] The ocean sometimes sent its glories right into cabins, leaving everything soaked. Madge Preston and her mates persuaded their steward to leave a porthole open, promising to close it if necessary. They awoke to six inches of water. When the steward answered their call for help, he found them all "convulsed with laughter" despite their wet clothes.[66]

Captains and crewmen could laugh at minor mishaps, but as revenues from tourism increased, efforts to make passengers as comfortable as possible grew in tandem. Women rarely had reason to criticize the man in charge of their ship. One who did assumed her ill-tempered captain was angry about an accident early in the voyage.[67] Julia Haylander concluded the suspicious woman sharing her antebellum ship was the captain's mistress which "destroys all comfort" as "the very thought makes everything unpleasant."[68] Such trysts were likely more common in the years before captains were employees of competitive ship companies, but there were still occasional complaints in later decades. Helen Gould ruefully noted that the captain of her ship spoke to no one else but was "devotion itself" to an attractive woman on board.[69] Eliza Gardner, who had likely heard tales of amorous captains, praised the man in charge of her ship as "rarely seen except when anything is required of him & [one who] looks after his ship instead of making love to the ladies."[70]

Most women were satisfied that the men in charge took good care of them. Praise for captains included "good [and] kind," "just as jolly and nice as he can be," "quiet, dignified [and] gentlemanly" and "the finest man in every way I ever met."[71] Helen Gould's English captain frequently escorted his female passengers on deck and brought them rugs (ship vernacular for heavy blankets); she extended her praise of him to all Englishmen who, she conjectured, respected women more than other men did.[72]

Ship captains commanded a hierarchy of crewmen ranked from first to fourth, as well as cooks, stewards and, especially on larger ships, stewardesses, plus a number of sailors who tended to the variety of chores necessary for a successful voyage. Most female passengers either praised or ignored crewmembers, but occasionally one was singled out for complaint. An antebellum traveler on the clipper ship *Young America* found the first mate's flirtation with a female passenger "shocking dalliance," especially since it occurred "while on duty!" The captain's repeated demands that he desist were to no avail so he confined the miscreant to quarters until he could be sent ashore.[73] Caroline White objected to the quantity of alcohol the crew consumed, but she also objected when the third mate beat his sailors for being intoxicated.[74] Madge Preston complained that after her stewardess fell victim to seasickness she "left unmade our beds and neglected other duties very necessary to the attended to both for health and cleanliness."[75]

Even those blessed with a more attentive stewardess could find maintaining cleanliness challenging. Ruth Church learned too late that seasoned travelers, privy to the efficacy of tipping, were rewarded with favored bath hours. Her uninitiated family was allotted the ten-thirty slot which, she complained, ruined their mornings.[76] A generous tip would not have solved Isabelle Busbee's problem; she was awakened one morning by someone shaking her shoulders and discovered it was a bath steward "so ugly he scared me."[77] These two women were unusual in mentioning private matters such as bathing at all; most maintained the silence that gentility dictated.

Typically Americans sailed with crews of native English speakers, but some first faced the challenge of coping with an unfamiliar language while at sea. Hannah Gould knew nothing of her crew's native tongue, but rationalized "the fact that the stewards are all Dutch makes the difficulty of getting what you want rather exciting."[78] Mary Elizabeth Gittings found her German crew kind and helpful, but preferred they ignore her since she could not speak their language. In time she learned that when a steward looked at her to just shake her head and say *nicht* which prompted him to touch his cap and respond *bitte*. The ritual worked so well that Mary Elizabeth concluded "it's nice to be a woman after all."[79]

If socially prescribed boundaries were respected, young women, especially those traveling in later decades, had some license to flirt with crewmembers. Jennie Young, sailing in mid-century, praised the "excellent kind captain" who took her on walks, read to her and escorted her to dinner. There is no evidence revealing what the other passengers thought of their relationship and Jennie offered no hint that his intention was less than innocent.[80] Nina Pape described a companion on her mid-century voyage as "lively as a kitten," who went around with the cook and sailors "as much at home as if she were one of them."[81] Probably she described a child, as it is unlikely she would have reported such familiarity between the crewmen and a young woman so uncritically. Not all of the young and unmarried, however, were strictly supervised. Mary

Stiles ridiculed those she chaperoned as "forever jabbering and giggling over the officers and telling each other which one they love the most."[82] Seventeen-year-old Julia Butler had "lots of fun with the fourth officer—very good looking and nice," but was less successful with the captain; when she tried to visit his cabin he "took me by the collar and put me out, much to my disgust."[83] Julia sailed in 1890, a time young women increasingly found the ship a place to test boundaries imposed at home.

Henrietta Frank reported from one of her several voyages that "about all we do is walking at intervals & eating at longer intervals."[84] A primary mandate of every crew was to assure passengers enjoyed abundant and appealing food during the long intervals. Harvey Levenstein suggests that as early as the 1830s "the transatlantic packets were already renowned for their munificent meals."[85] A Scotsman traveling with Cunard at mid-century offered firsthand corroboration, noting "how so many things can be cooked, how there can be so much pastry dressed up daily, is a standing wonder to everybody."[86] Antebellum shipboard cuisine, however, was not uniformly munificent; pastry every day would have certainly been a wonder to passengers on early sailing ships. Mid-way in Eliza Smith's voyage stormy weather inhibited the ship's cow from giving milk, forcing the crew to slaughter chickens prematurely to supplement a diet of sea biscuits.[87] Passengers on a crossing in 1836 missed an evening meal when the cook fell and spilled a tureen of turtle soup over his face and neck; he attempted to make amends by preparing a new batch the next day.[88] That decade Alicia Middleton enjoyed mackerel for breakfast as "quite a treat" after days of "nothing but mutton boiled, mutton washed & mutton stewed for four days & strong tough poor mutton."[89]

Even in later decades, when meals were elaborate affairs offering much greater variety than mutton, there was the inevitable fault finding. Elizabeth Nichols complained of "hurry and confusion and want of clothes and napkins."[90] Nearly a century after Eliza Smith made do with sea biscuits, Mabel Root described meals on her ship as "queer, but as good as you could expect, I suppose, on an Italian boat;" she did acknowledge that other passengers described "an astonishingly good table."[91] Variations of praise—"everything that one can desire in the eating and drinking way is to be had," "the jolliest dinners [with] such menus and such style," "food that was "abundant & luxurious" and "sumptuous enough to feed kings"—drowned out complaints on most postbellum voyages.[92]

Lavina Urbino described a typical day dining aboard her ship: "a hearty breakfast at eight; lunch at twelve; dinner at four, and tea at eight o'clock; supper for those who desired it." She singled out a fellow passenger "a lady—yes, and one of the so-called sick ones, too" for her breakfasts of "coffee, beefsteak, boiled eggs, hot biscuits, buttered toast, and fried potatoes, with one tumbler of punch and another of cider."[93] Teenager Bessie Horstmann skipped breakfast for a morning walk, ate lunch at noon, dinner at four and tea at seven, all eaten with "gusto as the salt air was very good for giving me a good appetite."[94] Ruth Church did not have the option of missing breakfast because her ship's buglers awoke passengers for their first meal. "At eight promptly," she recounted, "a gong sent a swarm of waiters down the aisles with the first course, [and] another sent them back to retrieve the dishes."[95]

The novel experience of men preparing and serving meals was a rare respite from the domestic obligations most women faced at home. Miss Davis offered a satirical assessment of this role reversal: "I have been reconsidering the principles of life ... before I have fully believed that the housekeeping and dishwashing were especially the province of women but the practical experience of the last fortnight has completely upset the views of a life time." She praised the captain for being "kindly as a woman," and reported "we had eaten but one meal when we knew our ground and were at home." She also praised the crew for "a splendid table[;] not a word of fault can be found." Miss Davis's tongue-in-check account concluded that "from this time forth be it known that I believe it to be a piece of usurpation for women to claim the housekeeping." She now assured no doubt "that a woman might learn navigation and command a ship," as "this is not so very difficult an affair after all," but also insisted that "to put all this hospitality and diplomatic management into execution requires a kind of cool nonchalance which women do not arrive at [at] an early age to say the least." No woman, she asserted, could deal with "guests unable to eat as dinner spoiled," or "the frequent crash of china."[96] This witty assessment reveals one woman's enhanced understanding of the contextual reality of gender roles often defended as immutable.

The dining room, the largest interior space on most ships, was the gathering place for meals as well as a variety of entertainment. Stephen Fox explains that "the first dinner at sea was a defining event" because tables were reserved for the entire voyage. Experienced and well-informed passengers marked their preferred place at table with a visiting card. A seat near the captain was coveted for status, but those anticipating the occasional quick exit might prefer close proximity to the door.[97] One father made the unusual request for new tables because men seated with his family made what he considered inappropriate remarks in front of his daughters; the captain deftly solved the problem by persuading the offenders to be more circumspect in their language.[98] Clara Ritchie endured men who "talk of nothing but pool and betting until we are quite disgusted," but she could at least rationalize they were "the only drawback to our pleasure."[99] Susan Hale described a man seated beside her as "a jackass, who on the strength of teaching French a few years at Harvard, proclaims himself Professor of that place."[100] Louise Keltner, always solicitous of her travel companions, siblings Lydia and John Morris, first regretted sharing a table with people "not at all agreeable" and resolved to deal with them "as a necessary evil and with all politeness of course;" by the end of the trip, however, "two ladies at our table are the only nuisance we have to put up with." When admirers sent flowers and fruit to Lydia, all three enjoyed the attention and Louise surmised that even their table steward was proud. On a subsequent trip, the captain switched two men who complained of a breeze to Lydia's table, likely a ruse designed to meet the attractive woman they continued pursuing throughout Europe.[101]

The sociability shipboard dining offered was constantly undermined by seasickness as most passengers suffered through days when they could not eat at all and some could only tolerate meals in the open air even when well. Mary Peirce and her companion, both awarded the sobriquet good sailor, often found themselves the only women in the dining room; one calm day it struck Mary as quite unusual and "so pleasant to have ladies at the table!"[102] After several bouts of seasickness, Susan Minor likened eating in the dining room to "death" so commenced taking her meals outside.[103] Emily Severance pondered if those at home could "imagine the ladies of the Clev. [Cleveland] party bundled up with hoods, waterproofs and shawls taking our dinner and supper on deck."[104]

Fin de siècle floating palaces offered private dining options that freed women from nuisances, gamblers and jackasses. On the ill-fated *Titanic*, for example, women could dine at small tables in the Parisian Café rather than share a table with strangers in the first-class dining room. Some ships even offered room service. Georgette Chamberlain opted for breakfast in her cabin so she could eat and dress at her leisure.[105]

Ship crews occasionally broke the monotony of routine with special dinners or parties and occasionally passengers orchestrated such events as well. Julia Rush attended a dinner exclusively for women which featured champagne punch and realized she was made "a great deal better by the frolic."[106] Female passengers on another voyage invited their captain to a party in the ladies' cabin; he brought them a peace offering to make up for his unkind (and unrecorded) comments about Americans.[107] The captain of the *S.S. Haverford* arranged a birthday party for several young women from North Carolina which their hometown paper described as "a beautiful one," complete with a cake, "a master piece of the chef's hands." Toasts and recitations enlivened the event, but rain precluded dancing on the deck.[108]

Modern steamships typically offered a Captain's Dinner near voyage's end. Mamie Parsons penned a witty description of one she attended: "The band stands behind the captain—the stewards all retire to the pantry. At a given signal the bandmaster strikes up—the head steward enters and advances to the captain—the band continues. More stewards enter—the band gets excited—the stewards to their particular tables, the fiddlers fiddle—the trumpets sound—the drums beat and we all eat soup to the time of the *Tannhauser Overture*. Then the roast beef gallops in—the fish (which is always no. 3) waltzes in. The salad has a ballet dance, and I tell Louise [the woman she traveled with] that they ought to usher us out with a funeral march."[109] Adelaide Werner's special dinner featured waiters carrying ice cream illuminated by Japanese lanterns, "one of the prettiest sights I have ever seen." When the orchestra ended the dinner by playing *Columbia* she reported that whereas "the Americans clapped their hands off and kept time with there

[sic] feet," several German passengers questioned if the song was appropriate.[110]

If the weather cooperated, the Captain's Dinner was often capped by a dance on the deck. Sarah Elliott described a "lively party" and, although the men "looked very Protestant," she did not protest at all.[111] When the majority on board, women may have welcomed even Protestant-looking men. Isabel Coleman danced with another woman until the captain introduced them to two young men; she "enjoyed it very much" with a male partner.[112] Isabel Busbee and her female friends, on the other hand, preferred dancing with each other.[113]

The success of dinners and dances depended a great deal on conditions at sea. One held around the turn of the century started with 250 guests, but ended with only 40 or so as one by one revelers had to shift their attention from the captain's celebration to Old Neptune's dictates. On her third trip to Europe, Louise Kellner was disappointed that bad weather forced the cancellation of the special dinner "with the illuminated ice cream at the end—the big dining room darkened and the stewards marching to the tunes of the music," as well as the ball planned for afterward.[114] On another voyage the ship approached England on a foggy night which mandated cancelling the dance to enable the crew to hear the foghorns.[115]

Holidays were usually a respite from the monotony of an ocean crossing. Even some European crews accommodated their largely American clientele by commemorating the Fourth of July. Abbie Perkins's crew launched fireworks "to remind us of the 'glorious 4th'."[116] Mabel Bragdon was "astonished & pleased" that the ecumenical sailors on her ship had decorated the dining room with both American and British flags and offered "all good American delicacies."[117] One captain made the unusual gesture of inviting children from steerage to participate in an Independence Day pageant. Sallie Wilbur, who represented American Indians in this morning show, also attended "exercises, toasts, music, ect [sic]" in the evening, "an elegant time" exclusively for first- and second-class passengers.[118] Passengers on a Dutch ship awakened to the *Star Spangled Banner* and discovered the dining room decorated for a celebration that began with a grand march around the deck followed by speeches (whether by the Dutch crew or their American passengers was not recorded).[119] Less obliging Europeans left it to their American passengers to celebrate if they wished. Herma Clark joined in setting off firecrackers and singing patriotic songs.[120] Emma Trexler and her shipmates made do with decorations and singing because their captain banned fireworks.[121]

No other holiday garnered as much attention as July Fourth because summer was the most popular time to sail. Mary Gay awoke to discover sailors had decorated her ship Christmas Eve night, but offered no organized celebration; in time she joined a group of women discussing their families and other domestic matters, "always an attractive topic to the feminine mind."[122]

Most crossings included varied evening entertainment intended to amuse passengers as well as raise money for seamen's widows and children. One program offered instrumental and vocal solos and imitations of a character dubbed "Rastus," a denigration of African-Americans for entertainment that was, unfortunately, welcomed on board.[123] After a benefit concert which included a man imitating a "negro preacher" delivering a sermon, Nina Pape, whose intolerance was racially inclusive, joined others for wine, but later complained, "if I had known who the company were going to be, I would have refused."[124] Martha Griffis enjoyed an evening of poetry readings, singing and "some racy witty anecdoks [sic] that kept us all amused."[125] Sarah Guild's father was in charge of a night's entertainment that featured a tenor "who sang gloriously," a speech, card tricks, a mimic who imitated a dogfight and a ventriloquist claimed as the world's most famous.[126] Early in the twentieth century Ginevra Freeman helped organize a musical that included awarding ribbons to all the women and toasts to President Taft and King Edward VII.[127]

Captains and their crews also improvised informal ways to keep spirits up during the tedious middle stretch. Heavy rain prompted Sarah Cleveland's captain to rig a large tent where "we went to house keeping immediately [which was] completed with buffalo skins & sofa cushions against the railings."[128] Conversely, Althea Harper's captain announced that due to exceptionally good weather he would pitch a tent on deck for a dance, news greeted with applause. The passengers were soon dancing and "laughing at our friends on shore who are no doubt thinking we are sea sick."[129]

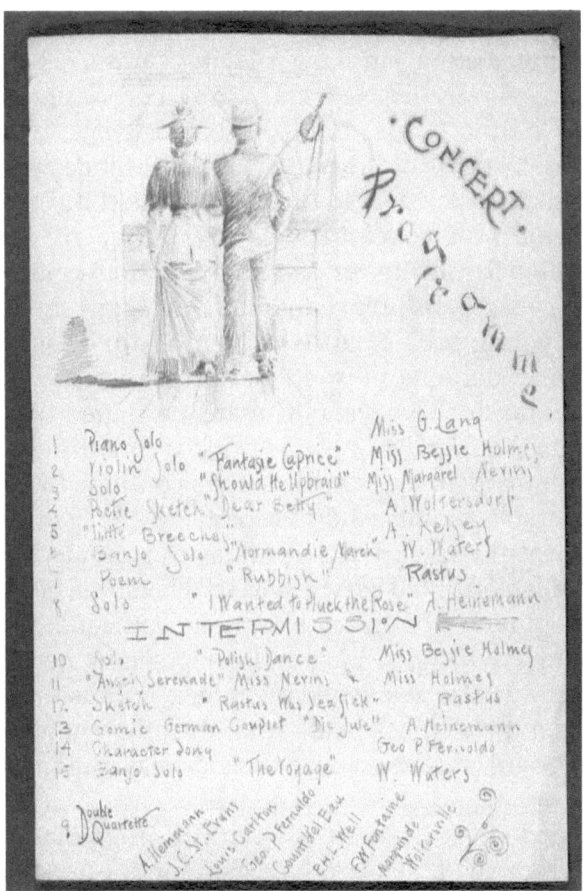

Program from a concert held on Susan Minor's ship in 1892
University of Virginia

Passengers also devised informal amusements that changed little across the century. Kate Jones assured "we spend our time delightfully," explaining "those of us well enough to be up [are] running up on deck, watching for sea monsters & ice-bergs—promenading, exchanging a pleasant word with each as we pass, playing proverbs, charades, solving riddles & at night most of [us] gather in the gentlemen's saloon and Dr. A. has prayer. This service concludes all our evenings. We sing too, a great deal."[130] Lizzie Van Benschoten, sailing a half century after Kate, described a similar day; "just imagine," she reported home, "about 150 persons on deck, some walking and others stretched out in chairs, talking, reading, writing, eating, smoking, playing games, joking & having a good time generally."[131] Near the end of her voyage Mary Hartt checked off "all the proper things[:] seen a whale, two steamers, a sailing vessel, shoals of porpoises and on Monday we slipped a big wave which took a whole line of unsuspecting people full in the face. Tonight the concert comes off and we are complete."[132] On a typical day Sarah Hunter, an early-twentieth-century traveler, "saw whales, read, [and] played games." At night she walked and watched the young people dance to the music of a bagpipe.[133]

In the early decades most ships observed the Christian Sabbath in some fashion. For years Cunard permitted only Anglican services until, Stephen Fox notes, "prickly Americans" protested; even when more inclusive, Cunard ships continued to be "floating bastions of established British Protestantism."[134] It was common for Sabbath observance to vary from Sunday to Sunday depending on who was available to hold services. Mary Flavelle reported one day with no recognition of Sunday except for someone "tooting on a cornet a hymn," which she blamed for worsening her headache.[135] Laura Libbey was also awakened by hymns, but discerned no other indication that it was the Sabbath until the following week when a minister on board, recovered from seasickness, began holding services.[136]

By the end of the nineteenth century, religious observation waned and services that were held became more varied. Herma Clark was amused that her fellow turn-of-the-century passengers refused to attend a sermon "given by a non-conformist."[137] Some ships did not even offer an unorthodox preacher. Complaints that it did not seem like Sunday, a common refrain throughout Europe, were honed in route. Hannah Gould criticized fellow passengers for organizing a party rather than being "as strictly observant of the Sabbath as we should have been." Days later, however, she rationalized that on the ocean "we are in a wonderful blue temple where it's easier to worship then most places & so Sunday gets distributed through the week."[138] In the early-twentieth century, an escort advised the young women in his charge that holding Sunday service on board was "considered affected" so no longer done.[139]

An American traveling to Europe in the mid-nineteenth century conjectured that life on board ship was an experience "annihilating the conventional distinctions, differences, and social distance between man and man."[140] In reality, extreme social distances prevailed largely intact. Passengers in first and second class had little contact with the poor in steerage struggling to improve their lives by going to America or re-crossing the Atlantic back to their homelands. Racial mingling was certainly taboo in the antebellum years and the taboo survived on many ships into the twentieth century. In 1845, famed black abolitionist Frederick Douglass's request for a first-class cabin was denied by Cunard's Boston office, forcing him to travel in crowded steerage instead.[141] A decade later the company's British officials acceded to American prejudice and confined Caroline Putnam's party, all of them of African background, to a separate table apart from the other passengers.[142]

In the early twentieth century, Mabel Root, unusual in her concern about the extreme inequity on passenger liners, questioned if "this is a shameful sort of ship" with 1,500 steerage passengers crowded into a fourth of the ship's space while the eighty people in first and second classes enjoyed the rest. Mabel's sense of shame did not, however, preclude contempt as she shuddered to be on "this wide lonesome sea" with steerage's poor "so near with their dirt and numbers and discomfort."[143]

Having a look at steerage was a popular pastime although it was generally expected that women who ventured there would be accompanied by a male escort; those who had a look were about equally divided as to whether steerage passengers were content or wretched. Ethel Dummer concluded that in first class "absurd unhuman conventionalities" inhibited socializing, but "below the peasants dance merrily to an accordion & the 2nd class folk gather in a group."[144] Idella Plimpton, on the other hand, thought steerage "a place for cattle instead of humans."[145] Ironically Idella wrote in 1869 and Ethel forty years later. Before 1880 many steerage passengers were from northern and western Europe and generally enjoyed better accommodations than those from southeastern Europe who followed.[146]

Ethel distinguished between first- and second-class passengers, but the two groups usually shared public spaces and socialized together. Passengers of more modest means might have at least limited interaction with the very wealthy and for the most part their relations were cordial. Nina Pape was unusual in her complaint that "on board ship rank seems to be set aside at table for one sits with all classes & conditions of mankind."[147] Clara Ritchie, from a wealthy Cleveland family, sailed with John D. Rockefeller and his family and found them "very unassuming."[148] Constance Harrison traveled with Astors and Vanderbilts who, she noted, "stay together but [are] not exclusive."[149]

In the mid-nineteenth century sectional conflict could be more polarizing than class status; as the debate over slavery intensified and finally brought war, northern and southern passengers grew more wary of one another, although they were rarely overtly hostile. In 1851 Kate Jones found that although she liked all of the passengers, she gravitated to her fellow Southerners. On one occasion they came together "all in a group talking of our beloved southern homes—our peculiar institutions, & one by one we began to tell anecdotes & incidents of our negroes—their sayings, [and] superstitions" and "have had so much fun."[150] Occasionally Northerners and Southerners sailed together during the war years. In 1864 a captain was warned that although two women traveling with him lived in San Francisco, they "are rebels & true to their native land," but he was also assured "their treason will only make them more interesting to you."[151]

Once the Union was restored, Southerners were no longer rebels liable to charges of treason. New Yorker Catherine Townsend, sailing only months after the war ended, described most of her fellow passengers as "disgusting" and "vulgar but amusing" except for a group of "secech people" from Virginia she thought "very nice."[152] In the winter of 1866, Ohioan Mary Jane Blair noted without further comment that the majority of passengers on her ship, including General P.G.T. Beauregard, Confederate commander in the war's first major battle, were from the South.[153] The only woman assigned to New Englander Eugenie Homer's table was "a determined conservative southern" who defended slavery; unfazed, Eugenie just concluded it was "very nice for us to have had her with her gray hair with us."[154]

A few years into Reconstruction Laura and Bettie Thomas and their escort found themselves the only Southerners on their ship.

Laura thought passengers from the North "seemed delighted to know us & are kind, polite and exceedingly attentive;" indeed, she and Bettie found the northern men so charming they "were tempted to get up quite a little romance."[155]

There were, however, Southerners with enduring memories who clung tenaciously to their Confederate identity. Three decades after the war's end, South Carolinian Eleanor Middleton decided that "one reason we find the voyage so fatiguing is the numbers and perpetual presence of the invading hordes of vulgar Yankees."[156] A decade later, when a crewman made the mistake of calling Mary Jane McMaster a Yankee, the diehard rebel threatened if "You call me a Yankee I'll wreck the ship. I'm a Southerner."[157]

Northern and southern Americans sailing to Europe were overwhelming Protestants, and some of them met Catholics, Jews and members of other religions for the first time on their voyage. M. E. Thompson listened so intently to a French Catholic explain his faith that she feared he concluded she had made a convert.[158] Louise Kellner was astonished to learn from the first Catholics she had ever talked to that they believed much the same as Protestants.[159] The Catholics and Jews who astonished Protestants could in turn be astonished themselves. Henrietta Frank had an enlightening conversation with Mormons, previously known to her only as believers in polygamy.[160] Most likely, a number of Henrietta's fellow passengers had never talked to a Jew before meeting her.

Not all Americans who mingled with passengers from other lands were impressed with the people they met.[161] In 1898 Annie Fields held a defensive debate with a Frenchman about her country's declaration of war on Spain as well as its past treatment of Indians.[162] When Susan Marsh Emerson met English people for the first time, she criticized them as rude for talking too much.[163] Mamie Parsons complained of fellow passengers who were "German Jews of the most horrid type."[164] Angelica Van Buren did not distinguish among nationalities, but simply concluded that all "foreigners are certainly destitute of natural modesty not to say decency."[165]

More women, however, responded positively to their ship's international flavor. Emma Traxel found French girls, with their "flirtation, singing and talking French," endlessly amusing.[166] Sarah Hunter, traveling with "a well-behaved crowd of simple German folk with a sprinkling of Hungarians, Poles, English, Americans and Italians," concluded that German ships had fewer "impossible people" than American ones.[167] Herma Clark's experience inspired her insight that "it is good for me to see people of different nationalities & religious affiliations in this way and realize that though there is so much difference in our ways, we are all trying to do what we can to make the world better." After watching passengers playing cards (she did not reveal their nationality), she decided it was not "a vital question at all, and that those who do play aren't necessarily a bit worse than we who don't."[168] Hannah Gould relished the "rare experience [of] a few human beings thrown this haphazard on an equal basis absolutely shut on all sides," and realized "I love it."[169]

Victorian Americans, even those tolerant of mingling with different nationalities and religions, were typically uneasy about men and women thrown together haphazardly. The unique nature of a ship voyage could remind women that as guardians of gentility they were not as free as men aboard ship, but the unfamiliar circumstances could also demand loosening familiar gender conventions. M.E. Winslow thought it "astonishing how intimate we get on board ship" as she came to "feel as if I had known the Dr. and Charlie all my life and we lie all in a heap on deck as it we were a nest of kittens."[170] Not many women, however, could describe their relationships with men recently met as feline-style intimacy. Most stepped on board assuming that accustomed gender relations would be observed, although, as Judith Rives so painfully learned while seasick, it was not always possible.

Ship companies, always concerned about their reputation, made sporadic efforts to minimize unfamiliar intimacy by designating a ladies' cabin and a gentlemen's cabin for daytime socializing, although these spaces were not always available for the intended purpose. Women on one voyage had nowhere to congregate at night because the stewards slept in their lounge; on another ship the women's parlor was used as a third dining room.[171] Eugenie Homer thought her ladies' cabin "as pleasant as one could expect," but noted the one designated for men was used as a dining room for children and maids.[172]

End-of-century floating palaces were large enough to segregate some space by gender. Maxtone-Graham explains that in 1910 "male and female passengers on the *Olympic* were neither encouraged nor expected to mingle in the hours between dining and retiring." The smoking room, the largest public space available, was reserved for men while the women made do with a reading and writing room and some outdoor space. The one public room open to both sexes was only large enough to accommodate about one-sixth of the passengers.[173]

Most ships, however, did not formally separate men and women, but left it to passengers to invent their own rules. In 1859 Susan Marsh Emerson described a woman traveling without companions as "a mystery lady" wearing a "shocking dress" who walked the deck by herself, leaving several men concerned that they were enabling her questionable behavior by ignoring her. Finally it fell to Francis Weyland, president of Brown University, to offer himself as her escort.[174] Taboos about women walking the deck alone did not much survive mid-century (and were not always observed even before), but the idea that men and women should not stray too far from familiar gender norms while crossing the ocean endured well into the twentieth century.

Generally older women preferred the society of their own sex, at least most of the time. In 1844, Sarah Cleveland observed "men [and] women very soon settle themselves into companions."[175] On Caroline Kirkland's ship, which also sailed in the 1840s, "walking, knitting and chess fill time of the ladies while gentlemen have shuffle-board;" when seas were rough "we ladies have been all lashed to the bulwarks with a long rope, to enable us to keep our places."[176] On one calm evening Eliza Gardner had "a pleasant chat with Lord Ashley" before taking her seat with the other women.[177] Sarah Shurtlef frequently joined a women's group while her husband socialized with the men; one afternoon, after hitting a high wave, they "all fell into a heap of women" and "all were laughing as the men came to rescue their wives."[178]

Men and women usually joined together for evening activities, but not always. Caroline White's husband joined a group of men to write and sing songs in their designated smoking room; the women "had the pleasure of hearing them all read tho' we did not hear them sung."[179] A female opera singer emboldened the women on

Hetty Kennedy's ship to join the men in a singing fest; the women retired at eleven thirty "but the gentlemen continued their merriment until a later hour or rather I should say to an earlier hour on Sabbath morning."[180]

Louise Jewett articulated the common conclusion that during a sea voyage "one may as well be sociable for the pleasures of solitude are not attainable."[181] Long hours between meals were filled conversing with fellow passengers and in the unique environment of a shipboard community gossip was inevitable. Typical descriptions of fellow passengers included: "a motley assembly" that was "more amusing than any novel," a "strange medly [sic] of odd people," of "very worldly people spending their time in eating, drinking & card playing," and as purveyors of conversation "bad or indifferent with a very little perhaps of good."[182] Elizabeth Ogden shared her "dreadful voyage" with passengers she found, "with the exception of one or two, ordinary to the last degree."[183] Nina Pape described two male passengers as "splendid company," but thought most of the others on board "are not, so to say, of our set." She did throw oranges to the children in steerage, an act of charity apparently deemed appropriate for her set.[184]

Especially in the early decades, when most reticent about improper association with men, women typically aimed their harshest barbs toward their own sex. Caroline Poor liked her fellow passengers, "the gentlemen especially," except for a woman, "one of the most inveterate talkers I ever heard," who "would always get some gentleman and talk to him by the hour together until he was utterly exhausted and would then fasten on to another."[185] Nancy Stoney criticized a married woman who dressed "like a guy in a short skirt!" and a young woman from Chicago who traveled alone and frequented the smoking room to play cards with the men. Nancy assured their parents that her brothers "disapprove of her intensely."[186] Caroline White decided a ship was an especially interesting place to study human nature; she analyzed Mrs. Howe as "not what she should be" and determined that "the blackness of Mrs. Coit's character" mandated avoiding "proximity to such a vile woman."[187] Althea Harper disapproved of a woman who "walked into the dining room as brave as if she was in the swellest room on earth in a very low evening gown" making her "the comment of everybody." Another " 'lady' [who] thinks it quite the proper thing to walk up and down the deck or sit in the smoking room smoking cigarettes," was also offensive.[188] Annie Ware, critical of the critics, despaired that "nobody is as wise as he otherwise would be [and] the whole condition is unnatural and upsetting;" she was candid enough to admit "I've gossiped till I could blush for shame and talked of food and ailments till I hated my fellow creatures."[189]

Fortunately relations among strangers thrown together for an ocean crossing were usually more amiable than shameful. Kate Jones added "some most delightful and valuable acquisitions to our list of friends."[190] Julia Rush claimed that "there were never a set of passengers who liked each other so much" and even came to love the ship as if it were a person.[191] Emma Clements enjoyed "an at home feeling everywhere as people settled themselves into their steamer chairs & drew their wraps around them."[192]

Men eager to please did not hesitate to invade exclusive female society. Mary Poor's observation that "all the gentlemen have made themselves agreeable" was likely apt for many voyages.[193] Caroline Farrar singled out a man who "carried extra shawls for their [the women's] exclusive use and wrapped them up with the most assiduous care;" she also praised him for "having an arm always ready not only to promenade the deck with the young ladies but to assist the forlorn & sea-sick old ones when they need."[194] Lizzie Van Benschoten was grateful to a man who "sees to everything we want & some things we do not."[195] Louise Jewett praised a male shipmate for being attentive, carrying things and tucking her and her companion in, yet also qualified her praise because "on the whole he is sometimes a little wearing."[196]

Young single women were less likely to find men's attention wearing. There were 180 women on Herma Clark's ship but only 60 men, not an unusual ratio. The gender imbalance assured "our masculines are in great requests for promenades, games, ect [sic]." Herma teased a male companion about "the young lady pedagogues with whom he sets out to watch the stars."[197] A female chaperone observed that whereas "I'm happier without having to depend on the male sex to entertain me," her charges "feel better & happier when they can have small and absolutely foolish talk with the men."[198]

Foolish talk and even full-blown courtships were generally indulged if properly conducted. Indeed, older and married women could find the flirtations of the young and single a source of amusement. On one of several Atlantic crossings she made, Henrietta Frank predicted that with so many single people on board "it would not be surprising if several romances resulted from this trip."[199] During the hours spent in her steamer chair, "my present comfort," Georgette Chamberlin watched as "couples in joyous moods are passing and repassing."[200]

Henrietta and Georgette could be more indulgent than parents and chaperones of girls on the cusp of adulthood. Herma Clark assured her mother "I have carefully heeded your injunction not to be too friendly with strangers."[201] Eugenie Homer assured her parents that without a male relative to serve as chaperone, "our conversations with any of the gentlemen are somewhat restrained, though not stiff."[202]

Some young women, however, were less willing to heed the injunctions of their elders. Clara Alexander, traveling with an older woman, was "almost vexed to think that she keeps such a vigilant eye upon me," because "I know there are some of the finest looking gentlemen aboard I ever saw. They are perfectly enchanting."[203] Nina Pape found it frustrating that she could only talk to men when her chaperone was seasick.[204] Annie Ware, on the other hand, was attracted to several Frenchmen on board, but deemed a courtship impossible without a chaperone. She considered her two female companions "rather dull" and most of the ladies on board "uninteresting" while "I have on the contrary too much energy." She longed for a friend, ideally male, because "if it were a boy, that would be perfect for then we could go about wherever I liked." Annie was, however, resigned that "I must perforce not wander all over the ship" so "I can't have the fun I want to." Towards the end of her trip she was emboldened to hold long conversations with a doctor from Brazil.[205]

The admonitions and watchful eyes of parents and chaperones did not invariably preclude shipboard romances. Harriet Rich pronounced her friend "the belle of the ship" who "has won the masculine hearts right and left."[206] Bessie and Mamie Horstmann, both in their early twenties, met a New Yorker traveling to see his family in Switzerland who was "very kind to us." On deck he tucked in their rugs and, Bessie recorded, "trotted me up and down quite a number of times." She surmised that another would-be suitor was searching for a reason to talk to her, which he finally "very conveniently" did by offering to move her chair out of the sun; in time she reported "he has been with us ever since."[207] Marian Nichols met no one "who seemed to me to have very fine character" until, despite teasing from her older sister Rose, she began socializing with Oswald Garrison Villard, grandson of abolitionist William Lloyd Garrison and himself a well-known activist.[208] Ella Cabot's shipboard courtship was acknowledged in a diary notation: "one must grow to know people intimately in such a life & I grew to know Eliott 'very' well." She did not write about him again, but a red check marked his name in her diary.[209]

Teenager Emma Witmer traveled with an unusually indulgent mother who placed few restrictions on her daughter's freedom to socialize with the young men on board. Emma was first attracted to two Princeton students, but soon concluded they were "perfect sticks—no fun—no anything." The man she nicknamed Achilles, on the other hand, became "a source of infinite amusement." One evening the two sat together watching the ocean's wake, sipping champagne and discussing "various topics." Emma judged the Virginia reel Achilles helped organize a bore; a subsequent disagreement left him in a "pea green fury." The next day they reconciled and spent the afternoon together; the day after Emma recorded "evening spent with same." Achilles visited her cabin when she was sick and shared his awkward wish that she were a young man whom he could faithfully nurse. Having him nurse her sick daughter was likely beyond Mrs. Witmer's tolerance, but she did allow the two to continue their courtship once in Europe. Emma realized "the embarrassment of traveling with a young man, a comparative stranger," but also acknowledged being "a little smitten at having the hotel Proprietor wish to give you a room together & your mother separate." As the two parted company they promised to write. When Emma received "the long delayed one from Achilles ... a crazy wild letter, just like him," she decided not to answer.[210]

Some shipboard courtships proved more successful and occasionally even culminated in marriage. Eliza Smith remembered years later how annoyed she was that her father asked her to interpret for a Frenchman on board, with "little thought that very man was to be my husband."[211] Mary Woodbury's fear of "seasickness, icebergs and all kinds of thing" almost dissuaded her from sailing. Once on board, however, Jamie Neilson's overtures left her wishing the crossing would never end as "we were enjoying ourselves quite too much to be in a hurry to separate." She cut short her plan to study music in Berlin, married Jamie there and moved with him to New Jersey.[212]

Not all young women were interested in a shipboard romance, at least not with the men available. Recent Swarthmore graduate Helen MacGill dismissed the single men on her ship as "not beauties by any means—indeed I think three less attractive specimens could not easily be found."[213] When Cornelia Chapin was pursued by a man who, "for some incomprehensible reason [has] taken an increased fancy to me," she realized "it rather vexes me to have him so constantly in my 'wake'."[214] Helen Gould first enjoyed exploring steerage with a doctor on board, but grew annoyed when he remained with her for the rest of the day and paid her compliments "so untrue that they sounded like mockery." When he took a deck chair beside her she ignored him, acknowledging "I felt hypocritical about pretending to be asleep but what can one do?" Toward her voyage's end Helen noticed, "a tall well built Scotsman" she regretted not meeting earlier.[215] Susan Marsh Emerson hid from the Englishman who wooed her even though fellow passengers assured her he was "splendid." Her reluctance was in part because she thought him too old, but she also doubted his interest would survive discovery that he pursued a lady's companion.[216] Clara Mitchell was first pleased when a German passenger took "a great fancy to me," but "soon took an unaccountable dislike to him" and even came to dread appearing on deck "for he invariably joins us." His fantasy that romance would result if she fell overboard and he rescued her left Clara "so wrought up that I never wanted to see a German again & didn't care even if we didn't go to Germany at all." Ironically, once there, she wanted to contact him, but having assured that was impossible, concluded "what a goose I always am!"[217]

By the *fin de siècle,* as gentility's mandates retreated, women were freer to be more playful with young men and with each other as well. Grace Taplin predicted "grand times" with eleven recent graduates of Wellesley College and early in their voyage reported all "nearly die laughing" at the English officers and stewards.[218] Isabelle Busbee and her friend Sadie alternated flirting with several men on board and laughing at them. One was labeled an "impudent suitor" even though he escorted Isabelle to the " 'fore' where the waves & the breeze were lovely." One evening they enjoyed the moonlight together and the next day she spent the afternoon with him; too much time together, however, left her concluding, "he isn't very exciting." Isabelle noticed another "real cute man," but was also "growing quite batty about Miss Hull" and her companion, Miss Paisley. Isabelle reported home "I like them both so much," and together they enjoyed "a grand time gossiping." During one night spent with her suitor, Isabelle grew jealous that her female friends might be having the better time so she sought an excuse to join them. The women "nearly killed ourselves laughing" over the way the dejected man walked; one ridiculed his coat tails which "flop in a most unseemly manner," prompting a companion's fantasy of sprinkling salt on the offending garment as if he were a bird to catch. Nicknames for male passengers and crew included "Brer Rabbit," "the Hottentot," and "the Pig." Isabelle described an officer she thought was flirting with her group as "the cutest little fat red-headed man you ever saw;" likely he was not one of the two men they fantasized about feeding to the fish.[219]

Isabelle sailed in 1906 on the S.S. *Haverford*, an American ship built with only first-class accommodations. That year the *Mauretania*, nicknamed the *Maury*, the first of the famous floating palaces, claimed by Stephen Fox as "the greatest steamship ever built," was launched by the British in an effort to deflect increasing competition from the United States, Holland and Germany.[220] Hannah Gould sailed on a Dutch competitor complete with writing rooms and a library trimmed with "beautiful wood work," which she thought "a queer[,] careless[,] luxurous [sic] place where every wish is gratified, even anticipated and where both space and time have become your slaves[;] there is nothing quite like it."[221] Another early-twentieth-century traveler described her cabin as "nice and even nicer than some of the best hotels." Her ship included a restaurant as an alternative to the traditional dining room, a swimming pool and an orchestra that played three times daily.[222] These opulent ships offered passengers such a vast array of entertainment that they hardly felt at sea.

Not all passengers could afford a room nicer than those in the best hotels. Ships continued offering a second-class option for passengers wishing to economize but unwilling to travel in steerage (which in the early-twentieth century was given the less demeaning name of third class). Mary McMaster reported a great time in second class but concluded of those in first: "to tell you the truth they don't look desirable."[223] Mabel Root and Charlotte Crawford booked second class in 1910, but rather than enjoying a great time, they were "terribly crowded and uncomfortable in our cabin," and found nothing to do but sit on deck from eight in the morning to eleven at night.[224]

Young single women traveling on the dawn of the twentieth century, many of them college students or graduates, were less reverential of gentility's norms than their elders had been. Traditional entertainment such as singing hymns and promenading gave way to college songs and athletic events. Pauline Biddle sailed in 1892 on a ship that offered a number of competitions, including a "very exciting" tennis tournament, as well as a ladies pond for bathing, a ship first.[225] Isabelle Busbee also enjoyed athletic competitions and games, although only two events, a potato race and a thread and needle race, were open to women.[226] Shuffle board (alternative spellings included shovel and chuffle) was a mainstay of recreation which, by the twentieth century, symbolic of more open relationships, had been transformed from a game for men exclusively to one played by men and women together.

Luxuries such as swimming pools and tennis courts could obscure the reality that crossing the Atlantic continued to involve a degree of risk. The *Titanic* disaster was a tragic reminder that even the most luxurious ships could not guarantee safety. Surely some Americans reconsidered their plans after the invincible ship sank, but over the next two years thousands still boarded luxury liners as well as more modest ships and headed to Europe. Clara Schmidt, traveling with her family in June 1914, found "the days are hardly long enough for all we want to do." Her niece, Alma, reported they were "always busy at something ... shuffleboard, swimming, contests." Clara described a day's routine: "We do practically the same things every day. I get up, at about ten or so. Then I walk twice around the deck, if there is time[,] and take breakfast. We never wait for each other which makes it much more comfortable. Consommé is served at eleven and then we swim until the one o'clock luncheon. I have rested once or twice in my room but usually prefer to be on deck." Near the end of the voyage Clara mused "when I think of all the luxuries with which we are surrounded I am really amazed at our civilization," and concluded, "the trip has been a glorious experience and I am really sorry that the voyage will soon be over."[227] Several days after reaching Europe, however, Alma and Clara learned that the European civilization they so admired was threatened by war. They could not have imagined that it would be of such magnitude that it brought the golden age of Grand Tours to an end.

They returned home on an emergency voyage carrying refugees away from the war zone. Before the summer of the guns of August, most women had a more conventional second voyage to look forward to or to dread. Mary Millis, unusual in writing during the return trip, found it delightful as "the weather was fine, the sun was warm, and though I had not enthusiasm for returning to the domestic scene, I reflected that there was still a week or more in which to enjoy my liberty in the great world."[228]

Mary's candid acknowledgment that she dreaded returning to the domestic scene offers evidence that domesticity's bonds were loosening as the nineteenth century gave way to the twentieth. Throughout the century women had to stretch the boundaries of domesticity to undertake a Grand Tour and decade by decade more were willing to do so. Their challenge to their accustomed sphere began with a voyage across the Atlantic Ocean, an experience that pulled them in two directions. The captains' authority demanded their submissiveness but, although men were freer to explore the ship and remain on deck when they wished, they too had to obey orders. In some ways life at sea reinforced hierarchical roles, but it also freed women from many gendered responsibilities. Most tried to maintain standards of gentility, and were critical of those who did not, but they were constantly challenged in the abnormal environment of an ocean voyage.

Whether they sailed on packets or floating palaces, when free of the agonies of seasickness, many women shared Mary's embrace of liberty. Another Mary, traveling in the 1880s, realized that "free from all conventionality, so careless and irresponsible, we almost shrank from the thought of entering again the busy life of the world."[229] Of course women were eager to enter the busy world of a Grand Tour; once their destination was reached they immediately confronted its challenging quotidian demands.

III

Getting Along the Best We Could: Quotidian Demands of a Grand Tour

On the last day of her voyage across the Atlantic, Emily Severance confided in her diary: "My heart almost flutters with expectancy at the thought of being so near Europe."[1] Ruth Church recalled of her first day in England: "we couldn't have been more excited and terrified if we had landed among hostile Zulus."[2] These two women articulated a common intertwining of excitement and anxiety as voyages ended and Grand Tours began. Whether they traveled in 1814 or 1914, whether they spent ten days or two months crossing the ocean, the first sight of the Old Country was a moment that left many hearts fluttering.

Once in Europe, American women constantly juggled familiar patterns of behavior demanded by genteel domesticity with the new demands of unfamiliar places and experiences. Women who dreamed for years of a trip to Europe were usually clear about the famous places they wanted to see, but often had at best only hazy ideas about the demands and realities of daily life on a Grand Tour. Travel imposed logistical challenges that women, especially, were unaccustomed to at home and hardly contemplated before arriving in Europe. Decisions had to be made about transportation, where to stay, what and where to eat, how to budget money, how to manage luggage and clothes and how to allocate time. Once abroad women had to deal with a variety of people in unaccustomed ways, often in countries with unfamiliar languages.

Women traveling with male companions were likely to depend on them to make their trip run smoothly. Those without male support might seek the assistance of men they met along the way or possibly that of a more experienced woman. A fellow passenger escorted Ellen Perry and her sister from Liverpool, pointed out sights along the way, arranged for a carriage in London and stayed with them until "he saw us safely in a coach & all our luggage arranged & told the driver through what streets to take us on our way to lodgings."[3] Laura Comer likewise depended on a male shipmate to help her with customs, buy her rail ticket and put her bags on the train to London. An English woman on the train accompanied Laura to a hotel where she enjoyed "every attention from proprietor and waiter I need."[4]

But Good Samaritans, male or female, were not always available; from the minute they stepped on shore, some women had to cope on their own the best they could. On their first trip abroad, Mrs. Van Rensselaer, along with her daughters, Catherine and Eleanor, had relied on her husband to handle most daily details; when the three women returned to Europe shortly after his death, they expected to find men willing to assume his role and help them out. Catherine soon realized, however, that "we had depended a little upon the assistance of Mr. Andrews or some of our friends but no, they never offered to lift a finger or even to tell us how to act." As a result, "E and I left to our own devices picked out our trunks, reserved our chair & with a few francs to back us got on very well."[5] There were women who never considered the need for even a little assistance. When a man on Clara Alexander's ship offered "to pilot us through the Kingdom and the Continent" she refused as "I am determined to have my own way."[6]

The Van Rensselaers disembarked in Havre, France, but most Americans ended their voyage in Liverpool. Wherever they landed, passing through customs was the first order of business, an obligation repeated at every border crossing. Obeying commands from men they did not know and who did not speak their language could be especially unnerving for women. Maria Bayard heard so many stories of customhouse horrors that in Havre she found herself "trembling like an aspen leaf;" a French woman came to her defense and threatened to "box their ears" if officials attempted to search the American.[7] Decades later, Emma Clements, dependent on her husband to deal with customs officials, observed "a young lady have a great deal of trouble."[8] Miss Abbott credited her brother, who "always bribed heavily," for the light examination of her trunks in Italy.[9] Louise Jewett reported "Mr. C. took beautiful care of us and we had no trouble in the custom house."[10] Although Clara Mitchell's male escort was in charge, she frequently joined him because "the scene was quite a fascination for me" and "the proceedings are so funny."[11]

Customs officials, sleuthing primarily for alcohol and tobacco, frequently ignored women's luggage since they presumed respectable women did not indulge in either vice.[12] Mrs. Hairston observed men's trunks were thoroughly examined while women only faced the formality of having theirs unlocked.[13] Mabel Bragdon also noted indifference about what women carried because "the cigar is the thing they are looking for."[14] In Queensland, Ireland, Mary Jane Blair's party prepared "to rush off American fashion" to their hotel until ordered to the customs station where "after a deal of squeezing & pushing we subsided." The women were ignored while the men, asked if they had tobacco products or firearms, assured on their honor as gentleman that they did not.[15]

Emboldened with experience, women could take advantage of official indifference. In the 1820s Swiss officials posted on the border with Italy threatened to confiscate Eliza Smith's new French silk dresses, prompting her fight "to convince the ignorant creatures that they had no right to them, as they were French & had not been out of my trunk." She kept her dresses.[16] Decades later, Mamie Parsons bragged that when crossing from Switzerland into France the customhouse officer was "satisfied by our bland and guileless smiles" because "little did he suspect that the big pocket of my cape contained 200 cigarettes and that the fashionable fullness of the back of Mrs. Andrews's jacket was in part due to a box holding 50 more."[17] When Clara Alexander was asked if she carried tobacco products "or '<u>sich,</u>' " a question usually reserved for men, she retorted <u>"of course not,"</u> which she underlined in her diary to underscore her outrage. Nina Pape admired her female companion for navigating customs "with coolness when most men would have got angry & cursed."[18] In the 1870s Adeline Trafton was amused when her hoop skirt "jumped out like a Jack-in-the box" and hit the man inspecting her luggage. Long after hoops were obsolete, Virginia McCormick was amused by "a frenzy of gesticulating French" observed as she passed through customs.[19]

Jane Eames and her companions, exempted from a search for tobacco, had it offered for sale. In response, "we drew ourselves up to our utmost height (we are both quite short) and said with supreme indignation, 'No! ladies in America do not use such things'."[20]

The unification of numerous small states into the Kingdom of Italy and, further north, into the German Empire in the 1860s and 1870s meant less time clearing customs, but the process was a nuisance of European travel into the twentieth century. In the 1890s Lucy Dudley complained "what nonsense it is for travelers, and what an annoyance it would be to go through that performance, when passing from one state to another at home." She was crossing from Austria into Italy when an officer entered her first-class car and "turned my pockets inside out and the cushions upside down, to see if I was smuggling cigars and whiskey." Since not "engaged in that delectable business" she strained to endure their intrusion unperturbed.[21]

Nineteenth-century European governments were more concerned with smuggled goods than with illegal entry. Passports, the modern version of the document needed to pass through *una porta* (a gate) of medieval Italy, were sometimes needed by one member of a party—usually a man with a family—sometimes by each individual and sometimes not at all. Before the First World War it was common to go abroad without a passport and acquire one only on demand.

Guidebooks perpetuated word-of-mouth confusion about passports. One published in 1872 suggested that a single passport was needed for a couple traveling together whereas a woman alone needed her own.[22] At the turn of the century, Mary Cadwalader Jones's guide for female travelers advised that legal documents were useful primarily to prove their owner's respectability.[23] Sometimes *femme covert* (married women) were required to have a passport and sometimes *femme sole* (single women) were not. Maria Bayard's party were ordered to present passports only after they had successfully navigated customs at the French border and were settled in Paris. Maria was not required to appear for hers so she waited in their carriage while her male companions went to the American consulate. When presented with her new document she was "quite amused with the description of myself as it is the first I have had drawn."[24]

Tourists in pre-Risorgimento Italy, a fragmented peninsula of rival states, were especially vulnerable to random demands for passports. In 1844 Sarah Cleveland's party was forced to remain in Civitavecchia for several days while their documents were corrected; their exploration of nearby Etruscan ruins was a silver lining in their delay.[25] There was no such positive outcome for Isabella Faber who complained while traveling through northern Italy the same decade that "there are so many little petty kingdoms here that it appeared to be every few [hours] our passports are called for."[26] In mid-century Mrs. Bullard was assured that traveling with her husband exempted her from passport checks so "congratulated myself upon being able to travel without one." When the couple attempted to pass from the Papal States into Austria, however, officials delayed them until an English-speaking German clarified that they were married.[27] When Emily Severance crossed Italian borders in 1867, Garibaldi's troops had successfully unified most of the country leaving only Rome independent. Emily made no mention of the Italian campaign for unification, but did think it worth noting that only men needed passports.[28]

Travelers crossing conflicted borders were those most likely to need documentation. In 1831, the year Belgium fought for independence from Holland, Judith Rives' husband was required to take a special passport with his family listed as "his suite" in order to cross this contested border.[29] When Nina Pape learned a passport was required to go from France to Austria as they battled for control of the Italian states in the 1860s, she posed as a maid who followed behind "with the parasols & bags & looking as humble as I could;" since servants were exempt from documentation her ruse worked.[30] Despite the rising tide of militarism in the wake of late-nineteenth-century European imperialism, passport requirements remained haphazard into the twentieth century. In 1890 Adella Hughes ignored the advice of relatives assuring she did not need a passport, countering it was better to have one even if it was never used.[31] The sudden outbreak of war in the summer of 1914 prompted teenager Alma Peterson to inquire if she needed a document to leave Germany. She was assured she did not.[32]

Europe's babel of languages made understanding procedures for customs and passport checks a renewed challenge at each new border. Most Americans began their Grand Tour in England, thus postponing the necessity of coping in an unfamiliar language. Fluency in European languages, considered an ornamental female accomplishment at home, proved a most practical skill once travelers crossed over to the Continent. Some women considered learning one or more new languages a priority of their Grand Tour and devoted a great deal of time in classes, with tutors or studying on their own. Grace Hutchins resolved to use every spare minute "grinding on an Italian grammar" because she was "very anxious to learn the language before I leave Italy;" it was a tenacity typical of many American women who had been exposed to European languages since they were schoolgirls.[33]

Women who lacked confidence in their ability to acquire new languages or not interested in hours poring over laborious grammar might opt to limit their trip to Great Britain or come to wish they had. After traveling from France to England, hearing their mother tongue was described in variants of "sweet to our ears" and "delightful to me."[34] The language barrier so undermined Harriett Rich's enjoyment of Paris that she longed for "solid old London where they speak a recognizable tongue and I am satisfied."[35] Most women, however, envisioned a Grand Tour including more than solid London so grappled the best they could with the unfamiliar sounds. Complaints about being "confused and helpless," of feeling "shut out and blank," of seeming like "a stranger in a strange land," and about being forced to silence "which is very provoking to say the least" were commonplace. [36]

Talking French, lingua franca of the day, was helpful throughout Europe, but even those fluent in it or other languages were rendered speechless at times. The Van Rensselaers spoke French and Italian but knew no German; they struggled in vain to tell their omnibus driver outside the train station in Vienna where they wanted to go until finally the exasperated Austrian put them out in the street, trunks and all. The three women stood guard while Mr. Van Rensselaer searched for a place to stay. Catherine described the situation as "quite ludicrous, as we could not help ourselves in the least not being able to speak."[37] Ruth Church spoke English then German and French, each language accompanied by pantomime, when attempting to buy shampoo in Italy, but to no avail.

At last the proprietor indicated his comprehension and sold her a small bottle. When her mother failed to get the presumed shampoo to lather, she added more. The two women finally realized their mistake, but it took days "to restore ravages of insecticide."[38] Mary Pierce also spoke French and German, but found herself "utterly hopeless" when Italian was demanded; frustration fueled her misguided indictment of Italians as "very stupid about understanding."[39] Florence Scofield, equally misguided, so disliked the people she encountered in Munich that she lashed out at "the barbarian language and the stupid people." [40]

Fluency in a second language was empowering. Martha Griffis, always aware that her brother had license to do things considered inappropriate for her, was especially proud to translate for him.[41] Sarah Elliott felt "quite well educated for once" when she translated for an Englishman in Paris.[42] When Marian Nichols translated both French and Italian for the men who accompanied her and her sister to the theatre, she realized "their difficulties helped to add to our enjoyment of the evening."[43]

Whether polyglots or limited to English, American women found ways to communicate in order to grapple with the quotidian demands of a Grand Tour. Once past customs, the first order of business was to decode the transportation system in order to reach the first destination. Clear memories of the long and arduous ocean crossing likely left many women sharing Sara Howell's sentiment that "I dread steamers and sea very much now."[44] Most kept their feet on dry land except for the unavoidable trip across the English Channel; even the shortest crossing of around two hours could restore the agonies of seasickness. Mary Ashhurst encountered seas so rough that she was forced to stretch out on a bench covered with shawls; she later recalled (apparently missing her ironic contradiction) that "every woman & almost every man on board with the exception of Alice and Mary were calling 'steward hassen, bring the basin'."[45] Mary Jane Blair watched women prepare for the seemingly inevitable, but successfully resolved, "there was not use being sick on a two hour sail." With the familiar hint of mirth, she noted that a male companion had "paid his respects to the old sea god."[46] Caroline Farrar found nothing humorous about her long Channel crossing as all the passengers passed "a sort of purgatory of a night."[47]

A few women once again faced the purgatory of traveling by water on the other side of the Channel. Frances Stevens, unusual in traveling from Italy's Civitavecchia to Marseilles by boat, found the first day pleasant, but the next "boisterous & rough to a degree anything but agreeable," prompting her vow to never sail on the Mediterranean again.[48] After traveling on the Rhone, E. Thompson complained that "<u>every man</u> I could almost say commenced to smoke cigars and actually thought nothing of puffing away directly in our faces." The women found no refuge in their exclusive cabin because "there the men, for I cannot so disgrace the word gentlemen, were actually playing cards."[49]

Women were usually spared card games when traveling in carriages, but not always smoke. A horse-drawn vehicle, classified as either a carriage or a diligence, was the only means of land transport until trains launched a transportation revolution in the 1830s; they continued to supplement trains until displaced by automobiles and buses in the early-twentieth century.[50] Carriages, the smaller of the two, only had inside seats, were usually hired privately, and traveled only by day. Wealthy tourists usually traveled by carriage until trains reached the places they wanted to see. In the 1820s Eliza Cox and her husband determined night travel was unsuitable for her and their children so paid $150 for a twelve-day trip from Paris to Switzerland in a private carriage.[51] Caroline Townsend's first carriage ride left her feeling like "a grand seigneur" which, for her, justified the additional cost.[52]

More women, especially those on a limited budget, concluded a diligence was grand enough. These stagecoach-like vehicles, first manufactured in France, were by mid-century a staple of tourism because they were cheap and went to a variety of places. Outside seating, both on top and along the sides, accommodated more passengers; they also traveled at night, which could mean a sleepless ordeal, but allowed reaching a destination in half the time it took by carriage. Mary Jane Blair described the first diligence she encountered as clumsy yet right away she sought to ride in one. Mary Jane explained to the uninitiated: "the seats are mostly on top, there are two divisions, the upper & lower, then there are what is [sic] called palors [sic] inside which is [sic] cushioned & made comfortable for the luxurious. Five horses are attached to this vehicle, 3 abreast & two back of them."[53]

Women who actually rode in one of the clumsy vehicles might be less sanguine about the experience. In their maiden years, diligences moved so slowly that for short stretches it could be faster to walk. In 1817 Eliza Rodman complained "how tedious it was to travel five hundred miles always at the same slow pace."[54] A few decades later, Miss Lawrence's brother walked so far ahead of the diligence she rode in that the two were not reunited until after dark.[55] Alicia Middleton's ride through Switzerland in one "hard as a common cart" left her protesting, "my bones were well nigh broken." Napoleon's ambitious road-building facilitated travel in France, but Alicia had an unpleasant experience there as well. A trip from Havre to Paris acquainted her with "the miseries of economical traveling" which was compounded by a bad headache and a "disagreeable impertinent coachman."[56] Isabella Faber's trouble in France was of a different sort; horses her party had reserved were given to others, leaving them briefly stranded and "sadly disappointed." While waiting in the station for replacements, she was at least compensated somewhat by boiled eggs served with bread and butter. Once underway, it took ten hours, including two stops to feed the horses, to travel from Avignon to Aix, a distance of about forty miles.[57]

Travelers in the first half of the nineteenth century were especially vulnerable to transportation horrors in Italy. In the 1840s Margaret Gardner's trip from Rome to Naples was delayed because the queen of Naples had commandeered all available post horses.[58] When E. Thompson visited in 1848, a tumultuous year of revolution and war, a washed-out road forced her party to wait in a small village for three days "in the midst of discomforts which we endeavored to bear with patience, but which we were truly thankful to leave behind, without much expectation, however, of finding much comfort until we are out of the region of Italian Inns." They met an American mother and daughter there who had been stranded for five days due to impassable roads. Thompson's party resolved that rather than risk the fate of these beleaguered women they would send their baggage on by boat and walk as far as possible. After crossing a river on an improvised bridge, they reached their destination fatigued and "fearing lest the morrow bring us news of greater obstacles."[59] Miss Lawrence decried that riding through Italy with frequent stops to change horses and check passports made sleep impossible and thought it "quite strange" to wait through one long stop in a café full of armed soldiers late at night, but was at least pleased to be served coffee.[60] Bettie Kimberly, visiting in 1859, so feared the hazards of Italian transportation that she questioned if it were not better to dream of the country than to actually visit; she explained and complained to those at home: "We do not travel upon wings but in a dirty old slow steamer upon the Mediterranean with your stomach heaving with every wave until you verily think that the next thing you will see are your toes peeping out of your mouth. Or in a carriage with slow horses over its long dusty roads sleeping at the little way side Inns in their <u>bad smelling</u> beds and half way eaten by industrious fleas & bed bugs and more over constantly expecting the pleasure of being invited by a band of robbers with pistles [sic] pointed at your head to yeald [sic] up money & trunk or life."[61]

Bettie's litany of complaints did not mention mountain travel, but it was a major challenge for horse-drawn vehicles. The Simplon Pass, completed in 1805, facilitated alpine travel from Switzerland to Italy, but mountains were still formidable barriers, especially when snow, which might fall even in the summer months, mandated replacing wheels with runners. Since it was customary that only male passengers walk up steep roads to lighten the load, Ann Marie Green thought it novel enough to record that German women joined the men walking through heavy snow.[62] Mrs. E.P. Thompson walked with all the passengers in her carriage down an especially steep descent in the Italian mountains.[63]

Spain's primitive transportation system deterred all but the most intrepid travelers. A woman who ventured there in the early-nineteenth century complained of the "horrors" of riding in a Spanish diligence "squeezed in with two big Spaniards and two Englishmen" on "disgraceful roads."[64] In 1866, another tourist to Spain recounted of her travels: "it was very cold during the night and the wind came in all the corners. We stopped nine times for fresh horses and every few minutes to put on the brakes so it seemed as though I got very little sleep. It was too compact and cramped to be comfortable."[65] Even approaching the twentieth century, Constance Harrison had reason to describe a Spanish diligence ride as "dreadfully rough, my head riding up and down on my pillow and my back-bone vibrating with the motion all night long—impossible to sleep, till weary nature was overcome toward morning and I dropped off." Not surprisingly, she concluded it was the "hardest journey we have made."[66]

Thanks to a more comfortable experience, or perhaps to a more cheerful disposition, some women took diligence travel in stride. In 1827 Sarah Tuckerman and two male companions resolved to make their long trip from the French coast to Paris a great adventure rather than merely an arduous journey. Once safely arrived she described their experience: "We were up by seven and had a good comfortable breakfast at eight (oh the delicious bread) & were off to take our places in the diligence at nine. Oh the diligence the ugly, lumbering, heavy, clumsy, huge, graceless diligence with the miserable, uncomfortable ragged looking horses & the harness so deplorable, so dirty so patched up of huge wooden collars old rusty, clumy [clumsy?] dirty leather & knotted broken cords & looking as if it were contrived & made before the flood. Oh the diligence the diligence! What scenes, what amusement what sport we had in that coupe." The coupe, she explained was "the forward of the three divisions of the moving mountain," and accommodated three which allowed her party to travel alone. "Suffice it to say," she reported home, "that we talked, laughed, slept, told stories, played games, read et [sic] & drank, all in turn & all in our petite coupe rarely alighting for anything." The trip took forty hours, from nine o'clock one morning to one o'clock the following night. Once safely there, Sarah affirmed, "we all bore it very well."[67]

Despite a difficult journey to Genoa, Kate Jones dismissed the discomforts she experienced "as part of the play," rationalizing "it gives us a little variety at least for until the last week we have known nothing of the annoyances of travel."[68] Caroline Farrar, who found diligence travel in Italy less onerous than she had feared, reminisced that her party started out in the early morning and watched "the cold gray descend over the hills and through dense clouds struggle into day."[69]

Steady improvement in carriages and roads assured faster and more comfortable travel. An 1867 edition of *Baedeker's* recommended if "ladies are of the party" a more expensive diligence with a coupe (enclosed seating for three inside) should be chosen.⁷⁰ In the 1880s one woman remembered traveling in a diligence through the mountains by day as "very delightful," although at night it seemed "a horror."⁷¹ Elizabeth Gilman realized that despite its deficiencies, traveling in one of the clumsy vehicles was practical; when a carriage arrived too late for her to catch a train to Innsbruck, she concluded, "a diligence may seem stupid but is sure."⁷²

Local diligences were usually sure as well although there were occasionally unfortunate accidents. Elizabeth's confidence in diligence travel was challenged when her family experienced a broken wheel outside of Sorrento, forcing them to wait in a small village while it was repaired. She described the women and children who came to have a look as "scurtizing [sic] us," but also appreciated their generous offers of chairs and water.⁷³ When the Cabot family's diligence overturned just as they passed Milan's famous cathedral, local witnesses helped them recover their belongings and return to their hotel, even carrying Mrs. Cabot in a chair. Ella Cabot praised her sister's "perfect unselfishness and bravery" for walking despite being badly bruised and minus a tooth.⁷⁴

Carriages and diligences barely survived the nineteenth century. In 1901 Hannah Gould described riding through Switzerland in a diligence drawn by six horses as "like a dream of the last century." Riding a modern electric tram up a Lucerne mountain inspired her conclusion that Swiss transportation "was quite a combination of the 19th and 20th centuries."⁷⁵

Trains spanned the two centuries and, once widely available, became the mainstay of European travel. The first European railroad, opened between Liverpool and Manchester in 1830, cut the time it took to travel between the two cities nearly in half; by the 1850s all of the major English towns and cities could be reached by rail.⁷⁶ In 1854 Elizabeth Eppes experienced a trip from Liverpool to London by train which she described as a "comfortable and delightful manner of travel."⁷⁷ Train travel was not a novelty for Lucy Dudley, wife of an American railroad executive; nearly half a century later she described her arrival in Liverpool: "the luggage was lettered alphabetically, and we all swore we had no spirits, cigars or perfumery, and then took the train for London, ordered a lunch basket, and began our first ride in England."⁷⁸

The French rail system, launched in 1840, soon radiated out from Paris in every direction. Once tracks were laid to Nice in 1864, tourists could traverse the country in less than two days.[79] Grand stations heralded a system that by mid-century accommodated over six million passengers.[80]

Through much of the nineteenth century, Italy and Switzerland, poor countries without strong central governments and with challenging mountainous terrain, lagged behind.[81] Napoleon gave the Swiss a boost when he built the Simplon Pass in order to move his army rapidly from France to Italy, but it was not until the late nineteenth century that Switzerland surpassed other European countries in the efficiency of its trains. A period of civil war in the 1840s convinced its leaders to create a more unified and centralized government for their multi-lingual country which facilitated building a tourist infrastructure. By the 1860s rail lines snaked through the major valleys and steamboats plied the lakes. Alfred Nobel's invention of dynamite in 1867 made it possible to tunnel through imposing mountains. In the following decade railroad mileage in Switzerland nearly doubled and funiculars and cog railroads were built to transport tourists at least part of the way up its famous mountains.[82] At century's end, geography lecturer John Stoddard could plausibly proclaim "how great the difference between Switzerland of today and that of fifty years ago!" He pointed out "where, formerly, a man would hardly dare to go on foot, trains now ascend with myriads of travelers."[83] In the early twentieth century an American women declared Swiss railroads as especially well run and without the problems of those in England.[84]

Conflicts among the principalities and states of the Italian peninsula inhibited the development of infrastructure there, but trains did follow in the wake of the successful Risorgimento. By 1870 it was possible to travel from Paris to Rome in two or three days by train, a trip that took two or three weeks by carriage. After Termini Station, named for the Terme (Baths) of Diocletian nearby, was completed in 1876, most tourists arrived in the city by train, and by the 1880s at least some of them were offered Italian-style luxury. On a trip from Florence to Rome, Marion Burgess and her fellow passengers each received a package containing a bottle of wine and a tumbler, bread, cheese, sliced sausage, a pear, an orange and "two thick pickles."[85]

Many Americans abroad had first experienced train travel in their own country. According to historian Amy Richter, American trains were "domesticated" as cars exclusively for women, sometimes referred to as home, assured them "public domesticity" where they could feel confident that rules of Victorian etiquette would not be breeched.[86] George Pullman facilitated the security of proper domestic space with the sleeping cars that bore his name as well as dining cars and comfortable seating, luxuries rare in Europe until the 1890s. That decade Lucy Dudley complained that European trains did not compare with America's "in size, or luxury of chairs, sleepers, buffet, dining and toilet rooms and general convenience."[87]

Pullman-style luxury was not unknown in Europe. In 1877 Mamie Haven described her first-class car in France as "paradise on earth" where she could delight in "hot lunches and dinner [and] everything in the way of books, papers, magazines and puzzles" found in the saloon car.[88] A decade later, when Helen Gould traveled from Liverpool to London, she was served a hot lunch on china and with crystal glasses that was delivered at one station and removed at another. The experience left Jay Gould's daughter questioning why these services were not possible at home.[89] By the turn of the century some European trains approximated the best in the United States. Inveterate traveler Henrietta Frank's first experience eating in a dining car was pronounced "not bad."[90] Sarah Ogden agreed that the food offered on French trains was good although she complained it was poorly served.[91]

A guidebook from the 1880s claimed most trains had one or more cars where "the sterner sex" was banned and that "even the offer of a piece of money, so potent in other matters, will not secure the violation of the rule."[92] In 1870 Catherine Van Rensselaer rode with her mother and sister in a first-class ladies car from Paris to Switzerland while her father made do in second class.[93] Not all women, however, were able or willing to choose the best. Mary Jane Blair reluctantly stretched her budget when traveling with "the gents [who] are very aristocratic & will not hear to a second class one [car]."[94] Not all first-class cars were gender specific and second class, the most popular choice, almost always accommodated both men and women. One guidebook offered the counterintuitive advice that second class was actually the better choice because in first class "a burly Englishman or stolid German wouldn't hesitate to take a timid woman's seat and women without escort will be insulted by [the] women with them" whereas people in second class would treat them with "utmost deference."[95] Lucy Chamberlain was not convinced; after traveling from London to Liverpool in the less exclusive car, she complained "it required a strong minded woman to get through all right for nobody seems to care whether you get your baggage or not, or indeed to help you at all."[96] Agnes Kummer, on the other hand, after several weeks abroad was "quite disposed to travel second class."[97] Elizabeth Nichols also found a second-class car adequate, especially if she was fortunate enough to find one empty; she assured her husband she was "perfectly satisfied with its comforts as we have never been at all crowded," but also confessed that on one occasion men in her compartment smoked and drank.[98]

Complaints about traveling with men deemed obnoxious and even feared threatening were not uncommon. Amy Aldis and her friend, Helen, traveled through Switzerland seated near a drunkard who "leered at Helen all the way till she was frightened."[99] Abbie Farwell endured an overnight ride from Switzerland to Paris with "a horrid Frenchman who would not leave us ladies to ourselves tho we all begged him."[100] Mary Olney and her six female companions were unusually good humored about sharing a car with strange men. They were traveling from Rome to Naples in a compartment filled with their luggage when "two strapping Italians climbed in" and all "had a great time making room for them and we and they all got to laughing."[101]

Male escorts might try but could not always deflect obnoxious behavior. Mary Pierce, her husband, Gus, and their female companion started an overnight trip from Amsterdam to Berlin in a car they shared with two German men. When Gus complained their smoking was offensive to the women, one rebutted that he did not care because "he was a German not an Englishman." Gus found a place for the women in another car, but had to rejoin the Germans who confided that they had bribed the guard to get the car to themselves and had smoked as a tactic to drive the Americans out.[102]

It was not always preferable to travel seated near European

women. Miss Marsh and her companions had to endure "a vile creature" who "caused some unpleasantness" and made the ride from Rome to Florence one of "great discomfort."[103] Catherine Van Rensselaer considered it a great improvement when "a disagreeable French woman" left her train and "three big burley Englishmen got in."[104]

Sharing a compartment with unpleasant companions was just one potential hazard of train travel. Laura Thomas was dismayed to discover that on the day she planned to journey through England the government had distributed free tickets to the poor, leaving little space for paying passengers.[105] Miss Marsh missed her train in Paris so had to remain an extra day; she was so overloaded with parcels in an Italian station that she lost her ticket, causing her "great anxiety and a great search."[106] Florence Alimnae's party discovered while in route from Switzerland to Florence that their reserved seats were in first class although they had paid the second-class fare. They opted to move rather than make up the difference, but were unable to find an available compartment so crowded in with a congenial group from Indianapolis.[107] Katherine Johnson was comfortably settled with her shoes off in route to Haarlem when she was unexpectedly forced to change trains in The Hague station. "I was quite disturbed by being ousted in this way," she groused, a disturbance exacerbated by her discovery that Hague officials only spoke their native tongue and that she had left her *Baedeker* on the train.[108]

Mamie Parson's most dire train misadventure occurred in Germany. "Just as we would get comfortably settled," she recalled, with "air cushions blown up, rugs spread (it was bitterly cold and raining in torrents)[,] guide books and maps unfolded — we would find ourselves stopping at some dripping little station and be told to bundle out." Mamie found the experience "too aggravating," but culled some humor from her travails. After an occasion when her party, which included a couple with three young sons, had to change trains unexpectedly, she wrote home: "If you could have seen us. Our Macintoshes got mixed — Miss W. got mine — which barely reached her knees. I got hers — and nearly broke my neck stomping on it as I was hurried out of the carriage, wildly clutching a *Baedeker* — a *Murray* [guidebook] — Lois's cushion — a basket of fresh figs and a parasol which I had grasped by mistake in the hurry." Once off the train "as I lurched forward, scattering *Baedekers* and *Murrays* all over the platform—putting my foot almost through Miss W's macintosh [sic]—I fell into the arms of two or three Merrill boys and a funny old officer who utterly disregarding the ruin of a beautiful new uniform escorted us each in turn through the hail and mud to the other train which was of course on the very furthest track."[109]

Frances Gaston also penned a humorous description of how three women coped with handling their luggage in train stations: "I have Anna's black bag,[—]fortunately she made it strong[—] packed till it looks like a black sausage, two umbrellas, a package of books and Mary's satchel. Mary follows with my linen carry all, umbrella, and more books. I forgot to say that Mary forgot to put in her best bonnet bought in Berlin. It is wrapped in brown paper and dangles from the string of my bag. Mary E. has bought an ugly black carryall that emigrants use, satchel[,] umbrella and book. Dr. Jones has an immense satchel. When we can[,] we get things carried, when we can't well, we are a sight[;] that is all."[110]

Passengers frequently grappled with excessive luggage and other small inconveniences, but only an unlucky few faced the trauma of being left behind. Louise Kellner joined John Morris to deal with customs in Liverpool while his sister Lydia waited in the train that would take them all to London; after finishing their business, the two discovered the train had departed without them. Several shipmates infatuated with the attractive single woman embedded themselves in her predicament; Louise later described one as "nearly wild with the thought of Miss Morris's misfortune." She and John were also worried, especially because Lydia had no money, "yet we could not help laughing," because "it was all so ridiculous." Eventually they boarded a train scheduled to couple with the one they had missed and "found our brave Miss Morris who, like a sensible woman, had sat perfectly still, and never lost courage."[111] After Mary Pierce was separated from her husband and friends she passed "an anxious night" alone in a car with strangers, which was surely even more stressful than her encounter with the German smokers.[112]

Overnighting by train was an improvement over sleeping in

a diligence, but far from comfortable until Pullman cars were introduced. Mary Sterling was convinced that after their ordeal sitting up through the night, she and her husband were "the dirtiest couple that ever travelled."[113] In the 1890s Jenny Tracy complained that travel to Spain required "sitting bolt upright all night with the company of smoking and spitting Spaniards."[114] A few years later Jane Adgar failed to book a sleeper to Madrid so endured "a rough and fatiguing journey" on an overnight train.[115]

Early in the twentieth century Grace Taplin found it funny that canal-laced Venice had "not a horse in sight."[116] Within a few years it would be funny to see a horse in any European city. By the 1890s automobiles (machines) and buses (auto diligences) were bringing about a transportation revolution that was both embraced and deplored by Americans seeking an Old World experience. Henrietta Frank praised automobiles for eliminating the necessity of being cooped up in trains "with others less exclusive."[117] Elizabeth Ogden, on the other hand, bemoaned the "awful noises and smells" cars brought to Paris.[118] Tour guide Willie Allen styled her group as "all automobile mad," but she regretted that the music of the past was being replaced by the noise of traffic and wistfully questioned, "do you know progress has killed the old Italy?"[119]

The naysayers were doomed to lose the fight as the noises and smells of cars quickly replaced neighs and manure. In 1910 Dolly Whaley surmised that a guide who ten years earlier had taken her around in a horse-drawn carriage had become very successful "because he has a beautiful machine."[120] Wilhemina Mathews appreciated that this new means of transportation made it possible to enjoy scenic views and explore small villages as she rode through southern France. She also recorded a new travel complaint: "our first puncture."[121] Tourists pioneering automobile travel sometimes had to face the hostility of locals, especially in rural areas where horseless carriages were rare and viewed with alarm well into the twentieth century. Elizabeth Stevens's party paid for a goose they killed and in another small village their car was hit by stones launched by angry locals as they passed by.[122]

Taxis, buses, tubes and trams transformed intercity travel. London's underground system, opened in 1863, was rarely used by tourists until the turn of the century. In 1908 Sarah Ogden reported traveling via the London Tube to watch King Edward open the city's first Olympic games.[123] Despite London's successful example and some local encouragement, Paris builder Georges-Eugene Haussmann evidenced little interest in underground transportation; the French system was not opened until 1900.[124] Isabelle Perkinson rode the underground in Berlin seven years after it opened in 1902 and was "fascinated by it—you go flying along and they have the nicest cars."[125] The more sentimental Mabel Bragdon found German trams convenient, but regretted they "have taken away much picturesque in Nuremberg."[126] Mary McLean ruminated that taxis were an extravagance, but grew resigned to paying the price after several attempts to use buses met with "questionable success."[127] Year by year taxis became less extravagant and more popular; by the second decade of the twentieth century they had almost completely replaced horse-drawn carriages for urban public transportation. Margaret Thomson was in Rome in 1912 when taxi drivers formed a union and took a day off. "It shows the sapping effects of luxury," she acknowledged, as "Claude and I had no idea what to do." Margaret admitted she was "absolutely spoiled" because she never considered walking when she could get a taxi "which is ninety nine times out of a hundred."

Whether they arrived by carriage, train or automobile, Americans frequently found themselves in a new and unfamiliar place with nowhere to stay. Likely Frances Gaston spoke for others when she identified the most "distasteful" part of travel as arriving at a new destination with "uncertainty as to where we shall go."[128] Few women were as adventuresome as Miss Davis who left Florence in the evening, "sped along valleys and through mountains in more than midnight darkness till two p.m.," changed carriages in Bologna and arrived in Venice at five a.m. where she and friends found shelter in a photographer's establishment.[129] Elizabeth Nichols found travel exhausting enough without "poor uncomfortable beds and stuffy, smelly passages," so resolved to stay in only first-class hotels. Choosing first class, however, did not always assure comfort; she was shown one place with that coveted rating only to discover "very common men are eating with their knives and everything smells of cabbage and onions."[130] Harriet Curtis was more fortunate with her Swiss hotel, the Splendide, which, she quipped, was "indeed splendiferous and costs a million a minute."[131]

Carriages arriving at a French hotel in the late-nineteenth century. *Library of Congress*

In the waning decades of the nineteenth century, luxury hotels throughout Europe joined Switzerland's best. In 1880 Ann Marie Green ranked English lodging as a century behind America's, but just a decade later Margaret Preston countered that America offered nothing like the "palatial hotels" Europe boasted in every major city.[132] London's Westminster Palace Hotel, opened in 1860, featured three hundred rooms, fourteen bathrooms, and the city's first elevator. At century's end, profits from Gilbert and Sullivan operettas financed the luxurious Savoy, one of the first hotels illuminated by electricity. Cesar Ritz's, so grand that it made his name synonymous with luxury, followed.[133] Their success in England won architects commissions for the Astoria and the Claridge in Paris.[134] The most dramatic spatial transformation occurred in Switzerland where by the end of the century luxury hotels were available even in remote Alpine villages. John Stoddard noted in 1897 that "on every prominent point commanding a fine view is planted a hotel" where, after a day in the mountains, one could "sit down to a well-cooked dinner, hear music on a broad veranda, consult the latest newspapers, and sleep in a comfortable bed."[135] The Grand, which premiered in 1905 as Switzerland's finest hotel, offered its clientele lawn tennis in summer and ice hockey in winter.[136]

Constance Harrison reinforced a popular European stereotype by advising that to make one's money last, "see where the Americans go, & then turn the other way."[137] In reality, many American tourists could not afford places that seemed to cost a million a minute so spent considerable time searching for less expensive accommodations guided by little more than tips from friends and fellow travelers met along the way and from guidebooks. Guidebook authors, resolute in assuming a male readership despite mounting evidence to the contrary, encouraged gentlemen traveling with ladies to take special care in finding proper accommodations. The 1891 edition of Morris Phillips's *Abroad and at Home* identified Hotel Albemarle in London, which boasted a ladies drawing room, and Hotel Meurice in Paris, as ones "the ladies in your party would find especially pleasant."[138] *Baedeker's* advised choosing only the best hotels "when ladies are of the party" whereas "gentlemen traveling alone" could be quite comfortable in cheaper places.[139] Even on the dawn of the twentieth century, the popular guidebook could hardly conceive of women traveling alone.

Women with a male companion were likely to leave the legwork necessary to find lodging to him. When Sarah Newberry and her husband arrived in Paris, she stayed in their hotel until he identified several apartments and then collaborated in choosing the best.[140] Helen Brooks also left it to her husband, acknowledging, "the dear fellow does all the work, and I criticize."[141]

Some women, however, took the lead in finding appropriate places to stay. Before its era of luxury hotels, a successful result could be especially elusive in Switzerland. In 1835 Alicia Middleton slept in a village hotel's servant quarters because all the guest rooms were taken; the bed was so dirty that she did not undress. Her next room was only "tolerably clean."[142] A woman visiting Switzerland about the same time complained her "lone hut" was "the dirtiest hole in the world," where "I fancy I should soon starve."[143] Caroline White and her husband converged in a Swiss village with another

American couple, but found there was only one room available in its sole hotel; the women shared the space while the men "rough it as best they may."[144] Mary Emma Sterling was dismayed to learn that despite a reservation, the Swiss hotel her husband had booked was full; fortunately they knew guests there who agreed to share beds and floors.[145] Even in the early-twentieth century, when Switzerland could boast some of the finest hotels in the world, it was not always easy to find a suitable place. Eliza Pool, there the first year of the new century, stayed in a Geneva hotel so crowded that she had to share her room with a Russian woman who spoke no English and only a little French; as a result, Eliza quipped, "our conversation was not brilliant."[146]

Difficulty in securing an available room could be only the first of a cacophony of problems. Frances Gaston described her Interlaken hotel as a "hateful place" and the bill "a gouge." Adding insult to injury, the hotel's carriage left her party stranded in the hot sun.[147] Laura Rutherford complained about a Swiss clerk who, despite repeated remonstrance, neglected her party, leaving them to "race ourselves to death."[148]

Complaints frequent in Switzerland were echoed all over Europe. After a tedious journey to Granada to see its famous Alhambra, Jenny Tracy and her husband joined a long line of weary people unable to find rooms until they were finally offered "a garret room devoid of locks where we slept very comfortable on two little camp bedsteads."[149] Caroline Farrar rationalized it would be sadder to leave Rome if her party had found decent housing there "but we can hardly fare worse."[150] Clara Ritchie longed for the good hotels she had enjoyed in London when in Paris she endured an uncomfortable bed, had only candles for illumination and encountered bed bugs for the first time. [151] Eleanor Middleton, resorting to an all too familiar bigotry, left a hotel in Germany made "intolerable from the vulgarity & the ill temper of those horrible Jewesses."[152]

Those with recommendations in hand at least knew where to start their search, although the advice they carried was not always reliable. Lavina Urbino and her husband were directed to London's Taverston Hall only to discover it excluded women. They booked the closest hotel that would, as Lavina joked, "accommodate female bipeds," although it did not allow them in the dining room, forcing the couple to take meals in their room.[153] Clara Reed's "good enough" room in Cologne was agreeable only because it was cheap; in Paris she was even less satisfied with "my dingy little room up three flights."[154] After inspecting what she had been assured was the best hotel in Bayreuth, Mamie Parsons ruefully recalled watching "Miss W. and Louise now—their noses turned up—their skirts gathered tightly but <u>loftily</u> about them picking their way over cabbage leaves—potato pairings—occasional onions and so on."[155]

Recommendations gleaned from guidebooks rivaled the wobbly reliability of word of mouth. Clara Alexander reserved a room in the only *Baedeker*-starred hotel in Coblenz, but no one met her at the train station; she did not give up on her German guidebook, choosing another place it recommended near the station.[156] Marian Burgess, another American wiling to embrace anti-Semitic stereotypes, complained that *Baedeker*'s only recommendation in Triberg was "a horrid place—dirty beyond words, kept by a Jew and filled with common, noisy people." Her party located an alternative in nearby Baden-Baden only to discover it catered exclusively to invalids. A large tip finally settled things although they had to take meals at a nearby hotel where they shared a table with an American woman traveling alone.[157] Guidebooks could disappoint but were still a critical tool in the oft-repeated hunt for somewhere to stay. Edith Dummer was chagrined to find the two-star hotel she chose in Reims full of fellow Americans who had also faithfully followed the same guide.[158]

Advance reservations could eliminate laborious hours spent searching, but the European reservation system remained hit or miss well into the twentieth century. On their second visit to London, Louise Urbino and her husband returned from the Lake District to find the room they had reserved was no longer available. They "went first to the Grand, but they were full up; then to the Metropole—the same; to the Victoria—the same." They finally found rooms in "a horrid little hole."[159] One party of Americans sent their courier ahead to make a reservation in Rome for the Christmas season only to discover on arrival that "some prince" had been given the room he had booked. A similar disappointment prompted one woman's nationalistic retort: "I could not help sighing my country! My country! Forever! Where I would not be turned out of a house for any prince or nobility but first come first served."[160] Eleanor Middleton missed spending Holy Week in Rome because, thanks to the "faithlessness of boarding house keepers," her party's rooms "were coolly given to other people" and it was impossible to find others.[161] When Martha Ann Tilton discovered rooms reserved in Venice had been given to a group willing to remain longer, she deemed it best not to argue with one "so devoid of principle."[162]

Members of the Women's Rest Tour Association assumed they had the advantage of their exclusive list of hotels. One member found an Oxford recommendation "simply adorable."[163] Frances Curtis offered up "three cheers and a squeak for the Association" when she found affordable lodging in an English village. On another occasion, however, she was told that its recommended boarding house in Monmouth could only accommodate one person at a time and a lengthy stay was required. Her group of four had to resort to the more common strategy of asking locals for suggestions; they took one recommended by the local postmistress that Frances thought "delightful."[164]

Women experienced searching for rooms could become savvy critics. Mary Millis praised a companion's ability to find unusual hotels "frequented by the citizens of the country rather than by swift moving tourists."[165] Ann Marie Green's party first had difficulty getting a suitable room in a Florence hotel, but "we had been traveling long enough by this time to understand matters and things." Faced with their threats to go elsewhere, the hotel owner suddenly remembered a room was available. Ann Marie also learned to buy candles ahead rather than pay for the expensive ones sold in hotels; she was pleased to learn that her hotel in Florence had gas lighting.[166]

Professional group tours, increasingly common in the twentieth century, alleviated frustrating searches for adequate rooms and finding candles to light them. In 1896 Florence Alimnae noted that everyone on her tour was delighted with their hotels.[167] A decade later, Grace Taplin praised Baker's World Tours for its hotels, especially because they all had electricity.[168]

Before the era of electricity, cold rooms were a major cause of complaint. In 1887 Maria Fahys's room in Paris offered only a small wood fire "and altogether a good deal of discomfort for one accustomed to steam, furnace, running water and gas;" she upgraded to one with at least a lamp, "a great luxury apparently."[169] Nearly a decade later, Mamie Parsons traveled with a woman whose poor health and depression made her especially intolerant of discomfort. Discovering her room in Naples lacked a fireplace, she responded by "boiling—sizzling—weeping—with rage!" With "great effort" Mamie found a warmer alternative.[170]

An unlucky few faced problems more serious than a cold room. Ellen Perry recounted "the horror of that night!" in Marseilles sleeping on a hard sofa while men "caroused" outside in the halls; she was first awakened by a sound fit "to curdle the blood" and again by footsteps approaching her door.[171] Louise Kellner endured a stormy night in a German-owned rooming house in Syracuse, the Sicilian treasure trove of Greek and Roman ruins; windowpanes broke, leaving her awake, cold and wet much of the night. When she reported her ordeal the next morning, the owners merely expressed gratitude that she had not disturbed the entire house.[172] Laura and Bettie Thomas's ordeal played out over several days. One winter night they were awakened by the smell of smoke and a voice commanding them to leave. The sisters were offered new quarters that included an anteroom with a fireplace; the next morning they returned from breakfast to find three men seated around the fire "not seeming the least bit disconcerted." They demanded yet another room where Bettie piled furniture against the door for fear the men might retaliate. Unbelievably, the morning after they awoke again to a fire alert; perhaps becoming jaded to danger, Laura drolly recorded "I never was out of bed & out of my room as quick in my life."[173]

Most hotels assured their guests a more tranquil stay and some even served as centers of social life. Sixteen-year-old Isabelle Perkinson met twelve Americans, "all nice girls," in her Roman hotel and spent evenings playing games with them.[174] Teenager Eleanor Joy embraced the guests in her Swiss hotel as like a family; they also played games and one night held a dance "where all the ladies and gentlemen were powdered & wore plasters." Eleanor was first disappointed in another place where she described a Virginia woman and her daughters as "rather common," but did meet Italians she certified as acceptable.[175]

Not all women readily embraced hotel society. Frequent trips abroad supplied Mamie Parsons with a long list of complaints. In one hotel she took an instant dislike to the forty-six females and lone male, members of the English Wintersdory Reading Club, and declined their invitation to a lecture titled *The Cockroach: A Primitive Insect*. Days later she was appalled to witness Americans at the Grand Hotel in Rome who "reached the climax of bad manners" by bicycling in the hotel corridor, the women in dinner dress. In another place she was seated next to a "very twangey [sic] Yankee woman who ate unlimited pickled beans and liked this hotel better than any of the other 36 she had been in this summer."[176]

Pickled beans were among the many unfamiliar European dishes that Americans tasted; they occasionally responded with compliments, but more frequently with criticism. Early in the nineteenth century, Judith Rives assured her family that in France "the table we found excellent and have had to complain about it nowhere in this country of Lords."[177] Praise of European food continued to be scattered through letters and diaries; one writer proclaimed French cuisine "elegant" and another found food in Germany "very nice indeed."[178] Compliments, however, were drowned out by a steady drumbeat of complaints. One woman even came to the startling conclusion that "the French don't know what good food is."[179] Disdain for Italian food inspired descriptions including "wretched"and "horrid."[180] European bread was ridiculed as "made in the last century" as "hewn from a quarry in the Sierra" and "out of the pyramids."[181] There might be too much spice or not enough. Mrs. E.P. Thompson and her friends ordered *mous a la provencale* in a French café, only to find "to our great consternation" that they had ordered "cod fish highly seasoned with garlick [sic]."[182] Eliza Marshall, on the other hand, complained that Europeans did not use enough salt. After seeing large salt cellars fashioned from precious metals and jewels that had belonged to royalty—perhaps she saw Cellini's famous cellar in Vienna—she quipped that maybe "the royalty consumed all the salt in those days as so little of it gets into the food nowadays."[183]

Even the limited praise American women offered European food was often qualified. Constance Harrison thought Spanish fruit and vegetables delicious, but she condemned the fish and meat as vile.[184] Phoebe Pember, who singled out cherries and cake as the only good things she had to eat in Dresden, looked forward to Munich "to be with nice American people and eat nice American food."[185]

Distaste for what was served abroad exacerbated nostalgia for accustomed fare at home. One Massachusetts woman craved her state's famous baked beans. A fellow New Englander noted with disdain that the English knew nothing of "doughnuts, fritters, cream toasts and the dozen little knickknacks that every Yankee cook considers indispensable in her pantry."[186] A southern woman longed for "above all broiled & fried chicken, which we have not seen since leaving home," and another realized a year into her trip that she was desperate enough to offer "my soul for a buckwheat cake or my birthright for a mess of oysters."[187] Northerners and Southerners alike defined corn on the cob as the quintessential American food; Sarah Smythe described Germans eating American-style corn as both ridiculous and amusing because, she claimed, they ate the cob.[188] Clara Mitchell dreamed of corn and sweet potatoes as "I haven't tasted such good things anywhere in Europe."[189] Clara Ritchie missed "sweet corn, good bread, pumpkin pie, beans, catsup, cider, peaches and Catawba grapes." She did rate German chocolate and fruit as the best she had ever eaten and decided that while some might find it dreadful, eating dry bread all day was agreeing with her and was perhaps healthier than her diet at home.[190]

In the last half of the century some European chefs tried catering to American tourists by making American food available on Thanksgiving. Caroline Farrar described the Thanksgiving meal she shared with nearly eighty Americans in Berlin as "rather stupid."[191] Clara Ritchie, another critic, missed "that informal manner among the people and that open-heartedness that we would find at a similar gathering at home."[192] Most American women, however, enjoyed a special Thanksgiving meal with traditional food. One who spent the day in Valencia suggested "we enjoyed it more than the good people at home, their turkey & cranberry sauce."[193] Ann Marie Green discovered an American-owned hotel in Florence where she feasted on "turkey, plum pudding and mince pie."[194] Isabelle Perkinson was not so lucky; when she asked for cider in an

Anglo-American supply store, hoping to make it seem more like Thanksgiving, the clerk did not know what she was talking about.[195]

One woman's offer of "a big sum for a good drink of American ice water" articulated a perennial complaint.[196] Some women were concerned that wine and beer were too readily available, but for others these libations were a novelty to embrace. Mariana Starke's 1826 guide maintained that it was common for ladies to drink alcohol in the evening while abroad.[197] A half century later, however, Morris Phillips counseled that whereas English women enjoyed alcohol, "American women will prefer something weaker like soda."[198] Mary Chafee may have been unique in finding beer for breakfast "very satisfactory," but more than a few American women discovered they preferred something stronger than soda.[199] Mary Watson Gay confessed after a dinner in London that "considerable wine and beer was made way with."[200] While there, Laura and Bettie Thomas were invited to join a group of men in their coffee room for a glass of wine, "a thing not ever done there before." "Ladies," Laura explained, "are not allowed in the Club & we of course considered it an especial honor & enjoyed very much the nice time."[201] Mary Bradbury thought most English mealtime customs "very queer," yet reported home "we have also begun our wine and have our bottles of claret every day."[202]

American women were even more likely to consume alcohol on the Continent. Jennie Reizenstein drank beer with her sauerkraut and wurst in Germany and found that "for the first time in my life I really enjoyed the brew."[203] Eleanor Rutledge was also in Germany when she reported to her family "we have fallen [sic] easily into the habit of the country & drink our tumblers of red wine with much gusto."[204] Susan Smythe even questioned if she could adjust to dinner without wine once home.[205]

As the twentieth century dawned, some young women drank as much to rebel against convention as to enjoy European-style dining. Teen-ager Isabelle Perkinson enjoyed a "splendid evening" sitting out on a Parisian street where she "had a great big glass of beer and saw all the people go by."[206] Gena Trumbull was ridiculed for ordering milk in a Munich beer hall so took a sip of her mother's beer; she continued drinking through "a most genial, wholesome evening," which made her realize that "we people in America are no judges of what it means to drink beer over here."[207] Edith Stedman's less indulgent mother made her twenty-three-year-old daughter promise not to touch alcohol while she toured Europe in the summer of 1912, a promise Edith frequently broke. Seeing an older woman she traveled with drink excessively dampened Edith's own consumption for a time, but she was soon enjoying wine again because "I can't help myself." After sharing several bottles of Sorrento wine at dinner, which "made me feel silly," she confided in her diary that "Betty and I acted like perfect idiots." Edith reminded herself that "Mummy was worried about my drinking wine over here and I gave her my word not to touch it." Perhaps she resolved once again to honor her promise after an older companion became "so pickled" at Christmas dinner that she could not talk straight, prompting Edith to leave the table in embarrassment.[208]

Most women drank in moderation or judged alcohol as just one more thing wrong with Europe and did not drink at all. The early-nineteenth-century temperance movement, an effort to curb excessive drinking in the United States had, by the end of the century, grown into a nation-wide effort evolving from temperance to prohibition. The Woman's Christian Temperance Union, founded in 1874, stigmatized drinking as a male vice that women, the guardians of genteel morality, should challenge. Those sympathetic to the cause carried their opposition to alcohol abroad. When Lucy Dudley realized that lunch baskets in England always included a bottle of claret, she questioned why "it never seems to dawn upon anyone here that there is anything to drink except something spirituous, only at five o'clock tea."[209] Eliza Marshall defiantly ordered ice cream in a German beer garden and criticized her companion for imbibing. She also ridiculed Germans for the quantity of beer they consumed, claiming that as a result "you often see beastly looking men & women about the shape if not the size of the Heidelberg Inn."[210] Cornelia Upton reported "the usual fight about wine" in Berlin because Germans thought it inconceivable that Americans did not drink with meals.[211]

As American women adjusted to European customs concerning food and drink, they also had to consider propriety about where and when to dine. Restaurants, named for the *restorants* or bouillon prescribed in eighteenth-century France to restore good digestion, first appeared in Paris in 1766 and in London only a century later. Initially Parisian restaurants were exclusively for men; a 1788 guidebook warned that "honest women, and those of good reputation, never go there."[212] By the early-nineteenth century, women were beginning to patronize restaurants, but the idea that they were novel spaces that were somewhat inappropriate and not really compatible with gentility lingered through the century. Mariana Starke's guide assured women that they could go to Parisian taverns "without the smallest impropriety," but nearly a century later another guide author warned that although there were numerous restaurants and cafes in the city, "there are none to which it is pleasant for ladies to go by themselves and you had better avoid them."[213] In the 1830s Alicia Middleton found it "unpleasant to dine at a public table" in Paris's restaurants which she thought dirty.[214] Two decades later Kate Jones's family conformed to the French practice of stepping "from the sublime to the ridiculous and from the Louvre to a Restaurant." Observing French women in cafes prompted her conclusion that "with us, it would be thought [a] very equivocal position, but in Paris the motto is _honi soit—qui—mal—y—pense_ [shame to him who thinks evil of it]."[215] Caroline Farrar and a female friend made the mistake of going to "a miserable hole" and only with difficulty ate their "miserable dinner;" to compensate both ordered a glass of whiskey.[216] Laura Thomas "wished myself out twenty-five times" while dining in Munich; the ubiquitous smokers prompted her to also wish that "the German people would learn refinement."[217] Ann Marie Green complained of moderately priced restaurants that "though the food was often good the rooms were dirty and no places for a lady."[218]

Women concerned about the propriety of patronizing restaurants could opt to eat in their hotel, although some found this style of dining, with its unfamiliar customs, also unpleasant. Cadwalader Jones advised her readers to "bow slightly to the others at table both before taking a place and when leaving," and warned that failing to do so would be considered especially rude in Germany. She also advised that a woman seated beside a male stranger should speak first.[219] Frances Stevens preferred remaining silent, explaining to her husband "I was seated between persons unknown, [and] there I have sat for 1 1/2 hours without uttering a word."[220] Clara

Ritchie and Martha Maltby only dined in their hotel on Sunday because they found meals there much too long and tedious.[221] Laura Thomas objected to serving herself, "that being considered the thing to do," but "something I had been taught from my earliest youth as being ill mannered." Laura was candid enough to admit that Germans "thought us wonderful barbarians as we thought them."[222]

The variety of restaurants available by the end of the century transformed dining out making it easier and cheaper. The Ritz popularized separate tables where women could take their meals without the risk of associating with people they found objectionable.[223] In 1888 Helen Culbertson discovered "a very neat and nice" Dutch café in Paris with thirty-cent meals which allowed her to live there on her budget.[224] In the early-twentieth century, Gena Trumbull was introduced to automated restaurants in Germany and "to our joy, we found it GREAT."[225]

American women were as ambivalent about Europe's fashion as they were its cuisine. Before leaving home they had to make decisions about what clothes to take on a trip that might last a year or more. The majority of guidebooks assumed a male readership so were of little help to women. *Harper's* advised its presumably male readers to carry some kind of firearms, leaving it to women to decide for themselves what to carry. Henry Morford candidly admitted his book was "for the male sex," but assured women that they could easily adapt it to their needs.[226] The *Satchel Guide* justified writing solely for men as "we have not the masculine presumption to dictate to the ladies." The author did suggest that women read Miss Trafton's *An American Girl Abroad* for its "excellent counsel—if the male human creature may judge of these things."[227] *Osgood's Complete Pocket-Guide to Europe* repeated the refrain of ignorance about female fashion yet did offer "our injunction concerning plenty of wraps, and to hint that thin shoes should not be worn in travel."[228] Thomas Knox's guide was at least somewhat more inclusive, suggesting that "for ladies, a traveling-dress, a walking dress, and a black silk dress may be considered the minimum," assuring that since he was "neither a lady nor a lawyer" he had sought advice from both groups.[229]

Since their needs were largely ignored by the most popular guidebooks, women had to depend on the few written especially for them, the advice of experienced friends or their own imaginations. Katherine Ledoux, who published *Ocean Notes for Ladies* in 1877, offered the unusual and likely unnerving advice that, since accidents did happen, women should always dress well on board ship because "I have always felt that a body washed ashore in good clothes, would receive more respect and kinder care than if dressed in those only fit for the rag bag."[230] Ann Marie Green, less morbid and more practical, advised that "a lady needs but two dresses, a good stout wool for traveling and a dinner dress of black silk or cashmere" and assured that "with nice collar and cuffs added she can always appear respectably at table d'hotel or in the parlor;" she also counseled that the "less superfluous trimming a lady has upon dress or hat the better she will look and feel after a few weeks of travel." Ann Marie also recommended "stout walking boots" and "a waterproof and shawl" as important practical additions to a traveling wardrobe.[231]

Young women, especially those traveling primarily to socialize, were least likely to heed such practical advice. Louise Jewett concluded, "the prettiest clothes one sees in Paris are those of the American girls who have just arrived."[232] Frances Curtis, one of five sisters who made frequent trips to Europe to enjoy its social life, implored her mother to dismiss their father from the room while reading a letter detailing the many clothes their daughters had bought. The expense was justified, Frances argued, in light of "the strange fact that when living & not sightseeing & moving in very fashionable company one requires more clothes."[233]

Those who did not move in fashionable company were frequently critical of those who did. Martha Griffis claimed American women abroad were noted for "their extravagance in dress and their extreme fashion" and sarcastically described "some exceedingly stylish New Yorkers whose chief object seems to be a grand display of dress and a great deal of their conversation is on this deeply interesting topic."[234] Catherine Van Rensselaer complained about "dressy American girls who seem to think that Switzerland was only meant to show off their fine clothes." She described the walking suits her parents bought their daughters as "really resplendent in silk and velvet with cloth overskirts & jacket," but rejoined it was "extravagant and foolish to think so much of dress."[235]

Remaining stylish while traveling was a constant challenge, especially in the first half of the nineteenth century when female fashion embraced extremes of impracticality. In his study of Victorian women, Duncan Crow suggests that in the 1830s "women's dresses were almost theatrical in their exuberance."[236] They became even more so in the 1840s when hoops, collapsible steel or wooden frames, were introduced, making it possible to extend the diameter of a woman's skirt to more than five feet. According to historian Drew Gilpin Faust, "hoops were a product of early Victorian ideals" because a woman who wore one "transported her enclosed, private space with her."[237] A campaign in mid-century to reform women's clothing attracted more scorn than success. The Bloomer costume, billowy pants largely covered by a knee-length skirt, named for dress reform advocate Amelia Bloomer, evoked such ridicule that even its most ardent champions soon abandoned it. Women continued packing corsets, hoops and petticoats until modest reform in the last decades of the nineteenth century made female dress at least somewhat more practical.

In 1866 Georgians Eliza and Janie Lamar tied their hoops on the back of their mules when out riding.[238] Mary Jane Blair, in Europe the same year, wore her hoops often enough that she thought it worth noting that on a mountain excursion in Ireland "I had on my large hat, woolen dress, no hoops."[239] Idella Plimpton took her contraption along in 1869, but rarely wore what was no longer the fashion in Europe.[240] By the late 1870s it was no longer fashionable in the United States either, but even relieved of their hoops and voluminous petticoats, women struggled to be well dressed on a lengthy trip.

Isabelle Perkinson thanked her mother for picking out just the right clothes, assuring her "all that I have has been just what I wanted—and so stylish and tasteful looking." When her mother offered to send her money to replenish her wardrobe, Isabelle insisted that except for underclothes, she did not need anything, that "really clothes do not come first with me just so I am clean & neat."[241] But staying clean and neat was a constant challenge. Frances Stevens and her daughter cast off so much worn-out clothing that by the end of their trip they only needed two small trunks to carry a traveling dress, a black silk and one additional dress each; they arrived in Paris, their last destination, "to be sure rather shabby but determined to make things hold on."[242] Holding on was essential for those unable or unwilling to buy new clothes. When her companion was still wearing her "July dress" in December, Mary Gittings silently wished for someone to steal the offending frock.[243]

Dresses worn from summer to winter had to be cleaned and mended from time to time. In the 1820s Eliza Cox joked about limiting her wardrobe to mourning clothes since washing was such an expense."[244] Nearly half a century later, however, Ann Marie Green found washing so inexpensive that she advised future travelers to bring few undergarments. Watching Swiss women "soaping, banging and pounding" taught her why buttons were often broken or missing.[245] Mamie Parsons echoed from Germany, "European washing leaves the dirt and removes the garment."[246]

Most women had to occasionally devote a day to replenishing her wardrobe. Mamie, refusing a friend's offer of maid service, took up her own mending; "you should just see the patches and the darns and the re-linings and the re-bindings that I have performed," she bragged to her mother. "My stockings are positively lovely with embroidered toes and heels that would thrill you."[247] Clara Reed endeavored to maintain her forlorn clothes by mending and "putting a braide [sic] on my blue dress which I have worn almost constantly for weeks."[248] Shortly after arriving in Italy, Ellen Hammond despaired of "literally dropping to pieces;" her companion's cashmere was "so defaced with travel [in] the dusts of the desert & of Mt. Etna as well as spotted from dirt and horses that it must be thoroughly cleansed & made over."[249]

An unfortunate few experienced fashion disasters more dire than forlorn clothes in need of remaking. When her cabin flooded, a woman sailing with more extravagant clothing than most found her red evening dress had run on her hand-painted yellow satin, ruining both.[250] Clara Reed's party was caught in the rain walking along the Champs Elysees, resulting in the "loss of feathers—dress—shoes ect [sic]" just before "an invitation for the theatre tonight—lunch tomorrow—dinner tomorrow and Wednesday!" A shower at Ascot left her white crepe de chine without any semblance to a dress so it became a dressing gown.[251]

While moving from place to place, women frequently sent

trunks ahead and made do with what they could carry in a small bag for days at a time. Eliza Lamar complained that traveling without her trunk for five days left her "so uncomfortable always in the same dress."[252] Mary Sterling managed without most of her clothes for seventeen days and more nonchalantly noted it was "quite a while for a lady to be with only hand luggage."[253] Making do was certainly less stressful than having luggage disappear altogether. When Elizabeth Adams trunk was stolen she was forced to indulge "in that heathenish pastime of buying clothes."[254] Phoebe Pember also suffered a theft that left her temporarily without even a nightdress or toothbrush.[255]

Those unaccustomed to walking for hours had to learn and sometimes re-learn advice that thin shoes were unsuitable. Mamie Parsons found Germany especially hard on shoes, but only reluctantly bought sturdy boots with buttons after wearing out two pairs.[256] Catherine Van Rensselaer's father bought her shoes in Scotland she praised as "splendid thick ones, regular 'Clydes'." When he offered her new ones in Dresden, Catherine rejected popular French shoes with pointed heels and chose instead "a boy's pair with flat broad heels."[257]

Catherine most needed her boy shoes in Switzerland. There, especially, women were compelled to challenge dogma about proper female dress. Innovative dress reform gained popularity in tandem with the popularity of mountain hiking. In 1844 Sarah Cleveland cut "holes in the belt of my dress into which I put strings [through] thus tying up the skirts in 4 fine scollops [sic]," which enabled pulling up her skirt up when necessary; she also put nails in the soles of her shoes.[258] To facilitate hiking, Mary Bates bought calfskin shoes that laced up the front male-style. Her aunt shortened a blue flannel which they initially agreed was only suitable for mountain excursions. Mary did not have a dress to spare so settled for tucking up her traveling dress when climbing and letting it down for regular wear. This improvisation worked well enough until a seven-hour hike in Engadine left her skirt soaked; she reconsidered that a short skirt was appropriate for dining and followed her aunt's example. After days of mountain hiking, Mary reported the two were "perfectly independent, coming and going as we please, wearing our thick shoes and short dresses into breakfast, etc."[259] Laura Thomas,

Marian and Rose Nichols, on the right and left, wearing hats they bought in Salzburg in the 1890s
Schlesinger Library

who wore a dress she had hemmed when climbing up Vesuvius, later recalled "what a picture we were, a sight for the gods, with our short dresses, showing our feet to full advantage, although we endeavored to envelop the latter in shawls."[260] Women not bold enough to wear short skirts innovated the best they could. Bettie Amis endured a climb to Mer de Glace by holding up her dress from behind with one hand and holding her stick in front with the other.[261]

In Europe's more formal venues women were constantly challenged to keep themselves groomed and stylish. Bettie described herself and her companion as without "one particle of vanity left" because they only kept their hair tightly coiled.[262] Most women, however, bowed to vanity. Hats were often essential for being well coiffed, but Europe offered mystifying customs about their proper use. In one country hats were obligatory on streets and in churches, but banned in theatres; elsewhere it was quite the opposite so new rules had to be learned for each new country. In the 1820s Catherine Pritchard failed to procure a proper bonnet so declined to attend church in England.[263] By century's end proper bonnets were banned in many English venues. Nina Halsey and her friend, Sissy Jenkins, were adorned with hats as they entered London's Covent Garden, but failed to persuade an usher they were necessary camouflage for unkempt hair. An Englishwoman chimed in that Americans should not be expected to know local customs, but failed to sway him. The women finally surrendered their hats only to be aggrieved anew when a dressing room maid demanded a shilling to mind them. Nina was self-conscious sitting among English women in full evening dress, but also amused to see "Sissy's hair in a little topknot."[264] Marion and Rose Nichols confronted the opposite dilemma when attending the theatre in Naples; they arrived without hats only to discover that Italian protocol demanded them.[265]

Confusion about proper haberdashery was but one of many fashion challenges American women faced. They constantly had to balance conforming to European customs while maintaining their own style. In the 1820s Eliza Cox dressed her daughters, the youngest only three, in the corsets thought "indispensable in Paris."[266] When a decade later Mary Ronalds was unexpectedly invited to a concert in Rome, she searched "the miserable little stores," but failed to find a dress she thought suitable so sent her apologies.[267] Despite access to Paris's grand department stores, Gert Parsons feared she could not match the gorgeousness the Ritz demanded so turned down an invitation to dine there.[268] Mary Jane Blair discovered English women wore low-necked dresses with short sleeves to the opera so stayed away to avoid feeling out of place.[269] Jane Cowl, on the other hand, determined that if "one <u>has</u> to wear low dresses at the opera" she would cut the yoke out of her evening gown and go.[270] Cornelia Upton attended an opera in Germany, but felt so conspicuous wearing a colorful dress and jewelry amidst local women all dressed in black that she "surreptitiously unfasten[ed] a rose at my throat and hid it in my pocket and a moment later my bracelets went in after it."[271]

Fortunately there were times and places where fashion could just be ignored. In Lucerne, Clara Alexander joined women with shawls thrown over their morning dresses and men without collars to see the sunrise.[272] Alicia Middleton and her female friends found it acceptable to dine in their traveling clothes when no other women were present.[273] Caroline Farrar, on the other hand, realized that away from men "the way you need not dress is perfectly inspiring."[274] Although Paris was unquestionably Europe's fashion capital, Sarah Smythe discovered that among crowds of tourists there "we are nobody" which made it a nice place to wear old clothes.[275] Eliza Howell designated Florence as Europe's most casual city because "dress is not the subject of <u>importance</u>—one wears just what one pleases."[276]

Nineteenth-century women rarely wore just what they pleased, but the era of the New Woman did introduce more practical clothing suitable for athletic pursuits. Tennis dresses and golfing skirts appeared on packing lists. Near century's end, Isabella Curtis, inspired by seeing European women wearing trousers and riding bikes, ordered a bicycle suit with "<u>hot</u> blue velvet knickers."[277] The transportation revolution also affected fashion. In 1906 Wilhemina Matthews spent a morning at the Bon Marche shopping for an automobile hat.[278]

Along with their clothes, women had to pack enough toiletries, medicine and other necessities for a lengthy stay. In 1886 Sara Elliott assured her mother she was supplied with: "one candle and matches, laudanum, [made from alcohol and opium and used for a variety of ailments], mustard plasters, hot-wax box, whiskey, quinine, ipecac [used to induce vomiting], a pen, ink and paper, a flannel wrapper, a French dictionary, an Italian dictionary, a guide book, a Bible, hypophosphites helphile soda [for nerves] and cholera medicine." Her husband carried a few other medications and more whiskey.[279] Sara may have been especially well stocked, but most women brought along the array of supplies they deemed essential.

It was impossible to transport enough for a trip that might last months or even years so of necessity women shopped along the way. In the early-twentieth century Cadwalader Jones advised that "young and strong" women would need only two dollars a day (the equivalent of about forty-six dollars today), but an older woman would need at least five dollars to be comfortable.[280] When Mabel Root, one of the young and strong ones, realized she could manage on three dollars a day, she proclaimed it "fine and marvelous."[281] Whether they had to budget carefully or enjoyed abundant funds, many women found handling money a new and empowering responsibility. Before traveler's checks became widely available in the early-twentieth century, Americans abroad typically carried certificates of credit, which were promoted as especially advantageous for women. These certificates, issued for at least $500 and registered by number, were presented to European banks in exchange for cash; if the owner lost hers, she telegraphed her home banker who immediately notified his correspondents abroad not to issue money on it. Male bankers in the United States and Europe thus served as the financial protectors of female travelers.[282] Mary Millis's father gave her a letter of credit worth $1,000 for her to spend in Europe until it was used up.[283] Before Emma Clements's husband returned to the United States, the couple went to a London bank to put their letter of credit in her name "& I received instructions for its independent use."[284]

Not all women embraced independence with such confidence. Married women were especially inclined to write home for advice. Mrs. Hunt complained "I hate to spend money & wish I did not have to—that frets me," prompting her husband to admonish her for worrying.[285] Frances Stevens prevailed upon her husband to increase her funds while also assuring him "I shall endeavor to keep within bounds and not take advantage of your kindness to me." After she was forced to borrow money in Paris, Frances urged him to send more, appending "I feel very unpleasantly at having overdrawn my account." In time, however, she was emboldened to conclude that when making financial decisions "I must rest on my own responsibility."[286] Constance Harrison assured her husband that despite tempered use of her letter of credit she had "traveled comfortably, lived comfortably, seen all I set out to see, and have my way liberally everywhere." She confided to a female relative, however, that in Rome she bought "a good many things I could not resist and I find that travel for two ladies, first class everywhere, runs away with the cash in a surprising manner."[287] Elizabeth Nichols, who regularly reported her expenses home, acquiesced to her husband's leadership in their financial affairs, but also defended her own ability. After losing her certificate she confessed, "there is no excuse for carelessness," but also reminded him "that such lapses occur occasionally to most of us, not excluding yourself." She concluded on the more contrite note that "naturally this has been a lesson to me."[288]

The more time they spent abroad, the more confident and proud women became handling money. When watching her mother manage their expenses, Gena Trumbull found it "a joy to listen to her and add an encouraging word now and again."[289] Mabel Root bragged of going alone to a Cook's office where "I counted mine all by myself and got it alright."[290] Laura Thomas lacked the right change to pay her Italian driver, who "ranted and ranted as only Italian coachmen know how to do;" she went to a nearby store to get what he demanded "as independent as if I had been a boy of sixteen—instead of a stranger in a strange land."[291] Occasionally a female traveler found herself in the unfamiliar situation of assisting a man with his finances. When Edinburgh banks closed unexpectedly, Nina Halsey offered a loan to her tour leader "to help him out of his difficulty."[292]

Travelers with enduring dreams about famous places in strange lands often arrived without knowing how long their trip would last or exactly which countries they would visit. Weather, epidemics, illnesses, wars, news from home, a variety of circumstances affected plans. Alicia Middleton found herself at a loss whether to winter in Italy or return to Paris and "earnestly desiring to be directed right by Providence." She (or Providence) chose Italy.[293] Leaving decisions to divine intervention, whim, or the counsel of others was not uncommon. When Kate Jones also faced the choice of going to Rome or abandoning "that delightful portion of our anticipated pleasure," she chose Rome, only to find herself disgusted with the modern city.[294] Half a century later Gena Trumbull's family realized while planning that "everything is if Italy." They finally agreed to visit Venice which Gena found "glorious."[295] M.E. Winslow and her companion spent time while crossing the Atlantic to constructing an itinerary which M.E. predicted was so grandiose that they could not accomplish half of it; they finally decided to postpone final deliberations until in Liverpool."[296] After landing in Ireland, Laura and Bettie Thomas joined their escort in "a council of war" to decide whether to go to Switzerland and Italy, a decision they also delayed until in England where friends could advise them.[297]

Guidebooks supplemented advice gleaned from friends. Sarah Cleveland, traveling in 1844, grew so dependent on the guides that John Murray and his son published that she pondered "what I shall do when I get home without a guide book [as] there is such a pleasant completeness when you have seen—done up—all that's put down."[298] The Murrays also published Mariana Starke's *Letters from Italy*, one of the early guides designed for Americans and perhaps the first by a woman. The third John Murray in the business produced books with such practical advice that by the 1840s they were the ones most popular with Americans. When German bookstore owner Karl Baedeker realized Murray's books sold especially well in his shop, he launched a competing series which soon surpassed them in popularity. In the 1860s Baedeker began publishing in English and added a chapter on the Atlantic crossing for his American readers, assuring his red-leather bound guides were their first choice.[299] Mary Gay was "armed" with her "invaluable" *Baedeker's* in France as she "sallied forth in search of new worlds to conquer." [300] Constance Harrison chided the English who "clutch their little red *Baedeker*s," but also acknowledged "(as indeed we do, life would be insupportable else)."[301] Henrietta Frank realized "my friend *Baedeker*" was vital for touring the palaces of Venice and carefully studied another volume "with a view to an invasion of Belgium."[302]

Those reluctant to depend entirely on printed advice could hire locals, although *Harper's Hand-Book* recommended avoiding them "unless you are with ladies."[303] More than a few ladies preferred to avoid them as well. After working with several guides, Frances and Mary Gaston complained "how they gouge and we so helpless."[304] Mary Hartt's guide for Louis XIV's Versailles Palace was so old and lame that he had trouble keeping up and his "information became more and more infrequent;" her party finally "managed to lose him entirely and surveyed the palace on our own hook."[305] Ann Marie Green and her husband rebuffed a man who wanted to show them Rome's Palatine, evocative site of ancient Roman homes and palaces, as they preferred to walk about "without having a continual stream of jargon pouring into our ears."[306] Laura and Bettie Thomas enlisted their printed guides as shields; when "harangued on all sides by the most awful & horrid men" they keep their eyes focused on their books, their "faithful friends, [which] saved us from & helped us out [of] many a difficulty." In Venice the sisters again avoided guides "as though they were serpents," but on their own hook became lost. They first "hauled out our *Baedeker* & *Murray* [and] searched and searched," but unable to navigate in the labyrinth of canals, bridges and streets, finally decided to hire someone local to lead them.[307]

Some were pleased with the locals they engaged. Florence Scofield and her mother found exploring Munich without information at hand unsatisfactory so hired a man for a day.[308] Isabelle Busbee described the guide she trailed in Versailles as "the cutest guide you ever saw" who every few minutes would say "now, my ladies."[309] Isabel Rogers was unusual in hiring a woman, whom she found "a great aid to us, indeed," for touring Germany.[310]

Guidebooks and local guides helped women find and appreciate the sights they had long dreamed of seeing, but were of little help with the myriad challenges a Grand Tour entailed. Finding hotels and palatable food, mastering transportation, keeping clothes clean and mended, handling finances and dealing with it all in unfamiliar languages in strange lands could be more than some women could cope with. They might opt to hire a courier, usually a

European man who spoke English and offered a variety of services. Alicia Middleton engaged a man with thirty-two years of experience and fluency in several languages who could manage passports and customs houses and was "a respectable middle age."[311] The courier (they used the French term *valet de place*) Kate Jones and her husband engaged in Paris was "a quiet, gentlemanly old man of fifty five or sixty" who would "accompany us in all our excursions—either shopping—sightseeing—opera." Kate concluded right away "he will prove a treasure to us." She found him especially useful for scolding dressmakers although she feared he sometimes used harsher language than she intended.[312] When Ellen Perry's courier left unexpectedly, she realized "it has taken much of the bloom off the first days in Europe to be left at the mercy of strangers instead of travelling with N. as we expected & going in a leisurely way."[313] Frances Stevens was advised a courier was essential so resolved to make up the additional expense with fewer purchases, to "get accustomed to self-denial." But the man she hired did little more than buy tickets and weigh luggage, leaving it to her "to plan journeys, visit bankers [and] search railroad guides;" she finally concluded that "to depend upon ones [sic] self is best—after all it takes away all obligation," and let him go.[314] Laura Johnson reluctantly hired a courier in Paris, but found the relationship "horrid" so paid him a month's salary for only a few days of service. Although she thought him "a good sort of man," she also found it "a bore to me to have someone always about with us who did not belong to us."[315]

Not all couriers were good sorts of men. Helen Gould complained "the fleecing is enormous," but tried rationalizing that her courier averted enough trouble to be worth it.[316] Anna Fahnestock's family discharged a man who cheated them even though it meant the loss of wages already paid.[317] Elizabeth Horstmann depended on the man she hired through the difficult days her husband and daughter were dying from cholera, but even in the midst of tragedy she had to confront his dishonesty.[318]

Women hired to help with daily chores were usually called maids even if the tasks they performed approximated those of couriers. The multi-lingual maid Catherine Brooks engaged to accompany her to Dresden took good care of her clothes yet, Catherine fretted, "her ways would never answer in America." The perceived infractions grew serious enough to prompt her conclusion that all French maids were "a perfect nuisance." She tried dismissing the woman only to relent when confronted with her tears.[319]

Some European maids had ways that better suited the Americans who hired them. Catherine Van Rensselaer's mother took on a woman in Paris over her daughter's objection. Catherine soon warmed to the arrangement, however, because the woman spoke no English, forcing the family to practice French with "our constant guide, companion and protector during our sojourn here."[320] Frances Gaston realized her maid was "no sinecure" because she "hunts up railroad times, pays and sees to everything and more than all keeps my bonnet straight."[321]

Some young women, or their parents, preferred Americans who were seasoned travelers rather than couriers to take care of all aspects of their trip. Mr. and Mrs. Corsons agreed to escort two, an arrangement they all came to regret.[322] Charlotte Crawford and Mabel Root, on the other hand, enjoyed such a satisfactory arrangement with their American escorts that mid-way through the trip Mabel described their foursome as "perfectly harmonious."[323]

By the late-nineteenth century, tour companies offered another alternative for women who felt gouged and helpless traveling with couriers, hiring tour guides or trying to do it all on their own. Englishman Thomas Cook, pioneer of group touring, started leading excursions to British temperance meetings in the 1840s. The low-cost leisure tours that he subsequently offered throughout Great Britain were especially popular with women. By the 1860s Cook's Tours, with offices all around the world, was attracting American business for services that helped simplify the logistics of travel.[324] At century's end Constance Harrison proclaimed Cook's was "the most universally useful and acknowledged power—everybody goes to them—they are banker for all the world, and always civil and helpful everywhere."[325] She joined a growing number of Americans who used the English company to buy tickets, change money, plan trips and even send and receive mail.

Americans tended to be dubious about organized tours until the end of the century when the desire for convenience began to overwhelm the stigma of mass tourism. The popularity of Cook's services convinced some Americans that traveling with them might be preferable to going it alone. Laura Libbey advised a Cook's tour was "a most satisfactory way of travelling and a great saving of troubles and expenditure besides."[326] After six weeks traveling independently, Sarah Shurtleff's party "put ourselves under Cooks [sic] guidance for our near journeyings."[327] Laura Rutherford's group was so pleased with a short Cook's tour over the Simplon Pass that they signed up for a longer excursion.[328] Henrietta Frank was not as impressed. She had already visited Germany several times before joining a tour, but the experience prompted her complaint that "I did not see some of the sights that our neighbors at table saw, who took *Baedeker* & their Yankee ingenuity as their guides instead of the man from Cook's."[329]

American companies could not rival the British giant, but did offer some successful alternatives. Baker's World Tours offered its largely female clientele several itineraries to choose from, each guaranteed at less than $500 for a two-month trip; one included twenty-five cities in forty-six days.[330] In the late-nineteenth century Henry Gaze founded the Teacher's Grand Vacation Excursions to Europe which accommodated approximately 300 teachers annually, each paying $160 for a short trip.[331] Women also capitalized on the growing popularity of group travel. Elizabeth Adams, a teacher at the Women's College of Maryland, and Florence Bright, a Smith College graduate and high school teacher in Pennsylvania, offered a sixty-five day trip that included eight European countries, as well as short stops in the Azores and Gibraltar, for $560. They promised "to present much that is beautiful and worth while in Europe," and boasted that the charm of their tour lay "in the variety of its interest—in facination [sic] of art[,] the appeal of history and the grandeur of natural scenery;" they also assured there would be no sightseeing on Sunday.[332] Willie Allen resigned from her position teaching school in Birmingham, Alabama, to lead European tours. Several years of guiding convinced her "there is much money in this business and I feel that another year may see great developments;" after a decade in the business, however, she found the job so stressful that she gave it up.[333]

Even the most enthusiastic travelers longed for home at times. Mary Frazier's admission that "I feel very much like having a fit of homesickness" revealed a common emotion.[334] Most women were homesick occasionally, but for a minority, yearning for home was a chronic condition. Susie Silver's companion grew so depressed that Susie predicted she "will never want to hear of Europe again."[335] Others suffered more from travel weariness than from longing for home. Frances Gaston realized her dependency on letters "which comforted us amazingly for strange as it may appear we are almost weary of wandering and will gladly return to our duties."[336] Elizabeth Nichols went to Europe frequently, usually with pleasure, but in the midst of one trip tried to convince her husband that she should return home because "this knocking about isn't by any means all fun and I could go home tomorrow without any real regret, though I appreciate that I am having advantages not open to many."[337]

Grand Tour denizens who did not appreciate their advantages left scant record. Isabelle Curtis, one who did, admitted after several days in Paris, as to the sights "dare I breathe it that I have not seen a one." She had opened her *Baedeker's* guide for France for the first time the day before and was resolved to commence sightseeing soon in St. Germain, the old quarter on the Left Bank that includes the Luxembourg gardens.[338] Eliza Marshall shared her conviction that there was "no danger of my becoming spoiled & preferring the 'old world' to the 'new' at least under present circumstances!" After "swallowing ... daily museums, mummies, masterpieces & antiques of every description," she carped that "sight seeing is a bore & that I will never leave home any more!"[339] After five months in Europe, teenager Henrietta Schroeder found sightseeing so tiresome that she questioned if "any human being has ever suffered as much as I have!!!"[340]

Women who found it all tiresome are known primarily through the words of their critics. Mary Hartt expressed her disdain for "unadmirable specimens" of Americans, "grumpy fault finding people who think more about their meals than anything else and regard three cathedrals a moderate dose for one day."[341] Clara Werner condemned as "wicked" the reality that some women had "all the money they want and absolutely no strength or capacity to appreciate this wonderful place, while you [her family] who are so temperamental and appreciative cannot be with me."[342] Gena Trumbull concluded the woman she traveled with "would be far better back in New York instead of worrying through Europe—blinding the eyes of her children to the beauty of the world and the knowledge to be gained in this."[343] Caroline Farrar criticized a companion for worrying constantly about costs yet finding nothing of much interest except the shops; Caroline did give the woman credit for candidly acknowledging she "can't bear old things."[344]

Women eager to see Europe's treasures far outnumbered those who could not bear old things. Most women anticipated bouts of seasickness, but at least hoped that once on land they would be well enough to enjoy the Old World's galleries and churches. Inevitably, however, most who undertook a lengthy trip experienced illnesses or injuries from time to time. Anais Bliss and her husband planned only a day in Nice, but were there for ten more after she fell ill.[345] Catherine Van Rensselaer, constantly concerned about her mother's poor health, fretted one hot August day how "I wish this exacting neuralgia would go away. It worries me greatly besides making Mama so thin & suffering." Weeks later she despaired again that "Mama [is] not at all well[,] so much pain."[346] Mrs. Steedman was injured in a fall in Switzerland and a few days later was diagnosed with sciatica.[347] Eliza Marshall had a tooth incorrectly treated in Edinburgh, forcing her to visit an American dentist in Paris daily for a week.[348] Annie Spalding was delighted with Europe until pregnancy brought the agonies of morning sickness and with it her conclusion that "there is only one place for anyone in this condition & that is home."[349] These were among the many ailments that could inconvenience or even ruin a Grand Tour. Of greatest concern, however, were deadly epidemics that periodically swept Europe and occasionally included Americans among their victims.

Cholera epidemics were intermittent and unpredictable calamities of the nineteenth century. This highly lethal disease, which originated in the Indian subcontinent, reached Europe and the United States in the early 1830s; hundreds of thousands of victims died over the next two decades. Between 1863 and 1875 there was a second pandemic. Because cholera affected all classes, this second outbreak spurred a determined middle-class demand for a solution. By the mid-nineteenth century the link between drinking water and the disease was clear in medical circles, but the conviction that it was airborne proved stubbornly persistent. Even toward century's end travelers could have trouble collecting mail that had to be fumigated as a precaution.[350] Until it was widely accepted that clean water would eradicate it, cholera continued to claim victims, including the occasional American tourist.

Sallie Horstmann and her father, a wealthy Philadelphia businessman, were two of the unfortunate Americans who were victims of cholera. Elizabeth Horstmann took her four children—three girls on the cusp of adulthood and a younger boy—to Europe in April 1869, and her husband, Sigmund, joined them four months later. Bessie, the middle daughter, kept a diary chronicling her family's Grand Tour that began as a high-spirited adventure. Shortly after their reunion, the Horstmanns left their son with relatives in Germany and settled in Rome with their daughters for the winter. Bessie enthused after their first weeks there that "no one could have enjoyed themselves more than we have," that "everything has been so bright and happy before us." This bright and happy time, however, turned tragic in early March when first Mamie, the eldest daughter, then Sallie and finally their father fell victim to cholera. Elizabeth devoted herself to caring for them with the help of live-in nurses and a doctor who came daily. Bessie was sent on walks around Rome alone or to visit Americans who befriended the stricken family. She bought flowers for her sisters, but could do nothing to stay the relentless course of their illness. On March 23 Bessie recorded that "Sallie was very ill all night long and this morning at 11 minutes after 7 o'clock she passed from this world to another, very happy and ready to go." Three days later Sigmund Horstmann's brother arrived from Germany; in the sickroom he sang *Nearer My God To Thee*, a gesture as heartfelt and as futile as Bessie's flowers. He died unaware that his youngest daughter had preceded him in death days before; Bessie again turned to her diary, recording that her beloved Papa "went to meet Sallie in heaven." A service for father and daughter was held in Rome's American Chapel. The bereaved family had to remain in the city where their lives had been shattered until Mamie recovered. When she was well enough "Mama told Mamie the sad sad news this morning, poor child[;] it was very hard for her but she bore it very well." Bessie acknowledged "we long so for home now." When their return voyage was delayed, she despaired: "Oh! How dreadfully disappointed we were. I could have screamed! But it cannot be helped so we must take if for the best." Finally on June 18, 1870, fourteen months after their tragic trip began, Elizabeth Horstmann and her three surviving children sailed for home.[351]

Fortunately the Horstmanns' ordeal was uncommon; far more tourists were inconvenienced by the threat of cholera than were its victims. Kate Jones and her family first canceled plans to visit Italy due to a cholera outbreak (they did go later) and when new cases were reported in Paris, they shortened their stay there by twelve days.[352] Rumors of cholera convinced Mary Hartt's party that "we are not so eager for Paris that we cannot forego it."[353] June Spencer also shortened her stay in Paris and avoided Italy altogether due to an epidemic there.[354]

In 1892 Europe's last major outbreak was only serious in northern Europe.[355] Precautions left Harriet Blanchard "rather fearful of annoyance from fumigation and detention in crossing the line between countries." She heard Germany and Holland were especially unsafe so decided to avoid those countries and go to Paris "notwithstanding cholera prevails but we think not to a dangerous extent & it is now diminishing."[356]

Maria Bayard, who traveled in Europe before cholera reached its shores, had more reason to fear robbery in the English countryside than deadly epidemics.[357] In the 1830s rumors of bandits stealing money and jewelry left Mary Ronalds afraid to travel through rural Italy at night.[358] In subsequent decades, however, most American women felt safe in Europe's popular tourist venues. Violent crime was rare, although some trips were marred by petty theft. On their second European tour the unfortunate Horstmann sisters had their trunks robbed in Munich.[359] Elizabeth Ogden guessed that the trunk she lost in Genoa was stolen since she castigated Italians as "notorious thieves."[360]

Only one woman represented here was clearly the victim of a violent crime. Mary Flavelle, a sixty-year-old widow when she made her second trip abroad, was a cautious traveler who only reluctantly traveled alone because there was no one to join her. After landing in Naples, she rarely ventured far from her hotel, but braved traveling by train to Rome because she was eager to spend Easter there. In route, an Italian student, later indicted as "crazed," shot and robbed her as she sat alone in a train car. When Mary seemed to be recovering a friend came to escort her home; shortly after she arrived in Chicago, however, Mary Flavelle died from her wound.[361]

Fortunately, most women enjoyed a healthy and safe trip, a happy homecoming and a lifetime of remembering their experience of Europe. There is scant record for most women in the years after their tour ended so we can only speculate about the specific impact of the experience on each individual life. Surely most women were changed in subtle ways and some more profoundly. Travel abroad presented challenges to accustomed roles and the dictates of gentility. Women faced the demands of custom officials with ruses including smuggling cigarettes and posing as maids. Those fluent in one or more European languages could be empowered by their role as translator. They adjusted to the vagaries of transportation by walking up slippery slopes and tolerating the presence of unfamiliar and sometimes unpleasant men. Rather than enjoying the familiar domestic space of home, women abroad had to constantly seek new shelter and deal with leaky and cold rooms, fires, sharing with strangers and the presence of men thought menacing. Rather than serving familiar food in their own homes, they dined on unfamiliar fare amongst strangers and in restaurants deemed questionable for ladies. Women who had viewed alcohol consumption as a male vice came to drink beer and wine with gusto. Constant travel, including hiking in mountains, made dictates of fashion seem questionable, even foolish. Women largely ignorant of their family economy learned how to manage letters of credit and deal with unfamiliar currencies. Some hired maids or couriers, but even those who did grew more confident in their own judgment to deal with the myriad quotidian demands necessary for a firsthand look at the treasures of the Old World.

IV

My Dreams Were All of London, Paris, Rome: Itineraries of a Grand Tour

Each woman's trip was unique in its details, but most itineraries followed a predictable pattern inherited from the British Grand Tour and inspired by a Europe-centered education. When Ann Marie Green reminisced "my dreams were all of London, Paris, Rome" she articulated the goals of many nineteenth-century American women longing to see the Old World.[1] The cities she dreamed of, the linchpins of most Grand Tours, were combined with other places in England, France and Italy as well as in Scotland, Ireland, Germany, Spain and other parts of Western Europe.

Great Britain

Americans typically began their Grand Tour in a place they still called the Mother Country. Some Americans visiting England in the early decades of the nineteenth century remembered when they were subjects of George III, nemesis of Revolutionary America, who, despite arsenic-induced madness, remained on the throne until his death in 1820. A second war with Great Britain from 1812 to the closing days of 1814 failed to deter Maria Bayard from traveling there, but most trips awaited the Treaty of Ghent ending this war and the final defeat of Napoleon at Waterloo months later, which ended the intermittent warfare that had convulsed Europe for over a century. Pax Britannica assured a relatively peaceful Europe until the early twentieth century. After the brief monarchies of George III's two sons, his eighteen-year-old granddaughter was crowned Queen Victoria, beginning a reign that lasted from 1837 into the next century. The Victorian Era, marked by staid attention to propriety, was ceding to the more convivial Edwardian Era, named for Victoria's son and successor, well before her death in 1901. American society mimicked this British cultural shift. Throughout the nineteenth century American women traveled primarily for self-improvement, a Victorian trait, but by the dawn of the twentieth century a more Edwardian-inspired quest for pleasure and adventure was becoming an equal partner in motivating Grand Tours.

American ambivalence about their relationship could inhibit acknowledging Britain's cultural influence, whether Victorian or Edwardian. As Daniel Kilbride points out, in the first decades after the Revolution "hatred toward England was never far below the surface and "was rekindled by the second war to address unfinished business from the first."[2] This postscript to colonial revolt was settled by restoring the antebellum status quo, although Americans pointed to the decisive thrashing Andrew Jackson's improvised army inflicted on crack British troops in New Orleans a month after the Treaty of Ghent ended the war to anoint themselves the true victors. The subsequent rise in American nationalism and self confidence made Americans less defensive although throughout the nineteenth century it was popular to "twist the lion's tail," the phrase commonly used to describe Americans giving the British their comeuppance whenever possible. Shirley Foster, author of a short study of nineteenth-century American women abroad, explains that after the last Anglo-American war, England elicited both "feelings of belonging and estrangement."[3]

The British also carried ambivalence into the years after their final conflict with their former colonies. Jackson's success hardly dented their sense of superiority. An American woman visiting London during the impeachment trial of President Andrew Johnson complained, "John Bull [a fictional character similar to Uncle Sam] seems to be exulting over our troubles as she [sic] always does."[4] Even in the early-twentieth century, a few British shops prolonged the antipathy by displaying cards reading "American trade not solicited."[5] Expressions of overt hostility, however, were rare. The English disdain for their former colonies declined in tandem with the decline of American Anglophobia. In 1825 Cornelia Grinnan was delighted to find that English animosity toward her country had noticeably waned.[6]

In the post-War of 1812 decades, despite lingering vestiges of hostility on both sides, nineteenth-century Americans typically felt on arrival a special connectedness to England, and were far more likely to describe a gracious welcome than to complain of hostility. Sarah Endicott, there in the 1840s, vowed to never again criticize the English as "they have been so very kind to us."[7] From mid-century on common usage of the adjective "merry" and other terms of endearment, frequently partnered with "old," revealed deep ancestral affection. Women recorded awe when "my foot pressed the shore of Merrie England," of feeling "quite at home," in "our mother country," of touching "English soil that dear old ground," of being "much at home here," and enjoying "every moment of my stay."[8] Hannah Gould was "filled with joy to see this country which I have read & heard & thought about for so many years."[9] Many American women appreciated England all the more after traveling on the continent where they confronted unfamiliar languages, the dominance of Catholicism and more visible entrenched poverty. Britons met in non-English speaking countries often seemed as kinsmen which fueled Anglo-American rapprochement.[10]

Most Americans first touched English soil in Liverpool, one of the nineteenth century's busiest ports which early that century saw approximately forty percent of the world's trade, including many slave ships, pass through.[11] The minority of Americans who stayed more than a few hours in a city dubbed the New York of Europe may have encountered the Irish and other immigrants flocking there, although some may have been as blind to them as they were to the steerage passengers who had shared their Atlantic crossing. One woman, unusual in remaining four days in Liverpool, singled out a statue of Lord Nelson, the admiral who defeated Napoleon's navy, as the only thing worth noting.[12] Most Americans left for London as soon as possible or stayed only overnight.

Typically Americans began their tour of the Old World in London where they encountered an urban space energized by the activities of women and steadily more amenable to female travelers. Literary scholar Sally Ledger explains that throughout Europe "it was the emergence of women in the modern city which threatened the patriarchal construction of the Victorian metropolis."[13] American women became increasingly comfortable in these modern cities where they observed their European counterparts working and socializing as a matter of course.

They were especially comfortable in the English capital which combined the novelty of a foreign place with the ease of a shared language. In the 1890s geography lecturer John Stoddard proclaimed, "of all the great cities, London is the greatest."[14] It was certainly the greatest in size. When Maria Bayard visited in 1814, London was home for 1,200,000 people; one hundred years later, on the eve of World War I, the population had passed 7,000,000 compared to a population of 5,000,000 in New York City, its closest rival. In the late-nineteenth century Jennie Reizestein marveled that its "bigness is all pervading," and found it "a never ceasing wonder."[15]

The nineteenth-century London Americans encountered was largely a new city, built after the devastating Great Fire of 1666. Much of what tourists saw in the bustling, growing city dated back no more than two centuries. Westminster Abby and the Tower of London, two exceptions built during Norman times, were the most famous structures that survived the conflagration to become tourist meccas. Christopher Wren's re-designed St. Paul's, one of the first buildings restored, opened in 1697. Two centuries later an American woman proclaimed Westminster "a noble Gothic building," and St. Paul's "a most noble edifice."[16] The British Museum, housing collections that grew in tandem with British imperial success, opened in a seventeenth-century mansion a half century after the new church. While proud of their numerous famous sights and their treasure trove of antiquities, nineteenth-century Londoners shared with Parisians the compulsion to destroy testimony to their past to make way for the future. "It is difficult to exaggerate the Victorian hatred of the past," London biographer A.N. Wilson writes, "particularly of the eighteenth century." Much of the city on view for tourists was built during Queen Victoria's reign. "Victorian London," Wilson adds, "was a permanent building site."[17]

Nineteenth-century buildings—including the National Gallery, the Marble Arch, Westminster Palace and the Victoria and Albert Museum—changed the face of the city. This new London was also made familiar by negative images, drawn especially from the novels of Charles Dickens, of the poor struggling to survive in a city some called Babylon and compared to ancient Rome. The Bank of England, monument to the city's worldwide financial supremacy, was adorned with Roman arches, temples and baths that exemplified this imperial analogy.[18] American tourists saw the grandeur of this new Rome, but rarely glimpsed its poor who, Ackroyd explains, "departed into areas of misery created by the slum clearances of the new city."[19]

An American woman visiting in the late-nineteenth century intuited that the London she encountered was "a thousand times more beautiful" than it had been a century before.[20] Most critics, however, did not place London's nineteenth-century buildings among the world's great architecture. In Stoddard's opinion, even St. Paul's Cathedral usually disappointed.[21]

Perhaps he was right that London's architecture could disappoint, but the city overall rarely did; most American women touring Europe were eager to visit and once there were delighted with what they found. In the 1830s a woman complained about traversing muddy streets and breathing air fouled by the constant burning of coal.[22] Only a decade later, however, Sara Cleveland described London as "clean—endless—& magnificent," a city that "surpassed my expectations decidedly."[23] Agnes Kummer, there in the midst of her own country's domestic war, reiterated the complaint that "the dirt & rags & poverty can be equaled no where in the world," and found the city "dingy," "smoky" and "muddy," yet she loved "Dear Old London for all that."[24] Frances Gaston arrived prejudiced against the English city, but left realizing "the whole sentiment of the place has entered into my soul." Her daughter, on the other hand, found London "an interesting old city but dull."[25]

Martha Ann Tilton did not find London dull at all but reckoned a lifetime was needed to see everything of interest; her enthusiasm was only challenged at the Tower of London, a place of "dreadful" stories about the two young princes allegedly murdered there by their uncle, Richard III, in the fifteenth century.[26] Adelaide Werner, on the other hand, was eager to see the infamous Tower she had heard about from childhood.[27] Caroline White proclaimed a visit to Westminster Abbey was "one of the 'eras' of my life."[28] Louise Jewett, usually rigid in her refusal to sightsee on the Sabbath, was so eager to see Hampton Court, home of Henry VIII and the last five of his six wives, that she begged those at home not to think her wicked for going on that day.[29] Mary Kent Stone singled out St Paul's as a highlight although she refused to climb its dome; she also visited Highgate Cemetery and some nearby ruins.[30] She did not mention the British Museum, but most American women recorded one or more visits there. After the Elgin Marbles, masterpieces from the Greek Parthenon, were acquired in 1816 they joined the Rosetta Stone, key to Egyptian hieroglyphs, as the museum's most popular holdings.[31]

Although London's famous sights were widely praised, its famed art could offend women who embraced their moral authority to assure genteel standards. Julia Haylander, there in the 1830s, was dismayed to encounter a gallery of statues "entirely in a state of nudity" and refused to enter with her two male companions, but looked on from a nearby reception room as men and women alike "amuse themselves." While conceding some of the female statues were "splendidly and finely executed," Julia was "too much shocked even from my concealment to enjoy them."[32]

She was a few years premature to be shocked by statues of wax. Madame Tussaud's figures joined the list of popular London stops after Marie Tussaud, who was taught the art of wax modeling while a servant in the home of a French physician, opened her permanent collection in 1835. A Baltimore woman visiting in the 1850s was pleased to see wax renditions of the first American president, George Washington, and sitting president, James Buchanan, mingling with European royalty.[33] Not all American visitors agreed they were well represented. In 1877 Ann Marie Green, "vexed to see three mean ill dressed statues bearing the names of Abraham Lincoln, Andrew Johnson and Gen. Grant," fantasized about smashing "this disgrace to the name of Americans."[34]

The Crystal Palace, an iron and glass structure adorned with 300,000 window panes that graced nearly twenty acres, built for the Great Exhibition of 1851, was a popular display of British industrial achievement which attracted thousands of Americans eager to enjoy its fountains and gardens. Agnes Kummer left pondering, "how delightful it would be to have something of this kind in America."[35] Mary Hartt, who also imagined taking some of London's famous attractions home, quipped, "I'd like to import Westminster & the

Tower, for winter amusement, but I'd rather live in Buffalo."[36] Catherine Van Rensselaer, on the other hand, thought Westminster Abbey and other famous buildings and statues "too old to be very interesting as the marble figures are all black with age," so best left where they were.[37]

Catherine may have found a visit to Parliament more to her liking. A common language and a long history as British colonies made current affairs in Great Britain especially accessible to Americans. Attending a session of the Lords or Commons was popular with women despite the second-class treatment that protocol demanded. Some may have been familiar with a women's gallery in their own national Capitol that was maintained into the twentieth century, but it was not strictly segregated as male escorts were allowed to join women there.[38] The British Parliament was less tolerant of the sexes mingling. In mid-century Harriette Kidder was separated from the men in her party, taken down a long passage, up a flight of stairs and seated in a gallery near Victoria's throne. Rather than protesting her isolation, Harriette rationalized that this "post of obscurities was very favorable."[39] Clara Ritchie, there nearly four decades later, likewise rationalized it was "a great thing for a lady to get in there and we felt highly honored notwithstanding the fact that we were obliged to go up in the topmost gallery and sit behind an iron screen where we could look down upon the law makers & hear a little of the discussion that was going on."[40] Louise Robinson attempted to dilute mandated segregation with humor by describing sitting behind the iron barriers as like "being placed, front side out, in a bread toaster for we are separated from the M.P.'s by metal spokes."[41] Elizabeth Cady Stanton, who near century's end attended a session of the House of Commons with Susan B. Anthony, her partner in the fight for women's rights in the United States, was less willing to rationalize with humor, but declared segregation by sex "a disgrace to a country ruled by an Empress."[42]

The British love of their popular queen may have dampened criticism of Parliament's exclusory rules. Americans embraced condemning monarchy as their birthright yet also found the British royals irresistibly alluring. Allison Lockwood suggests in her study of American tourists in Great Britain that they "devoted considerable energy to catching a glimpse of Queen Victoria."[43] Ellen Coolidge, in London the year after Victoria was crowned, realized "a feeling of <u>loyalty</u>" she hoped other American women shared because "we are so seldom called to fill high places that our hearts are stirred at once with pride & love when we see the destinies of a great people are nominally committed to heads like our own."[44]

More than a glimpse of the queen usually required an elusive ticket. Mrs. Bullard felt fortunate to obtain one until dismayed to discover it was stamped "no lady admitted except in full dress."[45] Most lucky enough to obtain an audience, however, likely agreed with Louise Moulton that it was worth wearing uncomfortable attire if necessary to see royalty.[46]

Most had to settle for a brief and distant sighting of Victoria or a member of her family. Frances Morse had only tipped her hat to Victoria's daughters before, with capital letters underscoring her excitement, she "SAW THE QUEEN."[47] Ester Lindsay was disappointed that instead of her schoolbook image of "a dignified, modest girl," she saw "a fat old lady."[48] Charlotte Conant, on the other hand, who saw Victoria only months before she died, thought she "looked very kindly & far brighter than her pictures."[49] Constance Harrison was disappointed to miss even a glimpse of Victoria at her birthday ceremony, but thought it some compensation to see other royals driving up to Buckingham Palace. At a Covent Garden performance of *Lohengrin* she was seated near the Prince and Princess of Wales, as thrilling to her as Wagner's opera.[50]

Interest in the royal family waned after the popular queen's death on the dawn of the twentieth century and the ascent of her son, Edward VII. Laura Rutherford judged his royal procession as "not as brilliant as it should have been."[51] Mary McMaster dismissed it as "queer to see him talking & meeting his friends, just like any other elderly man." [52]

Although Parliament's exclusion revealed British intolerance of women's rights, American women visiting London in the nineteenth century encountered a women's suffrage movement more muscular than its counterpart in the United States. American leaders for suffrage worked primarily through the political process while their English counterparts, notably Emmeline Pankhurst and her daughters, countenanced violence to publicize their demands. Isabelle Perkinson described fences encasing government buildings filed down by police to remove militant women who chained themselves there.[53] Edith Stedman, surprised by a conversation with a supporter of the British suffrage movement, concluded it was unusual "to meet a man as young as he is so enthusiastic over such things."[54]

Most American women never mentioned the violent tactics of their English counterparts or encounters with pro-suffrage men; shopping merited far more space in their letters and diaries. In the 1840s, a walk down Regent Street left Margaret Gardner "forcibly struck with the superior magnificence of the shops of London compared with those of Paris."[55] After the Bon Marche and other great Parisian stores revolutionized consumerism two decades later, however, commercial London fell to second place. Elizabeth Porter Gould offered the minority opinion that London's Peter Robinson's was more pleasing than the Bon Marche.[56] When Elizabeth Adams decided to look for a riding habit in London she speculated, "Papa will sigh and ask in a dismal manner why we did not do all our shopping in Paris."[57] The majority who thought Paris the world's shopping mecca, however, typically frequented and praised London's stores as well. Harriett Bradbury was pleased with the bargains offered on Oxford Street and in Peter Robinson's reveled in "gloves, silk stockings and the best of all sorts of things."[58] When she learned that London shops would be closed for several days, Edith Stedman "went off like mad at heat of day—squandered my subsistence and had a beautiful time at Crosses & Liberty's."[59] When shops closed several days for Easter, Anna Wilcox fumed that "of all dumb places London is the worst—all shops closed from Thursday eve until Tuesday morning."[60] Lucy Baxter, on the other hand, may not have even noticed lengthy closures as she was "most too busy seeing sights to go in any shop or store at all."[61]

Most American women made London their only English stop, but some included long day trips or a few nights elsewhere. Elizabeth Grinnell was disappointed that Stonehenge seemed "nothing but some gray large stones nobody knows anything about."[62] Most women, however, had a more positive reaction to what England offered beyond its famed city. Shakespeare's home of Stratford was described as "where all good Americans go" and "a shrine."[63] Elizabeth Adams and her friends saw Oxford best Yale in rowing on the Avon and then "did our duty to Mr. Shakespear [sic]."[64] Sallie Wilber's "jolly time in 'Merry England' " included the "immensely pleasing" Lake Country.[65] Chester, surrounded by Roman and medieval walls and styled by one as "like a toy city," was another popular overnight destination.[66] Caroline Farrar doubted that even Rome would please her as much.[67] Lucy Dudley thought Canterbury Cathedral, revered by pilgrims since Archbishop Thomas Becket was murdered there in the twelfth century, the most impressive place in England.[68] Sophia Boardman visited Stoke Poges, both site of Gray's "Elegy in a Church Yard" and his burial place; she also went to the Isle of Wight which she thought one of the most beautiful places in Europe.[69]

Nineteenth-century Americans rarely referred to Great Britain (the union of England, Scotland and Wales in 1707) or the United Kingdom (the union of Great Britain and Ireland in 1801), but generally wrote as if Scotland, Ireland and Wales were separate countries. From colonial times, many Americans felt they had more in common with the Scottish than with the English and well into the nineteenth century some described the Scots as more welcoming.[70] M.E. Winslow found Scotland "so bright[,] the air so invigorating & the people so pleasant & hospitable."[71] Fans of Scottish literature, especially Sir Walter Scott's novels and Robert Burns's poetry, were inspired by what they read. According to Mary Kelley, Scott "had no rival as antebellum America's most celebrated literary figure," and he continued to be popular later in the century as well.[72] Helen Brooks enjoyed a pleasant stay, "Sir Walter making it so of course."[73] Lucy Culler hiked to the summit of Arthur's Seat, one of the hills around Edinburgh which was the setting for *The Heart of Midlothian*, her favorite Scott novel.[74]

Martha Ann Tilton described Glasgow as one of the best-governed cities in Great Britain (she was unusual in using that name) and Edinburgh as one of Europe's most "romantically beautiful."[75] Eliza Marshall, a rare American critic, found nothing romantic in Scotland but complained, "after you have seen one 'Ben' and one 'Loch' you have seen it all."[76]

Irish literature awaited an invigorated international Irish identity enhanced by the publications of James Joyce and other twentieth-century writers to rival that of Scotland and England in inspiring travel. In 1890 Kate Logan sought information at Dublin's Trinity College about her Irish grandfather, but only after World War I, when they were more securely integrated into American society, did large numbers of Irish-Americans search for their roots in their ancestral homeland.[77] American tourists who included Ireland in their itinerary often disembarked in Queenstown (renamed Cobh in 1922) rather than continuing on to Liverpool. Blarney Castle's fabled stone was the Emerald Island's most popular attraction. Mary Pierce watched her husband perform the ritual kissing, but admitted, "none of the ladies were bold enough to perform the feat—which requires some stretching over a dangerous looking aperture."[78] When Amy Smith's companion proved bold enough, Amy assumed people below were "aghast to see half the figure of a lady projecting over the high crumbling old wall."[79] Fannie Smith also climbed the castle's winding stairs and "kissed the bona fide blarney stone with my own two lips."[80]

Catherine Brooks found Ireland "delightful," but not all Americans agreed.[81] Mary Jane Blair concluded people in Catholic Dublin were especially ignorant whereas those in Protestant Belfast were more industrious and so more like Americans.[82] Octavia Jones, who embraced Paris as paradise, thought all of Ireland closer to purgatory and begged from there: "Take me away-take me away."[83]

France

Octavia was not alone in declaring Paris near paradise. France was typically the second country visited on a Grand Tour itinerary and, just as England usually meant London, it was largely experienced in Paris. Levenstein explains that by the 1850s "Paris, which had been originally seen as mainly a way station to Italy ... became a major destination"and rivaled Rome as Europe's most popular city.[84] Thousands of tourists mingled with the numerous American artists who lived in an American enclave described as "a little city within a big one."[85]

On a fall day in 1814 Maria Bayard entered Paris at dusk and declared it "impossible to imagine anything more elegant." Her diary reveals no interest in the historical events swirling around her that were transforming Europe. Earlier that year Napoleon, whose power had spread through much of the Continent, had been captured, forced to abdicate as emperor of France and sent into exile on Elba Island; Paris had surrendered to European countries allied to prevent French domination a few months before the Bayard party arrived. While her male relatives watched a review of troops defending Louis XVIII, the restored Bourbon king, Maria went alone to a fashionable milliner's shop. When news reached Paris that Napoleon had escaped and commanded an army near Lyon, less than 300 miles away, she tersely noted, "it caused a great alarm here." In the subsequent period known as the Hundred Days, Napoleon briefly ruled again, but after his defeat at Waterloo he was permanently exiled to Saint Helena. Maria was unperturbed about visiting a country at war, but was occasionally inconvenienced by the death throes of Napoleonic France. Her party was warned to always carry passports and to wear an American eagle pin to signify they were not belligerents.[86]

Historian Colin Jones explains that Parisians were no more enamored of the Bourbons than they were of Napoleon and, accordingly, met his defeat "with a great deal of indifference."[87] It was an indifference Maria seems to have shared; her diary reveals greater interest in fashion and theater than Napoleon's fate. She tried to conform to Parisian style "as I am too much English to appear in the streets as they laugh at them." She praised the city's women as elegantly dressed "except [for] their bonnets which are of an immense height." Although Maria was there decades before Paris became the fashion capital of the world, she enjoyed shopping, musing "the only thing one wishes is a purse without an end to the money."[88]

The end of the Napoleonic Wars introduced a century of relative peace only briefly interrupted by revolutions around 1848 and by the Franco-Prussian War in 1870, as well as occasional short-lived, localized skirmishes. Peace was a great boon to tourism; many of the Americans who visited Europe in the century before the outbreak of World War I were women and most of them visited France's famous capital city.

When she arrived on a spring day in 1828, Abigail Mayo "could hardly believe that I was in Paris!" and proclaimed it "Queen of the world."[89] Not all Americans confronting Old Paris shared Abigail's lofty opinion; despite the music, theater, art and architectural beauty it offered, the early-nineteenth-century city could be slow to work its charm. Indeed all of France, a country that evoked deep ambivalence, was a challenge for Americans. Daniel Kilbride explains that in the early-nineteenth century, "if Americans had trouble making sense of France, it was because its complexity pulled them in many directions simultaneously."[90] Appreciation of the country's artistic treasures and gratitude for its support during the American Revolution were offset in many minds by a distrust of Catholicism and a fear of political instability in the wake of the French Revolution, which some Americans felt had been transformed from a revolution emulating their own to one perverting its ideals. "The marriage of revolutions," historian Susan Dunn claims about the late-eighteenth-century French and American experiences, "ended in divorce."[91] General Lafayette was largely above reproach thanks to his service during the American Revolution, but Americans viewed other well-known Frenchmen from Voltaire to Napoleon as either radical democrats or dangerous tyrants. One woman visiting in the 1830s even questioned of France, "Oh! Why is this lovely country not a Christian country."[92]

Despite her disdain for all things French, Eliza Cox lived there with her family for nearly a year in the 1820s; she assumed relatives reading one of her letters would be "surprised at seeing this dated Paris not withstanding the disgust I expressed at the idea, before we left home." She was willing to set aside her Francophobia so her children could acquire the adornment of fluency in French. Eliza reported after a few weeks that living in Paris "gives all the blues," although she conceded some beauty, especially the gardens. Spring so improved Eliza's mood, however, that she could write, "the season is most delightful [so] even Paris has become less obnoxious."[93]

Before mid-century, Paris, a city largely built in medieval times, was more likely described as dirty than delightful. Judith Rives, there a few years after Eliza, was disappointed with monuments "all encrusted with the accumulated dirt of centuries and some of them so entirely covered with green mold as to render the effect almost powerless."[94] Caroline Cushing thought the city she visited in the 1840s "dingy and somber ... very far from elegant and pleasing to the eye."[95] Emma Willard walked streets that "seemed anything but the elegant Paris of my imagination."[96] Sarah Cleveland, already enamored of London, found "as a whole Paris positively disappointed me," which was "in all dispassionate unprejudice for I went expecting to become captive."[97]

In the second half of the nineteenth century "gay" began replacing "dirty" as the adjective considered most apt for Paris, although at least in one child's eye it was preferred even earlier. Twelve-year-old Ann Page described a "large and gay city" when she visited in 1837.[98] Sarah Tuckerman, there the same year, also challenged the negative impressions of her contemporaries, describing the shops under the Arcade of Palais as "all brilliantly beautiful" with goods displayed in a "most tasteful manner" and the streets as "a perpetual comedy."[99] Her only complaint was that not one of the thousands who watched the comedy "knew what Sunday meant." Despite her disdain for its capital's dirty monuments, Judith Rives still concluded "of all that I have seen of Europe, with all its faults, France is the best part of it."[100]

Judith joined the majority of Americans who found Paris the best part of France. Annie Fields credited Napoleon Bonaparte with making the city an "earthly Paradise."[101] Some of its artistic treasures were thanks to his looting in Italy and elsewhere, but the new Paris was more to the credit of his nephew, Napoleon III, who was elected president in 1848 and three years later crowned Emperor, and to Baron Georges-Eugene Haussmann, the man the new emperor commissioned to transform the city. Most of this transformation happened between 1851 and 1870, the period of the restored monarchy known as the Second Empire. Historian Colin Jones describes it as "a program of urban renewal perhaps as ambitious and as far-reaching as any in western history."[102] Wide streets and boulevards were designed to beautify the city as well as inhibit popular uprisings. The Louvre was at long last completed and slums between the museum and the sixty-seven acre Garden of the Tuileries, the city's premier garden and meeting place, were cleared. Around Notre Dame, according to Paris biographer Alistair Horne, "Haussmann now conducted a massacre as if an atomic bomb had exploded." He suggests the opera house, opened in 1875, best epitomized the new Paris with its "florid magnificence."[103]

In 1855 an international exposition was held to showcase the evolving magnificence that was Paris and, according to Jones, "the world was duly dazzled."[104] Three years after the second exposition in 1867, however, war threatened to destroy Haussmann's dazzling city. Prussia's Chancellor Otto von Bismarck ignited widespread Francophobia in an effort to unify the Germanic states; France likewise embraced war as a tactic to curtail Prussia's resurgent power. Conflict over the Spanish throne enabled Bismarck to maneuver France into declaring war in 1870. The superior German army quickly overwhelmed its neighbor and lay siege to Paris. Most Americans caught up in the conflict fled the beleaguered city. Medical student Mary Putnam was among those left to experience the starving time that reduced the city's citizens to eating rats and zoo animals. One night she was forced to join hundreds sleeping in the crypt beneath the Panthēon, an ordeal that left her dreaming of "white bread, café au lait and green vegetables."[105]

The outbreak of the Franco-Prussian War was so sudden that Americans contemplating a Grand Tour that year were oblivious to the possibility. Mary Woodbury, on her way to Berlin to study music and German, had crossed the Channel from London to Rotterdam where she was informed that the outbreak of war made continuing on to Germany impossible. Mary recoiled at remaining in the Netherlands because "<u>Dutch</u> is no language and music is not where [sic] I imagine." Tourists were soon ordered back to England, assuring her time there was as short-lived as she hoped. There was little Mary could do to reverse what initially seemed the greatest disappointment of her life, but she clung to hope that a swift end to the conflict would allow her to reach "my Germany and my music and all my 'fond ambitions'!"[106] In the fall of 1870 Mary did reach Berlin, but new hopes and dreams compelled her to return home just two months later, a story for Chapter VI.

The keen interest young women expressed in contemporary European affairs undercuts the image of shallow American daughters. Catherine Van Rensselaer's family, in Brussels when the war broke out, abandoned plans to travel up the Rhine and returned to Paris instead. Catherine, unhappy to be back in the city she thought "so wicked it will certainly fall like Babylon before long," penned one of her typically unyielding opinions: "I would not have believed it possible that such a state of things would have existed a fortnight ago. I hope Prussia will win although I very much doubt it for the

French are determined to extend their border to the Rhine. France is altogether too independent. What right has she to dictate who is to be on the Spanish throne? I do hope she will be defeated." The Van Rensselaers found the French capital filled with troops, all singing the *Marseilles*, which reminded Catherine of "the terrible revolutionary day," but also made the city she wanted to hate seem exciting, at least at first. Despite her keen interest in the conflict, however, she found it increasingly stressful to be in the midst of a war; excitement gave way to yearning for home. The Van Rensselaers left France and settled in Scotland where Catherine issued a gratuitous warning that French leaders must "make peace on any terms or else the beautiful wicked city will be destroyed." When the French did surrender, she gloated over their fate, underscoring her glee by adding "Hurrah! Hurrah!"[107]

Not all Americans were on Prussia's and Catherine's side. Teenager Grace Bigelow was in Germany when the war broke out, but longed to be in Paris "ready to give my whole life to the Imperial cause." The French surrender left her despairing "my heart feels as if it would break" and commiserating with the "many sorrowful hearts" in Paris.[108] Sixteen-year-old Julia Newberry first opined, "if Paris surrenders. I shall be utterly crestfallen;" when her fear became reality she penned just three words to vent her frustration: "Defeated! Betrayed & Crushed."[109] Laura Johnson criticized France for declaring war, but was even more critical of Bismarck, "the arch aristocrat," explaining, "I hate no one but I come as near to it with him as is possible." Laura wanted to believe that "poor France will be able to keep her Republic so long desired," yet reluctantly predicted "I fear for it, with the odds so strong against her."[110]

In the wake of defeat, Napoleon III's Second Empire collapsed, and was replaced by the Third Republic. For many Parisians, the shock of loss soon gave way to relief. Alistar Horne explains that even under the shadow of defeat, "all Paris took to the streets to celebrate its most gratifying revolution." The new republic, however, had to endure four months of a German siege and the humiliation of troops entering Paris. France surrendered in January 1871; the victors underscored their triumph by announcing the creation of the German Empire in the Palace of Versailles.[111]

The American women who sided with France may not have

recognized the deep internal divisions within the country they championed. The religious and conservative countryside harbored intense suspicion of more secular and liberal Paris. The vacuum following the Second Empire's collapse empowered the Commune, a revolutionary quasi-socialistic government in Paris, which was opposed by the new republic and much of the rest of the country. The ensuing struggle led to a frenzy of destruction. More than 20,000 Parisian rebels were killed in a week and others were arrested. Executions occurred in public places, including the Luxembourg Gardens where only recently tourists had strolled. Once the Third Republic had suppressed the Commune, it commenced a regime that lasted over seventy years.[112]

Most American tourists recorded more concern with their own travel woes than with France's political future. Laura Thomas supported France yet fretted that if she was unable to visit Paris her trip would have been in vain. Rumors of a surrender she had recently opposed left her musing, "I can scarcely think it true but tomorrow we will know." The fight against the Commune, however, forced Laura to postpone travel plans yet again, "as things are not as quiet there as we would like & we are afraid to venture, unless all is perfectly tranquil." Their chaperone agreed it was not prudent to visit France so traveled in Germany while Laura and her sister waited in Italy. In June the three concluded it was safe at last and Laura could rejoice to reach Paris, "that pleasure of pleasure." It was not, however, the pleasure it had been just over a year before. Many famous sights were closed and under guard or, like Palace d'Orsay, destroyed.[113]

At least Laura could enjoy Paris minus the usual crowd of fellow tourists as most Americans avoided the ravaged city for months after peace was restored. Those who came found little reason to choose the familiar adjective of gay. Bettie Amis described a city as "in an awful condition," and warned would-be visitors that many famous sights were in ruins.[114] Annie Bradley confronted the unhappy reality that in the Jardin des Plantes, which housed both a botanical garden and a zoo, most of the trees had been cut down for firewood and the animals eaten."[115]

Alistair Horne reinforces contemporary accounts that in 1871 "Paris presented a dreadful sight," yet he also suggests that more of the city had survived than many people feared. When Venus de Milo was removed from hiding and returned to the Louvre, "it was like a symbol of the return of life to Paris herself." "Indeed," Horne continues, "normality seemed to be restored with remarkable speed."[116] At year's end, Grace Bigelow reported, "Paris is changed & not as gay or as attractive as formerly," but "is far more so than when we first arrived."[117] Katherine Johnson, who returned more than two years after fleeing the city, realized "what a departure of despair and an entry of hope."[118] After 1873 none of the American women represented here described war damage. In 1875 Jacques Offenbach brought *La Vie Parisienne*, his light opera starring the notorious can-can, to the United States to convince any remaining skeptics that they would find Paris gay and attractive again.[119]

In retrospect it is clear that the German invasion followed by devastating internal fighting was but a brief hiatus in the transformation of a city that dazzled the world. To be sure, as it was transformed some Parisians mourned the loss of their old city. Novelist Homophile Gautier bemoaned, "this is Philadelphia, it is Paris no longer!"[120] To Americans, however, whether dazzled or dismayed, Paris was most definitely not Philadelphia. Horne describes the late-nineteenth-century city as "the summit of gaiety and frivolity, the music of Offenbach, the rediscovery of a joyous world in the unfettered splashes of Impressionist colour, and sexual liberation."[121] American women who scorned frivolity, preferred the German and Italian repertories to Offenbach, sought classical painting while ignoring or deploring the avant-garde Impressionists and were little past the sexual views of their Puritan foremothers, were more likely to call Paris wicked than gay. But at century's end, as Victorian sensibilities were challenged and upended in the more freewheeling Edwardian era, more women than not embraced the transformed French city. Indeed, as historian Charles Emmerson suggests, Paris served as "the antidote to American puritanism and the narrowness of its commercial spirit."[122]

Angelica Van Buren left no comment on Haussmann's rebuilding underway all around her when she visited Paris in mid-century. Her trip was marred by disappointing opera and theater, constant rain, and the stressful demands of both shopping and sightseeing. Her carriage broke down during an outing to Versailles, forcing passengers to walk part of the way home. Her Irish maid was "as a devil to us." It all added up to "a harried life." A cholera outbreak was the straw that broke Angelica's will; she reckoned she had never left a place "with more satisfaction than I did Paris."[123]

Too much rain and the threat of cholera could discourage even the most intrepid tourists. Most visitors in the last decades of the nineteenth century, however, were more fortunate than the hapless Angelica and were far more likely to regret leaving Paris than to leave with satisfaction. Kate Jones, who arrived with her family just as the rebuilding was underway, reported "all delighted with Paris." The spectacle of Parisians dining and socializing outdoors prompted her conclusion that "they really do seem to enjoy life, or rather the <u>time present</u> more than any people in the world."[124] Caroline Poor decided Paris, where "all is bright and gay," pleased her more than London although she also speculated that it might be "too gay" for some Americans. Observing Parisians at the opera left her pondering, "what our strict Bostonians would say to see ladies in low necked dresses and [with] bare arms."[125] Bostonians and women from elsewhere, however, were as likely to be enchanted as shocked. Laura Johnson described Paris as "very gay and beautiful" and speculated there was nothing like it in the world, but echoed Caroline in questioning if it might be "too splendid."[126] Clara Alexander thought it "a <u>very</u> handsome city—much more so than London," and speculated that Parisians were surely content with "lovely parks and gardens freely opened to their use containing works of art and nature in such abundance."[127] Mamie Haven joined the chorus describing the city as "paradise," enthusing "you can't imagine anything more exquisite."[128]

The Third Republic embraced Haussmann's legacy and, although the post-war regime forced him from office in 1871, his work was carried on with much of the city he planned completed in subsequent decades.[129] Each year American tourists encountered a different Paris as post-war expositions resumed showcasing the city-in-progress to the rest of world. In 1889 the ambassador to France reported Americans were flocking to the city's latest exposition "as if Paris were another Oklahoma."[130] The United States contributed a Wild West show featuring Buffalo Bill and Annie Oakley as well as the American Corn Palace; the show was a great

Visitors to the Paris Exposition of 1889 stroll under the Eiffel Tower
Library of Congress

success although the pink and white popcorn balls on sale were less so. Not all Parisians readily embraced Gustave Eiffel's tower, centerpiece of the fair which surpassed the Washington Monument as the tallest man-made structure in the world. Critics circulated a petition claiming "even money-grubbing America ... would not want it." In reality, Americans were well represented in the mix of two million visitors who gladly handed over their money to see Eiffel's work, and many of them joined the crowds riding the new American-made Otis elevators to dine at the top.[131] Lucy Dudley thought it a marvelous attraction, but was incredulous that anyone would risk going that high.[132] Clara Ritchie did, but the experience left her amazed that more people were not killed.[133]

Over time the controversial tower was embraced as the city's symbol, but the Louvre, opened in the 1790s, was still its most popular attraction. Napoleon's defeat compelled the return of some of his looted treasures to Italy, but even deprived of a portion of this booty, visitors to the museum were privy to the most outstanding art collection in the western world.[134] American women schooled in European studies from an early age were knowledgeable about Europe's art treasures and seeing them was a high priority of their trip. Most noted at least one visit to the Louvre and many went multiple times. One woman recalled "looking forward to this day for many years" and another described seeing "wondrous things" she had "longed to see for years."[135] Constance Harrison, unusual in seeking out the Impressionists who were revolutionizing western art, explained that after a feast of classical fare in Rome, in Paris "I am every day getting the best of modern production in music, drama and painting."[136]

To be sure, some women did not care about the best of art, whether old or new. Even in the last decades of the nineteenth century some women were as shocked by artistic nudity as Julia Haylander had been decades before. After visiting Luxembourg Palace, second to the Louvre in art, Helen Culbertson complained that the naked women on display "would have looked just as well with a little something over them."[137] Year by year, however, gentility expanded its range of tolerance. Mary Pierce, in Paris a decade before Helen, thought Titian's *Venus* the most beautiful painting of a naked woman she had ever seen and so justified in being without clothes.[138] By the late-nineteenth century, most who shunned Europe's galleries found them more tedious than scandalous. Mary Hartt, proud of an education that inspired her appreciation of art, wagged her finger at the "many dull people 'doing' the pictures with a long suffering expression."[139] Clara Ritchie spoke for the long sufferers when declaring it "so tiresome standing and looking at nothing but paintings."[140]

Depictions of Paris as gay were more a response to risqué entertainment than to nude art. One visitor reasoned that cabarets "represent Paris to many gay Americans."[141] The Folies Bergere initiated the association of "Gay Paree" with titillating dancing, but it was never as popular with Americans as its rival, the Moulin Rouge. Established in 1889 and notorious for the can-can, it quickly became the most famous cabaret theatre in the world.[142] Kentuckian Nina Halsey agreed to chaperone some of the younger people on her tour for a night in the Parisian demimonde. She watched female performers disrobing and "displaying the most exquisite under clothes," and then "higher would go their clothes and leg until it became simply horrible." Nina's shock rose in tandem with the performers' legs; she vowed she had never seen anything "so low and vulgar." It only went lower and became more vulgar still. She stared horrified as dancers "slap their behinds and say something in French that got great applause" and at "women sitting in men's laps, smoking & doing anything in their power to entice the men." Capital letters dramatized Nina's final verdict on Paris's gay entertainment: "I HAD RATHER BEEN LAYING ON A SLAB IN THE MORGUE unknown and unloved than [be] one of these women. Oh it was an experience that will do for a lifetime. I felt ashamed of my sex that they could become so low & degraded." Young men with her made it seem more degrading yet by claiming what she saw was tame compared to the infamous cabaret's usual fare.[143] Emma Witmer, the young woman whose mother indulged her unconventional shipboard romance, was another reluctant patron of the Moulin Rouge; after seeing "young ladies expose their unmentionables with pride" she insisted on leaving before the show ended.[144]

As new views about human sexuality were ushered in with the twentieth century and norms of gentility relaxed their grasp, Americans were not so easily scandalized by Parisian entertainment. On the dawn of the twentieth century, Abbie Farwell and her companions decided to be "wickedly gay" and go to a music hall unescorted, but found it "disappointingly respectable" so left early, thus ending "our only taste of wild Parisian pleasure."[145] After her second trip to the Moulin Rouge in 1895, Mary Mclean recalled that several years earlier she had been "too much shocked ... to enjoy myself for a minute," yet this time "was able to enjoy a good many things."[146] Some of the young women traveling with Willie Adams insisted on an evening there even though warned "what a dirty place it is."[147] Elizabeth Ijams described a performance as merely "an eye opener" and once back at her hotel at two a.m., described herself as "much the worse for wear."[148]

Risqué cabarets were but one of the eye-opening venues Paris offered. Edith Parsons attended a play she thought "perfectly awful but so cleverly acted and so convulsingly funny that it was impossible not to be amused," and pondered if "the French stop at nothing[?]"[149] Sarah Elliott assured her mother that the French ballet she attended was both decent and beautiful, but also admitted that in the audience "the older the women the fewer clothes they had on!"[150] Isabelle Perkinson watched an outdoor theatre that offered singing, dancing and acrobatic performances by girls with "mighty good looking clothes" but "<u>very</u> short skirts and in once case <u>low</u> couldn't express it." She revealed her twentieth-century temperament when assuring her mother "I am getting very used to things of that kind now [and] if I am not as broad minded as a plank by the time I come home, it will be a pity."[151]

Whether they were broad minded enough for risqué entertainment or not, most Americans women spent hours in Paris's famous stores and with its dressmakers. Parisian department stores were ushered in with Haussmann's rebuilding and emerged as centers of a consumer culture unknown in Old Paris. In 1821 Eliza Smith overcame her fear of being run over and ventured out alone to shop "which I did not know was not the thing to do in France." She was perplexed by the curiosity she evoked until advised it was considered inappropriate for women to go out unaccompanied.[152] Two decades later Caroline Kirkland reported seeing no one shopping in Paris.[153] From the 1850s on, however, rituals of buying were increasingly popular and by the end of the century almost obligatory. Some American women came to Paris primarily to acquire the latest fashion; in the 1880s a French newspaper claimed that Americans spent more money there than all other nationalities combined.[154] For many American women, however, shopping was an onerous obligation and for a small number of no interest at all.

In 1869 the Bon Marche, first of the modern department stores, opened a new era for Paris as the center and symbol of consumerism. Rosalind Williams begins her study of mass consumption in late-nineteenth-century France by quoting Denise, a character in Emile Zola's *Au Bonheur des Dames*, who exclaimed on observing Parisian-style merchandizing, "Now, there is a store." Denise's "initial encounter with a department store," Williams writes, "dramatized the way mid-nineteenth-century society as a whole suddenly found itself confronting a style of consumption radically different from any previously known."[155] According to historian Michael Miller, the Bon Marche, "the quintessential big store," became "the world of leisurely women celebrating a new rite of consumption."[156]

American women were key players in this new rite. In 1874 travel writer Charles Fulton identified "an American invasion" of Paris led by women. "It is easy to get to Paris," he concluded, "but very hard to get away again, as most of the Americans now congregating here find, especially if there are ladies among them." American women were keen on the city, Fulton speculated, because "there is no place for the lady tourist like Paris ... its attractions being so novel and varied and its stores so brilliant and extensive in their display of all manner of fabrics."[157] Two decades later Elizabeth Nichols corroborated his impression, recording that she saw "any quantity of American women [but] not many men except such as have some study to pursue here."[158] Tour guide Willie Allen clearly had women in mind when she reported "an American in Paris gravitates invariably toward the Bon Marche, the Magazines de Louvre or the beautiful Avenue de L'Opera."[159]

The reality that most women shopped has fueled the erroneous impression that this was the primary and for some even the sole reason they went to Paris. An image of shallow American women flocking to the French city to acquire its goods and style was reinforced by philosopher Thorstein Veblen's portrayal of the conspicuous consumption of the Gilded Age's leisure class. Fiction has also fueled the stereotype. Henry James's *Daisy Miller*, published in 1879, introduced the self-possessed but shallow daughter of a wealthy man who came to represent the stereotypical American girl in Europe. In the early-twentieth century the New York *Herald* introduced Fluffy Ruffles, another fictional character described by journalist Hebe Dorsey as "the archetype of the young, pretty, naïve but sassy American girl, eager to acquire the famous Parisian chic."[160] Blanche McManus, who published an account of her trip in the early-twentieth century, referred to Fluffy's real-life counterparts as "dollar princesses" who were watched "with interest and curiosity" by Europeans.[161] Historians have also played a role in perpetuating a one-dimensional image. Foster Rhea Dulles, author of one of the first studies of Americans touring abroad, largely ignored the female experience except for his one-line claim that "the women—and a surprising number of them recorded their travels—

invariably went shopping."[162] Thus fictional and historical studies alike have used the female consumer, spending to display her father's or her husband's wealth, to symbolize the hegemony of the American bourgeois class and the character of American women abroad.

The majority of American women did shop in Paris, but most of them fall well outside the stereotype of dollar princess. The city's big stores were places where women were expected to spend time without men and were accordingly as much agents of independence as venues for flaunting wealth. Sally Ledger explains, "department stores, like the arcade, boulevards and cafes, constituted a half-public, half private social space which women were able to inhabit comfortably."[163] Some women were content walking through stores that seemed like dazzling small villages, although most wanted to take home some of the novel goods they displayed. For some women shopping joined great museums and monuments in making Paris an attractive destination. Soon after they arrived, Eliza Homans and a friend "(woman like) drove to the Bon Marche" where they "determined to do or die as to bonnets."[164] Elizabeth de Peyster relished trips to a department store, "a world within itself" and "a fascinating place," because "the time passes so rapidly when one is looking at so many pretty articles."[165] Those with limited means had to resign themselves to just looking, at least most of the time. One young woman carried a letter of credit designated for a velvet street costume. Parisian cuisine, however, proved more enticing than its couture and her credit steadily eroded until she had to confess she had "devoured the underskirt and was about to attack the overdress."[166]

The minority who thought great stores the city's primary attraction could become targets of scorn by others who considered shopping decidedly secondary. One woman acknowledged her contempt of the "many people [who] think because it is Paris they ought to buy."[167] Another mocked women who insisted on a carriage for sightseeing, but were "very strong when shopping, walk many miles."[168] Willie Allen, first amused "to see how crazy we are over the shops," realized "not an hour passes but someone comes in with a remarkable purchase—usually the value of 18 or 19 c[ents]." In time, however, her sense of humor worn thin, she confided to her sister "we have been here six days and not one single solitary remark has been made by my young ladies as to anything around Paris, except the shops and dress-makers. They absolutely care nothing for what you or I would call travel."[169] Kate Field also criticized American women she thought came to Paris only "for what is elegantly termed 'a spree'."[170]

For many American women, however, a spree was in reality a chore. Caroline Townsend exemplifies those who viewed shopping more as an onerous obligation necessary to acquire a stylish wardrobe than as a pleasure. Caroline, fatigued on arrival and concerned about her ailing mother, felt "rather homesick." The first week she avoided stores and stayed in "as if there was nothing in this world ever to be done in Paris." One Sunday she joined her mother at church and then visited American friends, prompting her wish that "all the days were filled like this." But the compulsion to acquire French fashion was powerful and Caroline could not put off the inevitable indefinitely. Entries over the next ten days include: "Shopping. French people will be the death of me. They are infamous;" "I hope my friends will put on my tombstone <u>died—of commissions!!!</u>;" "Shopping;" "Shopping again!"; "I will be glad when we leave Paris. It is so tiresome here," and finally "shopped & wore myself out."[171]

Caroline's litany of tiresome shopping-filled days may have been excessive, but it was not atypical. After a week in Paris in the early 1860s, Caroline Farrar despaired of having "seen nothing—done nothing—read nothing—enjoyed nothing as yet [but] corsets, petticoats, shops & weariness to the flesh;" she could at least append the cheerful postscript: "city right pleasant—new looking."[172] Elizabeth Adams shopped even though "I hate it beyond words" as "It brings out my evil temper and makes me hot and cross and tired."[173] Marion Nichols admitted a compulsion to buy, but it left her longing to leave Paris "as we have spent the ten days in a most stupid way doing the necessary shopping."[174]

Mamie Parson's patience was stretched thin by a female companion with "no talent whatever about ordering clothes and [who] has so little money to spend that everything has to be carefully considered;" Mamie found going alone far more appealing and successful; she sent home a witty description of her shopping experi-

A Mary Cassatt drawing of dressmaking
Library of Congress

ences: "The purchases are beginning to pour in and my conscious [sic] is beginning to prick—My room looks like the Bon Marche turned loose. To get to the washstand I must jump 3 hat boxes—to open my trunk I must demolish a leaning tower of lingerie—to write at my table I must insert my blotter between piles of gloves, handkerchief boxes, etc. [,] to open the wardrobe I must stand on a chair and to get into bed I must put on the floor one or two charming gowns that I have already [had] sown [sic] from Mme. Lebonnere."[175]

Dressmaking, a specialized part of the shopping ritual, lacked even the fascination afforded by the sights in large department stores. Some wealthy Gilded Age women made annual trips to Paris to be fitted by the couturier Charles Frederick Worth, described as "the very emblem of good taste in New York and San Francisco," or one of his high-priced rivals.[176] Women of more limited means made do with Mme. Lebonnere or other less-famous choices. Elizabeth de Peyster concluded dressmaking was the mainstay of conversation for American women; if so, they were surely conversations laced with complaints. Elizabeth endured the process as a "torment" and "a bore" and wished dresses "could be made by magic." She engaged one of Paris's most renowned seamstresses only to conclude it was "wicked to pay the prices she demanded." Despite the torment and cost, however, she took "this opportunity for replenishing our wardrobe" and visited a dressmaker almost daily for a month.[177] Mrs. Hunt's dressmaker came to her hotel but, finding this arrangement little better than going out, she fumed that "I never got so tired of seeing one before" as "she is to [sic] slow & I am so impatient." Rising frustration with her sartorial obligations was vented in frequent diary entries: "this dressmaking business completely unfits me—I hate it," "what a waste of time," "these miserable French women," and "I would much prefer sightseeing to such a waste of time." Mrs. Hunt was candid enough to acknowledge, "I expect I am hard to please."[178] Laura Thomas, perhaps unfamiliar with the famous male designers, was more surprised than disgusted when introduced to her dressmaker. "I was quite astonished at seeing a man," she later recalled, "but he seemed to understand & I stood perfectly still as though it was no novelty."[179]

In the early twentieth-century American women felt

less compulsion to shop in Paris as stores in New York City and elsewhere began offering comparable goods. In 1910 a New Yorker maintained that stores in her city were replacing those in Paris for style and variety although she did acknowledge many of its goods did come from the French city.[180]

Italy

Her parents' mandate that she have dresses made prompted Catherine Van Rensselaer's confession: "I inwardly rebel & could be contented I think to be myself & unstylish." Weeks in Parisian stores only left her longing to give up "this shopping brilliant frivolous city" for Rome.[181] Rome was traditionally the quintessential goal of a Grand Tour and an obligatory stop long before consumerism became intertwined with learning and tradition and made Paris a popular rival. It remained the favored destination of women seeking monuments to the past more than present-day fashion. Naples, Florence and Venice were also traditional stops inherited by Americans who visited Italy.

Before 1870, when the Risorgimento, the movement to create a unified Italian Kingdom, was completed, what Americans called Italy was in reality a number of separate political entities. The Congress of Vienna, held in 1815 to draw the map of post-Napoleonic Europe, replaced France's relatively lax control over much of the Italian peninsula with the more autocratic rule of Austria's monarchy. In 1847 Austrian Prince Metternich, mid-century's most powerful European diplomat, famously quipped that Italy was but "a geographical expression." But Italy was also an ideal; the Risorgimento, inspired by Giuseppe Mazzini and fought for by Giuseppe Garibaldi, sought to turn a mere expression into a unified nation with Rome as its capital.

In the last years of the 1840s the revolutionary movement that spread across Europe and centered in Italy made it a particularly inconvenient time to travel there. Deep divisions over its future ignited sporadic skirmishes throughout the peninsula. In 1847 King Ferdinand effectively suppressed a revolt in the mainland portion of his Kingdom of the Two Sicilies. The following year, revolutionaries in Rome declared a new Roman Republic, forcing Pope Pius IX to flee until French and Austrian troops arrived to restore the Catholic Church to power and join King Ferdinand in the fight against the would-be republic's affront to monarchy. Margaret Fuller, who reported from Rome for Horace Greeley's New York *Tribune* from 1848 to 1850, informed her American readers "the struggle is now fairly, thoroughly commenced between the principle of democracy and the old powers," and presciently predicted that it "may last fifty years, and the earth be watered with the blood and tears of more than one generation" yet "the result is sure. All Europe ... is to be under republican government in the next century."[182]

The intermittent violence dissuaded some Americans from venturing abroad, and some who did avoided Italy. E. Thompson resolved to carry through with her Grand Tour despite feeling "a little foreboding of evil from the troubled state of affairs in Europe." As her party contemplated leaving Paris for Italy, she worried it was "imprudent to say the least;" several men traveling with her queried officials at the American embassy who convinced them it was safe. Once there, however, they found themselves so close to the fighting between King Ferdinand and the revolutionaries that they could see royal troops passing by their hotel and smoke from the battlefield. They were forced to cancel plans to visit Sicily, but were assured Pompeii was safe. E.M.'s party was in Milan in time to observe rejoicing over Austria's defeat; little boys ran along side their carriage shouting *"Viva L'Italia, Viva il Pio Nono."*[183] The bambini realized only half of their wish; Pius was restored, but Austrian troops soon reestablished control.

Throughout the years that Italians warred over their peninsula's fate, American tourists continued to come, although they were forced to modify plans from time to time. In 1851 Kate Jones opined from Rome that "constant watchfulness is required ... I shall not feel safe until we are out of Italy."[184] Seven years later Louisa Smythe, prevented from going to Venice when conflict between France and Italian nationalists erupted there, joined Americans fleeing to Marseilles where she heard "nothing but Garibaldi and Victor Emanuel."[185] The next year Bettie Kimberly was confident enough traveling in Italy that she encouraged her family to join her, but also assured them that if the conflict worsened she would come home immediately.[186]

The same year Bettie declared Italy safe, Austria's mobilization in the North left Hattie Trowbridge's fearful about traveling to Milan, at the center of the fighting, so she resolved to wait patiently until the situation was resolved. She reluctantly gave up Venice because of its unsettled state. Hattie was in Florence when its grand duke was forced to flee in a bloodless revolution. Once convinced it was best to leave Italy altogether, her party traveled first to Genoa where they encountered French soldiers filling hotels and streets; the men felt safe walking around the city, but the women feared joining them. Confined to her room, Hattie vented her pro-French sentiment, penning: "Viva La France. God give them victory." The number of troops on the train to Turin left her fretting, "I am sure I don't know where we shall go to." Once there, the women, finally emboldened to venture out, found French troops all around drinking and gambling, a scene, Hattie realized, "such as I never beheld before."[187]

Americans in Italy during the Risorgimento read about scenes never beheld before at home as well. In the years Italy was becoming unified American unity was shattered by southern secession and civil war which likely kept more Americans at home than did the conflicts in Italy.[188] In the early years of the Civil War, some Northerners feared Great Britain, and possibly other countries, would recognize the Confederacy, resulting in a European war as well. Some travelers, especially young men eager to enlist, departed for home when they learned their country was splintering into North and South. Especially in the last years when casualties touched almost everyone, most likely many Americans who contemplated a Grand Tour decided that it was inappropriate to enjoy that pleasure in the midst of so much tragedy.

Anna Marie Fahnestock and her husband were in Germany when they received word of the conflict over Fort Sumter, federal property just miles from Charleston, the fire-eating center of the South. They were especially worried that European involvement would make it impossible to return home, a concern exacerbated by Mr. Fahnestock's serious illness. Anna Maria explained to her children that because their father's nervous system was greatly unsettled by the news, they hoped to soon re-cross the Atlantic as "the wear and tear of his mind would not be worse than sitting here thinking of the war."[189] After Caroline Farrar read letters from home "awful enough to make us blue," she sanctioned her male relatives' decisions to return home and join the Union Army.[190] Frances Duer began interspersing her diary entries about Europe with comments about troubles at home. Two weeks after Savannah fell to Sherman's army she presciently proclaimed it "the beginning of the end," adding the postscript: "thank heavens."[191] Mr. and Mrs. Edward Ogden brought their daughters to Europe in 1864 to mourn the death of their only son in one of the battles Grant and Lee waged in Northern Virginia; tragically the grieving parents both died there.[192] The magnitude of this protracted war made it inevitable that the usual camaraderie Northerners and Southerners had enjoyed abroad was shattered. A New York *World* reporter observed sectional animosity replicated in Europe as tourists, once united as Americans, began "looking upon each other as enemies."[193]

Lee surrendered to Grant on April 7, 1865, but President Lincoln's assassination a week later erased a short-lived spirit of reconciliation and plunged the nation into the traumatic period of Reconstruction. The southern planter class began coping with the diminution of their wealth and millions emancipated from slavery began building precarious lives as free people. Some southern white women retained the means to travel and those who did were more inclined to vacation in Europe than in once popular Northern destinations such as Niagara Falls and Saratoga Springs. Northern women, less affected by the war and its aftermath, began returning to Europe in steadily increasing numbers.

In the years the United States struggled over the state of its union, the Kingdom of Italy was formed and expanded. When the Most Serene Republic of Venice, independent for more than a thousand years until conquered by Napoleon, joined in 1866, only the Papal States remained apart. Annie Fields, who closely followed events at home and in Italy, concluded that the only thing more interesting than the pending liberation of Romans from papal control was the emancipation of American slaves.[194] Emily Severance was also cognizant enough of contemporary affairs to note in 1867 that "Rome seems to be dying and Popery too."[195] She exaggerated the dismal fate of the Catholic Church, but correctly grasped that profound change was imminent in central Italy. Its war with Germany forced France to withdraw from Rome, allowing Italian troops to enter in their wake. The loss of French protection forced Pope Pius IX's retreat to the Vatican, an exile that lasted nearly sixty years; he retaliated by claiming papal infallibility. Catherine Van Rensselaer was delighted that "Rome is the capital of Italy! Victor Emmanuel entered it today;" the serenely opinionated twenty-year-old also noted that "the goose of a Pope has declared himself infallible," but insisted "it does not matter much after all what one bigot chooses to call himself."[196] Victor Emmanuel I, the man whose triumph she celebrated, was named the first king of unified Italy and took up residency in the Quirinal Palace, the former residence of the pope. After 1870 Rome was physically and spiritually divided between the heirs of Caesar and the heirs of Christ.

In the years after the Franco-Prussian War, American tourists were only occasionally inconvenienced by small conflicts until 1914 when long-simmering nationalism erupted into a European-wide war that eventually engulfed the United States as well. In 1898, for example, Italians rioted over food shortages, and in Milan alone over 500 people were killed or wounded by their government.[197] An American woman there at the time reported the trouble "was quelled very quickly and although it prevented many people from coming into Italy and probably sent many out it didn't alter our plans."[198]

For the most part, American tourists experienced secular Rome much as they had when it was part of the Papal State. Clara Mitchell, unusual in admiring the post-Risorgimento city, thought it "about as modern a looking city as you'd want to see," and "a very fine one too, with nice wide well paved streets & large handsome houses."[199] Eleanor Middleton, on the other hand, not as impressed with the secular city and convinced that Romans hated Piedmontese and despised Neapolitans, concluded "the costliness of a monarchy seems worse than the waste and corruption of the Papal states."[200] Most American women, however, looked past modern Rome and rarely concerned themselves with its politics.

They came searching for an ancient city of nearly two millennia earlier still in evidence amid layers of subsequent Romes. James H.S. McGregor, historian of Roman architecture, explains that, "unlike Haussmann's Paris, Rome has never been subdued to a single overarching vision or plan of organization," but, to the contrary, is "an agglomeration of historical cities."[201] Post-Risorgimento Rome searched for its own place among the architectural and artistic treasures of Ancient, Medieval, Renaissance and Baroque Romes; it also had to struggle against nearly two thousand years of Catholic hegemony. Historian Christopher Duggan explains that despite ambition to make the capital of united Italy into a major metropolis, it struggled "to emerge from the shadow of the papacy and establish a new identity for itself." From the mid-80s on, massive building projects did begin transforming the city in ways that Duggan points out were "deeply dispiriting to many observers."[202] After 1885, tourists encountered the Vittoriano, a monument to Victor Emmanuel I that was ridiculed for its resemblance to both a wedding cake and a typewriter and even called *pisciatoio nazionale* (national urinal), rising up to dwarf ancient buildings with its starkly white visual dominance.[203] By the turn of the century the Tiber River, favored dumping ground for murdered Romans and popes alike, had virtually disappeared below embankments built to control periodic flooding.

American tourists largely ignored the intrusive monument looming over them as they walked about the Forum and had little to say about the vanishing river. But almost every Protestant American criticized markers of Catholicism that overlay ancient ruins. Anti-Catholicism, which crossed the ocean with the first Protestant colonials and was exacerbated by the nineteenth-century influx of Catholic immigrants, including millions of Italians, was virulent in nineteenth-century America. Protestants carried prejudices honed at home across the ocean largely intact. Catholic rituals encountered abroad were denounced as "pomp and nonsense," "mockery," "a delusion," "humbug," with corruption "only too apparent," and for "ignorance and superstition." [204] Several weeks in France and Italy left Charlotte Horlbeck feeling "more thankful every day that I was born in a Protestant country."[205]

Caroline Farrar was a rare Protestant who praised the sincerity and simplicity of Catholic worship, and even wished for a church as grand as the Milan Cathedral at home so she could make an annual pilgrimage.[206] Some women, although less willing to concede sincerity to Europe's Catholics, joined her in what art historian

John Davis has labeled "Catholic envy."[207] Mary Hartt exemplifies those whose intellectual rejection of Catholicism did not preclude an emotional attachment; she acknowledged, "our thirst for cathedrals is never fully appeased & I don't know how we shall get along without them."[208] June Spencer regretted that the Cologne Cathedral, one of Germany's most popular sights, was Catholic, but also acknowledged, "Protestantism would never have raised it."[209]

Throughout Catholic Europe, and especially in Rome, American women struggled to reconcile their distaste for the displays of Catholicism all around them with their appreciation of the artistic treasures it had inspired. In his magisterial study of America's Rome, William Vance explains Americans confronted Italy as "the Other, both in the knowledge and beauty that it offered and in the horrors of its spiritual and social condition."[210] In her study of the nineteenth-century Protestant response to Rome, Jenny Franchot concludes that "travel narratives of the period contradictorily advertised the triumph of Protestant history over the visible evidence of contemporary Italy's pagan ruins and allegedly Vatican-induced poverty while acknowledging the overwhelming force of the visual encounter with classical and papal Rome."[211]

When seeking the ancient city, these American women were guided to certain sites and in their responses to them by the Romantics.[212] Despite their perception of horrid social and spiritual conditions, most were overwhelmed by a more emotional reaction to the Eternal City than they experienced anywhere else in Europe. Angelica Van Buren, relieved to leave Paris, overlooked the poverty around her in Rome sufficiently to determine "it would have a refining influence upon one's nature to live in such an atmosphere of ideal beauty."[213] Modernization of the city in the last decades of the century hardly blunted the encomium. Louise Kellner realized within days of arriving that "my eyes, my brain, my head and all the awe and wonder that I am capable of feeling are in a constant whirl."[214] As she prepared to leave Rome, Laura Thomas reflected on "a place to dream over the days that are no more[,] the centuries that have rolled away & and of which now & then you see a reminiscence in form of an old ruined arch or the ruined tower or the huge crumbling mass of some Imperial home."[215] Clara Ritchie, there with Martha Maltby, loved the city "so much I cannot bear to think of leaving but we shall both drink of the Fountain of Trevi [the Baroque fountain completed in 1762] before we leave which is said to insure a return to Rome."[216]

It was the ruins of ancient Rome, especially, that prompted such affirmations of love and longing to return. Laura Libbey, who had read for years about "this most ancient city, its seven hills, its palaces and its temples, its walls and its battlements," was first disappointed to arrive at a modern train station; discovering the famous ruins at last prompted her postscript: "our disappointment vanished and we felt that we were indeed looking upon ancient Rome!"[217] Constance Harrison, who encountered the ancient city right away, exclaimed "nothing quite hit the bull's eye like running over the Tiber at midnight and beginning to catch glimpses of ruins that told us we were nearing Rome."[218]

Excavation of the Roman Forum, begun during Napoleonic hegemony, slowly revealed surviving remnants of ancient Rome's heart. Nathaniel Hawthorne, there with Sophia in 1859, estimated that in March alone they were joined by fifteen hundred fellow Americans exploring the site; he described Basilica Julia, a public building dating from the early Roman Empire, as "heaps of bricks, shapeless bits of marble and granite, and other ancient rubbish." Nathaniel was disgusted by the human waste around the Arch of Titus, but amused by clothes and sheets flapping around the ruins where they were left to dry.[219] Even a decade later the Forum was still dubbed *campo vaccino* (Cow's Field) as cows and sheep grazed among the ruins. Most visitors overlooked the dross of humans and animals in a place they came close to sanctifying. Enough was visible—including the Arches of Septimius and Titus, pillars that once framed the House of the Vestal Virgins, the Temple of Saturn first built in the fourth century BCE and the iconic Phocas Column, built a thousand years later—that women steeped in the history of the place were deeply moved by what they saw. Laura Thomas, an especially poetic traveler, recounted growing "sadder and sadder at each thought for what a garden spot of art what a place for learning & culture—what a place to dream over the days that are no more[,] the centuries that have rolled away & of which now & then you see a reminiscence in form of an old ruined arch or the ruined tower or the huge crumbling mass of some Imperial home."[220] Idella Plimpton stood at the rostrum "to imagine how Caesar felt

The Coliseum in 1875. *Library of Congress*

when, standing in the same place, he delivered his oration against Cataline [sic]."[221] Indeed, imagination was needed to appreciate the scattered ruins. Ann Marie Green was typical in acknowledging she would not have understood what she saw without her "red covered book" (*Baedeker's Guide to Italy*).[222]

Guidebooks were not as essential for making sense of the largely intact Coliseum.[223] This iconic symbol of Rome's ancient glory and decadence, built in the first century as an arena for gladiatorial games, had, by the nineteenth century, survived an earthquake, the ravages of scavengers and even aborted plans to turn it into a wool factory employing prostitutes or a bullfighting arena. "Of all the ruins in Rome," a visitor declared in the 1860s, "none is at once so beautiful, so imposing, and so characteristic as the Colosseum."[224] Anne Bense enthused over "the noble old Coloseum [sic]" which "impresses one more and more as it rises from the mists of the centuries into the vision of the present."²²⁵ Appreciation of this most famous symbol of ancient Rome was often mingled with sad reflection on the legend that Christians were martyred there. Nina Halsey joined others delighted to see "the grand old Coliseum," but was also aggrieved to confront the place "where thousands of Christians were [torn?] by wild beasts for the amusement of the Emporers [sic] of Rome."²²⁶ Lucy Dudley could find no redeeming quality at all in the venerable arena which "stands alone, different and useless except in its lessons of power and martyrdom."²²⁷

Constance Harrison, as eclectic in her response to Rome as she had been to Paris, thought the Baths of Caracalla, ruins from the third century CE where Shelley penned *Prometheus Unbound*, more impressive than either the Roman Forum or the Coliseum.²²⁸ Marion Burgess claimed the Pantheon, a Roman temple that was saved from destruction by consecration as a Christian church in the seventh century, as "the most splendid monument of antiquity in Rome."²²⁹ Until 1883 visitors saw it topped off with "asses ears," the local nickname for the two belfries Bernini added in the sixteenth century in a misguided effort to improve the magnificent ancient building. When Mary Elizabeth Gittings visited two years after the eyesores were removed, it was the "big eye at the top," the oculus that allows in light (and rain as well) that caught her attention; she also singled out the "grand old equestrian statue" of Marcus Aurelius in front of the Campidoglio, which dates back to the second century and is the only equestrian statue from the Roman Empire to survive.²³⁰ On the day she visited the Pantheon in 1900, Willie Adams could only admire its exterior because "thousands of dirty people" were crowded inside to view the body of King Umberto I, lying in state after he was assassinated by an anarchist.²³¹

Ancient ruins held little attraction for Eleanor Middleton, unusual in her preference for the Vatican Museums and St. Peter's Basilica.²³² Others were more ambivalent about these legacies of Roman Catholic power and genius. The overlay of Catholicism, which sometimes co-existed with ancient ruins but could overwhelm them, nearly ruined Rome for Kate Jones who arrived mid-century assuming "it would be "that 'mecca' of our fondest anticipation." A few days in Rome, however, served "to sicken & disgust me with the place." She speculated "if I could visit the <u>ruins only</u> & forget that I am in modern Rome, perhaps I might wish to prolong my visit—but to look around, see the priests by scores—at all points—hear the miserable tales of crime and degradation, and almost utter absence of everything like a virtue and religion. O! it is enough to make the Christian weep tears of blood."[233]

Most women did not become so overwrought, especially not after 1870 when the papacy was confined to the Vatican and Rome became visually more secular. But others also struggled with the disquietude they felt when the Catholic city and the contemporary city impinged on their experience of ancient ruins. Constance Harrison, uneasy with even the grandest monuments of Catholicism, realized she could do without "the marvels of Renaissance art [but] those of the Ancients—never!"[234] Alice Carter also thought the Colosseum and Forum made a trip to Rome worthwhile, but found St Peter's "<u>very</u> disappointing" and "nothing but a monument to popery."[235]

A majority of Protestant women, however, even those who condemned what they called popery, embraced St. Peter's Basilica, the Vatican Museums and other treasures of Catholic art and architecture as integral part of experiencing Rome. St. Peter's, designed by Bramante and completed by Michelangelo in the sixteenth century on a site where a Christian church had stood for more than a thousand years, rivaled the ancient ruins in familiarity and popularity. Mrs. Thompson reminisced that on seeing the church "my lips were dumb—& my heart stood still."[236] Isabella Faber realized she would never forget entering the holy edifice familiar from childhood but, revealing typical ambivalence, she also realized "I cannot tell all the pomp and nonsense I saw that day."[237] Some women thought it humorous to kiss the toe of St. Peter's statue, a custom of pilgrims dating back centuries, but Clara Ritchie countered it was "the most superstitious and degrading thing we have seen done."[238] Caroline Corson shared the majority view that the church was "vast & beautiful," but also realized it "did not impress me devotionally in the least."[239] Catherine Van Rensselaer agreed it was "Oh so grand and splendid," but fantasized about the day "when it will be turned into a Presbyterian meeting house."[240]

Mary Ronalds, traveling a decade before American women began organizing to demand rights at home, singled out the Catholic

Church's treatment of women for criticism; she claimed the Vatican policy of excluding her sex from certain places, including the pope's antechamber, was evidence that it was "genuinely afraid of women" even though "all their tombs have at least two and their finest pictures are of women." When barred from St. Peter's underground rooms, she protested, "ladies do not hold their proper places in society in Rome," a sure sign, she thought, that Romans were "uncivilized and unenlightened."[241]

In contrast to Paris's Louvre, there was no major Roman museum that housed the lion's share of the city's wealth of art; seeing Rome's most famous treasures necessitated numerous trips to galleries and churches scattered throughout the city. Constance Harrison singled out the Vatican, the Capitoline and the St. John Lateran museums as her first choices.[242] Marion Burgess, more in line with today's taste than many of her contemporaries, named Michelangelo and Raphael as favorites, but Guido Reni, a now obscure seventeenth-century Bolognese artist, exceeded these Renaissance masters in popularity throughout the nineteenth century.[243] His fresco *Aurora*, a classical allegory covering the ceiling of the Palazzo Rospigliosi (rarely accessible and virtually unknown today) surpassed the Sistine Chapel ceiling in popularity; almost every woman touring Rome saw it and lavished praise on what she saw. To Margaret Thomson, long familiar with the copy in her home, the original seemed like "an old friend."[244] Sarah Newberry found Michelangelo's *Last Judgment*, culminating his work on the Sistine Chapel ceiling, "displeasing," but thought *Aurora* "exceedingly beautiful."[245] Mary Olney described Guido's most famous painting as "pure beauty" and thought it "worth breaking one's neck to see."[246] For Eliza Marshall seeing *Aurora* was reason enough for a trip to Rome, but she was disappointed in Guido's *Beatrice Cenci*, symbol of aristocratic privilege which then hung in the Barbarini Palace.[247] Mary Elizabeth Gittings, on the other hand, thought this portrait "the most haunting picture I ever saw."[248] Grace Bigelow was unusual (and also more in accord with contemporary taste) in insisting that Raphael's Madonnas were superior to Guido's famous works.[249]

Most Protestants could look past their Catholic origins and appreciate paintings of the Madonna and saints, but human relics were another matter. Constance Harrison chided a friend with "a taste for horror" for taking her to see the Church of Santa Maria della Concezione's display of the bones of thousands of Capuchin monks arranged in decorative patterns.[250] Bettie Thomas was so alarmed at the sight of the ornamental skulls that she "screamed aloud & left the old crypt."[251] Harriet Blanchard just dismissed the church of bones as "a strange place."[252]

Some Protestant women embraced the Catholic celebration of it, held in February or March just before Lent, as harmless fun, but others rejected it as just another display of Catholic decadency. In 1867 Harriet Blanchard was disappointed that only tourists were taking part in Rome's Carnival until told Romans were boycotting to demonstrate their opposition to Pope Pius IX's resolve to retain control of the Papal States.[253] Caroline Farrar denounced Carnival as "humbug;" the sight of men dressed in women's clothes prompted her verdict that it was "stupid" as well. But she also accepted that "our first principle being in Rome is to do as the Romans do" so "stood it out bravely."[254] Hattie Trowbridge was amused by Carnival thanks to her success confounding friends with her disguise and by speaking French; it made the day "a merry one and not soon to be forgotten."[255]

Protestants generous with their criticism of Catholic rituals, yet afflicted with a measure of Catholic envy, were often eager to obtain an audience with the pope or attend a Catholic service. Dolly Whaley was likely correct in her conjecture that most who did were inspired to go more out of curiosity than reverence.[256] After her audience with Pius IX, Idella Plimpton declared herself "blessed by him as well as I could be as I was too much Protestant to kneel before his majesty;" watching Catholics who did kneel left her criticizing "the most idolatrous miserable means of influencing a people by display that I have ever seen here."[257] Caroline Farrar found the pope's blessing of the candles "a gorgeous ceremony," but thought it too theatrical to experience again.[258] Euphemia Olcott condemned the service she attended on Christmas Day as "a painful exhibit of Christianity" although she thought the music splendid.[259]

Whether motivated by spirituality or curiosity, women who wished to participate had to conform to the protocols of Catholic services. Willie Adams borrowed the requisite black lace veil from her chambermaid.²⁶⁰ Lucy Baxter, whose party of eight had only four tickets for an audience with the Pope, realized winning one was a mixed blessing because it necessitated buying a black dress.²⁶¹ When Mamie Parsons joined women wearing the mandated attire for a morning service, she concluded, "a good many of them <u>looked</u> as foolish as I <u>felt</u> and doubtless looked."²⁶²

Some American Protestants suppressed their curiosity and deemed it entirely too idolatrous to participate in Catholic rituals. Grace Roberts and her sister were invited to a ceremony in the Sistine Chapel, but their father refused to go and their mother judged it inappropriate for them to go alone; finally a friend agreed to escort the two. Grace was impressed enough to be "thankful we did not miss seeing this grand ceremony."²⁶³ When Catherine Van Rensselaer's father received an invitation for his family to meet the Pope, it was the daughter who refused to go. Catherine, who described her family as "free born American Presbyterians," admitted, "I like the old man! And as a sovereign would not mind being presented to him," but criticized fellow Protestants who had their "heads completely turned and act like fools." Her father and sister assured her afterwards that their visit with the "extremely sweet and gracious" Pope was a success so Catherine joined "the two Popesites opposite and got some ice cream."²⁶⁴

Rome denied Catherine's wish to turn her back on all Catholic rituals. The spectacle of pilgrims climbing on their knees up St. John Lateran's Sancta Scala, which legend holds were from the palace of Pontius Pilate and once climbed by Christ, and kissing the steps as they ascended, left her wishing for "a chance of trying to convince them of the absurdity."²⁶⁵ Mary Pierce watched the spectacle as well and singled out one man she judged as "too sensible for such foolery."²⁶⁶

Of course American Catholics who came to Rome (six are represented here) found it all more splendid than absurd. Mrs. Beckley felt she was on "holy ground," and offered rosaries from friends at home for blessings.²⁶⁷ Isabelle Perkinson left a service at St. Peter's convinced "it would inspire anyone with reverence and devotion" as "it is so impressive and everything about it had so much dignity." She traveled with Protestant relatives and so relished time to be "with some good Catholic people."²⁶⁸

Catholics and Protestant alike, those who sought ancient Rome and those who preferred its Renaissance heritage, had to confront the city's poor. Bettie Kimberly joined in the hosannas to the ancients, acknowledging, "there is much in its past history to make us love & honor it," but also found "more in its present to make us shut our eyes & turn from it in disgust."[269] Hattie Trowbridge rationalized that "over this squalid Italian poverty there is a poetry and romance hovering."[270] A decade later Laura Johnson also looked away the best she could and "in spite of dirt, discomfort and depression we had a delightful time in Rome."[271]

Isabelle Perkinson found Rome so interesting that she stayed while her relatives traveled south.[272] Most women, however, were anxious to see Naples's fabled scenery, including Vesuvius and the ruins of Pompeii nearby. Ann Page, who had already experienced France and several Italian cities when she arrived there, declared Naples the best place she had seen since leaving Philadelphia.[273] Mary Ashhurst embraced the majority opinion that Rome had more to teach yet Naples's splendid vistas made it her favorite Italian city.[274] Anne Bense, dazzled by how "the brilliant sunshine gleamed on the cream-colored walls of the houses" and "everything pulsated and danced with the joyousness of Italian life," concluded "there is nothing like it in the earth."[275]

For some, southern Italy's all-pervading poverty, more dire than that confronted in Rome, made it difficult to appreciate the city's natural beauty. The ubiquitous poor, Ruth Church acknowledged, "sickened us."[276] Emily Severance joined in celebrating Neapolitan scenery, but thought its people "the lowest dregs of humanity that we have yet seen."[277] One woman even decided Neapolitans were "more poverty stricken than our Negroes."[278]

Florence, less scarred by confrontation with poverty and largely unscathed in the fight for Italian unification, was as popular as Naples.[279] Ella Cabot exclaimed on arrival: "the goal of our desires, reached at last!"[280] Hattie Trowbridge, who celebrated her eighteenth birthday in Florence, liked it more than any city she had visited "of course excepting Paris."[281] Laura Johnson praised the Tuscan city as clean and comfortable, but also thought that this made it "not like Italy."[282]

Tourists confronted centuries of history in Rome, but in Florence they found the Renaissance. Michelangelo's famous *David* greeted them from the Piazza Della Signoria until 1873 when it was moved inside the Accademia for protection from the elements. American women may have been shocked, perhaps too shocked to comment in their letters and diaries, that the seventeen-foot-high statue was minus the strategic fig leaf they were accustomed to seeing in pictures. John Stoddard's popular lectures on Florence, for example, offered readers a small likeness of David allowing them to see all of the nude but what the leaf covered.[283] Jennie McGraw found the Uffizi Museum and the Pitti Palace, Florence's most popular galleries, delightful although too cold for a lengthy stay.[284] Laura Thomas complained that crowds of Americans diminished her enjoyment of the Pitti Palace, a problem she likely confronted in many of Florence's famous artistic sites.[285] Constance Harrison was unusually tenacious, as she had been in Paris and Rome, in seeking out lesser-known treasures. She was pleased to find Giotto frescoes, liberated from their whitewash prison in mid-century, adorning a wall of the Franciscan Basilica of Santa Croce. She was also fortunate to visit Florence after Fra Angelico's masterpiece frescoes in the Monastery of San Marco were opened to women.[286] Sophia Hawthorne had been keenly disappointed several decades earlier because she was refused permission to enter the famous painted cells.[287] Mary Pierce singled out Ghiberti's baptistery doors, labeled by Michelangelo as "the Gates to Paradise," as so familiar to her that "I felt I had seen them before."[288] Young Eleanor Joy thought the "dear old Boboli Gardens," the sculpture garden behind Pitti Palace, the best Florence offered.[289] Some women considered the city not only a treasure trove of art, but a shopping mecca as well. Eleanor Middleton, however, feared time spent in stores would mean less time in "those glorious galleries."[290]

Venice was a respite from the intellectual and emotional energy demanded by Italy's ancient and artistic cities; it was a place to simply be enjoyed. This labyrinth of canals and old palaces has recently been labeled "a paradise of cities" and so it seemed to many nineteenth-century American women.[291] Martha Ann Tilton had heard about Venice all her life yet realized on arrival, "I had no idea of the beauty and novelty of the place."[292] Caroline Farrar, on the other hand, found the "city of my dreams" exactly as she had imagined it. After a gondola ride on the Grand Canal, an experience "I have always longed for," she enthused that "Venice sufficed to make us contented."²⁹³ Catherine Van Rensselaer, as usual out of step with popular opinion, found St. Mark's "old & dingy" and was sure nothing could persuade her to live in its city. Yet even Catherine could not resist the enchantment of floating down the Grand Canal Venetian-style with a "glorious full moon" and the sight of "old palaces [that] looked very majestically down with their deserted balconies and open windows."²⁹⁴ Harriett Kimball, another rare critic, thought Venice interesting for a few days until "we have seen about all there is to be seen unless it is churches and we have seen churches until we are sick of them."²⁹⁵

Early in the twentieth century Dolly Whaley reported traveling "tourist style" through Italy, meaning she visited a variety of places for a short time.²⁹⁶ Tourist style became increasingly popular as improved transportation made Italy's wealth of artistically rich and beautiful towns and cities more accessible. Mary Ronalds, there in 1836, was unusual among antebellum travelers in venturing beyond the most popular cities; she climbed Pisa's famous tower, spent a day in Siena, a beautiful town even more redolent of the late Middle Ages and early Renaissance than Florence, and made a short trip to Viterbo to see Etruscan ruins.²⁹⁷ Nearly a century later Ruth Church joined throngs of Italians and a sprinkling of fellow tourists in Siena for the Palio, the famous horse race around the Campo, the city's shell-shaped piazza, held since the mid-seventeenth century.²⁹⁸ Isabelle Perkinson found herself before "the thing that I have wanted all of my life to see-the Leaning Tower," and thought it as fascinating as she had predicted.²⁹⁹ Elizabeth Gilman singled out the Franciscan town of Assisi for its charming architecture, which she thought "in keeping with the sympathetic saint."³⁰⁰ When Miss Davis's dream of seeing Milan's gothic cathedral came true, she found it even grander than she had imagined.³⁰¹ Miss Marsh enjoyed a day "of great pleasure" viewing *The Last Supper*, Leonardo's masterpiece adorning a wall of Milan's Santa Maria delle Grazie.³⁰² Savvy art critic Constance Harrison described Leonardo's fresco as "one of the greatest and saddest pictures of the world."³⁰³

Italian towns did encounter the occasional naysayer. Mary Gaston enjoyed riding though Italy's Alps, but after a visit to Verona advised others to "let the old mouldy [sic] place go."[304] Nina Halsey was ready to let all of Italy go; although charmed with "the peculiar & strange sights" she encountered "too many fleas—too much dirt and filth and bad odors."[305]

Germany

Nina might have found German orderliness and efficiency more to her liking. After studying French in Paris for several months, Sarah Tuckerman speculated, "what would I not give for such a residence in Germany."[306] Although not as integral a part of a traditional Grand Tour as England, France and Italy, Germany's romantic image as the land of Wagnerian opera, beer halls and castles along the Rhine assured a steady stream of tourists. Americans there before the wars and genocide of the twentieth century found Germany a happy and even carefree place. Mary Elizabeth Gittings praise of the country as "free" and "delightful" was a typical reaction.[307] Cadwalader Jones touted it as an especially good place for women traveling alone because "the customs are simple and the scale of expense not high." [308]

Until the 1870s, what Americans called Germany was in reality a loose league of states; Germany, like Italy, was a geographical expression. Americans traveling in mid-century, who might have confronted fighting in Italy, also had to dodge battles in Central Europe when the struggle for the region's future turned violent. Mary Jane Blair encouraged her party to go early in 1866 "before the war spreads more & traveling becomes troublesome." In late July she was relieved to report that Prussia had defeated Austria and the Seven Week War was over.[309] After the Prussian-led defeat of France in 1871, the German Empire unified all of the major Germanic states except Austria, made Berlin its capital and crowned Wilhelm I as emperor. Although they were more fixated on the British monarchy, Americans were curious about their German cousins, these new royals. Mary Jane's encounter with the future emperor prompted her boast: "Hurrah! I have been on a train with the King of Prussia." She was confident that Americans were held in such high esteem that once the fighting for unification ended, she could travel through the country freely.[310] In 1889 Mamie Parsons

A stereoscope card with a duel image of
Berlin's Brandenburg Gate in 1902
Library of Congress

described an encounter with Wilhelm II, who had become Germany's third emperor the year before: "My Yankee mind has never been able to separate the idea of royalty from a crown and scepter and it seemed impossible to believe that the nice looking fair haired man driving himself was really the Emperor. What he saw was two exhausted Yankees—one [her companion Louise] with great presence of mind making him quite a fine curtsey—the other [Mamie] standing bolt upright—clutching a beloved red *Baedecker* [sic] in one hand and gazing at him open-mouthed."[311]

Berlin did not dominate the tourist itinerary as London, Paris and, to a lesser extent, Rome, did in their countries. It was hardly even a city until the mid-eighteenth century when Frederick the Great located the Prussian capital there. But Berlin grew rapidly after it was anointed the capital of the German Empire in 1871, and, as Charles Emmerson explains, became a "world city just as Germany aspired to start to become ... a world power."[312] Berlin joined Cologne, Dresden, Frankfurt, Munich, Hamburg, Heidelberg, Nuremberg and a number of smaller cities as popular destinations. Jennie Reizestein, who visited more German cities than most, thought Hamburg "beautiful" and richly deserving of its title *"Garten Stadt Deutschlands,"* found Nuremberg "a wonderful place," and praised Wiesbaden for arranging splendid fireworks and music to celebrate the Fourth of July for its American visitors.[313] Elizabeth Gould thought Munich "a wonderful city," one free of poverty, where "you feel the discipline, order, system in everything" and "everybody looks happy and prosperous."[314] Not all visitors were as impressed. Mary Hartt thought German cities "monotonous" compared to those in other European countries.[315] Catherine Van Rensselaer praised Munich's wide and straight streets, but missed the "dirt and antiquities" of Italy.[316]

Protestant Americans carried their relentless harangue against Catholicism into Central Europe; they also confronted Judaism where the overwhelming majority of Western European Jews lived. Occasionally Jewish sights were deliberately included in sightseeing itineraries; in the 1830s, for example, a guide offered to take Judith Rives and her husband to the Jewish synagogue in Amsterdam and, "having some curiosity to see the mode of worship among the Israelites of the present day," they agreed.[317] Scattered comments about the Jewish ghetto in Rome were usually negative. Those on a Grand Tour were more likely, however, to observe Jewish life and worship in Germany than elsewhere. The Jewish Quarter in Frankfurt was close to popular tourist sights so more American tourists commented on seeing Jews there than anywhere else during their travels. Laura Johnson found Frankfurt more interesting than she had anticipated primarily because of its Jewish population.[318] Clara Alexander, on the other hand, thought its Jewish Quarter "a miserable place swarming with people."[319] Catherine Van Rensselaer described the synagogue in Berlin as "a superb building" and found it a great relief to find no signs of Catholicism in this largely Lutheran city.[320] A decade later Julia Severance and her devout Christian family attended a service in a "beautiful Moorish Jewish synagogue" in Germany's capital.[321]

German-American Jews, pioneers of Jewish immigration to the United States in the mid-nineteenth century, also led the return of Jews to Europe as tourists (five are represented here). Ironically, despite the virulent anti-Semitism that waxed and waned in nineteenth-century Europe, some American Jews felt more welcomed in its fashionable tourist venues than they did in those at home.[322] Henrietta and Henry Frank, both descendants of German Jews and fluent in German, spent most of their time in their ancestral homeland during their numerous trips to Europe. They occasionally confronted hostility; during a visit to the German Reichstag Henrietta realized "a disagreeable sensation when the guide mentioned the Anti-Semitic Party." When she chatted with a German woman who sprinkled the conversation with negative comments about Jews, however, she acknowledged "as we had made similar remarks to one another, we could not take offense." The Franks were usually comfortable as Jewish tourists. On one trip they dined in a kosher restaurant in Berlin and the next day visited a synagogue in Leipzig. Henrietta was not always pleased with Jewish observation in Germany; Yom Kippur "did not seem as festive as at home" and the couple declined to attend services if men and women were separated. They were observant enough, however, to refrain from traveling on Rosh Hashanah. A Christian service in Westminster Abbey that included readings from Esther and the singing of Kedushah left Henrietta feeling like "I was at a good old Jewish service."[323]

The Franks usually included a visit to Germany's legendary river because, Henrietta enthused, "I love the Rhine and always greet it as an old friend."[324] Literature and music, notably Heinrich Heine's poem *Die Lorelei* and Richard Wagner's opera *Das Rheingold*, popularized the river. Mary Fraser commenced a trip through the Rhine Gorge convinced that New York's Hudson River was more beautiful, but "had to give up my prejudice in favor of my own country."[325] Harriet Johnston singled out the beautiful castles along the river as "long of interest and romance."[326] Mary Few was unusual in finding the Rhine disappointing although she thought Germany "a delightful land."[327]

Whether they preferred its major cities or villages along its famous river, it was Germany's, as well as Austria's, music that most captivated American visitors. In the early-nineteenth century the Italian repertory was dominant in the United States so most familiar to Americans abroad. When Sarah Cleveland heard Giuseppe Verdi's *Foscari* in Rome in 1844, she declared him the best Italian composer (although what is proclaimed his best work, from *Macbeth* to *Falstaff*, was yet to come).[328] A few years later E. Thompson enjoyed Donizetti's *Lucia di Lammermoor* in pre-Haussmann Paris.[329] From the time his first operas were heard in mid-century, however, Richard Wagner successfully challenged the preeminence of the

Italian masters, as well as the French master, Georges Bizet. Elizabeth Gilman found Bizet's *The Pearl Fishers* "a strange contrast to German opera which I greatly prefer."[330]

By the turn of the century many Americans not only preferred Wagner to the Italian and French composers, but to other Germanic musical geniuses, including Bach and Mozart, as well. Joseph Horowitz, author of *Wagner Nights: An American History*, suggests that because of its "predisposition to Wagner ... to a remarkable degree, America remained a musical colony of Germany until World War I." Horowitz associates Wagner with female listeners, claiming his music "powerfully infiltrated the women's movement" and that "most American Wagnerites were female." He argues "Wagnerism in America did not, as in Europe, herald an iconoclastic modernism ... [but] to a remarkable degree ... was absorbed within the dominant genteel traditions."[331] Historian Jackson Lears concurs that Wagner was especially popular with women, explaining that the therapeutic culture of the late-nineteenth century, a culture dominated by female patients, was especially receptive as "Wagner gives expression to that which is repressed." These German operas, he argues, "gauged the emotional repression they [women] suffered," and the music "fulfilled fantasies of liberation and violated taboo."[332]

Americans could hear Wagner's music throughout Europe, but France, especially, was resistant to this German dominance. After attending one of his operas there, Marian Nichols condemned "a few idiots who pretend to be patriotic [and] want to prevent his opera being sung in Paris."[333] A few years later, however, after seeing *Die Walküre*, Constance Harrison reported that "Paris is wild over it and seats are hard to get." She also enjoyed a performance of *Lohengrin* at London's Covent Garden.[334] After attending opera in both countries, Hattie Trowbridge described operagoers in Italy as "all fire and enthusiasm" while those in Germany were "so quiet and appreciative."[335]

Whether they were more enthusiastic or quietly appreciative, Americans were especially eager to hear the native music of Germany and Austria in its homelands. Laura Rutherford's first order of business in Berlin was to buy a ticket for *Tannhauser*.[336] Wagner made Mary Boit "perfectly wild" and a performance of *Die Walküre* was "two [sic] swell for words." It was all so swell that she gave up opera for Lent.³³⁷ Mamie Parsons, among the fortunate Wagnerians to hear his operas sung in Bayreuth, the city where Wagner spent his last years and made the preeminent venue for his oeuvre, feared she was "selfish and mean" for sending enthusiastic letters home about her experiences.³³⁸

Knowledge of opera did not assure familiarity with the customs of European opera houses. In time Mamie laughed about an opera misstep that began when her party arrived late after the lights were already dim, forcing them to grope their way to their seats. In the process they encountered "a general stumbling over swords which we afterwards discovered were attached to 3 gorgeous officers." The Americans first thought the Germans were in the wrong place, but after arguing with an "ancient usher" learned that in Berlin entire boxes were not reserved and the extra seats did indeed belong to the three men. Once she understood it was a shared space, Mamie reached for what she thought was her chair only to discover it was the epaulette of an officer who "with German stolidity and excellent manners" did not even smile.³³⁹

Not all women were convinced that opera houses were venues for fun. Mamie enjoyed a performance of *Siegfried* in Hamburg, but her companion "took a comfortable nap whilst the dragon was being slain."³⁴⁰ Kate Jones knew she would not become opera mad because "there is too much unnecessary & disgusting exposure, too much to tinge the cheek of the modest & refined woman with the blush of shame."³⁴¹ Mary Gaston, in Europe forty years after Kate, was less prudish, but also resolved "never, never shall I care for opera as I do for the theatre" as "I cannot endure to see people trying to die and sing at the same time. They are sure to do one or the other badly." Her mother was more favorably disposed although she declined to attend a performance of *Lohengrin* as "we have not been quite long enough in Germany not to mind a little obstacle like Sunday."³⁴²

The uninitiated who slept through opera or refused to attend at all may have favored the ubiquitous informal venues crowded with Germans enjoying music. Mamie observed all classes displayed "a mania for their beer gardens."³⁴³ Anna Rew described for her father a visit "with a splendid band playing Wagner, people around us smoking and drinking mild beer, having a simple happy time," and shared her fantasy that "when I find a gold mine I think I shall build a German concert hall and teach Americans how to enjoy life."[344] Nina Pape likewise praised "the very novel sight" of Germans "sitting out under the fresh trees & God's blue sky with nature all around & enjoying oneself [sic]."[345]

Abbie Farwell wrote "Kaiser Wilhelm's Country" to described for St. Louis *Dispatch* readers the "wild joy which filled our hearts when we mustered up courage to be really wicked and Bohemian; when we found ourselves sitting in one of the cozy little sidewalk beer gardens in Strasburg [annexed by Germany after the Franco-Prussian War, but today again part of France], with a small portion of meat and a very large mug of beer on the table before us. We wondered what we should think at home to see two unattended ladies drinking spirits in a public street; we wondered what our gentle and scrupulous mothers would think to see us so. But no one else seemed to find it at all strange; in fact, every one was doing likewise, and the band played meanwhile."[346]

Abbie could have penned a similar account about the country of Austrian Emperor Franz Joseph I, whose sixty-eight-year reign lasted into the First World War. Fewer Americans went to Austria than to Germany, but those who did also praised evenings spent drinking beer and listening to music. Gena Trumbull was pleased to spend time in a Salzburg beer hall although she feared her grandmother would be scandalized to learn she had done so on Sunday.[347] Caroline Farrar's visit to a beer hall in Vienna, the "city of my dreams," inspired her to join the chorus urging similar facilities at home.[348]

Beer halls and evenings outdoors made the Germanic countries especially appealing to college students who steadily swelled the ranks of Americans in Europe as the nineteenth century gave way to the twentieth. Grace Taplin joined friends for an evening dancing in a beer hall in Austria's Tyrolean Alps where local men were happy to entertain the young American women. She felt sure "I or none of the rest of the people will ever forget to their dying days" as "we danced so fast that I just spun around like a top, barely touching the floor, [and] everyone just laughing fit to kill themselves [sic]." Her Austrian partner insisted he usually danced much faster.

Grace's embrace of German-style entertainment continued in Munich where adults "insisted I must drink bere [sic] too;" she did even though "I hate the stuff." Grace was sorry to leave Germany after "a perfectly dandy time."[349] Twenty-year old Clara Ritchie likewise discovered on departing: "You know I dread to leave Deutschland."[350]

Germany's reputation as a carefree and happy country waned in the early-twentieth century as rivalry with other European countries ignited increased militarism. Americans typically made little distinction between the two German-speaking countries they visited, but thirteen-year-old Edith Rosenshine, visiting on the eve of the First World War, decided she loved Austria where "everything seemed so easy going and gay," but hated Germany where "oppression [was] in the air."[351]

Spain

The Iberian countries lagged behind in developing the infrastructure tourism demanded so few American women visited Spain and even fewer went to Portugal. In 1898, the year the United States defeated Spain in a four-month war that destroyed the last vestiges of its empire, John Stoddard noted that "not many years ago, a tour of Spain was regarded as a dangerous enterprise."[352]

Four decades before Stoddard's description, Ellen Perry and her sister experienced "cold, fatigue [and] hunger," resulting in a "terrible journey." Despite the hardships, however, Ellen was delighted to be in "romantic Spain, the goal of our wishes, the land of promise to us." A trip to the Royal Museum (now the Prado) in Madrid prompted her conclusion that whereas America had the greatest natural beauty, Europe had the greatest art.[353] Harriet Allen did not find it so romantic, but criticized the interior of Spain as "barbarous" with "the inns little better than stables and swarming with vermin, so that travelers enter them as rarely as possible."[354] Ellen Moulton, in Burgos in the 1880s, reflected on "the delicious strangeness and quaintness of it all."[355] Mary Elizabeth Gittings, in Spain about the same time, had a more ambivalent response to Toledo "with its narrow streets, beautiful buildings, queer smells, unusual food, and above all its degraded aspect of Roman Catholicism." She concluded that Madrid, although ugly in comparison, was also "comically homelike and pleasant," that the cathedral in Cordova was right out of Arabian Nights and that Granada's Alhambra was "a perfect delight."[356] Near century's end Constance Harrison realized traveling in Spain was still difficult yet "delightful to me [because] its tracks have not yet had all the green beaten out of them by the feet of tourists."[357]

It is unlikely that Spain's iconic sport was often scored as delightful. Jane Adgar questioned how anyone watching a bullfight "can retain any refinement or delicacy of feeling."[358] E. Thompson accompanied her husband to one, but almost immediately wanted to be "as far as possible from that horrid arena." As disgusted as she was, she conceded it was "an important feature in the sights and habits of Spain." Paintings by Bartolome Murillo, seventeenth-century leader of the Seville Baroque School, were more to her liking and made her difficult journey worthwhile.[359]

Europeans

Alexis de Tocqueville, who continued scrutinizing Americans once back in France, claimed they made "invidious comparisons and lofty boasts" to assure both their hosts and themselves that theirs was the superior country. The letters and diaries used for this study suggest that nationalistic boasting waned through the decades and was rarely as invidious as Tocqueville suggested, but they also reveal that he was not entirely wrong. Boasting could serve to camouflage uncertainty as to which side of the Atlantic could claim the superior culture. Foster Rhea Dulles found the ambivalence Americans felt in Europe was an effort to balance "a reluctant appreciation of the Old World's highly developed artistic culture" with "a deep and abiding scorn for its outmoded political system."[360] American nationalism, born of the American Revolution and maturing decade by decade, predisposed Americans to claim their republic's superiority to aristocratic Europe. An education that focused on Europe as the fountainhead of their culture and manners, however, undermined nascent nationalism. Richard Bushman captures well these conflicting viewpoints, explaining Americans were preoccupied with "the aristocratic past at the same time as they were rushing into a democratic and capitalistic future."[361]

It was difficult for most American visitors to analyze in depth how Europeans grappled with the transformative nineteenth century because they spent limited time with anyone except couriers and maids. Accordingly, their assessment of European gentility—of their religion, work, gender relations, manners and appearance— was based largely on what they observed in public spaces.

As we have seen, the most common criticisms American women (and likely American men) articulated concerned religious practices that seemed too lax, too theatrical and even un-Christian; Catholic emotionalism and exuberant displays were condemned as incompatible with gentility and even European Protestants were found wanting in their observation of the Sabbath.

Criticism of religion was, for the most part, gender neutral. When critiquing more secular matters, however, American women were more likely to single out their European counterparts. Their greatest indictment was directed at the hard agricultural work they observed European women doing. It was, of course, criticism blind to slavery as well as to the hard work that was the lot of freed African-American and other poor American women. Racism clouded the eyes of Northerners as well as Southerners. In the 1830s, a decade in which more than a million African-American women struggled with the brutality of slavery, New Yorker Fanny Hall despaired upon seeing French women labor in fields: "Oh shame. Shame! To 'such civilization and refinement' may my happy country long be a stranger."[362] In the years just prior to the Civil War, as her native South became increasingly defensive about its peculiar institution, Kate Jones, who readily defended her family's exploitation of enslaved people, questioned why France, "the politest nation in the world," allowed women "to perform so much manual labor" and let the poor live "by the sweat of women's brow."[363] North Carolinian Bettie Kimberly, abroad on the eve of emancipation, indicted Germans for treating women like "a useful domestic animal," even claiming, "our Negro women are queens in comparison."[364] Virginian Alberta Taylor made an equally indefensible observation a half century after emancipation when she described German women harnessed to wagons pulling heavy loads as engaged in work "our southern darkies would not touch."[365]

Women dubious about the organized demand for women's

rights that accelerated after the Seneca Falls convention in 1848 also pointed out the hard work they observed European women doing to discredit the growing demand for improved opportunities in their own country. New Yorker Caroline Farrar satirized that "the staunchest champion of woman's rights would I think be satisfied with the right to labor equally with men accorded to the weaker sex here." [366] Nearly thirty years later Elizabeth Nichols echoed, "if women want equal rights with the men they certainly have it here."[367] Mary Gibson, in Europe in 1909, offered a contrasting perspective; she found Europe's women so superior to its men that "I am more in favor of woman's suffrage than ever, especially for Belgium and France."[368]

American women abroad constantly observed European women, but rarely talked to them; accordingly, their observations tended to fixate on appearance. Blanche McManus voiced the common opinion that "no nation can send out [women] into the world so correctly and appropriately dressed for the journey as can America."[369] Turn-of-the century travelers described the French as "gaudily dressed," wearing "strange unbecoming things" and as "dressed very curiously."[370] English women, the most frequent targets of American ridicule, were criticized for dressing "so badly," of having "a want of finish," as being "perfect frights," dressing "in miserable taste" and as "such ugly girls."[371] Mary Elizabeth Gittings admired the hair and eyes of young women she saw working in a tobacco factory in Seville, but otherwise found "not a great deal of true beauty." After attending a performance of *Carmen,* an operatic accounting of Seville's factory women, she again described "so many ugly women."[372] Mamie Parsons thought German women dressed "hideously" except for "very smart Jews from Frankfort [sic]."[373]

Some claimed not only the superiority of American women's appearance but their manners as well. In the early-nineteenth century Anne Eliza Rodman disparaged French women for shocking "American ideas of propriety."[374] Decades later Laura Thomas urged young English women to "come to America to learn modesty for their boldness does not come up to my idea of refinement."[375]

Refinement's mandates centered on relationships between women and men; time spent abroad could scramble norms dictating proper interactions between the two sexes. Some women thought they mingled too freely in Europe, but others praised freer interaction as a sign of greater female independence. In the 1840s Sarah Newberry grew increasingly at ease as the sole woman in the company of men because "so much more a female has of independence in France than with us."[376] Laura Thomas, revealing commonplace inconsistency, thought seeing "ladies & gentlemen—all sitting in the same room smoking—and drinking," was "as much as I could stand." Yet she also thought it absurd that in German Lutheran churches men and women could not sit on the same side or even stand in the aisles together. After months of observation, she concluded that young European girls were "caged like some wild animal" until "some man is willing to loose your [sic] bonds."[377] In the 1880s Helen Gould bordered on hating French men for disrespecting women, but admired the freedom married French women had to move about without an escort.[378] Suffrage leader Elizabeth Cady Stanton was impressed that men and women mixed freely in business and amusements in France, more so than in England.[379]

A mixture of praise and criticism was directed at specific nationalities irrespective of gender. English men and women alike were criticized for "extraordinary slowness in taking in an idea," for being "perfect egoists, bullies and cowards," as "self opinionated" and were called "such memorable queer people;" they were also depicted as "polite," "kind" and "courteous and well-bred."[380] Sarah Elliott decided many of the English she met were "very stupid," but thought their country "like some higher sphere" compared to others she had visited.[381] French people were depicted as "too idle," "horribly untidy & shockingly immodest," "fearfully excitable," "noisy" and "thoroughly corrupt." Helen Gould found them "a queer people—so savage with a polish over them."[382] They were also praised for being "clean and neat and very polite," of having manners "full of grace and sweetness," for their "lightness and gayety," and for the "brightness" of their lives.[383] June Spencer questioned how anyone could be in Paris long "without acknowledging that the French are a wonderful people." "French manners" she exalted, "take my heart by storm."[384] Gena Trumbull claimed Germans, with their "substantial, unpresuming, honest manner," were the politest Europeans.[385] Catherine Van Rensselaer also preferred them because "there is so much that is substantial about them & different from French and Italians." Germans were also praised as "intelligent & civil," as "very amiable" people who "do anything to oblige you," and as "kind & hearty." Ruth Church liked individual Germans, but "as a race we did not admire them." Negative assessments also included "impertinent," "stupid," the "rudest people," "barbarian" and displaying "the most appaling [sic] table manners." The best one woman could say about Italians was that they were "less irritable" than the French. They were criticized as "slippery," but also praised as "graceful and charming" and friendlier than the Swiss.[386] Even though Switzerland was her father's native land, Frances Stevens found its people "an uninteresting race" and inferior to Germans.[387]

Americans strained to invigorate nationalism abroad, but some were willing to concede points of European superiority. Hannah Gould concluded "that great as our country is there are things on this side just as beautiful, just as great, just as choice as anything we can boast." [388] The English were praised for "leisurely habits and quiet composure" in contrast to "the nervous restlessness and excitability of the American people" and for being "moderate" compared to the "rush and hurry" in New York.[389] Italians were also praised for avoiding "the rush and hurry of American life."[390] Europeans were collectively noted for eschewing "foolish etiquette" and for enjoying outdoor exercise."[391] Frances Stevens admired the strong middle classes in Germany and Switzerland, claiming they had "power unknown to us where only money and the Irish rule."[392]

More frequently, however, comparisons lauded American superiority. Mary Few, in Europe when her own country was not yet a half century old, "never ceased thinking of "my home [as] the most delightful in the wide world" and was sure she would return "a better American."[393] Sentiments sprinkled in subsequent letters and diaries include: "I glory in my country;" " I would live no where but in America;" I love "our own dear land the best—with its progress and plenty;" "oh sweet America ... what a great privilege to have been born there in that blessed country;" and thanks "that I am a citizen of the Republic."[394] Martha Griffis bragged Americans were "the neatest and most refined people to be met with anywhere."[395] Ann Marie Green concluded, "the attractions of the old world, when compared to the luxuries and comforts, the energy and thrift of the new, are a light weight in the balance."[396] Anne Heroy's assumption of America's superiority was more practical than grandiose; when her trip was over she realized "it did seem fine to be at home once more & have good American cooking … & American beds are the best in the world."[397]

Ellen Perry was unusual in centering her claim of national superiority on the natural beauty of the United States.[398] June Spencer offered the more typical view after a trip on the Rhine when she acknowledged "I fear I have gone over to the enemy and abandoned all allegiance to my own country in the matter of scenery."[399] Most American women who made a Grand Tour were from the eastern states and many of them were more familiar with the Alps than with their own snow-capped Rockies. The Romantic poets assured that when Americans sought the sublime, they had Europe in mind. Poetic renderings of the Alps, the Rhine and other natural sites assured they were places American women dreamed of seeing.

V

In the Land of Tell: Outdoor Adventures on a Grand Tour

After arriving in Switzerland in the summer of 1844, Sarah Cleveland enthused to those at home that "no possible idea can be received through books, or pictures or words in any way of the mountain scenery in Switzerland and even in the midst of it, it seems so incredible that I felt as if walking in a heavenly vision." A day there was "full of satisfaction—full of delight—full of wonder—a day never to be forgotten—a day unsurpassed." Time only enhanced her wonder; a hike up Lucerne's Mt. Rigi left her exclaiming that "I was never so satisfied & enchanted with any one thing that I undertook to do—as jumping, running, stepping down these steep paths of ice to the music of our guide who yoodled [sic] delightfully. The day was crowned by a view of Mt. Blanc in all his glory!"[1]

Decade by decade more Americans resolved to see this heavenly vision for themselves. In his history of vacationing, Orvar Lofgren writes that in the early-nineteenth century "the most sublime mountain sceneries were those of the [English] Lake District and Scotland," making them the most popular outdoor destinations, but "Switzerland's peaks shortly took precedence," and the "quest for mountains meant a redrawing of the tourist map in both Europe and North America."[2] Many European countries welcomed tourists to their mountains and other places of natural beauty, but Switzerland emerged as the quintessential mountain venue and attracted the most visitors. Geographer John Stoddard speculated that *fin de siècle* Switzerland, "of all the countries in the world, is the one of which the traveler is likely to tire least."[3]

The popularity of romantic mountains presented women, long designated the weaker sex, an especially daunting challenge. Girls growing up in nineteenth-century America confronted conflicting advice about proper physical activity. Early-nineteenth-century lore claimed female reproductive organs were damaged by more than minimal physical activity. Through the century, however, new insights into health and physical fitness challenged taboos concerning exercise and athleticism. Historian Frances Cogan explains that by mid-century "for some the ideal girl of this period was a stalwart specimen." A vigorous debate pitted those dogmatic about females curtailing activity against challengers who championed a stalwart ideal. Warnings about over-taxing the female reproductive system steadily gave way to advice that exercise was critical to both physical and mental health.[4] In 1856, Emily Thornwell advised in *The Ladies Guide to Perfect Gentility in Manners, Dress and Conversation* that the best activity for young women was "vigorous walks for two to four miles or, if unwilling to walk, to ride horseback at a stiff canter for an equal distance."[5] Most female academies advocated physical activity—boating and gymnastics were especially popular—as part of their curriculum even earlier. Antebellum southern schools usually included a walk as part of their daily routine.[6] St. Mary's Academy in North Carolina required its pupils to take two hours of exercise daily, possibly by walking twice around the grounds.[7] The women's colleges that mushroomed after the Civil War likewise offered a variety of physical activities for their students. Vassar, founded in 1861 and a model for other women's colleges, declared physical education "fundamental to all the rest."[8] The small number of late-nineteenth-century female physicians, those who took up the pioneering work of Elizabeth Blackwell, were particularly outspoken in challenging the injunctions of some of their male counterparts that women were too delicate to endure the rigors of higher education or strenuous physical education. By the late 1880s, even S. Weir Mitchell, leading advocate of the rest cure for women diagnosed as hysterical (and scathingly profiled for this advice in Charlotte Perkins Gilman's *Yellow Wallpaper*) was exhorting mothers to "crave, then, for your girls strength and bodily power of endurance."[9] In the 1890s artist Charles Dana Gibson's "Gibson Girl" successfully challenged the mandate of fragility by popularizing the counter ideal of an athletic woman who routinely engaged in physical activity including riding bicycles and playing golf. The

Gibson Girl emphasized conformity to femininity, but in expanding its boundaries to offer greater self-assurance and athleticism, compelled a late-nineteenth-century challenge to the domestic ideal of the past. As Dorothy Middleton writes in her study of female travelers at century's end, "women were learning to bicycle and to climb mountains."[10] British women were especially renowned for embracing outdoor activities. In 1879 Isabella Bird, the most famous of them, published *A Lady's Life in the Rocky Mountains* which offered her American sisters an example of one of their own climbing their country's highest peaks.

Schoolgirls learned to appreciate mountains decades before they could conceive of climbing them; geography lessons often included Europe's Alps and Italy's famous volcanoes. In 1817, for example, Connecticut schoolgirl Eliza Ogden recorded in her geography notebook: "In Switzerland the greatest curiosity was the Alps, being so high and always covered with snow."[11] As they grew older, some girls imagined someday seeing these curiosities for themselves. Maria Degen, one who did, described the Alps she saw as "the place of my most ardent longings for years and years."[12]

Literature transformed facts learned in geography class into vivid images that stirred imaginations. The Romantic Movement, led by British and German writers in the early-nineteenth century in reaction to Enlightenment rationality, fostered a love and appreciation of a natural world frequently described as sublime.[13] Many of the popular Romantic poets who celebrated nature as the path to the divine penned verses about the Swiss Alps. Friedrich Schiller's 1804 recounting of William Tell's exploits dramatized the legend of the Swiss mountain man forced to shoot an apple off his son's head to save both of their lives. His writing about resistance to tyranny, loaded with implications for nineteenth-century European history, also presented Americans a vivid impression of these faraway places. One American woman defined her trip to Switzerland as a chance to "see all the places that are associated with Tell."[14] Elizabeth Prentiss realized such emotion on seeing the Alps that she counseled a friend at home that "with your enthusiastic temperament, artist eye, and love of nature you never would survive even a glimpse of Switzerland—the land of Tell would be the death of you."[15]

The British Romantics also popularized Europe's natural scenery. Lord Byron's *The Prisoner of Chillon* and *Childe Harold*, both mainstays of academy education, joined Schiller in introducing Americans to Swiss history and nature. When she first saw Europe's mountains, Augusta Arnold recollected that "Chillon like Mt. Blanc & the Mer de Glace have been places in my imagination since I was a child," as "we had a picture of Chillon & I read my Byron's paen [sic]."[16] American women, guardians of genteel ideals, generally separated Byron's poetry from his scandalous lifestyle of debts, affairs and self-exile. Quaker minister Eliza Germey, for example, praised *Chillon*'s merit, but "utterly condemn[ed] Lord Byron's course."[17] Percy Bysshe Shelley's poem *Mount Blanc* and Samuel Taylor Coleridge's *Hymn Before Sunrise, in the Vale of Chamouni*, were also popular and romantic portrayals of the Alps.[18] When she first encountered Mt. Blanc, Margaret Preston "kept repeating over to myself Coleridge's hymn—realizing 'now' its truth and splendor, as well as that of 'thy bald, awful frown, oh Sovran [sic] Blanc!' "[19] Elizabeth Prentiss had anointed Paris as the epitome of European beauty until she saw the Alps, "handiworks of God," and "straightway all its palaces and monuments and fountains faded into insignificance."[20] Abbie Farwell Brown embraced nature "unknown of Cook" as "we get so tired of being in droves and herds and flocks that we are fain to crawl into a glacier crevasse and be lost just to escape the thud of his hoof and the chatter of his mount."[21]

Mt. Blanc was the Alpine peak most celebrated in literature, but the more accessible Mer de Glace, Europe's second largest glacier, on the French side of the border, was more popular with tourists who wanted more than looking from afar. John Stoddard, who included it in his published lectures on Switzerland (most Americans placed it there as well), wrote of the glacier: "It is well called 'Sea of Ice,' for its irregular surface looks precisely like a mass of tossing waves which have been crystallized when in their wildest agitation."[22] Tourists were occasionally injured and even killed when blocks of ice fell without warning. Despite the hazards, however, in the last decades of the nineteenth century so many Americans decided to include the sea of glass in their itinerary that it became an integral part of the American Grand Tour.

Men and women hiking on Mer de Glace in the 1860s.
Getty Images

The Alps elicited more emotional responses, but at least for Laura Thomas going up Mount Vesuvius was "the grandest experience ... I ever had or expected to have had."[23] Anne Bense described Vesuvius as "the dread of Naples and its suburbs, the topic of the ancients and the dream of the tourist."[24] Ascending to the crater, infamous for the eruption in 79 CE that destroyed the nearby towns of Pompeii and Herculaneum, was the most popular European hike outside of the Alps. In the mid-eighteenth century the two towns were rediscovered and excavations began. Schoolbook pictures of the long-buried ruins left indelible impressions of the volcano's destructive power as well as glimpses of everyday life in ancient Rome. After the 1834 publication of Edward Bulwer-Lytton's *The Last Days of Pompeii*, a fictional account of the deadly eruption, tourists began flocking to the emerging city. Emma Cordozzo reported that in the 1880s "Pompeii is still being excavated but slowly;" she also visited artifacts from the emerging town housed in the archeological museum in Naples.[25] Roughly once every ten years the volcano erupts again; in 1906 one hundred people were killed by one of its most powerful eruptions.

In the last decades of the nineteenth century, mechanized transportation facilitated mountain excursions for those eager to ascend

Europe's glaciers and volcanoes. In 1880 a funicular opened to carry sightseers part of the way up Vesuvius, but a few years later it was destroyed by a Luddite-style protest. Clara Mitchell's party had to abandon plans for an ascent because "guides destroyed Cook's Railroad & its [sic] too unpleasant, or too far or maybe both, to ride there."[26] By the turn of the century the lift operated again; Grace Hutchins reported going up the volcano "by dog-cart, our own two feet, a perpendicular railway and feet again."[27] The eruption in 1906, however, put the funicular out of commission for several more years. A railroad track completed in 1909 made it possible to travel from Chamonix to a station overlooking Mer de Glace, greatly reducing the time and effort necessary to see the popular glacier.

Well into the early-twentieth century, however, most mountain destinations were accessible only by walking, riding pack animals or human portage. Women who wanted to see Europe's Alps or its most famous crater—and many visited both—struggled to balance their adventuresome spirit with fear of the hardships involved. Mary Gaston, facing the possibility of climbing to Mer de Glace with her mother, weighed that on the one hand not to do it "would be an eternal regret on mother's part" yet on the other "to attempt it unwisely might mean almost anything dreadful." Frances finally resolved "to do or die" and unilaterally hired three mules with guides. The daughter, however, took charge at the top and mandated against crossing the glacier. Frances reluctantly agreed yet fretted "it could not have been much harder than the descent" so "we might as well have done the whole business."[28]

Doing the whole business was especially overwhelming for women unaccustomed to strenuous activity. Catherine Brooks questioned as she reflected back on her first outing: "how I have managed to climb mountains and endure the fatigue I have, I cannot understand."[29] Mary Bates struggled with the dueling emotions that "I don't want to over do and yet I want to gain all I can by exercise in this pure mountain air." When a male companion undertook a particularly difficult climb, one Mary knew several women had accomplished, she regretfully declined to join for fear that the snow was too deep.[30] Caroline White loved the Alps enough to be "a little frightened now & then—for the sake of looking upon their indescribable grandeur."[31]

Yet even decades prior to the athletic Gibson Girl's entry into popular culture, some women rejected an ideal of female fragility and set their sights on challenging mountain experiences. In 1836 New Englander Fanny Hall bragged of her confidence traversing Switzerland's glaciers, explaining that "at an early age, [I] acquired the somewhat 'unfeminine' accomplishment of walking and sliding on the ice."[32] A few years later Margaret and Julia Gardner determined to climb to the top of Vesuvius with their father "in spite of the remonstrances of the guide, who declared the attempt impracticable, for no lady had ever ventured before;" their "horror-struck" mother also reasoned in vain against the climb. The sisters were vindicated by success.[33] Two decades later, when Idella Plimpton was warned that a single misstep could mean death, she simply

A fanciful drawing of Swiss men carrying a woman in a sedan chair as a Swiss woman looks on. *Victorian Picture Library, London.*

resolved she "didn't intend to fall;" some of her companions grew more terrified the higher they climbed, but Idella remained fearless and convinced that the view was well worth the trouble.[34]

Sedan chairs offered those less bold or confident an option although not one that allayed all fears. Even into the twentieth century the most popular sites offered rides on these open seats or small cabins attached to poles and borne on the shoulders of two or more men. In centuries past, sedan chairs had been a stylish means for transporting the wealthy through city streets. Colonial Americans would have been familiar with the contraptions in their cities; one was included in Benjamin Franklin's will. By the nineteenth century, however, they were known only from pictures and associated with faraway and exotic places, at least until American women contemplated the possibility of ascending Europe's peaks.

In 1873, Caroline Carson was transported about Pompeii in a sedan chair which, she reported, made it possible to see everything without fatigue.[35] Most women, however, chose this unorthodox means of conveyance only if they felt physically incapable of reaching the high places they longed to see by pack animal or on foot. Sarah Cleveland described her transport as "a most ludicrous vehicle low as a chair" designed to be "as uncomfortable and impractical as possible."[36] The discomfort often compelled women who chose sedan chairs to alternate their use with walking and riding animals. Ann Page's "very interesting" trip up Vesuvius included four miles on horseback before she joined other girls and women riding chairs close to the crater. She feared it "was very laborious to the poor men who carried us," but thought it "justified for the magnificent view."[37] Harriet Blanchard started up Vesuvius in a chair, but for the last stretch "all walked, some quite alone [and] others with the assistance of the guide who puts a strap around his shoulders which they hold on to." Her conclusion that "it is very hard work" was likely apropos of the women hanging on to the straps rather than of the men who pulled them.[38] Tales of women walking up mountains inspired Mary Pierce to try, although her companion, Alice, insisted on a chair. Mary walked until exhausted, acknowledging she would not have made it as far as she did without one guide pulling her with a rope around her waist and another pushing from behind. In time the two women traded places with Mary sitting "perfectly limp" in the chair while Alice "tried the climbing and pushing process."[39] By the time Dolly Whaley ascended Vesuvius by chair in the early twentieth century—"born along like a princess with one man in front and one behind"—it had become a novel sight. Dolly was concerned enough about one man "puffing and panting" that she joked she should get out and carry him for a while.[40]

Some women were dubious that riding in chairs carried on the shoulders of men was a luxury fit for a princess or even the easiest way up. Likely Anne Bense's disdain for women "who submitted to being carried over God's free acres in a chair" expressed the sentiment of quite a few others.[41] Some who did submit came to regret their decision. Louisa Smythe, only thirteen when she was carried up Vesuvius, thought it "a terrible scramble and more than once I wished myself out of that chair." Her brother walked along beside, giving her some sense of security "helpless as I as in the hands of those wild, scowling, jabbering men."[42] Sara Newberry and her female companions started out riding animals, but switched to chairs; she was soon "well neigh [sic] frightened to death" so demanded to be let down. When exhausted from walking, she opted for a chair again, but advised women who followed in her path to forgo such conveyance, ascend only as far as they could walk and wait there for the men with them to descend.[43]

Women who feared or opposed being carried in a chair born by men and unaccustomed to strenuous walking could opt to ride a horse, mule or donkey, animals available for hire in the most popular sites. Emma Clements was willing to endure the hardship if necessary to see France's famous glacier, but her husband, Frank, while allowing their eleven-year-old daughter to ride a mule, insisted she go up in a chair. One was not available so Emma reluctantly "gave up the trip & let them go without me, my husband's fears to have me go on a mule, having prevented that." Her disappointment, however, soon gave way to determination that she would see the sea of glass after all; she hired a mule and a guide and for two and a half hours rode behind the others. Emma found the ascent fatiguing but not frightening and justified by the views. She caught up with her family just as they arrived at the summit and "greatly astonished & delighted them by my appearance;" Frank was "charmed" and "glad that I had had pluck to venture."⁴⁴ She was pluckier than some women faced with the same choice. When Susie Silver and her companions found chairs were not available, they paid men to carry them piggyback.⁴⁵

Not all women who chose to ride were as adaptable as Emma Clements. Judith Rives had had experience riding on her family's Virginia plantation when her party opted for mules to see Mer de Glace; she urged family members to think of them "mounted on these long eared affairs, with a man at the bridle rein to guide and direct their course—at least of mine and that of Mrs. Francis for the gentlemen of the party disdained such aid." Judith questioned whether she would have agreed if she had known the difficulty, but despite this postscript of caution, she rode up mountains several more times. In Martigny she had so much trouble staying on her horse that she opted to walk; her guide tried to keep her spirits up by telling her she "walked like a chamois." Judith thought her male companions found climbing less laborious, but also assumed "they (of course) scorned to complain."⁴⁶

Alicia Middleton begged against a riding excursion, but her children prevailed. She and her daughter each had a man to guide their mule while her son took charge of his own. In places too steep for riding the two women walked, which Alicia found extremely fatiguing.⁴⁷ Kate Jones was nearly thrown over her mule's head while descending a mountain near Mt. Blanc; she concluded, "the terror of ascending and descending almost destroyed the pleasure of the visit," so she decided to walk.⁴⁸ Susie Silver, fortunate to have a rubber pillow for her saddle, described the women with her as almost dead from walking because they were "so raw they could not ride."⁴⁹ Sarah Bradley walked while the rest of her party rode; when one of the men joined her, she concluded he "insisted on being polite and walking because I did[,] much to my annoyance as well as to that of his gouty toe[,] I suspect."⁵⁰

With practice even novices could develop pride in their equestrian skills. After a few outings, Mary Jane Blair bragged she had become "quite a rider" who no longer needed a guide.⁵¹ Florence Alimnae continued to prefer the security of a guide's lead, but reevaluated riding as "wonderfully easy" and even realized "the spice of danger added to our pleasure."⁵² Anna de Yoe also grew comfortable viewing the "joyous sight" of the Alps on the back of her donkey although she did wish it would stop occasionally and "give me time to try to think, connectedly."[53] Maria Degen, a better equestrian than her husband, reported "all this mule riding I bear very well," but "it fatigues excessively Mr. Degen." When the couple had to dismount and walk, she indulged in bragging that she "went on famously with my man & waited at the top for Joe, to come along by slow stages with his."[54]

Since no mule was available, Mary Pierce rationalized she was "pleased to try my walking powers." Her female companion was less pleased, but agreed that "there was nothing else to do—if we would see the mountains we had come for." After three hours of hiking, the women were so exhausted that a horse was found for them. Mary was uneasy riding sidesaddle on a man's saddle so "sat astride and went on triumphantly." Her party was briefly lost and were back at their hotel after dark, "safe but fearfully demoralized as to the advantages of climbing mountains on foot."[55] Laura Thomas was transported by chair in Switzerland, but disliked it so that she walked up Vesuvius. Later she recalled how amusing it was to see "B [her sister] & myself hanging on the arm[s] of two ugly dirty guides in shirt sleeves—but it was these escorts or none as Mrrs. Allies and Broadus [the men with them] found it as much as they could do to take care of themselves."[56]

Antebellum women were those most familiar with their designation as *the weaker sex*, but some of them ignored the implications and embraced the experience of mountain hiking. In the 1840s Sarah Cleveland and her sister-in-law resolved to attempt a difficult climb, one her brother predicted would leave them both bedridden for days. Sarah successfully trumped her brother's opposition and starting at three-thirty a.m., along with guides, hiked two and a half hours in the dark before stopping for breakfast. The others refused to continue, but Sarah was determine to reach her goal; she modified her skirt and shoes and with "my alpine [stick] I defied the very idea of slipping—and for 2 hrs. ½ we walked upon the ice." During one stretch she had the sensation of climbing a ladder as the guide put one hand behind to take hers and pull her up, with a stop every forty or fifty feet to breathe. Her guide proclaimed the four hours and forty minutes it had taken was "very good indeed for a lady" since it usually took a full five hours. Sarah was elated that "I had accomplished a true alpine excursion." She rejected the guide's proposal that she next climb Mt. Blanc, at nearly 16,000 feet Europe's tallest mountain, but did record with pride that a woman had recently done so.[57] Bettie Kimberly's husband bragged she was "active as a cat ... [who] can scramble among these mountains as nimbly as a deer" and with special shoes, "regular stompers ... fears neither mud, rain or snow." Bettie supposed those at home "would hardly believe me when I tell you of the walks we take—for the last three days we have walked from seven to eight miles a day."[58] Caroline Farrar and her companions dismounted below the summit of Mer de Glace "and took to our alpine sticks and feet." Caroline "quite won my guide's heart by springing over the chasms and on the narrow passes without assistance."[59]

Not every woman was as fearless or as fortunate. Amy Aldis was hiking near Chamonix with two female companions when the temperature dropped precipitously and it began to snow. They sought shelter where she had to lie down and drink brandy, missing the view of Mount Blanc.[60] Ellie Pierson could hardly walk after her inaugural climb and a subsequent one left her able to "barely hobble along." It was her last hike.[61]

Anne Bense's misfortune was more dramatic, but proved she was of sterner stuff. She was hiking with a friend she called King on Switzerland's Rhone Glacier one August day when a storm blew in; she recalled: "The mountains were hidden! Icy winds blew! Our gloves were soaked! Our raincoats were bedraggled. In such guise we wandered." When safely back to their hotel, the two "sank down among the blankets" relieved that "all's well that ends well!" Despite this harrowing experience, Anne and King were out again the next day. They rested at the snow line in a herdsman's hut before pushing on in snow up to their knees; she recalled "on and on and ever upward we toiled our strength failing and seized by an intolerable thirst, the summit was reached at last." There the wind was so biting "that my breath seemed to leave my body and I fell, gasping against a rock just as our guide called loudly 'Edelweiss!'," an exuberance about alpine flora Anne was unable to share. King found a rock shelter and dispatched their guide to find a horse. The stricken woman remembered being "possessed by one overwhelming desire to sleep and end it all." In the sanctuary of a nearby hut, "wet to the knees, shoes soaking wet and as cold as an iceberg," she was forced to acknowledge, "how ashamed I was!" of this "terrible plight." As news of the unfortunate visitors spread, the small room filled with curious men and children (the women were working in the hay fields); Anne thought them "rude" yet "kind." Her hosts built a fire and served her warm milk while she "suffered and bore the pain and publicity grimly." The men offered to carry her down in a chair, an irony, she realized, as "I! I!, who had laughed at others who submitted to being carried over God's free acres in a chair was to receive retribution." She avoided the humiliation by recovering sufficiently to ride again. Indeed her recovery was rapid and "perfectly fit I mounted my steed [and] together we rode at the sunset hour over the rough trail." King insisted Anne rest the following day, but the day after she was up at five o'clock, once again delighted to ride "along high places and look into the great depths and up the greater heights." Hiking to Mer de Glace left her convinced "I have never enjoyed anything as much as this dangerous exploit of springing through space."[62]

Gena Trumbull, her mother and three younger sisters show off dresses they had made in Nice in 1908. *Cornell University*

Teenager Gena Trumbull was another young American woman confident hiking in Europe's wild places. Her family often traveled with the Browns, a couple Gena thought a perfect fit, especially because Mr. Brown shared her love and appreciation of nature. When they were apart, Gena longed "to get out on these alpine hills with a stick and Mr. B. as a traveling guide." When reunited, they often arose early to see the sunrise as they hiked to summits, sometimes sitting in silence and at other times reading together John Ruskin's paeans to nature. One long outing left the two "absolutely silenced with the rapture" which, Gena described as "<u>sublime</u>." They eschewed guides even for a particularly difficult hike in Germany where "you had to draw yourself up by an iron rope (no steps only slippery rocks) to the very top."[63]

Most women preferred guides for even less challenging climbs. The many poor mountain dwellers assured a ready supply of those eager to earn money from tourists. David Birmingham's study of a Swiss village reveals that in the early-nineteenth century craft industries created wealth in urban Switzerland yet chronic poverty prevailed in many Alpine communities. As a result "child beggars preyed on the conscience of the first generation of tourists seeking pure mountain air."[64] Americans who visited Switzerland before mid-century frequently commented on goiters, a swelling of the neck caused by iodine deficiency that afflicted many of the poor. Judith Rives recounted with amusement the legend that they were "superstitiously believed by the ignorant inhabitants of the mountains to be the peculiar favorites of heaven."[65] Mary Fraser, not convinced that divine favor was at work, realized seeing so many afflicted with the malady "quite cured me of all inclination to live there."[66] Only late in the century did Swiss poverty (and goiters) all but disappear, in part the result of the wealth generated by tourism. Southern Italy, long one of the poorest areas of Europe, also had an abundance of locals eager to guide tourists up its volcanoes and to other outdoor sites.

Guides carried women in sedan chairs, led them astride animals, pushed and pulled those on foot or simply walked alongside. The best of them enhanced the experience for their clients. Judith Rives described the man she hired as "the good old patient guide."[67] Miss Lawrence praised those who "held us as they ran along with us and for many yards at a time our feet never touched the ground," and delighted in "flying in this way without helping ourselves at all."[68]

But complaints were more commonly dispensed than praise. Antebellum traveler Margaret Gardner found herself "surrounded by hundreds of mules, asses and horses, and guides of all descriptions, crowding upon one another, and uttering the most horrible execrations," a "savage and lawless looking set."[69] Would-be guides were still pestering tourists decades later even as Switzerland became a more sophisticated tourist destination. Idella Plimpton sparred with guides there who "bothered my life out of me nearly—trying to make me think I needed their help;" whenever she stopped to rest, "they would immediately commence their tune" as "one said I was dying—another that I would faint and then they would appeal to Mr. Bowen [her male companion] and wonder that he would allow me to go without help."[70] Elizabeth Nichols complained about eager guides who "swarm around us like beggars;" the one she reluctantly hired was "ugly [and] half-drunken."[71]

Sometimes the swarm of guides included women who, one potential client claimed, came to tend the mules while "the lazy husbands were resting."[72] Occasionally a woman was entirely in charge. Mary Bates's guide to a waterfall near Italy's Lake Como was "a fine looking middle-aged woman."[73] Apparently Capri had an unusually large number of female guides. Eugenie Homer reported "the donkey boys in Capri are women and girls also, and very bright and entertaining."[74] Anne Bense praised her "donkey girls," there, but thought the donkeys themselves "looked mouldly [sic] enough to have carried old Tiberius himself."[75] Caroline Farrar, on the other hand, wished "for the boys to come back" because her experience with women guiding only evoked "pity for unprotected females generally."[76]

Capri's Blue Grotto is one example of a popular venue outside of mountainous areas that demanded physical exertion. Elizabeth Ogden and her mother were drenched in route so tried first in English and then in French to convince their guides that "nothing under the sun could decoy us into that Grotto." They finally persuaded the men to turn back "which they did reluctantly, very reluctantly."[77]

Bavaria's largest salt mine was also a popular attraction. Maria Bayard, there in 1814, decided "a little want of courage should not deprive me of seeing what perhaps I might one day or other regret;" she agreed to be wrapped in a blanket and hoisted down in a bucket with her brother and a local woman sent along to assist her. They "went slowly down and I thought we never would get to the end." Once there she discovered "a terrible looking place" filled with "half naked men."[78] By the time Caroline Farrar visited a half century later, the mine was better prepared to handle tourists. The descent was "altogether unparalleled in our previous adventures" and Caroline was convinced it would give her children "a store of ludicrous pictures of their old mother in her bloomer costume sliding down a rail sufficient to keep them with a fund for merriment for a long while to come."[79] Twenty years later Abby Quincy explained that "the ladies took off their petticoats all but the flannel & put on thick white linen trousers & then a thick flannel tunic, belted at the waist & reaching to the knees, a leather apron tied behind, to sit upon when we went down the slides. A jaunty black cloth cap bound and trimmed completed the costume." She was incredulous that women and men were offered the same clothes for the descent.[80]

The Scandinavian countries were rarely a part of Grand Tour itineraries, but did attract some of the more adventuresome women. Despite advice that it would lead to "all manner of evil," Jennie McGraw joined her friend, Emily, for a strenuous trip in Norway which she hoped would be "unlike anything I have seen." Jennie tried to assuage concern from home by promising "we shall do nothing rash or imprudent," and assuring "we get on just exactly as well so far as if we had gentlemen escorts." She regretted that friends "fond of nature, bracing air, good roads & fast horses" could not share her adventure. On some days the two women and their guides plus a post boy rode more than sixty miles. Jennie discovered a taste for reindeer meat. Reaching Jostedal Glacier, Europe's largest, required rowing forty miles followed by an arduous ten-mile hike so Jennie reluctantly sought male companions. Fortuitously, two British men also eager to see the glacier were available and agreed to join the two women. Jennie teased her worried friends at home: "Oh, if you knew how early one must rise in Norway to make required stations for the night & then sometimes how woefully one's dreams of comfort are dispelled by surrounding circumstances on arrival." They rode fifty-six miles one day only to find the sole hotel at their destination full so "a wretched place was found for Emily & I [sic] in the magistrate's house & our six gentlemen friends slept on hay in the cow house." They dined on coffee and biscuits as well as tongue the Scotsman had brought along for emergencies; the food and shelter "combined with philosophical minds, good jokes, etc," made possible "the merriest evening." The two men left the next day leaving Jennie to muse "it will seem lonely I imagine." A few days later the two women also parted company with their guides and were left to "the responsibility of ourselves."[81]

Mary Woodbury enjoyed riding and hiking in Norway so much that she "decided to turn over a new leaf in that respect for I am growing woefully lazy." One day her party rode twenty-five miles until "obliged to walk two miles over the roughest of stones and hills" in order to see Jostedal. Mary concluded that although she finished exhausted, it was "as pleasant a trip as I ever made in my life."[82]

By the last decades of the nineteenth century a variety of organized athletic events offered women a new type of physical challenge while abroad. The five Curtis sisters traveled more for sports than for sightseeing. In 1907 Peg and Hat, both competitive golfers, played in the Ladies Golf Championship in London as well as in a tournament in Newcastle, County Down, Ireland.[83] Elizabeth Adams, another golf enthusiast, realized while visiting in Biarritz, a French city on the Spanish border, "I must play golf if I wish to enjoy myself."[84] Ellie Pierson usually played tennis with an American friend, but also taught the game to French women so she could practice speaking their language. She played croquet with French men, but when they insisted on different rules for the two sexes, she "learned to rail against things in French."[85] Isabelle Perkinson never imagined rowing on the Avon before leaving home yet it was a highlight of her time in England.[86] After riding thirty miles into a strong head wind on a biking trip through Germany, Mary Whitney arrived at her hotel tired and wet but determine to reach Munich on schedule; reports home told of "perfect days of wheeling among the mountains & such mountains."[87] A day-long biking trip in England left Jane Cowl barely able to walk, but she persevered and another day cycled from Southampton to Salisbury, nearly twenty-five miles.[88]

In 1878 Elizabeth Nichols, mother of three small children, was sent by her doctor for a rest cure in Europe. Seeing "fine looking English girls who tramp about splendidly" prompted her resolve to return "to this bracing air ... to walk and to teach my daughters to do the same." She did return with her three girls several times. Marian joined a tennis club in Italy and played mixed doubles in England; Margaret, the youngest and most athletic, always insisted that rowing, golf, and biking were included in the usual fare of museums and monuments. She was exhausted after rowing across Austria's Lake Grundlsee yet played tennis the next day. A few days later she climbed Rhone Glacier with her father and then joined him for a weeklong walking excursion in Spain. When the rest of her family visited the British Museum, Margaret opted for golf, which she enjoyed "though quite alone." Another day in London was given over to a long bike ride.[89]

Eleanor Joy, Margaret Nichols's kindred spirit, hiked in the German mountains free of chairs, horses and guides. "The air up here is really doing me good," she exclaimed, "for I climb about almost as much as when I was still half a boy in America. Sig. Hen. and I go out together [and] when we are out of sight of people we tuck up our skirts & scramble all of the mountains scarcely ever following any beaten path."[90]

It was especially difficult to replicate accustomed norms of domesticity when tramping in the bracing air and scrambling up mountains. Margaret Nichols and Eleanor Joy are representative of the late-nineteenth century's New Women, the Gibson Girls who stretched traditional assumptions about women's sphere. They sought outdoor and athletic activities, modified their clothing to be more practical and disdained being treated as fragile. Many American women were willing to take unaccustomed risks if necessary to see scenes familiar from their earliest school days. More than anywhere on their Grand Tour, they stepped outside the boundaries of genteel domesticity in Switzerland's Alps and Europe's other wild places.

Women on a Grand Tour had to constantly negotiate with friends and family about climbing mountains as well as what museums and churches and even what countries to visit. Every day abroad a myriad of quotidian details had to be negotiated by relatives and friends who traveled together. Some women even made the unorthodox decision to travel entirely alone. Relationships with others and grappling with solitude were integral parts of a Grand Tour.

VI

Wondering at Myself for Being Here: A Grand Tour Alone and Together

In the spring of 1840 Elizabeth Cady Stanton and Henry Stanton celebrated their marriage with a trip to Europe planned to correspond with the World Anti-Slavery Convention in London. Elizabeth's high spirits during her first Atlantic crossing drew charges of inappropriate familiarity with the crew. Once in London, however, her exuberance gave way to anger over the exclusion of women from a meeting held to champion freedom. Elizabeth joined Lucretia Mott, who also traveled with her abolitionist husband and was barred from the meeting, in vowing that once home they would organize a convention to address the oppression of women. After the proceedings in London adjourned, Elizabeth accompanied Henry on a lecture tour through Great Britain and France until a host family's perceived rudeness compelled her return to London where she was alone for ten days. When Henry rejoined her, the couple—described by Elizabeth as "self-reliant and venturesome"—made a walking tour of Scotland. On their return voyage Henry succumbed to protracted seasickness, leaving his wife to read, play chess and walk the deck.

Elizabeth's first trip abroad, one of emotional highs and lows, was a brief respite from the demands of domesticity that few women in the early-nineteenth century, even those as wealthy, well educated and self assured as she was, could escape; the first of the couple's seven children was born within a year after their marriage. The demands of her growing family forced Elizabeth to delay initiating the promised convention for eight years. In 1848, over 300 people—Frederick Douglass was among the approximately fifty men attending—met in Seneca Falls, New York, and launched a movement to fight for women's rights. Included in their resolutions was the claim that man had "endeavored in every way that he could to destroy her confidence in her own powers, to lessen her self-respect, and to make her willing to lead a dependent and abject life."[1]

In 1892, more than half a century after she was banned from the London convention, Elizabeth addressed the annual meeting of the National American Woman Suffrage Association, newly formed to unify the two groups that for years had competed for control of the women's movement. On this occasion Elizabeth was allowed to speak, but most in the audience found her advocacy of female independence and solitude so foreign that her words were met with as much incredulity as her presence in London had been years before.[2]

Perhaps it was remembering her own voyages (she had returned to Europe several times) that prompted Elizabeth to articulate her thoughts with nautical imagery. In her oft-repeated speech, "The Solitude of Self," Elizabeth argued that self-autonomy was as important for women as for men, that being alone could be a path to self-fulfillment, and that "no matter how much women prefer to lean, to be protected and supported, nor how much men prefer to have them do so, they must make the voyage of life alone, and for safety in an emergency they must know something of the laws of navigation." She insisted that the demand for women's rights was justified "because of her birthright to self-sovereignty; because, as an individual, she must rely on herself."[3]

When in 1830 Alexis de Tocqueville coined the word "individualism" to describe the attitude Americans had concerning their relationship to society, he only had in mind the male half of the population. Romantic poets who popularized the solitary soul as a heroic, often brooding, figure also thought about men exclusively. Readers understood that when Wordsworth wrote of the "bliss of solitude" and Shelley of how "I love tranquil solitude," they praised solitary men.[4] When Emerson penned an ode to self-reliance and his protégé Thoreau retreated from society to Walden Pond, these American authors likewise envisioned an ideal male. Women may have been consciously or unconsciously excluded although it was well known that they were avid readers of Romantic writers. Elizabeth Peabody communicated with Wordsworth and studied with Emerson; their ideas fueled her radical opinion that as every person is an "inalienable, absolute being," women as well as men must be free to cultivate an "inward soul."[5]

Even into the twentieth century, few men or women joined the two Elizabeths in romanticizing an ideal of female *individualism*. Whether they sailed in 1814 or 1914, most women had little thought that they were asserting their independence or seeking solitude, but once in Europe they did confront their relationships with others in new and often unanticipated ways. Alone, a word frequently called upon in letters and diaries, was sometimes underlined to accentuate its novelty. Mary Suzanne Schriber suggests that in the nineteenth century, " 'lone' female traveler" meant "unaccompanied by a male" rather than entirely alone.[6] It often did but not always; context created gradations of exclusion. Alone can be coupled with a singular pronoun and verb—"I was alone"—but also with plural ones—"we were alone." Women used the word to mean without men, without other Americans, without anyone but family, as well as without anyone else at all. Reporting to her parents that she had attended the opera, Mamie Haven bragged, "yes I did! Just me, and I alone." A few sentences later, however, she revealed that for her alone meant without a family member since she did have a male escort.[7] Most women preferred to be alone with someone else, yet a Grand Tour prompted them to think about solitude in new ways and many of them discovered that although they might fear it, they could also relish the experience.

Consciousness of being alone, whatever the context, was in some measure a response to the waning of strict protocols concerning chaperonage. In the early-nineteenth century it was commonly mandated that in certain circumstances a respectable female, especially one on the cusp of womanhood, should be accompanied by a man as she moved from place to place. During the Civil War, however, both northern and southern women found themselves traveling alone in unaccustomed ways—to fill jobs demanded by war, to tend the sick, to bring home the dead—because men, away in armies, were not available to accompany them. Southern women, and some in the North as well, had to move from the path of warring armies. Once peace was restored, the idea that there were inappropriate places for women to go without men revived, especially in the South, but in both sections it only survived in diluted form.

Georgian Eliza Lamar's European diary, written the year after the Civil War ended, reveals one young southern woman's struggle to reconcile traditional mores concerning proper female behavior with the unaccustomed freedom a sojourn in Europe afforded. Eliza was raised a daughter of the planter class in the waning years of a slave society dogmatic in its commitment to hierarchical relationships. A social order demanding rigid racial subordination of necessity demanded rigid gender subordination as well. Women with Eliza's background would have found Stanton's concept of a birthright to self-sovereignty especially difficult to fathom. Planter-class females, defined by their relationships with others, were not expected to spend time alone or even think of themselves as autonomous individuals. Eliza did not, however, categorically reject new norms in the unfamiliar environment of Europe; her diary reveals tremendous ambivalence about the propriety and safety of being a woman alone without a proper chaperone.

Eliza was eighteen and her sister, Janie, a year younger when they joined a constantly improvised group of relatives and friends on a trip their father had promised them before he died. Their only constant companion was their aunt, Annie, who, at twenty-one, hardly qualified as a matronly chaperone. Eliza embraced their first days in Europe as "one of the happiest times in my life," and wished to always be "as free from troubles and cares as now." When picnicking by a lake in Freiberg on the edge of Germany's Black Forest the three had "no difficulty in doing without a gentleman." Left in a casino with an American man, Eliza noted his surprise that his charge "was not frightened at being alone with him as if I was a chicken to be frightened by a hawk." Although bouts of homesickness left her musing at times "how happy I shall be when I get on my native soil," she also yearned to learn French and Italian for "what a nice time I could have if I should come back here again." A carriage ride to Paris with Janie as her only companion left Eliza pondering "what would my dear Da-ma [grandmother] have thought of her pet being sent off in this way, when she did not allow her to go about alone, even at home!" When the sisters were ordered to remain in their hotel to mourn their uncle's death, however, Eliza, now less concerned with her grandmother's sense of propriety, rejoined, "I am not one of those to make a nun of myself, especially when there are so many things we have to see before we go home."

Eliza's confidence continued to wax and wane. She was certain it would have been a better trip if her father had lived to bring his daughters to Europe—apparently assuming he would have retained his antebellum wealth—as "everything we fancied we would have had and never any such things as accounts to worry you." She enjoyed an outing to Versailles with several other women yet fretted about traveling at night without a protector. Dining with only Janie and Annie in a Paris café prompted her resolve: "<u>I never never</u> will place myself willingly in the same circumstances as I am now in," because "it is not thought right for [the] three of us to go out by ourselves[.]" Less emboldened with time, Eliza came to wonder "what in the world are we to do, [as] we cannot stay in the house by ourselves and we have no one to go out with."

It was a constant challenge to find suitable people to take them out. Eliza was infuriated when a northern escort criticized atrocities at Andersonville, the notorious Confederate prison located in her home state. Mr. and Mrs. Schley next took charge of the three young women, but Eliza also quarreled with them and finally concluded they were equally unqualified to be in charge. When they permitted a Sunday drive, she pondered that her mother would have never allowed such an outing on that day; when they were taken to a race, she was even more aggrieved to indulge in what her mother would have prohibited on any day. Eliza next complained of a filthy hotel she was sure relatives would disapprove of. Receipt of a message "that <u>no gentleman</u> would have sent" left her despairing "I shall feel so relieved and happy when I have someone to protect me from all such insults ... I now feel almost alone and deserted and I think the sooner Janie and I find someone to take care of us the better." Janie, however, was more reluctant to give up the unaccustomed freedom of European travel. When she ate in a café where she was told "no <u>lady</u> ought to go" her older sister could only protest, "I do not like her going."[8]

Eliza was especially conflicted, but many other women struggled to maintain familiar proprieties in an unfamiliar environment. Women traveling with their husband experienced the least disruption of accustomed gender roles and unease about appropriate behavior, but they also faced challenges to assumptions long thought immutable. In the unfamiliar environment of Europe, husbands sometimes acted in unpredictable ways. Sarah Newberry, in Paris with her husband, John, while he studied medical practice there for several months, was often alone and homesick. On a day John was late coming home, she "got very tired of waiting, very lonely, and very homesick so I had a good cry." On another occasion she "wanted to go out very much" so "at twelve began to fiddle because he did not come" and "by one was quite excited and at two desperate;" finally she "made a bold sally into the street." John was at least sorry to have disappointed her.[9]

Caroline White was also frequently disappointed, but her husband was never sorry. The couple made the first of several trips to Europe in 1854. When Frank went alone to London saloons on two consecutive nights, Caroline tried rationalizing that at least the second place was "not of so low a character" as the first. He toured Salzburg with friends while Caroline remained in their hotel and sewed. After he traveled to Kiel, a picturesque Danish town on the Baltic Sea, Caroline recorded her loneliness, but also her hope that "he will enjoy this bachelor trip." Frank returned from a solo outing to Chester praising its cathedral ruins as the most beautiful thing he had seen in England, leaving her to only imagine what she had hoped to see. On subsequent trips abroad Frank again left Caroline behind occasionally while he traveled with other men or alone. One rainy morning in London with friends, "the gentlemen left us ladies to amuse ourselves" which they did by writing letters. Subsequent entries noted "we girls have been out by ourselves," "we women went out together" and "Frank has been independently [sic] of any of us."[10]

Charlie Parsons sometimes left his wife, Rachel, behind without so much as revealing his destination. On one occasion she returned to their Paris hotel after a day with a dressmaker to find eight hundred francs and a note assuring his love. Only days later did she learn he was in London and would go from there to Frankfurt alone. Rachel's niece found her "disgusted and so disappointed" since she had hoped they would enjoy the English city's theatres and cafes together. In her niece's opinion, Rachel retaliated by spending a great deal of money; she explained to their family that her aunt "is so devoted to Uncle C. but I fear that she has had a bad time over the Paris bills—and she must always be ready to go anywhere—at a moment's notice."[11]

Most husbands were too considerate to leave their wives behind or dictate that they travel on a moment's notice. Couples traveling together generally enjoyed congenial relations and collaborated on planning their itinerary, clinging to familiar gender roles while also adjusting to a new environment. Georgette and Frank Chamberlain rented an apartment in Paris suitable for preparing meals which facilitated establishing accustomed routines. Frank went early to a nearby market for fresh eggs while Georgette made coffee; she cooked the eggs he brought and once ready "we sit ourselves down to breakfast—and such enjoyment." On one typical morning she washed dishes while Frank sat outside reading *Les Miserables.* Once her familiar domestic chores were complete, Georgette gathered up her guidebook and became "his ready companion;" "Frank places my arm in his" and "we are skimming over the ground with spirits buoyant."[12] Anais Bliss bragged that her husband was determine "to save me the slightest trouble or inconvenience." When ill health forced her to remain in Nice for days, she urged him to go to Monte Carlo alone, but he refused to leave her side for more than short walks.[13] Annie Spalding's husband also took walks alone, but always returned with "something pretty."[14] Henrietta Frank agreed to her husband's proposal of a second trip to Europe "as I never contradict especially when he proposes a great many agreeable plans." When they disagreed about how long to remain in Brussels, Henrietta suggested they leave if it rained, but stay an extra day if good weather and "the dear man agreed to the proposition."[15]

Every night Isabelle Perkinson's cousin planned the following day's activities, but frequently his wife rejected his itinerary the next morning.[16] Isabella did not report how her relatives resolved their disagreements, but likely most couples found ways to compromise. When Judith Page Rives toured Europe in 1829 with her husband, William Cabell Rives, during the weeks before he took up his duties as United States Minister to France, he usually took the lead in planning, but accepted her request to spend time "rambling among the romantic regions of the Alps" rather than visiting "the more fertile but probably less reviving country of our forefathers

[England]."[17] To her husband's dismay, Althea Harper resolved that they would both climb up St. Paul's Dome; part way he insisted they had gone far enough, but she "had my way and we started again." Althea also had to persuade him to go to the top of the Eiffel Tower, but this time he was glad she did.[18]

David Harris required little persuasion, but readily left most decisions to his wife, Caroline. Shortly after arriving in Europe they invited Louise Jewett, art professor at Mount Holyoke College, to travel with them. The women made short outings together while David stayed behind to study and write. When he did join them, he was "as amiable as possible and lets us plan to our hearts content."[19] Annie Spalding discovered on their wedding trip that her new husband had no plans, but left it all to her. A friend described Mr. Spalding's interest as of "a passive, if not negative, kind [so] the lady had the whole disposition of the entire affair."[20] Gus Pierce's interest in Europe was decidedly negative; his wife planned what ruins and museums to see because, "poor Gus gets no fun from Rome. He drags through a few things but looks as though he'd rather be at home."[21] Fred Sterling, unfortunate in visiting Europe during an unusually hot summer, was quite clear about where he wanted to be. His wife, Mary, complained to relatives that he talked constantly of home and "thinks a man must be a fool to try this thing over again," leaving her to bemoan that they would never bring their children abroad.[22]

A Parisian observing Americans in her city in the 1890s flippantly claimed "it is only when his daughter is bored, or when she wishes an aristocratic marriage, that the American head of the family makes up his mind to leave his absorbing and intoxicating business for a few months and takes her to Europe."[23] Young, unmarried women were more likely to travel with their mothers, but fathers frequently joined them and sometimes traveled with only their daughters; most of them were neither bored nor anxious to find a titled husband, but eager to learn what Europe had to offer. Mildred Cox, who traveled with her sister and both parents, usually opted to spend time with her father whether he visited banks or art galleries while the other two women shopped.[24] During the months before Bessie Horstmann's father joined his family in Europe, she grew "so tired of being without him" that when he arrived she "could not get enough of him or kiss him enough."²⁵

Likely most young women traveled as amicably with their father, but clearly some did not. A companion pitied Miss Folger, a "poor unfortunate traveling with an irascible father and an eye rolling step-mother."²⁶ Charlotte Horlbeck, eighteen when she traveled with her parents and sister, sometimes found her father irascible as well. After weeks together, he was not "any better a travelling companion." Charlotte groused after seeing too many of Rome's ubiquitous churches that "all you can do and say is of no avail[;] he will hop into every one he passes by." The teenager longed for "a pleasant companion, which I certainly have not got in our crowd."²⁷ Helen Gould usually enjoyed a more congenial relationship with Jay Gould, but at times found his supervision trying; she found shopping with a maid "great fun—much more than going with father."²⁸

Brothers and sisters were also usually compatible, although the advantages male siblings enjoyed could spark resentment and even conflict. Maria Bayard acquiesced to staying alone when her brother and cousin did things deemed unsuitable for ladies. While they reviewed French troops, she found women to join her shopping. She also sought female company to avoid dining with a group of men, but the host insisted she join and "was so positive I could not get off." Her experience prompted the ambivalent postscript: "I spent a very pleasant day tho' I could not do otherwise."²⁹ Sarah Elliott identified her brother as her antidote for homesickness and usually deferred to him to plan their travels, although she was sure their mother would be shocked that he took her to "such an awful place" as Paris's morgue.³⁰ Martha Griffis was frequently alone or with a female companion when her brother, Willie, went his own way. They were together in Paris, but Willie spent so much time walking around the city—his sister described him as "a wonderful walker" who "can accomplish wonders"—that she spent hours by herself in their hotel. When he announced his intent to leave France without her, Martha realized "the thought of staying <u>four weeks alone in Paris</u> is not a pleasant one" so demanded he clarify their unsettled plans. They agreed he would go to northern Italy while she stayed in Paris until escorted to Geneva. Willie would join her there and the two would go to Karlsruhe, a German border town on the Rhine, where she would stay while he toured Switzerland. They would then travel up the Rhine together before re-crossing the Channel and returning home. Martha agreed to frequent separations even though emotionally dependent on her brother. When he left Paris she was "quite lonely" and when he unexpectedly returned early it was "much to my surprise and joy."[31]

Women traveling without men were hindered in seeing the sights by lingering assumptions concerning their proper behavior. After several days abroad with her daughter, Frances Stevens reported that "without a gentleman to accompany us we have of course left unseen a great deal."[32] Bessie Horstmann's family also found it "very hard to go round without a gentleman" so "wait to see a great deal until Papa comes."[33] Even in the early-twentieth century, some women were timid without men. After Adelaide Werner's father was called to Scotland on business, his wife and daughters only left their London hotel to go to the National Gallery.[34]

Late-night events and those likely to attract crowds were deemed especially questionable for women. Susie Silver eagerly awaited a Parisian fireworks show, but her husband mandated "the crowd would be too great to take ladies out;" his rave review of the evening surely exacerbated her disappointment.[35] Mary Bradbury, who traveled with her brother, Charlie, and his wife, reported that Charlie did most of the planning with a new itinerary presented each morning. In Spain it included a bullfight for him, but he "would not allow any of us."[36] Custom connived with men's dictates to inhibit some women from going out at night. Mary Jones, whose traveling companions were all women, wanted to see a grand review of troops in Berlin in 1894, but, a friend explained, "she is a woman & so can't go unless attended."[37]

Some women, however, were emboldened to see a great deal. Mary Boit first felt "a little queer" going to the opera with only a female companion, but on discovering most German women were unescorted she dismissed her initial concern as "absurd." At a serenade for King Albert of Saxony, she was initially embarrassed by her proximity to strangers until she realized they were quiet and restrained. The experience left her speculating that "such a crowd at home would mean a mob, in which a man would very unwillingly take a woman & as for women going alone [it] could not be dreamed of." Mary and her friends grew increasingly emboldened as she realized breaking rules learned at home "amused us immensely."[38]

In the last half of the nineteenth century a number of female authors capitalized on the disquietude that men and women alike felt about lone women traveling and especially a woman traveling entirely alone. As Leo Hamilton points out, these authors "created a small but impressive library of first-person narratives that combined genuine learning with the spirit of individualism." Accordingly, "the once-lowly travel book, rather unexpectedly, became an important instrument for the emancipation of women."[39] In the 1870s, Adeline Trafton published *American Girl Abroad* in which she described herself and her female companion as "two anxious, but by no means aimless[,] females, knowing little of the world, less of travelling, and nothing whatever of foreign ways." Yet when asked if they were afraid to travel alone, her answer was simply "no."[40] Mary Wheeler's book, published around the same time, dismissed claims of women being unsafe going out alone as "absurd."[41] At the turn of the century, Mary Ninde recounted in *We Two Alone in Europe* that she and a female friend faced "one seemingly insurmountable obstacle" when they ruminated about going abroad: they had no one to accompany them. Finally they prevailed on "pater-familias" to escort them to London and oversee their first weeks there. Mary made it clear, however, that all along this concession to paternalism was meant to be temporary; once they had a "foretaste of the Old World" they "set forth alone," all over Europe. When they ventured to Scandinavia, Mary satirically queried: "Go to Norway? Two girls and alone! Who ever heard of such a thing?" Of course, they did go there and to Sweden and Russia as well.[42] In the 1890s, "Elino," pseudo-named author of a series of letters titled "Edith and I in Paris: The Experiences of Two Bright American Girls in the French Capital," argued that it was perfectly safe and respectable for women to spend time in Paris without men as long as they did not patronize unfamiliar cafes, go far from the main roads, or go out alone after dark. Elino admitted some women had "wild tales to tell," but assured that they were only told by those who violated these rules.[43] Abbie Farwell's trip to Europe at century's end inspired *Bachelor Girls*, a series published by the St. Louis *Globe* intended to inspire women to travel without men; she warned that it would not always be easy. Abbie wrote from Scotland that it was "a bewildering experience for four unsquired dames little used to travelling to find themselves stranded in a foreign city long after what would be 'dark' at home, with no prospect of finding lodging for their weary bones." Of course, lodging was found and the women "resolved to show the world how gloriously and triumphantly four lone lorn females can fend for themselves."[44] In *Waymakers Or Sola in Europe* Josephine Tyler offered her unusually radical opinion that women should even spend some time traveling entirely alone, "sympathetically independent," as she and her companion did to avoid their "mutual tyrannies."[45]

Women who never intended to publish their letters and diaries also chronicled their experiences traveling without men, not to convince the world but to convince themselves and their families that they were safe and respectable. As Frances Stevens grew more emboldened traveling with her daughter, she assured her husband that when locals met unescorted women "they seem to double their civilities."[46] Eleanor Middleton was convinced she was safe alone because "people are accustomed to independent American women," although she thought those she met were "mostly uninteresting."[47] In the early-twentieth century, Edith Parsons styled herself and her sister "two of those queer traveling American spinsters from California."[48]

Divergent needs compelled some wives and husbands to go their separate ways at times. When Helen Brooks went alone to study German in Dresden she was "perfectly surprised to find how easy it is, how well I can make myself understood and how entirely comfortable I am." During her first days apart from her husband she resolved to be "temperate in my doings," but in time became emboldened to go alone to art galleries. On a subsequent trip, Helen again went her own way, this time to Leipzig where she realized that, "although everything goes as smooth as wax work," yet "I get more excited when I am alone."[49] Caroline Corson had traveled several months with her husband when she made the decision to remain alone for several additional weeks. As they parted company she realized "it was awful to see him go off and to turn back alone into the night, the noisy London Night. I never knew before what real loneliness was!"[50]

John and Bettie Kimberly were forced to separate after their yearlong wedding trip was unexpectedly upended by her pregnancy. Their daughter was born in Europe and John's faculty position at the University of North Carolina mandated his return before the baby was old enough to travel. A transatlantic debate ensued as to whether he would re-cross the ocean to escort his family home or the two would come without him. She was determine to save the expense so urged him to "let a willful woman have her way for once and not drive me to extremity." She muted her assertiveness with assurance that she still depended on him to guide her financial decisions, but more candidly confided to her sister: "I am very much opposed to his coming for I can just as well go home without him as with him, though he flatters himself that I could not possibly cross the ocean without his valuable assistance." Bettie asked her sister to intercede because "I had much rather save the four or five hundred dollars it will cost and do without his company for a month longer." Bettie, emboldened by her time alone, finally prevailed and in the spring of 1860 returned home with their baby daughter.[51]

Wives who made their entire Grand Tour without their husband often sought advice from home. Frances Stevens's father, Albert Gallatin, secretary of the treasury in the Jefferson and Madison administrations, had taken her to visit his native Switzerland when she was a child. Although she had long dreamed of returning, she only reluctantly left behind her husband and sons when a trip was recommended for her daughter's health. Soon after arriving she confided to one son: "You cannot realize my dear Eugene what it is to me—the separation from your father and other dear ones in America. I had[,] as you know[,] always desired to re-visit Europe but certainly never anticipated doing it under the present circumstances. I did what I thought was right—but believe had I had more time for thought would not have come. But as your father says we must not look back." After several days in Paris she traveled with Josy through Belgium and up the Rhine "without any drawbacks or inconveniences." Yet Frances continued to suffer bouts of unease; she confided from Berlin: "I hope my dear husband you will approve what I am doing. I have no one to consult and must rest on my responsibility." The two women determined to suppress homesickness and uncertainty and "take the pleasure, profit & enjoyment which our travels are so capable of imparting." As her self-confidence rose, she even teased her husband that "you would not know your wife, she has become so active & energetic." After weeks of wavering between embracing her newfound independence and turning to her husband for guidance Frances struggled to convince herself that "to depend upon ones self [sic] is best."[52]

Ethel Dummer also fluctuated between accustomed reliance on her husband and a new appreciation of her independence. In 1909 she took their two oldest daughters to Europe while he tended to business and oversaw the younger two in boarding school. Even while still at sea she second-guessed "how I ever plucked up courage to make the journey[?];" after several weeks in Europe, Ethel still battled homesickness, but the tug of home competed with a growing conviction that the trip had been a wise plan. The family was briefly reunited when Frank brought the younger girls over; after he left, Ethel realized anew "nothing is really very easy here even for a party of women folk" and "how hard it is to have the ocean between us when there is always so much to talk about." The girls were "full of fun and mischief," prompting her to joke she wanted to "send them all home by American Express & continue the trip with Goethe." Ethel assured Frank during days she hiked with the girls in the Dolomites that "we are longing for your return" and queried "do you know I was quite courageous to take this trip alone[?]" In mid-July Frank did return to travel with his family and escort them home.[53]

Emma Clements and her husband, along with their daughter, Helen, started out traveling with a larger group until Helen became ill, forcing them to remain behind in Venice. Emma first found it "odd to feel us alone in this far off strange place," but came to appreciate independent travel so much that she decided to remain in Europe with Helen after her husband and the others left. The day he departed she realized "it is very hard to let him go without us, but it seems best for us to stay while he must go." On their first day alone they started out early "Helen & I to go our independent way." They traveled through Ireland and then crossed the Channel to Holland; Emma found The Hague so charming that she spontaneously added an extra day there. Mother and daughter then traveled through Germany for a month and spent a few days each in Paris, London and Glasgow before returning home.[54]

Some women never questioned their competence to travel independently. In 1898 Mary Harding took her four daughters, ranging in age from twelve to twenty-eight, on a Grand Tour, leaving her husband and sons at home to pursue their careers. Her oldest daughter Margaret's diary reveals no hint that Mary ever second-guessed the arrangement or sought her husband's advice. The five Tilestons traveled harmoniously, visiting some sights together and others in smaller groups or alone. When her daughters went to San Miniato, the Romanesque basilica overlooking Florence, Mary chose instead to explore Santa Croce, the city's major Franciscan basilica. On another occasion she bicycled with the younger girls until she parted company with them to explore a nearby palace. One day in Rome, Edith and Eleanor walked in the Borghese Gardens, Amelia explored the Roman Forum and Coliseum with her mother, and Margaret stayed in to "puzzle over accounts." To celebrate Christmas the sisters went to St. Peter's, two by carriage and two on foot; their mother went elsewhere alone. In Assisi she stayed behind while her daughters undertook the long climb up to the Castello, a castle above the Franciscan city; only Margaret and twelve-year-old Eleanor made it to the top where they "scrambled around under the fort and picked flowers." After Margaret and Amelia returned home, Mrs. Harding remained another month in London with her younger girls.[55]

By the last decades of the nineteenth century mothers and daughters traveling together epitomized an American Grand Tour. Laura and Bessie Johnson were an especially close example of this iconic pair of travelers. In 1869, shortly after the death of her husband, Laura took teenager Bessie and her eight-year-old sister, Laura, abroad, leaving her son, Oliver, to matriculate at Harvard College. Higher education was increasingly available to women in the post-Civil War years, but was still novel enough that instead of making it available to her bookish daughter, Laura decided that for her travel was "best, nay almost necessary."

After a few weeks in England, which Laura disliked, the family settled in "gay and beautiful" Paris. She hired a watercolor teacher and rented a piano for Bessie and resolved to take her to the opera as often as possible; their first performance was Beethoven's *Fidelio*, Laura's favorite composer's only operatic composition. Evenings at home might be spent reading favorite literature, including English poetry and Thomas Carlyle's history of the French Revolution. Laura recorded her delight that "Bessie and I are in such perfect accord and sympathy that everything we do together we enjoy tenfold;" she proclaimed their trip "a perfect success" as she watched Bessie "grow like the grass in a warm spring rain."

Their idyll was unfortunately undermined by news from home that Oliver had been suspended from Harvard for fighting. Watching her daughter thrive while her son floundered forced Laura to evaluate the gendered realities of her children's lives. She confided to a family friend: "It is a pity Bessie were not the boy and Olly the girl. Bessie is morbid and restless for more to fill her mind. A college would have been just the place for her. She can never have study or ideas enough. She beats against the trammels of a woman, and wants[,] as the common phrase is[,] a 'career.' She has only too much thought and conscience. Madam, her German teacher, used to say every day, 'what a pity that she is not a boy! Such a head as she has! She might make anything.' "

As Laura wrestled to reconcile the needs of her two oldest children, she weighed that "to stay here longer would be good for her," yet "<u>if</u> I can do Olly any good, that is the first thing." Ironically, her dilemma was solved by the needs of her youngest child who contracted scarlet fever, making it impossible for the family to return to New York for six months. Once home, Laura again focused on her restless older daughter, vowing that after a brief respite, she would take her to California.[56]

Laura and Bessie exemplify the many mothers and daughters who enjoyed traveling together, but of course there were exceptions. Mrs. Marsh, for example, had a strained relationship with her daughter, who grew so "severe in her remarks" that the mother yearned to go home "to free her of my weight."[57] Female relatives generally might find that harmony enjoyed at home could be eroded by the stresses of travel. After weeks traveling with an aunt whose compatibility she enjoyed at home, Elizabeth Gould complained "if

I have to stay another day, I think I shall kick a bit—I am so sick of it—of being contradicted." When she was finally able to go her own way, Elizabeth wrote home "strictly confidential" that "it was <u>such</u> a relief to be 'un famille' " after "Aunty T's constant contradictions and monopolizing Harriet made the day seem night, and our spirits released from this incubus soared to a great degree."[58]

Women without female relatives to travel with or who anticipated conflict sometimes sought a traveling companion. When twenty-year-old Clara Ritchie joined her father and his business associates on a trip to Europe, Martha Maltby, a few years her senior, was engaged as a companion. After a few days together, Clara assured her mother that "Miss Maltby is delightful company and we are both '<u>old</u> maidish' enough to get along well together." Their compatibility inspired a trip to Scotland together while the men took care of business in London. After rejoining them in England and then traveling together to France, Clara concluded that in contrast to Martha "who knows how to travel well," her father's companions were "perfectly helpless."

The two women remained in Europe after the men departed because "it seems like too good an opportunity to loose [sic] now that I am over here." Clara assured her mother that "if sure of our money we can get around almost anywhere." They reluctantly let others join them on occasion, but always preferred their society of two. "Miss Maltby and I have had so much pleasure by ourselves and felt so free and independent to go where and when we like that we hate to loose [sic] any of that freedom," Clara explained to her parents. "We have learned that we have a much better time when we are entirely at liberty to do as we like. <u>Two</u> can go anywhere."[59]

Finding congenial friends was a challenge which could require considerable improvisation; women without family often shifted from one group or individual to another and occasionally found they had no choice but to travel alone. Constance Harrison reluctantly left behind her husband, Burton, and their sons, promising "I shall put in my time with friends and never allow myself to be alone." After a difficult journey through Spain, France and Italy with two women, one with a young son, Constance was happy to report "all has gone well and smoothly between [sic] us," and concluded "we could never have accomplished such an extensive itinerary except in a party." She assured Burton from Rome that "such hardened travelers, Mary and I [are], that nothing now daunts us, and we had no fears of not going right."[60]

Martha and Willie Griffis traveled for several days with a woman they met crossing the ocean who asked to join them because her first party was too large and too expensive and "she feels more at home with us."[61] Henrietta and Henry Frank agreed to travel with a young Jewish woman from their voyage; on parting company, Henrietta praised her as "most agreeable all the time we traveled together," and reflected on "how near one becomes to people whom you know slightly when you meet as strangers in a strange land, especially if you belong to a minority."[62]

Mamie Parsons first traveled to Europe with her parents, but on subsequent trips improvised a variety of travel arrangements. One trip started off with two "delightful companions" who, "tho' they can't do tours in 17 minutes like Papa ... do in the end get to see everything, and see them [sic] intelligently." After they parted company, Mamie looked for a family "willing to take charge of me." When her mother insisted she not travel alone, Mamie countered she should not worry because "I am old enough and quite ugly enough to take care of myself and am having a very good time now."[63] Similar to Clara Ritchie's rationale that seeming an old maid protected her, Mamie projected a mantle of unattractiveness as a means of asserting her independence.

Phoebe Pember, seventy-two when she made her first trip abroad, was certainly old enough to take care of herself, but could rarely report a good time whether alone or with others. Two months traveling with Emma and her children left her with "nothing but worries." Emma also had worries with the arrangement so finally asked Phoebe to leave the apartment they shared in Dresden; Phoebe reluctantly agreed and with "extreme nervousness" searched for her own place. When friends urged her to visit favored sights, she questioned if they understood the challenges one faced traveling alone in foreign countries with unfamiliar languages. She enjoyed "nice American people" in Munich, but thought those met in Dresden "common." Phoebe went alone to Germisch, a scenic town nestled in the Bavarian mountains, which was so pleaasing that she stayed an extra week. She also found a companion there, a young

American woman who was "kind and obliging" and "relieves my loneliness and does not scream which is a god send."[64]

Young women not so willing to go it alone might make arrangements with a man or older women to serve as chaperone on their Grand Tour. Mabel Root and Charlotte Crawford traveled with Dr. and Mrs. Forman. Charlotte right away analyzed Dr. Forman as "the sweetest, most thoughtful person you could imagine" and described their foursome as "perfectly harmonious." When her tardiness caused them to miss a train in Palermo, Charlotte realized "great unhappiness on my part," but "angelic forbearance on Dr. F's." Three months into their tour the young women were asked to help plan and lead outings to allow their leader some rest. Mabel reported that on her assigned day all were "happy and jolly and I especially for I love to be conductor." Likely the group's compatibility was enhanced by their mutual willingness to part company on occasion. When Dr. Forman "balked on churches and picture galleries" in Rome, Mabel went alone. On another occasion the Formans sought out Etruscan tombs while Charlotte and Mabel visited the Ville d'Este gardens and fountains in Tivoli. On their return voyage, Dr. Forman was comfortable enough with his two charges to play tag on deck; Mabel described him as "just like a funny boy" who "can run like a streak."[65]

Sisters Laura and Bettie Thomas hired Mr. Broadus (called Mr. B) and enjoyed a usually harmonious, albeit, at times trying, relationship with him. When early in their trip he briefly went his own way, Laura appealed to those at home: "Well! Alas! Alas! If you have tears prepare to shed them now" for "Bettie and myself [are] left here in the great city of Dublin all alone." But the experience taught them that they could cope on their own. When Mr. B. fainted in a Dublin bank, Laura helped him home, revived him with whiskey and returned to conclude their business; she confided in her diary: "Mr. B. doesn't know what to do[,] what is good for himself or much about himself." In Holyhead, a Welsh seaside town, Laura and Bettie took responsibility for finding lodging. When the three realized they had the wrong train tickets for London, Mr. B. fell into such "a state of excitement running to & fro" that Laura "couldn't help laughing;" she suggested they simply exchange the tickets, thus "putting his mind at ease." After spending a few days alone in London the sisters rejoined their escort and traveled to Belgium where, "to our chagrin and grief," he was again sick. They agreed to go it alone, resolute that "travelers we are & [with] only a little time to spare we concluded to try." In Rome they rejected time to be lonely with "so much to do & see & study." The two declined an invitation for a second trip to Germany with friends although Laura "was too too sorry about it, as I would have liked much to have traveled with them." Instead they spent the summer of 1870 in Florence awaiting resolution of the conflict in France. Laura bragged to her nieces and nephews, "you ought to see your Aunts, how independently they walk about Florence." She was not as independent as her boasting implied, however; after a month in the Tuscan city she acknowledged "I have done very little for some time in the way of sightseeing as B. [Bettie] has been unable to go with me & I could not go by myself." Hiring a local maid finally allowed "quite a tramp with this woman at my heels as a protector—all about Florence." The guide understood enough of Laura's limited Italian that they "got along very charmingly." Not so charmingly, however, that she replaced Mr. B.; when he decided to rejoin them later than planned, Laura groused, "he has no idea what a disappointment it is." When their erstwhile leader finally returned, the three traveled through Switzerland, then to Strasbourg, Baden-Baden and finally to "that pleasure of pleasure," Paris.[66]

Not all chaperones and their charges were as compatible. Mary Millis thought it a "marvelous good fortune" when arrangements were made for her to travel first with Mrs. Laidlaw and then with Mrs. Minis and her two daughters; she left home convinced that Laidlaw's experience would greatly enhance her trip, but the relationship quickly soured after the older woman questioned her relationship with a visiting suitor. When ordered to her room, Mary retaliated by joining the Minis family earlier than anticipated. "Not accustomed then, as I subsequently became, to going alone in foreign cities" she "signaled with some diffidence to a cabman" to take her to their hotel. The Minises were Orthodox Jews, unlikely traveling companions for a young Protestant woman, but Mary found them amiable enough. They agreed that she could sightsee alone if she left behind a description of her route, promised not to deviate and kept her "red *Baedeker* prominently displayed under my arm and opera glasses in hand," — in other words " 'anglese' from top to toe." When time to return home, Mary hired two English women, both "tall, gawky, and silent," as escorts to London and "some kind of professional chaperone" to accompany her on to Liverpool where "I was duly turned over" to the captain.[67]

Caroline Corson and her husband agreed to escort two young women for six weeks, a commitment Caroline came to regret because, although "apparently under our guidance," the two were financed by a relative so "free from any pecuniary obligation." When her charges decided to go to Austria alone, Caroline countered that if they deviated from the original itinerary, there was no need to maintain the six-week contract and asked to terminate it with compensation for organizing the trip. The two women agreed, but remitted only fifty dollars. Later they reversed course and asked to return, leaving Caroline to assume "they got scared ... at being left to themselves and came to me begging to go back on the decision." She struggled over what to do, weighing concern that "to refuse might have caused me terrible regrets should they get into some awful scrapes" with equal concern that "to accept was a painful piece of weakness on my part." The Corsons reluctantly agreed to renew the contract with young women Caroline thought "like two spoiled children let loose in a candy shop [who] ... crave everything they see and do not see."[68]

By the late-nineteenth century large tour companies were an emerging alternative to improvisation and private arrangements. Professional tours, however, grappled with their own array of problems. Nina Halsey, the woman so offended by the Moulin Rouge, first praised her tour leader, Dr. Robert S. Barrett, as a good manager who "arranges everything with apparently little effort on his part." Subsequently, however, her complaints mushroomed: She had to help him out of financial difficulty; she had to leave historic sights early to join a group lunch at the hotel; he knew little of *The Last Supper* even though he had seen it six times; he had no program; he offered no information or direction; and, most serious of all in Nina's eyes, although married, his attention to Ruthie Kyle became "very pronounced." While visiting Italy's Lake Como, Nina observed the two "sauntering around through the grounds together" with attentions "too marked." From Venice she complained that one evening Mr. Barrett offered no advice or directions to his group before "leaving in a gondola with Miss Kyle" and the two "enjoyed the evening to themselves." In time, as Nina's criticism grew more inclusive, she also complained that "some of the party [were] very congenial [but] others [were] continually complaining of being hungry, tired—hot & etc." In contrast, she boasted of caring "little of the body & creature comforts [because] my mind [is] too absorbed with the present & with the past."[69]

Mrs. D.A. Tufts was apparently spared the discomfort of traveling with an amorous leader, but developed her own litany of complaints. She especially fumed about the unfairness that she and others had inferior accommodations "where good are to be obtained by a little looking into matters." An ever-expanding list of irritations prompted her to resolve never to travel in a party again because "one may be willing and should be to share the good and that which is not quite so good but it becomes one-sided when a few have always to take the worse of accommodations." She also regretted having "a conductor [who] does not give you his evenings unless he feel [sic] inclined." Mrs. Tufts candidly acknowledged, "it is not an easy matter to keep in good humor a party of women & I feel that I must not do any fault finding to add to the many annoyances which our conductor has." She resolved to keep her criticism to herself, but confided in her diary: "If I cannot travel hereafter by myself or without a conductor I will stay at home" as "there is something about a large party very repugnant ... the herding and numbering and follow-my-leader sort of fashion takes away the dignity of a party." [70]

Tour guide Willie Adam had a different perspective on the pluses and minuses of group travel. After successfully leading several summer excursions, Willie left her position as an Alabama high school teacher to lead tours in Europe full time. Her experiences guiding groups made up primarily of women elicited the gamut of emotions. During one trip she confided "my party is not hard to handle but oh! How ignorant and dead spiritually." In Scotland she poured over her *Baedeker's* while despairing of clients who "never bought a guidebook—do not intend to and have about as much interest in Scottish history as Old Pat—not as much possibly." She tired of a "coarse and ignorant and 'getting' " couple in one group as well as a man "about to kill me," because he had "never heard of the French Revolution in all his life—Louis XIV and Marie Antoinette are as new and startling to him as Sewall of Maine [Arthur Sewall, the Republican candidate for vice president in 1896] was to me." Willie hoped to visit Oxford alone, but had to reluctantly conclude, "I cannot trust my party to get safely across the Channel without me." Fortunately another group proved "so kind and intelligent that my duties are light," but they were the exception; after more than a decade leading trips abroad and "tired of the restless, omnipresent tourist," Willie gave up guiding. On a final trip she enjoyed a respite in Rome's Protestant Cemetery, final resting place of Shelley and Keats, where she "rejoiced that I was alone." [71]

Not all women rejoiced in solitude, but the vagaries of travel compelled many of them to grapple with being alone. In 1814 Maria Bayard thought it worth recording that in Bath "I went out alone."[72] Diary keepers echoed Maria into the next century with the word *alone* often underlined to emphasize the novelty. In the 1820s, a decade especially rigid in mandating female chaperonage, Mary Few proudly reported to her mother, who "always prophesized that I would make a poor traveler," that "I have never regretted my having determined to set out on my own account."[73] Decade by decade such resolve grew more common. Annie Winsor, in Europe in 1885, dreaded the constant proximity of others that travel demanded because without solitude she felt "confused and inobservant."[74] Mamie Parsons established a morning routine in the Bavarian spa town of Kinssingen to assure herself time alone. After breakfast she would take "my embroidery, a German novel, a little German dictionary and Heine's poems, and go to a certain bench in the shadiest allee of the Kurgarten." Mamie assured her parents "it is quite proper to sit there alone and such a comfort for I thoroughly enjoy it and get so much fresh air."[75] Anna de Yoe preferred visiting famous sights alone; at Versailles she compensated for her lack of French by using signs and pointing at her guidebook. Naples seemed more daunting than Paris and initially she feared even venturing alone to church there; in time, however, the city grew familiar and Anna was emboldened to go alone to see "coral stones, picture stores [and] Il Castel Dell'Ove [the city's oldest castle]" and then "took via along the bay & [had a] long long look at Vesuvius."[76]

Young women, especially, felt empowered when they explored on their own. After a few days in London, Herma Clark bragged, "I feel quite proud that I can go about so much by myself in this big city. It is really fun, I think." [77] Abby Quincy was proud of shopping "all alone;" she went to the Pincio, the gardens near Rome's Villa Borghese with a splendid view of the city, again underscoring that she had done so "<u>alone</u>." [78] Fifteen-year-old Isabelle Perkinson readily embraced going out alone, boasting "I walked this morning all by my lonesome but I had no trouble at all;" she assured her mother "I am getting very used to trotting off to church by myself now." As her trip neared its end, Isabelle realized "I am always glad when I can go alone … I don't know why but I am."[79]

Charlotte Crawford's long day alone garnered no such positive memories. None of her companions shared her desire to visit Lerici, Shelley's villa on the Gulf of Spezia, so she resolved to go without them. After Dr. Forman helped her plot the necessary connections from Florence, she "set out for Spezia <u>sola</u>." On the boat to the villa she was surrounded by young Italian men who "looked curiously at me (a young lady alone is a <u>rara avis</u>) and made efforts to pick me up." Charlotte "froze them off" even while eavesdropping to improve her Italian. When a wave pushed her into the arms of the most forward man, he harassed her all the more; when she confessed she was traveling alone, he pestered her to spend the night with him. Charlotte finally reached the villa only to find it closed to the public. To avoid a repeat of her earlier travails, she walked to a trolley for her return to Spezia, but one of the men continued his pursuit. Workmen nearby refused to help, leaving Charlotte fuming "how I hated all Italians!" and longing for "one good American or Englishman! Or a Greek!" When "the creature laid hands on me" she "slung him across the road, to his great surprise." Once safely in Spezia's train station, Charlotte shut herself in the women's toilet, "a ghastly malodorous refuge," rather than risk further harassment. On board she found herself the sole woman among "a noisy crowd of merry makers" and "the whole thing began all over again." She arrived back in Florence late at night "almost hysterical" and "tucked myself into bed at last."[80] Charlotte's rather light-hearted account of her solo adventure reveals anxiety and even fear, but offers no hint that she was concerned about violating proper genteel behavior. She personifies the New Woman increasingly emboldened to pursue adventures well outside the traditional restraints of domestic gentility.

Not all women traveling on the cusp of the twentieth century, however, easily embraced a new persona. On her second trip abroad, Constance Harrison, who had earlier bragged of her success traveling with only female companions, spent most of her time in England alone until a woman joined her for meals. When invited to attend Oberammergau's famous Passion Play, a depiction of the life of Christ staged in the Bavarian city since the mid-seventeenth century, Constance had to confide to her husband: "I have not the courage to return from there alone to England and have therefore reluctantly declined, for you know [I] had wanted to do it." Left behind in the English countryside, she realized "I can't stand being <u>alone</u> in these quiet country paradises (where I hear my heart beat and the clock tick)." Constance decided to return to London and await her two sons, assuring her husband "when my lads arrive I shall be perfectly happy and envy no one their lawful companions as I find myself doing at points along my road."[81]

Likely it was not uncommon for those who traveled solo to have bouts of envying others their companions. When Eleanor Middleton failed to engage a companion for a trip through the Dolomites, she set out alone. She fretted "I shall feel most lonely without Eliza & that all the best part … of my enjoyment will be wanting," but had encountered "so many forlorn women travelling that I am not <u>afraid</u> & it is the lot of some people to be lonely always." After traveling solo for several days, Eleanor joined an American couple, a "comfort and distraction to me in the midst of my loneliness for I was awfully tired of my own company & as melancholy and depressed." Their time together was short lived, however, because "a donkey cannot [run?] with a race horse" and "that is about the position my resources bear to theirs & I should only be a drag & clog on their movements."[82] Mary Pierce described a trip from Vienna to Dresden without "a soul for company all night except two fleas" as "unpleasant."[83] Katherine Johnson relished time alone in the British Museum, but was distressed to be alone at night. In Rouen, Normandy's capital along the Seine, she chose a small hotel, assuming it would be less dreary than a larger one, and found to her joy that there was another woman there. They dined between an Englishman and Frenchman who debated what was proper conversation when dining with ladies.[84] Elizabeth Nichols became "quite proud" after traveling alone for several days in Belgium and Holland, but confided to her husband that "although I am well treated and have had no trouble I find that the forlornness and peculiarity of traveling alone detracts a great deal from what I should otherwise enjoy and I want to get to London as soon as I can." She hoped to find a companion there, but assured her confidence that if she did not "I have somewhat learned the lay of the land and shall do very well alone."[85]

Some women were confident without qualification that they could do very well alone. After traveling from Liverpool to London, Abby Choate bragged that friends thought her "very smart and courageous to go out alone so quickly but I found no trouble." In route to Edinburgh she stopped at York Minster where "as I was alone & early they began paying me great attention;" she assured her family that she dined in the Peacock Inn with "two ladies opposite."[86] Emma Traxel joined an organized tour in Italy, but it did not include Milan's famous cathedral in the itinerary so she struck out alone to see it. Americans she met in route assured her she was safe and she in turn assured her family that throughout her two-day solo trip she "met friendly people along the way."[87] Sarah Elliott, traveling alone after her brother fell ill, assured their mother from London, "I think I have fallen on my feet—what do you think[?] I came all the way from Austria by myself—had no difficulty—was not sick over the channel."[88] When Clara Reed learned Wagner's *Tristan and Isolde* would be performed in Berlin, she resolved to travel from Dresden to see it even though her companion "felt very solemn at the idea of her 'fledgling' going off without her." Clara reported home that she was alone in a carriage in route, but met in Berlin so "I was not able to do much for myself, and it was not possible for anything very serious to happen to me."[89]

Not all parents of young unmarried daughters were as convinced that nothing serious would happen. Nancy Johnson's mother admonished her as she departed: "Now do be careful & do not travel alone;" Nancy dutifully promised she would always have a female companion.[90] Eugenie Homer made a similar promise to her parents, but was less dutiful. She stayed with a sister living in Paris only until she could find a room with a French family and then tried to convince her mother "I am pretty fortunate, I think, in being all alone here." She started off a trip to Italy with another woman, but in time parted company with her, promising her anxious parents, "whatever I do I shall keep with some friend for I do not believe in travelling for any length of time with mere travelling acquaintances, do you?" Despite her promise and feigned reluctance, however, Eugenie defended spending several nights alone in Switzerland. Her parents' unrelenting opposition prompted her to write her mother: "I do not know what you & father will say when you know what I have done, but it seemed so foolish to return to Paris & not by the Rhine & see the places I have seen & intend to see, that notwithstanding father's injunction a few months ago & that my conscious [sic] kept saying 'honor thy father & thy mother' I have used my own judgment & other's advice, & have undertaken to travel four or five days alone." Eugenie insisted she was "not in the least forlorn," but also admitted she would appreciate a companion. Once back with relatives in Paris, she claimed second thoughts, writing home, "I must confess to not being very fond of traveling alone though I am glad to have seen all that I have seen. But there is a point at which independence and having one's own way completely, ceases to be in itself a pleasure."[91]

Older women had less concern about their reputation and were not stymied by the dictates of parents, but they too could find solitary travel stressful. Laura Beecher Comer, granddaughter of prominent minister Lyman Beecher and niece of Harriet Beecher Stowe, had already traveled far from her New England roots when she married a Georgia cotton planter. In 1872, a widow without children, she resolved to make a Grand Tour, "the dream of my life," even though it meant traveling alone. Despite her regional apostasy, Laura was always deeply enmeshed in the religious sensibilities of her Beecher family; she opened her travel diary by writing "How wonderfully mysterious are God's dealings with us, his frail, finite beings!" Her own frailty, however, left her "completely exhausted—from fatigue of mind and body" so she spent hours alone in her London hotel reading her Bible, "my constant friend." She was rejuvenated by a trip to Windsor Castle where the attention of strangers reminded her "how precious to me is kindness!" The experience also left her questioning "why am I left, as it were, to encase myself in steel and fight the stern battles of life alone." Days in Paris offended her Puritan sensibilities and left her convinced "I shall rejoice when out of the city." In Geneva she realized anew "how delightful is social intercourse when one feels safe with friends—and not in fear of traitors." Traveling with friends, however, proved as stressful as traveling alone or facing traitors. Even in the midst of Alpine beauty Laura strained "to enjoy all I could as I went along not withstanding the discontent of others!" Cologne's cathedral inspired her to "bless the Lord that I have been permitted to see this day," but it may have been her only happy day in Germany. In Italy she planned to visit Naples and the ruins of Herculaneum and Pompeii and then "turn our face homeward," but the chance to join friends going to London proved more enticing than ancient sites. In route to England she poured into her diary her anguished realization that "being alone—a stranger[—]is bad enough for a man but for a woman it is terrible!—terrible!" After five months she ended her Grand Tour and returned to Georgia where "my heart is full to overflowing."[92]

Elizabeth Porter Gould, traveling two decades after Laura, never found being alone terrible at all. She joined an organized tour for three months, but favored sights were not included so she "started alone, at 9:50 a.m. from the Great Western Railroad Paddington in London (with only a handbag) for my trip through England and Scotland." Once in Oxford she looked back with pleasure that, "my first day alone had revealed much for which I was profoundly grateful." A trip to Kenilworth prompted some regret "that no one could share the pleasure with me," and a "longing at times for the soul to which I could say Oh Oh," yet she also realized "I was much happier being alone than with a petty being whose words of no real meaning flowed from an unappreciative nature." In the Lake District she was delighted to discover she shared her train compartment with the author of the guidebook she was consulting and together they enjoyed "the perfect September afternoon." On subsequent outings she met a woman who "proved to be most enjoyable" and "a genuine young woman I enjoyed very much." Elizabeth usually sought out well-educated and well-traveled com-

Jennie McGraw around the time of her second trip to Europe.
Cornell University

panions although in Glasgow she traveled third class "in order to see the people." Back in London she congratulated herself on becoming "a wiser, more self contained woman" who had "met with no accident, no delay, no frustration of plans by sickness, and no discourtesy." Elizabeth acknowledged her preference for traveling with a companion, but was also sure that "if I am denied the congenial other half which make travel ideal, this way of going was the next best thing."[93]

Most women determined it the next best thing only if traveling alone was necessary to see favored sites. There were some, however, who embraced solo travel as an escape from problems in their life. Jennie McGraw, the only child of a wealthy New York lumberman and benefactor of Cornell University, is one example. Jennie, born in 1840, was educated at the Pelham School in New Rochelle where she studied "history, physical geography, grammar, entomology, Latin, moral sciences, arithmetic, French composition, music and singing."[94] After completing her formal education, Jennie's life centered on serving as her father's companion. His death in 1877 left her wealthy but also bereft and feeling she no longer had a purpose in life. In the next few years, she made two trips to Europe, hoping that there she could re-discover life's meaning. She persisted in spending many months abroad despite the adamant opposition of two men at home who claimed themselves her paternal protectors. Her trip to Norway with a friend offered adventure and the security of companionship, but once it was over she was again alone and lonely. Jennie finally settled on "a sort of exile" with a French family because, despite her dread of being without an English-speaking friend, it was "the only way to accustom myself to speaking French." Although at times feeling "I shall die of the blues," she saw "no other way of conquering the tongue and my own foolish fright." Jennie traveled throughout France and to Italy, always in defiance of orders that she return home. She complained that her lawyer and would-be protector had "no faith in me & [I] worry you." In response to his demands that she come home, she questioned, "what do I go to? Where should I go?" Europe remained a refuge as she feared she had "no home[,] nothing but a few friends who would be glad to see me for a little time perhaps." As Jennie approached her fortieth birthday, she had to confront the reality that the ill health that had plagued her was ending her life. She abruptly married an acquaintance from Cornell who was also in Europe and returned with him to New York where a year later she died of tuberculosis.[95]

Europe also offered June Spencer a temporary escape, but in her case it was from the dictates of a domineering parent and for a measure of freedom before the restrictions her pending marriage would inevitably entail. Following the death of her husband when June was two, Cornelia Spencer provided for her only child by writing. When June completed her education, her mother mandated that she teach in Raleigh's Peace Academy near their Chapel Hill home until she married Lee Love. After a year of teaching, June successfully lobbied for a summer studying watercolor in England. Initially she was so overwhelmed by homesickness that she despaired that if given a second chance "wild horses could not drag me" to Europe. Her regret, however, proved ephemeral. After a week in England she abruptly left for Germany only informing her mother once there of her decision to remain in Europe, assuring her that "no doubt things will arrange themselves." Her mother's angry demand that she return home left June battling between contrition and defiance. She insisted "I am doing what I think is best as far as I can see," but also acknowledged "when I think of my having the <u>courage</u> to come to Europe <u>alone</u> I can scarcely believe it possible." Her mother's trans-Atlantic manipulation did successfully elicit June's promise to "never leave you for any such trip again," as "I wish I never had to be alone again as long as I live." Yet she refused to come home, insisting that "a special decree of Providence" had made her trip possible. Ill health reignited conflicting emotions. In a final letter, still insisting "I don't regret the trip to Europe," she also admitted that "nobody need tell me … that a lady can come to <u>Europe alone</u> & live & take <u>lessons cheaply</u>. She must have a companion who expects to do the same at least."

June Spencer published less-personal accounts of her trip in *The Presbyterian*, a paid series that Cornelia had arranged. She assured its readers, which, of course, included her mother, "the more I learn over there, the more I see and enjoy, the more eager become my wishes for others, for friends at home, to have the same enjoyments and advantages." She also expressed hope that "everybody will agree with me that I had a good time in Europe and have every reason to be thankful for my experience of foreign travel." [96]

June's defiance of domesticity and dependency was short lived. She returned to the United States, married and raised two children with the help of her live-in mother. The solitude of self she embraced for several months, albeit not always easily, continued to elude her and most women most of the time. In her fight for women's right to define themselves and to develop confidence in their own power, Elizabeth Cady Stanton surely knew that what she wanted for the female half of the population could evolve only slowly. Small incremental steps were taken in Europe. The idea that women needed to be accompanied by men to see the sights became inconvenient and even absurd. Women developed pride and pleasure in going about alone. On the dawn of the twentieth century so many women were finding Europe a springboard to independence that one could plausibly identify a "great army of globe trotting American girls who 'go it alone'." [97]

VII

How I Wish I Was Safely Out of This: The Titanic, the Great War and a New Grand Tour

As they anticipated the new century, members of Chicago's Hyde Park Travel Club organized a series of classes to help prepare for "the cosmopolitan era which 1900 would usher in." They joined a chorus of optimism heard throughout Europe and the United States because, as historian Geoffrey Blainey explains, "more was expected of the century than any other."[1] Henry Adams described the Paris Exposition of 1900, attended by thousands of Americans, as showcasing the transition from the old world represented by the Virgin to the modern world represented by the dynamo.[2] As if on cue, Queen Victoria, a woman of "uneventful stability," died the following year and her son Edward, a more modern royal who forsook his mother's "fusty heritage" for a life of fun, became King Edward VII.[3] The change of centuries did seem to indicate something new, something modern, was astir. World War I is often claimed as the swansong of the long-nineteenth century. But modernity, Philipp Blom persuasively argues, ushered in the new century; it "did not rise virgin-born from the trenches of the Somme."[4]

By 1900, Blom continues, Europeans (and, of course, Americans as well) had already experienced rapid change "and the most profound change of all is that in the relationship between men and women." Growth of industrialized society and shifting attitudes between the sexes, and about sex, "came by stealth ... no one great battle was fought over it ... ideals and expectations about men and women lost their anchorage and were cast adrift."[5] Yet if there was no one great battle there were many small ones; ideals and ideas about men and women were cast adrift only after intense struggle and constant backlash.

One of these small battles erupted in the spring of 1912 following the *Titanic* disaster. When Margaret Curtis, a frequent traveler to Europe, heard of the "awfully [sic] accident to the Titanic," she joined millions pondering how "such a thing should happen now-a-days."[6] The loss of more than fifteen hundred lives on a ship thought unsinkable and a marvel of the industrial age galvanized public attention for weeks. One *Titanic* chronicler claims that no single event in the twentieth century had "the breadth of its shock or the depth of its pathos."[7]

As lists of survivors and casualties revealed that most of the women and children in first and second class had survived while a majority of the men died, the pathos only deepened. Although not quite half of the women and children in steerage survived, their survival rate was also much higher than it was for men. It seemed that the law of the sea—"women and children first"—had prevailed.[8]

The perceived heroism of male passengers on the *Titanic* seemed to offer a shocked nation at least something positive to hold on to. It was especially reassuring to those anxious about an increasingly successful challenge to traditional ideals of womanhood that inevitably carried with it a challenge to ideals of heroic manhood as well. In the minds of conservatives, this example of men protecting women at the expense of their own lives was convincing evidence that traditional gender relations were natural and immutable after all. Women, so this argument ran, should demand not the equality of suffrage but the inequality of protection. A New Orleans paper proclaimed the *Titanic's* story made it clear "that man is eternally the protector of woman" and "woman accepts man's protection and obeys man instinctively." It was, accordingly, folly to believe in women's equality.[9]

In the first traumatic days after the disaster, women also pondered its lessons and some of them found great solace in stories of male sacrifice. All across the country, women contributed money for a statue "to the brave men of the *Titanic*" which one editorial praised as a gesture acknowledging "their womanhood [was] safe within the chivalry of men."[10] Several weeks after the *Titanic* sank, only half the number anticipated attended a long-planned suffrage parade in New York City, which, one woman articulated, now seemed "untimely and pathetically unwise."[11]

But some pointed to the heroic actions of the ship's female passengers, notably the unsinkable Molly Brown, and challenged this backlash; their interpretation of the tragedy accommodated the empowerment of women. Harriet Curtis, who, like her sister Margaret, had crossed the Atlantic several times, was at home when she learned of the *Titanic*'s fate. She found hope in "stories [that] are so magnificent and thrilling and inspiring" and enthused that "everyone is so proud of every one of the men from the band still playing *Nearer My God To Thee* to the millionaires tucking in the women in the boats." But Harriet's praise did not stop with wealthy and heroic men; she also acknowledged women for their "calm nerve and courage even when they saw the monster ship sink into the sea with all her lights still burning" including one who stayed with her husband, another who refused to overload a lifeboat, "her last chance," and others who "did finely rowing the boats from between 1 and 2 till 4:30 and later." "Truly," she proclaimed, "the world is better for being so stirred in learning of such heroism." [12]

Harriet easily embraced a concept of heroic women. Publicity about women such as Molly Brown reinforced the concept of a New Woman at the same time the celebration of men sacrificing their lives was used to resuscitate the ideal of female fragility. The ideal of a woman who was dependent on a man and who would obey him instinctively competed with the ideal of a woman who was well educated and sought control over at least some aspects of her personal and professional life. The New Woman, historian Nancy Cott explains, "stood for self-development as contrasted to self-sacrifice or submergence in the family."[13]

In just two years the tragedy of the *Titanic* would be overwhelmed by a far greater cataclysm that brought an end to the Golden Age of the Grand Tour. In the fall of 1911, a prescient Englishman sharing Hannah Gould's Atlantic voyage made the ominous prediction that Germany would soon declare war on Great Britain, that France and Russia would ally with the British, that Austria would support Germany and the resulting conflagration would eventually engulf the Unites States.[14] Hannah was more incredulous than convinced, but in the coming months Germany's resurgent economic and military power fueled growing concern that a major war might loom. In 1913 Elizabeth Gould, peering past

Germany's beer halls and romantic rivers and glimpsing its future potential, wrote from Munich that seeing Germany first hand also left her "feeling very shaky about free trade and having to compete with a nation like this—and a war! Impossible—I believe they'd beat any nation." [15]

There were early warnings, understood largely in hindsight, of Germany's ambition and potential power. Victory over France in 1870 assured its place as continental Europe's dominant country although an alliance between France and Russia, its western and eastern neighbors, maintained a tenuous balance of power that held into the twentieth century. The rise of nationalism, militarism and imperialism, the alliances that bound and divided European countries and conflicts in the Balkans and Morocco, were harbingers of war that most tourists hardly suspected.

In June 1914, a Serbian revolutionary, resolved to end Austrian control over the southern Slavs, assassinated Franz Ferdinand, heir to the throne of the Austria-Hungarian Empire. Americans continued coming to Europe, undeterred by what most thought was no more than business-as-usual in the Balkans. To the contrary, as news from Serbia rippled through Europe, entangling alliances transformed a local incident into a war almost identical to the one Hannah heard predicted. Germany supported Austria's effort to hold Serbia accountable for the assassination; Russia supported its fellow Slavs; France respected its alliance with Russia and Great Britain did likewise with France. On July 28th this house of cards collapsed and the Great War began. The lure of Austrian land persuaded Italy to abandon its allegiance to the Central Powers and join Britain and France. President Woodrow Wilson declared neutrality and for nearly three years the United States watched from the sidelines until German submarine warfare, especially the sinking of the British passenger liner *Lusitania*, resulting in more than a thousand deaths, including 128 Americans (out of 189 on board), prompted a declaration of war against the German coalition.[16] Over the next eighteen months, over two million American servicemen, dubbed doughboys, replaced tourists crossing the Atlantic. They offered Great Britain and France the fresh resources that enabled their long-elusive victory.

The day the war broke out Sarah Bolton noted in her diary,

"Mary Rice was to sail today to Europe, but this terrible war will prevent."[17] Mary joined thousands of Americans prevented from traveling to Europe for four years as the Western Front, a narrow swath of land in Belgium and France, became the scene of senseless slaughter. Approximately 120,000 Americans were in Europe in the summer of 1914.[18] One of them, Hatta Carolan, cabled her husband from Paris that she was "comfortable *et bien*," prompting his insistence that "you must come home as soon as you can." Assured she was safe, he acknowledged "you know better than we do the conditions there," but he still worried "about German dirigibles and a possible siege later on." [19]

Alma Peterson was visiting German relatives that summer. The day war was declared she assured her mother there was no danger. A few days later she added the more somber postscript that "everything is war here. It's the first thing we hear in the morning and certainly the last thing at night." For a few days Alma found the news intriguing, but by mid-August she was "most uncomfortable." As German soldiers marched across borders into countries initially thought safe, American tourists scrambled to leave the continent as quickly as possible. On August 24 Alma's family boarded a special train to Holland where they crowded onto an American ship filled with three times the usual number of first- and second-class passengers. Alma was relieved yet sorry to leave Germany, "a lovely country" with people "so heroic."[20]

She was among thousands of Americans who overnight had to grapple with the reality that they were now no longer tourists but refugees. One U.S. senator ordered the American ambassador in London to send his wife and daughter home on the first ship out, but even relatives of the wealthy and well connected could face an ordeal. Nancy Johnson, daughter of an influential congressman, fled from Switzerland to Venice and then to Genoa where she boarded a ship for home. Officials eager to please her father and aware she carried a letter of introduction from President Wilson made sure she was as comfortable as possible. Despite her privileged status, at times Nancy found herself in makeshift quarters, short of money and anxious about her future. She observed fellow Americans "walking about in Genoa's streets in a daze, without any place to sleep," some begging for money. Although shocked by the plight of others, when at last booked on the first ship out of Genoa, Nancy demanded first-class accommodation with space for all twenty-six pieces of her luggage.[21]

Many stranded Americans, including a number of schoolteachers enjoying inexpensive summer tours, faced the more mundane problems of securing food and shelter rather than where to put a mountain of luggage. Hotel owners accommodated wealthier patrons, but forced out those unable to pay. Many of the destitute found it impossible to get additional funds as the doors of banks and Cook's offices were closed indefinitely. Americans like those Nancy described were reduced to begging until funds sent from the United States finally stabilized the situation. By the end of September, almost all Americans who wanted to leave Europe had done so.[22]

Sisters Mary and Harriet Colles arrived in Brussels just two days before Germany invaded Belgium, which German strategy held was the best route into France. Once aware they were in a war zone, Mary and Harriet consulted the American embassy, which advised them to wait until things quieted down before attempting to leave; as a result of this questionable advice, they were still there when German soldiers entered the city. Within days American officials reversed their policy and issued a warning to the two women to evacuate immediately, frustrating advice since there were no longer any trains out. They had no choice but to remain. Mary poured anxiety into her diary as she pondered how they would ever reach home "for of course my return on the Hamburg American Line is no longer possible and our Express Checks are of no value. Nowhere are they accepted. What a situation of affairs!" The sisters watched German soldiers "coming into Brussels in legions!" and found "wherever we go we encounter them, men, horses and guns like an endless chain." Harriet returned to the American embassy to report her concern that their hotel would soon be taken over by German soldiers so "two lone ladies could not sojourn there under the circumstances." Although dubious about assurance that they were safe, Mary tried to convince herself that "here we are and here we must remain." The sisters waited days without news, prompting despair that "we might as well be living on another planet" since those at home knew more of what was going on in Brussels than they did. Mary even began to feel "not I but some character in a story or play" and as "living history indeed in this short space of time." The novelty of her situation, however, paled before her longing: "how I wish I were safely out of this!"

An Englishman finally made that wish a reality by agreeing the sisters could join the group he was evacuating if they took charge of a child in his custody. The Colles sisters left Brussels over a month after their ordeal began, very relieved to be on their way home and relieved as well that they could keep all of their luggage. The American embassy paid one hundred francs toward their hotel charge and they promised to pay the rest after the war. Once safely outside the city, Mary likened herself to "a prisoner released from captivity." They joined a group of twenty eight, including four performers known as the Tommy Texas Dancers and three other Americans, a group Mary thought "ill assorted" but "bound in good fellowship by a common danger and necessity." In time she pondered that "if one searched the world over they could not have brought together a more mixed set of people of every sort and variety! I laugh now when I think of the little Belgian Nun sitting in a cart with the Tommy Texas crowd!" An American flag attached to their wagon offered at least the illusion that they were "under the protection of the Stars and Stripes." The first night out of Brussels, a Belgian woman offered beds and served them bread and beer. The next day, carrying luggage that included "H's hat-box containing the apples of her eye, namely her two hats from Paris" which she guarded "as a hen her chicks," they took a second train to Ostend where they found a comfortable hotel. Their ordeal behind them, Mary and Harriet crossed the Channel to England and boarded a ship for home.[23]

Ruth Pike's party had just arrived in Interlaken when the war broke out. There they discovered that all banks including Cook's were closed, making it impossible to cash their American checks. The group went sightseeing for a few days, but transportation was difficult and food grew scarce in their hotel. On August 3 they traveled to Lucerne where they found that even in neutral Switzerland the train station and streets were filled with soldiers. "We are hemmed in by hostile countries," Ruth anguished, so "can not go to Germany, France or Italy." Her fears were assuaged somewhat by Swiss assurance that Americans would be allowed to remain in the country as long as necessary and that everything possible would be done to make them comfortable. The stranded Americans held meetings to consider their options and even arranged a patriotic concert in hopes that singing *Marching Through Georgia, Dixie, Columbia* and *The Star-Spangled Banner* would be reassuring; Ruth reported "we all had a thrill." As days passed with no clear plan to get them out of war-torn Europe, however, thrilling music gave way to "all getting restless." After nearly three weeks of anxious waiting, they were taken to Lausanne. Less fortunate than Nancy Johnson or the Colles sisters, they had to leave some of their luggage behind. The group crossed into France where, "after much bother," they obtained enough French francs to pay for a hotel room in Pontarlier. The next day Ruth's party "stood in a kind of stock yard like cattle" for nearly three hours waiting for a train. After changing trains in Dijon, Ruth found herself in a third-class car beside a man with what she feared was a bed bug walking on his coat, leaving her "on the jump every minute." Two men sitting by the window had "quite an odor to them," compelling one of her female companions to stand in the hall. They found a hotel room in Paris which Ruth described as dirty "but better than nothing." Following a day of sightseeing—for Ruth the highlight was Auguste Rodin's *The Thinker* which had been placed in front of the Pantheon eight years earlier—they traveled to Havre. After more long lines waiting to board, the beleaguered Americans enjoyed an easy trip to London; four days later they boarded the *Alannia*, its smokestacks painted gray to render it inconspicuous, and started the voyage across the Atlantic to home. The passengers initially enjoyed a respite from the war, but soon learned they had not left it entirely behind. Two German stowaways caught trying to send messages to their homeland were held captive for the remainder of the voyage. Once safely back in Boston, Ruth wrote of her ordeal: "Thus ended a summer I can never forget and [I] only hope another trip to Europe may be in store for me."[24]

If Ruth Pike was fortunate enough to revisit Europe, she found it looking much as she remembered; widespread physical destruction awaited the sophisticated aviation of Europe's next war. But behind the façade of buildings still standing, post-World War I Europe had changed profoundly—the enormous loss of a generation of men, the collapse of three great empires in central Europe, the rise of communism, the resentment of Germany and the resentment of Germans, the assault on aristocracy throughout the Continent—these changes were not immediately visible to Grand Tourists who continued to seek an iconic Europe. Tourists could not, however, avoid entirely confronting the misery caused by runaway inflation and food shortages or ignore the human cost of war as they shared the streets, buses and metros in Europe's cities with scores of maimed veterans.[25]

It took several years for the number of American tourists to return to pre-war levels. Even after the guns were silent, the disruption of ocean traffic and concern about the war's impact on infrastructure inhibited the immediate revitalization of Europe's tourist industry. But inexpensive tours became increasingly common in the 1920s and travel became more accessible for the middle class. In the decade called the Roaring Twenties, another new woman, this one dubbed a Flapper, emerged; she wore short dresses, bobbed her hair, smoked cigarettes and embraced a culture of fun. Harvey Levenstein explains that for post-war travelers, men and women alike, "cultural pursuits declined" and "sensual ones rose." *Paris Is a Woman's Town*, a guide written by two women in 1929, assured Flappers traveling abroad that they could go anywhere alone, offered advice about hiring gigolos for an evening at a dance hall and claimed "nobody but a minister's wife" would want to miss the Folies Bergere. They assumed women would drink in bars and cafes so instead of warning about the perils of Europe's bad habit, offered advice about selecting wine.[26] Male and female college students, the advance guard of study-abroad programs, began flooding Europe in the summer months. Germany, widely blamed for the cataclysmic war, was less likely to be described as carefree and less often visited but, for the most part, the core of the old Grand Tour remained intact. London, Paris, Rome were still the dreams of many American women.

In the Freudian post-war years, self-discovery through heritage joined searching for a common culture or seeking a sensual experience as a motivation to travel. Although Henrietta Szold's Grand Tour was in 1909, she exemplifies the post-World War I generation seeking personal identity through travel. She was Jewish and accordingly also exemplary of a travel experience that was becoming increasingly more inclusive. Henrietta's travels with her Austrian-born mother inspired appreciation on four levels. The two started in England where Henrietta discovered "my Anglo-Saxon education, my English language, my literary associations" which enhanced understanding of her own country. The second "family part" was in Vienna, where both of her parents had grown to adulthood and where she watched her mother discover memories of her youth; Henrietta realized that this was her mother's home "as England was home for me." She predicted before reaching Palestine, the third leg of their trip, that as Jewish women, there they would discover "the home of our race." Henrietta's trip ended in Italy where she was amazed at "how bewildered I am by all the wonders of European civilization;" a month of all things Italian left her feeling "as though I had been dwelling in wonderland." England, Austria and Italy all offered this Jewish-American woman lessons, but she correctly predicted that Palestine would affect her the most. She confided in Jewish friends from Rome that, for all its wonder, it was "their Eternal City, not yours and not mine." [27]

Henrietta was in the advance guard of a post-war demand that teaching about the wonders of civilization become more inclusive than traditional education had allowed. But there was a backlash opposed to inclusiveness as well. The rise of communism, the widespread unease that the war fought to make the world safe for democracy was being lost, spawned an upsurge of nativism, a Red Scare, in the United States. In 1921 and again in 1924 Congress passed legislation that sharply limited immigration, especially from countries outside of Western Europe. Ironically, restricting the number of people who could immigrate to the United States was a boon for Americans traveling abroad. Shipping lines tried to replace their steerage business by enticing tourists willing to travel in what was now called third class. One company lured hesitant passengers to travel by assuring them it was a space for "Students-Teachers-Tourists-Artists" and that "no others need apply."[28] The strategy did increase the number and range of tourists; they came for the culture sought by previous generations, but Jewish, Irish, Greek, Italian—a variety of hyphenated Americans—followed Henrietta in seeking their own roots as well.

Women who made a Grand Tour at least temporarily stepped outside their sphere of domestic gentility. Many of them left families, including husbands and young children, for months or years to embrace this experience. Even those who traveled with family members put aside the self-sacrifice that responsibilities at home demanded to undertake a journey of self-improvement that for a time and even for a lifetime, eroded the narrow circle.

In the 1840s Bessie Lacey could only read about faraway lands and wish she were a man, free to travel to places known from books. Clara Mitchell did travel to Europe nearly half a century later, but she also wished to be a man with the freedom to do as she wished. The process of first imagining and then experiencing travel, however, steadily pushed women from the narrow circle that Tocqueville described; travel became a prerogative of their own sex as well and every journey eroded that circle.

Leo Hamilton, editor of a volume of women's travel writing, posits that what they wrote abroad reveals "a freedom of action and thought unthinkable at home."[29] Of course, even while traveling there were limits to women's freedom of thought and action. As Monica Anderson points out in her book on the politics of travel, travel demanded a "balancing act between propriety and personal autonomy."[30] Each woman sought and found her own balance, but all were changed, some profoundly, others in more subtle ways. Probably most women boarded their ships with socially proscribed views about proper female behavior intact. The reality of their experience abroad, however, forced alterations, great and small, in their behavior and judgment. Bostonian Louise Jewett reveals one woman's changed perception. She refused her family's offer to come to New York to meet her ship, reasoning "a woman who could travel from Florence to Antwerp alone ought to get from New York to Boston without serious difficulty." It is one example, not of profound change, but a more nuanced feeling of self-assurance. This was the legacy of a Grand Tour.[31]

Epilogue

Laying Up Stores of Knowledge and Experience: After a Grand Tour

The nineteenth-century Grand Tour broadened the horizons of the small percentage of American women who had the means to travel. For the elite able to undertake a trip, the bonds of domesticity were loosened by each step taking them away from the domestic sphere. Most who traveled returned to familiar lives, but their studied preservation of letters and diaries written while abroad is testimony to the significance their trips held for them for the rest of their lives.

When Eliza Smith penned a memoir about her experience as one of the few women going abroad in the 1820s, she recalled that nothing "exceeded my joy at the thought of seeing the Old World;" across the decades she still embraced that joy as one of the defining moments of her life.[1] Caroline Kirkland realized her days abroad were a unique time free of the "petty cares of cooking and cleaning" allowing "more time for self-cultivation."[2] Annie Fields anticipated that her year in Europe would be "the jewel year" of her life.[3] Lucy Chase expected "the retrospect of this trip to last me for entertainment for the rest of my natural life."[4] June Spencer was convinced that she was "laying up stores of knowledge & experiences that will help to brighten my whole future life, wherever it is spent."[5] Ella Cabot described her "excitement, happiness & gratitude" for her trip and confidence that "real beauty never ends, it awakes and lives and gives us continual blessing."[6] Martha Maltby realized after returning that her travels with Clara Ritchie had inspired both with "a longing to do something worthy as well as to be better ourselves."[7] Augusta Arnold, who went to Europe several times around the turn of the century, was "sure these trips have been a good thing for me, opened new trains of thought & widened my horizons."[8] Delia Austrian predicted that in Europe she would not only gain greater knowledge but also "broader sympathy and new interests which will help me to understand myself and consequently mankind."[9] Ethel Freeman, connoisseur of all things Italian, visited Italy with her aunt in 1906; the older woman described her as "quite overcome" and found "it is impossible to put into language the growth, the awakening, the delight which she has had on this trip ... she will certainly not be content long at home after this."[10]

These women, who spoke across a century, represent thousands who understood their Grand Tour as a transformative event in their lives.

Notes

Preface: I Do Love Freedom So: Women and a Grand Tour

1   Alexis de Tocqueville, *Democracy in America* (repr. Garden City, New Jersey, 1969), 592.
2   In 1850 Caroline White, who is represented here, heard Lucy Stone speak against slavery and concluded that she was sincere, but "out of women's proper sphere." A few years later Stone countered that "too much has already been said and written about woman's sphere." In an important article on the rhetoric of women's history, Linda Kerber sides with Stone. She argues that the designation of separate spheres was, in the past, "primarily a trope" to reveal power relations and that its continued use by historians denies "the reciprocity between gender and society" and imposes "a static model on dynamic relationships." I may replicate the confusion Kerber claims sloppy use of this trope creates. As Caroline White's comment suggests, however, the designation "separate spheres" should not be dismissed from scholarship entirely since it was a term widely used in the nineteenth century. Separate ideals might be a more accurate way to grapple with mandated gender differences in the nineteenth century. The idealized male and the idealized female were profoundly different in the early nineteenth century, but those differences were under steady assault through that century and into the next. Since I study women who left their familial homes and their country (old spheres) and traveled (to new spheres) I have used the term here. Joanne Gray, "The Diaries of Caroline Barrett White," (MA Thesis, Clark University, 1990), 35-36. Linda Kerber, "Separate Spheres, Female Worlds, Woman's Place: The Rhetoric of Women's History," *The Journal of American History* (June, 1988), 9-39. Lucy Stone is quoted on page 9.

3 Clara Mitchell *Diary*, June 5, July 3, August 30, September 16, 27, 1888, Malcolm MacBeth Papers, Missouri Historical Society, St. Louis, MO (MHS). Clara never returned to Europe. She married two years after her trip and had three children when at the age of thirty-five she died in childbirth along with one of her newborn twins. Traveling was spelled with double l's in the nineteenth century so that spelling is retained and *sic* is not used.
4 The War of 1812 ended in December 1814 with the Treaty of Ghent, although fighting, notably the Battle of New Orleans, continued in early 1815. The Napoleonic Wars in Europe ended in June 1815 with the capture of Napoleon at Waterloo. Although 1815 might be the more appropriate beginning date, Maria Bayard's 1814 trip justifies the more felicitous "1814 to 1914."
5 The women studied here rarely used the term Grand Tour. I use it figuratively as a traditional designation.
6 Harvey Levenstein, *Seductive Journey: American Tourists in France from Jefferson to the Jazz Age* (Chicago: The University of Chicago Press, 1998), 107.
7 Blanche McManus, *The American Woman Abroad* (New York: Dodd, Mead and Co., 1911), 135.
8 Richard Bushman, *Refinement in America: Persons, Houses, Cities* (New York: Knopf, 1992), 440.
9 A statistical study of Americans going to Europe suggests women did not reach parity with men until after World War II. The authors counted people reentering the United States, whatever their reason for traveling. Most who traveled for purposes other than tourism such as business and education were male; if included, they inflate the number of male tourists. Furthermore, it is not certain whom government officials counted; it is quite possible that wives and children were not, thus deflating the number of females. There is considerable anecdotal evidence found in diaries and letters, passenger lists and other scattered comments that in the last decades of the nineteenth and the early-twentieth centuries, the majority of tourists were women. This statistical study claims that before the Civil War "only wives of a few wealthy men went abroad." There are thirty-three women in my study who traveled before 1860 and only approximately thirty percent of them traveled with her husband. This is evidence that this study did not use manuscripts to reach its conclusions. See Brandon Dupont, Alka Gandhi and Thomas J. Weiss, "The American Invasion of Europe: The Long Term Rise in Overseas Travel, 1820-2000," *National Bureau of Economic Research Working Paper*," (September, 2008), 10.

10 Mary Pike Conant, *A Girl of the Eighties at College and at Home* (Boston: Houghton Mifflin, 1931), 6.
11 Carol Berkin, *Wondrous Beauty: Betsy Bonaparte, the Belle of Baltimore who Married Napoleon's Brother* (New York: Vintage Books, 2014).
12 Cindy Aron's history of vacations in the nineteenth and early-twentieth centuries, for example, excludes Europe, claiming "only very wealthy individuals could have afforded European travel during this period." Cindy Aron, *Working at Play: A History of Vacations in the United States* (New York: Oxford University Press, 1999), 10.
13 There is information available for African-American women traveling in Europe in Dorothy Sterling, (ed.) *We Are Your Sisters: Black Women in the Nineteenth Century* (New York: Norton, 1984). Most went for formal education or professional opportunity so are not included here.
14 I was unaware that Helen Gould was Jay Gould's daughter until I had read her diaries. Her experiences were not especially different from travelers of more modest means although she offered occasional hints that her family was unusually wealthy. For example, they enjoyed a formal dinner with fine china and crystal while traveling by train in England and stayed in rooms in Paris that the Prince of Wales had recently occupied. Helen Gould *Diary*, 8, 20, Gould Family Papers, New York Historical Society, New York, NY (NYHS).
15 Matthew Sturgis, *When in Rome: 2000 Years of Roman Sightseeing* (Frances Lincoln Limited, 2011), 228-233.
16 John Sears, *Sacred Places: American Tourist Attractions in the Nineteenth Century* (Amherst: University of Massachusetts Press, 1999), 8.
17 Anonymous Diary (1843), Coles-Lippincott-Horstmann Collection, Historical Society of Pennsylvania, Philadelphia, PA (HSP).
18 Foster Rhea Dulles, *Americans Abroad: Two Centuries of European Travel* (Ann Arbor: University of Michigan Press, 1964). Dulles is an example of authors who included some individual women, but had little to say about travel as a female experience. Harvey Levenstein's study of Americans in France skillfully weaves a narrative that includes male and female experience and is a model for gender-inclusive studies.
19 Mary Suzanne Schriber, *Telling Travels: Selected Writings by Nineteenth-Century American Women Abroad* (DeKalb: Northern Illinois University Press, 1995), xvi.
20 Dulles, *Americans Abroad*, 3.
21 Ellen Walworth, *An Old World Seen Through Young Eyes: Travels Around the World* (New York: D&J Sadler, 1877), 2.
22 Elizabeth Nichols to Rose, August 13, 1896, Nichols Family Papers, Schlesinger Library, Harvard University, Cambridge, MA (HSL).

23 Frances Stevens to Alf, n.d., 1868, Gallatin Papers, NYHS.
24 Ann Marie Green *Diary*, 1, Ann Marie Green Papers, Western Reserve Historical Society, Cleveland, OH (WRHS).

Chapter I: A Trip to Europe Became the Great Desire of My Heart: Imagining a Grand Tour

1   Quoted in Steven Stowe, *Intimacy and Power in the Old South: Ritual in the Lives of the Planters* (Baltimore: Johns Hopkins University Press, 1987), 202, 208.
2   C.W.S. to Mrs. Vardry McBee, October 6, 1892, McBee Papers, University of North Carolina, Chapel Hill, Chapel Hill, NC (UNC). This letter, written by a woman who signed with her initials, inspired this book. C.W.S. did not express longing to see Europe, but did speak for legions of women who yearned to travel, whether to North Carolina's mountains, Switzerland's Alps or Europe's grand cities, yet feared that such places were too far removed from the sphere assigned their sex.
3   Mary Kelley, *Learning to Stand and Speak: Women, Education, and Public Life in America's Republic* (Chapel Hill: University of North Carolina Press, 2006), 67.
4   *Ibid.*, *Private Woman, Public Stage: Literary Domesticity in Nineteenth-Century America* (New York: Oxford University Press, 1984), 60.
5   *Ibid.*, *Learning to Stand and Speak*, 78.
6   *Ibid.*, 75.
7   *Ibid.*, 86.
8   *Troy Female Seminary Catalog* (1850), 20. Gutman Library, Harvard University (HGL).
9   Christie Anne Farnham, *The Education of the Southern Belle* (New York: New York University Press, 1994), 31-32.
10 Stowe, *Intimacy and Power*, 194.
11 Kelley, *Learning to Stand and Speak*, 92.
12 Joan D. Hedrick, *Harriet Beecher Stowe: A Life* (New York: Oxford University Press, 1994), 36.
13 Margaret Harding *Diary*, January 5, 6, 7, 10, 12, 16, 19, 24, March 31, April 1, 12, June 3, September 16, 20, November 3, 11, 29, 1881, Margaret Harding Tileston Edsall Diaries, HSL.
14 *Charleston Female Seminary Circular* (1870), South Carolina Historical Society, Charleston, SC (SCHS).
15 William H. Pease and Jane H. Pease (eds.), *The Roman Years of a South Carolina Artist: Caroline Carson's Letters Home, 1872-1892* (Columbia:

University of South Carolina Press, 2003), xxii-xxvii. Caroline became so enamored of things Italian that after her husband's death in the 1870s she moved to Italy.

16 C. Vann Woodward and Elisabeth Muhlenfeld (eds.), *The Private Mary Chesnut: The Unpublished Civil War Diaries* (New York: Oxford University Press, 1984), xix.
17 Elizabeth White Nims Rankin is my great-grandmother. Many of her books are now in my possession.
18 Anne Sinkler Whaley LeClerq (ed.), *Elizabeth Sinkler Coxe's Tales from the Grand Tour, 1890-1910* (Columbia: University of South Carolina Press, 2006), 2, 6.
19 Farnham, *The Education of the Southern Belle*, 132.
20 Nancy F. Cott, (ed.), *No Small Courage: A History of Women in the United States* (New York: Oxford University Press, 2000), 195.
21 Barbara Sicherman, "Sense and Sensibility: A Case Study of Women's Reading in Late-Victorian America," in Cathy N. Davidson (ed.), *Reading in America* (Baltimore: Johns Hopkins Press, 1989), 202.
22 Quoted in L.H. Signourney, *Letters of Life* (New York: D. Appelton and Co., 1866), 140.
23 R.W. Franklin (ed.), *The Poems of Emily Dickinson* (Cambridge: Harvard University Press, 1999),1286.
24 Sicherman, "Sense and Sensibility," 207-208.
25 Joseph Jay Deiss, *The Roman Years of Margaret Fuller* (New York: Thomas Crowell Company, 1969), 10-12.
26 Helen R. Deese (ed.), *Daughter of Boston: The Extraordinary Diary of a Nineteenth-Century Woman* (Boston: Beacon Press, 2005), 139.
27 Margaret Fuller Ossoli Cenotaph, Mt. Auburn Cemetery, Boston MA.
28 Megan Marshall, *The Peabody Sisters: Three Women Who Ignited American Romanticism* (Boston: Houghton Mifflin, 2005), 79, 83, 104, 125, 162-63, 183.
29 *Ibid.*, 147.
30 *Ibid.*, 265.
31 *Ibid.*, 3, 18, 47.
32 *Ibid.*, 138.
33 Thomas Wentworth Higginson, "Books and Reading" in *The Woman's Book* (New York: Charles Scribner's Sons, 1894), 361, 359.
34 Robert A. Leath and Maurie D. McInnis, "To Blend Pleasure with Knowledge: The Cultural Odyssey of Charlestonians Abroad," in Maurie D. McInnis (ed.), *In Pursuit of Refinement: Charlestonians Abroad, 1740-1860* (Columbia: University of South Carolina Press, 1999), 10.
35 Quoted in Wendell Garrett, "Introduction," *Ibid.*, 6.
36 Kelley, *Learning to Stand and Speak*, 15, 275.

37 Conant, *A Girl of the Eighties*, 37.
38 Farnham, *The Education of the Southern Belle*, 132.
39 Katherine Sally (ed.), *Life at Saint Mary's* (Chapel Hill: University of North Carolina Press, 1942), 15.
40 Farnham, *The Education of the Southern Belle*, 132-133.
41 Woodward and Muhlenfeld (eds.), *The Private Mary Chesnut*, xix.
42 Andrea Moore Kerr, *Lucy Stone: Speaking Out for Equality* (New Brunswick: Rutgers University Press, 1995), 17.
43 Sally (ed.), *Life at Saint Mary's*, xlix.
44 Marshall, *The Peabody Sisters*, 115.
45 Avriel Goldberger (ed.), *Corinne, Or Italy* (repr. New Brunswick: Rutgers University Press, 1987), xlix.
46 Marshall, *The Peabody Sisters*, 280.
47 Laura Johnson to Anne, March 23, 1870, Laura Winthrop Johnson Papers, New York Public Library, New York, NY (NYPL).
48 Frances B. Cogan, *All-American Girl: The Ideal of Real Womanhood in Mid-Nineteenth-Century America* (Athens: The University of Georgia Press, 1989), 76-77.
49 Schriber, *Telling Travels*, xxiv. Nineteen percent of the books men checked out were travel narratives.
50 Kelley, *Learning to Stand and Speak*, 178.
51 Katherine Johnson, "Record of Books Read, September 1868 to September 1871," Katherine Johnson Papers, NYHS.
52 Deese, *Daughter of Boston*, 4, 358.
53 Constance Harrison to Burton, May 8, 1891, Burton Harrison Papers, Library of Congress, Washington DC (LOC).
54 These paintings hung in my family's home.
55 Joseph Horowitz, *Wagner Nights: An American History* (Berkeley: University of California Press, 1994), 2.
56 Linda K. Kerber, "Why Should Girls Be Learn'd and Wise?: Two Centuries of Higher Education for Women as Seen Through the Unfinished Work of Alice Mary Baldwin," in John Mack Faragher and Florence Howe (eds.), *Women and Higher Education in American History* (New York: W.W. Norton and Company, 1988), 35.
57 Elisabeth Griffith, *In Her Own Right: The Life of Elizabeth Cady Stanton* (New York: Oxford University Press, 1984), 17.
58 Deese, *Daughter of Boston*, 11.
59 Wesleyan College in Macon, Georgia, and Mount Holyoke College in Mount Holyoke, Massachusetts, offered women what approximated a college curriculum earlier than Oberlin, but neither was credited as a college.
60 Susan Ware, *Modern American Women: A Documentary History* (New York: McGraw-Hill Company, 1997), 32-36.

61 *Minutes of the Hyde Park Travel Club* (1891), 48-65; (October 15, 1900), n. p., October 15, 1900, Hyde Park Travel Club Papers, Chicago History Museum, Chicago, IL (CHM).
62 Women's Rest Tour Association Papers, HSL.
63 Quoted in Levenstein, *Seductive Journeys*, 27.
64 The considerable attention very wealthy women, both fictional and real, have received has distorted the reality of the female Grand Tour. See, for example, Amanda Mackenzie Stuart, *Consuelo and Alva Vanderbilt* (London: Harper Collins, 2005).
65 Brooke Kroeger, *Nellie Bly* (New York: Random House, 1994), 9, 139-170.
66 New York *Herald,* December 18, 1865 (repr. *International Herald Tribune*), November 2, 2005.
67 Levenstein, *Seductive Journey*, 25.
68 Emma Cullum Cordozzo to Rebecca Huidekoper, February 5, 1866, in *Letters of Emma Cullum Cordozzo, 1842-1918* (Meadville, PA: E.H. Shartle, 1919), 26.
69 Guide to the Emerson-Nichols Family Papers, HSL.
70 Elizabeth Cabot *Diary*, March 21, 24, 25, 31, 1867, Elizabeth Rogers Cabot Diaries, HSL
71 Eliza Endicott to Mrs. George Peabody, October 27, 1832, Samuel and Eliza Endicott Collection, Peabody Essex Museum, Salem, MA (PEM).
72 C.M. Sedgwick *Diary*, 3, Massachusetts Historical Society, Boston, MA (MAHS).
73 Mrs. Herman J. Hall, *Two Travelers in Europe* (Springfield, MA: Hampden Publishing Co., 1898), 17.
74 Fanny W. Hall, *Rambles in Europe: Or, A Tour Through France, Italy, Switzerland, Great Britain, and Ireland, in 1836* (New York: E. French, 1839), 1.
75 Henrietta Frank *Diary,* 156-57, Greenbaum Papers, CHM.
76 Laura Libbey *Diary*, 1 (1992), NYPL. Libbey was a popular author of dime novels.
77 Eliza Gardner *Diary*, May 4, 1859, Gardner Family Papers, MAHS.
78 Madge Preston *Diary*, May 1, 1868, Madge Preston Diaries, Johns Hopkins University, Baltimore, MD (JHU).
79 Susan Marsh Emerson *Diary,* October 19, n.d., 1859, Susan Marsh Emerson Papers, PEM.
80 Margaret Ayer Barnes and Janet Ayer Fairbank (eds.), *Julia Newberry's Diary* (New York: W.W. Norton, 1933), 3, 68.
81 John Adams to Elkamah Watson, Jr., April 30, 1780, The Adams Papers, Vol. 9, Digital Edition.
82 When Frances Trollope visited the United States in 1832 she sug-

gested Latrobe's ears of corn were "the only instance I saw in which America has ventured to attempt national originality" and concluded "the success is perfect." Quoted in G. Martin Moeller, Jr., *AIA Guide to the Architecture of Washington, D.C.* (Baltimore: Johns Hopkins University Press, 2012), 21.

83 Daniel T. Rodgers, *Atlantic Crossings: Social Politics in a Progressive Age* (Cambridge: Harvard University Press, 1998), 34-35.

Chapter II: Prelude to the Unknown Joys of Europe: Across the Atlantic for a Grand Tour

1 Emily Eliot *Diary*, January 17, 1864, HSL. It is ironic that Emily chose the words "peace" and "comfort" during one of the least peaceful and comfortable years in her country's history.
2 Stephen Fox, *Transatlantic: Samuel Cunard, Isambard Brunel, and the Great Atlantic Steamships* (New York: Harper Collins, 2003), 196.
3 Edith Rosenshine, "Anecdotes of Our European Trip As A Thirteen Year Old Child," (typescript), 2, Rosenshine Papers, University of California at Berkeley, Berkeley, CA (UCB).
4 Eliza Leaycraft Smith, *Reminiscence of Eliza Leaycraft Smith*, (typescript), n.p., Robinson Papers, NYHS.
5 Levenstein, *Seductive Journey*, 15.
6 Anne Eliza Rodman to Aunt, October 21, 1817, Fenno-Hoffman Papers, University of Michigan, Ann Arbor, MI (UM).
7 Levenstein, *Seductive Journey*, 15, 20.
8 Fox, *Transatlantic Journey*, 5.
9 Schriber, *Telling Travels*, xiv.
10 Lynne Withey, *Grand Tours and Cook's Tours: A History of Leisure Travel, 1750-1915* (New York: William Morrow and Company, 1997), 173.
11 David McCullough, *The Greater Journey: Americans in Paris* (New York: Simon and Schuster, 2011), 210.
12 Florence Scofield, *Diary*, n.d., James Monroe Scofield Papers, New England Antiquarian Society, Worcester, MA (NEAS).
13 Fox, *Transatlantic Journey*, 128-132.
14 Wyn Craig Wade, *The Titanic: End of a Dream* (New York: Penguin, 1979), 214.
15 Eliza Leaycraft Smith, *Reminiscence*, n.p., n.d.
16 Judith Page Rives *Diary*, September 22, 1820, Alfred Landon Rives Papers, Duke University, Durham, NC (DU).
17 Catherine Pritchard *Diary*, 4, 26, Catherine McAlpin Wray Pritchard Papers, UNC.

18 Eliza Cox, *Paris Life and a Journey to Switzerland* (typescript), October 19, 1825, Cox Family Papers, HSP.
19 Fanny Hall, *Rambles in Europe*, 226, 4.
20 Alicia Middleton *Diary*, May 10-May 21, 1835, Alicia Hopton Middleton Papers, University of South Carolina, Columbia, SC (USC).
21 Sarah Newberry *Diary*, 6-7, Sarah G. Newberry Papers, WRHS.
22 Anonymous *Diary*, May 12, 1836, PEM.
23 Sarah Tuckerman *Diary*, August 4, n.d.,1837, George Becker Papers, LOC.
24 Sarah Cleveland *Diary*, May 17, 1844, Cleveland-Perkins Family Papers, NYPL.
25 Anne Eliza Rodman to Maria Fenno Hoffman, August 28, 1817.
26 Charlotte Horlbeck *Diary*, April 11, 1857, Charlotte H. Horlbeck Papers, SCHS. Charlotte did not elaborate on the unusual covering she described.
27 John Maxtone-Graham, *The Only Way to Cross* (New York: Barnes and Noble, 1972), 5-9.
28 Schriber, *Telling Travels,* xv.
29 Madge Preston *Diary*, May 1, 1868.
30 M.E. Winslow *Diary*, June 24, 1869, Winslow Papers, Columbia University, New York City, NY (CU); Delia Austrian *Diary*, May 7, 1902, Austrian Family Papers, University of Chicago, Chicago, IL (UC).
31 Catherine Van Rensselaer *Diary*, October 29-November 4, 1869, Erving-King Papers, NYHS.
32 M.E. Winslow *Diary*, June 24, 1869.
33 Mary Jane Blair *Diary*, n.d., n.p., Mary Jane Blair Papers, WRHS.
34 Isabel Rogers *Diary*, n.d., n.p., Rochester Public Library, Rochester, NY (RPL).
35 Allison Lockwood, *Passionate Pilgrims: The American Traveler in Great Britain, 1800-1914* (New Brunswick, NJ: Cornwall Books, 1980), 155.
36 Levenstein, *Seductive Journey*, 30.
37 Nineteenth-century editions of *Baedeker's*.
38 Mrs. A.T.J. Bullard, *Sights and Scenes in Europe: A Series of Letters from England, France, Germany, Switzerland and Italy in 1850* (St. Louis: Chambers and Knapp, 1852), 32.
39 Martha Griffis *Diary,* 125, William E. Griffis Papers, Rutgers University, New Brunswick, NJ (RU).
40 Mary Fraser to Mama, May 27, 1844, Mary DeSaussure Fraser Papers, DU.
41 Marion Burgess *Diary*, June 19, 1882, Rhode Island Historical Society, Providence, RI (RIHS).
42 Mary Jane Blair *Diary*, n.d., 1866.

43 Mary Watson Gay *Diary*, Part I, (1882), 5-6, Mary Watson Gay Papers, Vassar College, Poughkeepsie, NY (VC).
44 Fannie Smith sketch in *Chronicles of My European Tour*, (typescript), n.p. (1882), Fannie R.K. Smith Papers, Georgia Department of Archives and History, Atlanta, GA (GDAH).
45 Jeanette Aglionby to Mother, May 14, 1890, Frances Yates Aglionby Papers, DU; Ellen Prentiss *Diary*, June 26, 1890, Adella Prentiss Hughes Family Papers, WRHS.
46 Sarah Newberry *Diary*, 8.
47 Lizzie Van Benschoten to Dear Ones at Home, May 16, 1880, Tunis Van Benschoten Papers, NYHS; Florence Alimnae to Papa, June 22, 1896, Florence Floyd Merriam Alimnae Papers, Wellesley College, Wellesley, MA (WC); Mary Pierce to Dear Ones, November 5, 1876, Poor Family Papers, HSL.
48 Herma Clark *Diary*, July 2, 1907, Herma Clark Papers, CHM.
49 Sarah Newberry *Diary*, 27.
50 Isabel Rogers *Diary*, n.d., n.p.; Susan Emerson Marsh *Diary*, October 23, 1859.
51 Julia Brannan to Dodd, August 28, 1883, Mary Gardiner Marshall Papers, HSL.
52 Louise Kellner *Diary*, December 12, 1894. Louise Kellner Journals, HSP.
53 Mary Jane Blair *Diary*, n.d., n.p.
54 Jeanette Aglionby to Mother, May 20, 1890.
55 Louisa Stephens, *Golden Adventure: A Diary of Long Ago* (Pasadena: San Pasqual Books, 1941), 2.
56 Mary Bradbury, *Letters From Europe* (typescript), 3, Mary Robertson Bradbury Howard Papers, UCB.
57 Eliza E. Gardner *Diary*, May 7, 1859.
58 Martha C. Griffis *Diary*, 14.
59 Isabel Rogers *Diary*, n.d., n.p.
60 Joan Druett, *Hen Frigates: Wives of Merchant Captains Under Sail* (New York: Simon and Schuster, 1998), 28.
61 Alicia Middleton *Diary*, 15.
62 Kate Jones *Diary*, 3, Ann Catherine Boykin Jones Papers, UNC.
63 Anonymous Diary, July 3, 1897, Anderson Family Collection, Georgia Historical Society, Savannah, GA (GHS). The *Diary* was probably written by Nina Pape. I have referred to the author by that name in subsequent citations.
64 Frances and Mary Gaston *Diary*, April 18, 1894, Gaston Family Papers, RU. Frances and her daughter Mary took turns writing in the same diary.

65 Harriet Trowbridge, *Travels in Europe and the East* (New Haven: Tuttle, Morehouse & Taylor, 1879), 3.
66 Madge Preston *Diary*, 19-20.
67 Howard, *Letters From Europe*, 4.
68 Julia Ann Haylander *Diary*, 42, Charles Dewey Papers, UNC.
69 Elizabeth Ogden to Dear Loulie, November 19 (1893?), Elizabeth Ogden Adams Papers, MAHS.
70 Eliza Gardner *Diary*, May 9, 1859.
71 Sarah Tuckerman *Diary*, August 6, 1837; Anne Bradley *Diary*, August 4, 1872, NYPL; Madge Preston *Diary*, 7-8; Jennie Weeden *Diary*, March 27, 1882, RIHS.
72 Helen Gould *Diary*, 4.
73 Druett, *Hen Frigates*, 56.
74 Caroline White *Diary*, March 30, 1855, 10, Caroline Barrett White Papers, NEAS.
75 Madge Preston *Diary*, May 1, 1868.
76 Ruth Church *Diary*, 88, Ruth Church Papers, Oregon Historical Society, Portland, OR (OHS).
77 Isabelle Busbee *Diary*, June 6, 1906, Isabelle Busbee Papers, UNC.
78 Hannah Gould *Diary*, June 22, 1901, Gould Family Papers, Cornell University, Ithaca, NY (CNU).
79 Mary Elizabeth Gittings *Diary*, October 23, November 5, 1885, Harry Reid Papers, JHU.
80 Jennie Young *Diary*, October 22, 24, 28, 30, 1858, Jennie Young Papers, DU. His attention continued in London where they played the piano, sang and drank whiskey punch in her hotel.
81 Nina Pape *Diary*, May 13, 1867.
82 Mary Evelyn Stiles *Diary*, June 9, 1911, Mary Evelyn Stiles Papers, DU.
83 Julia Butler *Diary*, August 27, 1890, Francis Eugene Butler Papers, RU.
84 Henrietta Frank *Diary*, June 17, 1899.
85 Levenstein, *Seductive Journey*, 21.
86 Quoted in Fox, *Transatlantic Journey*, 208-209.
87 Eliza Smith, *Reminiscence*, n.d., n.p.
88 Elizabeth Thomas *Diary*, 3-4, Mrs. Evan Thomas Diary, Maryland Historical Society, Baltimore, MD (MDHS).
89 Alicia Middleton *Diary*, 21.
90 Elizabeth Nichols to Arthur, July 19, 1878.
91 Mabel Virginia Root, *Diary*, June 14, 1908, Mabel Root Papers, CNU.
92 Anonymous *Diary*, 33, Pauline Wright Davis Papers, VC. The author is only identified as the niece of Pauline Wright Davis. I refer to her as Miss Davis; Hannah Gould *Diary*, September 10, 1901; Mamie Parsons to Family, June 7, 1889, Parsons Family Papers, NYHS.

93 Lavina Urbino, *An American Woman in Europe: The Journal of Two Years and a Half Sojourn in Germany, Switzerland, France and Italy* (Lee and Shepard,1869), 2.
94 Bessie Horstmann *Diary*, May 21, 1869, Coles-Lippincott-Horstmann Collection.
95 Ruth Church *Diary*, 87-88.
96 Anonymous *Diary*, 33. Pauline Wright Davis Papers.
97 Fox, *Transatlantic Journey*, 198-199.
98 Kate Jones *Diary*, 5.
99 Clara Ritchie to Mama, August 12, 1889, Clara Belle Ritchie Family Papers, WRHS.
100 Susan Hale *Diary*, May 7, 1882, Castilian Club Papers, Boston Public Library, Boston, MA (BPL).
101 Louise Kellner *Diary*, 2, 4, January 6, 1900.
102 Mary Peirce to Dear Ones, November 3, 1876.
103 Susan Minor *Diary*, July 29, 1892, Minor Family Papers, University of Virginia, Charlottesville, VA (UVA).
104 Emily Severance *Diary*, June 20, 1867, Severance Family Papers, WRHS.
105 Georgette Chamberlain *Diary*, June 6, 1880, Georgette A. Chamberlain Papers, DU.
106 Julia Rush *Diary*, 51, Biddle Family Papers, HSP.
107 Ellen E. Perry *Diary*, n.d., Pierson Papers, PEM.
108 Newspaper clipping, n.d., Isabelle Busbee Papers.
109 Mamie Parsons *Diary*, June 7, 1889.
110 Adelaide Werner *Diary*, June 17, 1906, Adelaide Werner Papers, RU.
111 Sarah Elliott to Mother, November 27, 1886, Sarah Barnwell Elliott Letters, UNC.
112 Isabel Coleman *Diary*, n.d., Coleman Family Papers, DU.
113 Isabelle Busbee *Diary*, June 11, 1906.
114 Louise Kellner *Diary*, January 12, 1900.
115 Charlotte Coles *Diary*, March 25, 1902, Charlotte Berkeley Coles Letters, UVA.
116 Abbie Perkins to Dear Father, July 13, 1883, Cleveland-Perkins Papers, NYPL.
117 Mabel Bragdon *Diary*, November 30, 1906, Mabel Bragdon Papers, College of William & Mary, Williamsburg, VA (CWM).
118 Sallie Wilbur to Dear Friend, July 6, 1888, Aaron Wilbur Papers, DU.
119 Hannah Gould to Beloved Lass, July 4, 1901.
120 Herma N. Clark to Mama and Lo, July, n.d. (1907).
121 Emma Traxel *Diary*, July 4, 1905, CNU.
122 Mary Watson Gay *Diary*, Part I, 9.

123 Susan Minor Scrapbook, n.d.
124 Nina Pape *Diary*, July 9, 1897.
125 Martha Griffis *Diary*, October 5, 1869.
126 Sarah Guild *Diary*, May 27, 1871, MHS.
127 Ginevra Freeman *Diary*, November 25, 1909, Freeman Family Papers, RU.
128 Sarah Cleveland *Diary*, May 20, 1844.
129 Althea Harper *Diary*, April 29, 1901, Harper, Lathrop, Colgate Papers, NYHS.
130 Kate Jones *Diary*, 7.
131 Lizzie Van Benshoten to Dear Ones at Home, May 16, 1880.
132 Mary Hartt to Family, n.d., (1894), Charles Frederick Hartt Papers, DU.
133 Sarah L. Hunter *Diary*, July 1, 1902, Aaron Burtis Hunter Collection, North Carolina Department of Archives and History, Raleigh, NC (NCDAH).
134 Fox, *Transatlantic Journey*, 200-201.
135 Mary E. Flavelle *Diary*, 4. Mary E. Flavelle Papers, CHM.
136 Laura Libbey *Diary*, 5, 9.
137 Herma Clark *Diary*, July 7, 1908.
138 Hannah Gould to Beloved Lass, June 24, 1901.
139 Mabel Root *Diary*, 2.
140 Quoted in Fox, *Transatlantic Journey*, 199.
141 *Ibid.*, 200.
142 J.D. Thomas, "Cunard and Mrs. C.E. Putnam in 1859," Accessible Archives, September 10, 2012. Cunard's decision to pander to American prejudice met with considerable protest in England.
143 Mabel Root *Diary*, 6, 8.
144 Ethel Dummer *Diary*, November 12, 1909, Ethel Dummer Papers, HSL.
145 Idella Plimpton *Diary*, July 27, 1869, Idella C. Plimpton Papers, Mount Holyoke College, South Hadley, MA (MHC).
146 Fox, *Transatlantic Journey*, 330-331.
147 Nina Pape *Diary*, July 3, 1897.
148 Clara Ritchie to Mama, August 12, 1889.
149 Constance Harrison *Diary*, April 1891.
150 Kate Jones *Diary*, 8. Kate penned her most pointed criticism of Northerners from London, proclaiming: "I glory in my Country, her people (except the Abolitionists, poor things) & her institution; Kate Jones *Diary*, 148.
151 M.T. Fall to Captain Leeds, November 17, 1864, Hitchcock Family Papers, UCB.

152 Caroline P. Townsend *Diary*, December 21, 28, 1865, NYHS.
153 Mary Jane Blair *Diary*, n.d., (1866).
154 Eugenie Homer to Mother, October 17, 1878, Emerson-Nichols Papers, HSL.
155 Laura Thomas *Diary*, 1-5, Laura Thomas Papers, UVA.
156 E.M. to Harriet Middleton, April 22, 1895, Cheves-Middleton Papers, SCHS.
157 Mary McMaster to My Dearest Kin, July 5, 1905, Fitz William and Jane Macfre McMaster Papers, USC.
158 E. Thompson *Diary*, March 30, 1848, MAHS.
159 Louise Kellner *Diary*, January 15, 1900.
160 Henrietta Frank *Diary*, June 19, 1899.
161 Maria L'Hommedieu Fahys, "Two Years Abroad, 1887-1889," (typescript), 3, October 16, 1887, Maria L'Hommedieu Fahys Papers, CU.
162 Annie Adams Fields *Diary*, n.d., (1898), Annie Adams Fields Papers, MAHS.
163 Susan Marsh Emerson *Diary*, October 22, 1859.
164 Mamie Parsons to Family, n.d., (1889).
165 Angelica Van Buren *Diary*, June 15, 1854, Angelica Van Buren Papers, USC.
166 Emma Traxel *Diary*, July 1, 1905.
167 Sarah L. Hunter *Diary*, July 15, 20, 1907.
168 Herma Clark to Mama and Lo, July 4, 1907.
169 Hannah Gould *Diary*, 1.
170 M.E. Winslow *Diary*, June, 1869, n.d., n.p.
171 Susan Marsh Emerson *Diary*, January 23, 1859; Louise Kellner *Diary*, December 3, 1894.
172 Eugenie Homer to Mother, October 17, 1878.
173 Maxtone-Graham, *The Only Way to Cross*, 51.
174 Susan Marsh Emerson *Diary*, January 25, 1859.
175 Sarah Cleveland *Diary*, n.d., (1844).
176 Caroline M. Kirkland, *Holidays Abroad or Europe from the West*, (New York: Baker and Scribner, 1849), Vol. I, 10, 15.
177 Eliza Gardner *Diary*, May 10, 1859.
178 Sarah Shurtleff *Diary*, 19, Nichols-Shurtleff Papers, HSL.
179 Caroline White *Diary*, April 28, 1855.
180 Hetty Kennedy *Diary*, 77, Coleman, Twiggs, McEwen & Houston Papers, UVA.
181 Louise Jewett to My Dears At Home, August 13, 1886, Louise Jewett Papers, MHC.
182 Eugenie Homer to Mother, October 17, 1878; Sarah Tuckerman *Diary*, August 13, 1837; Harriette Kidder *Diary*, 245, Daniel Kidder Papers, RU; Annie Adams Fields *Diary*, June 3, 1859.

183 Elizabeth Ogden Adams to Loulie, November 19 (1893?).
184 Nina Pape *Diary*, July 3, 9, 1897.
185 Caroline Poor *Diary*, September 22, 1857, Caroline A. Poor Papers, NYHS.
186 Nancy Storey to Ladie, June 30, 1900, Smythe-Storey Papers, HSL. In the nineteenth century "guy," derived from Guy Fawkes, leader of a plot to blow up King James I and Parliament, meant someone with a grotesque appearance or in bizarre dress.
187 Caroline White *Diary*, 18, 24-25.
188 Althea Harper *Diary*, July 27, 1901.
189 Annie Ware *Diary*, August 14, 17, 19, 21, 1885, Annie Ware Winsor Allen Papers, HSL.
190 Kate Jones *Diary*, 3-7.
191 Julia Rush *Diary*, 60.
192 Emma Clements, *A Glimpse of Europe* (typescript), n.p., Helen Clements Kirk Papers, Bryn Mawr College, Bryn Mawr, PA (BMC).
193 Mary Poor to Dear Ones At Home, November 4, 1876, Poor Family Papers, HSL.
194 Caroline Farrar *Diary*, June 26, 1861, Caroline Weld Farrar Papers, University of Rochester, Rochester, NY (UR).
195 Lizzie Van Benschoten to Dear Ones At Home, May 16, 1880.
196 Louise Jewett to My Dears At Home, August 13, 1886.
197 Herma Clark to Mrs. Blair, July 2, 1907.
198 Mary Evelyn Stiles *Diary*, June 9, 1911, Mary Evelyn Stiles Papers, Virginia Historical Society, Richmond, VA (VHS).
199 Henrietta Frank *Diary*, July 12, 1899.
200 Georgette Chamberlain *Diary*, June 6, 9, 1880.
201 Herma Clark to Mama, July 2, 1907.
202 Eugenie Homer to Mother, October 17, 1878.
203 Clara Alexander to Mama, May 14, 1877, J. Park Alexander Family Papers, WRHS.
204 Nina Pape *Diary*, July 2, 1901.
205 Annie Ware *Diary*, August 14, 17, 19, 21, 1885.
206 Harriet Rich to Dick, September 12, 1886, Mary Robertson Bradbury Howard Papers, UCB.
207 Bessie Horstmann *Diary*, July 17, 1873. This was Bessie and Mamie's second trip abroad. The story of their tragic first trip is told in Chapter VI.
208 Marian Nichols *Diary*, November 12, 1893.
209 Ella Cabot *Diary*, May 2, 1885. Ella Lyman Cabot Papers, HSL.
210 Emma Witmer *Diary*, May 16-June 25 (c.1890s), University of Pennsylvania, Philadelphia, PA (UPA). Emma's undated diary was probably written in the 1890s.

211 Eliza Smith, *Reminiscence*, n.p.
212 Mary Woodbury *Diary*, July 13, 1870, Neilson Family Papers, RU.
213 Helen Macgill to Momma, September 12, 1877, Helen Macgill White Papers, CNU.
214 Cornelia Chapin to Mother, n.d. (1886), Cornelia Van Auken Chapin Papers, HSL.
215 Helen Gould *Diary*, 4-6.
216 Susan Marsh Emerson *Diary*, October 25, 1859.
217 Clara Mitchell *Diary*, June 28, July 24, 1888.
218 Grace Taplin to Mother, n.d., 1905, Grace Taplin Papers, BMC.
219 Isabelle Busbee *Diary*, June 2-June 11, 1906. Even in the early-twentieth century, young single women often referred to each other by their surnames.
220 Fox, *Transatlantic Journey*, 407.
221 Hannah Gould to Lass [?], n.d., 1901, to n. a., September 10, 1901.
222 Mary Pratt *Diary*, July, n.d., 1911, Herter Family Papers, MAHS.
223 Mary McMaster to My Dearest Kin, July 5, 1905.
224 Mabel Root *Diary*, 2.
225 Pauline Biddle *Diary*, June 20, 25, July 2, 1892, Biddle Family Papers, HSP.
226 Ship program, Isabelle Busbee Papers.
227 Clara Schmidt to Dear Sisters, July 10, 1914; Alma Peterson to Tessa, July 1, 1914, to Mother, July 12, 1914, Alma Schmidt Petterson Papers, Newberry Library, Chicago, IL (NL).
228 Mary Millis *Memoir*, 129, GDAH.
229 Mary Watson Gay *Diary*, 16.

Chapter III: Getting Along the Best We Could: Quotidian Demands of a Grand Tour

1 Emily Severance *Diary*, June 28, 1867.
2 Ruth Church *Diary*, 90. She revealed as well Victorian ease in denigrating Africans.
3 Ellen E. Perry *Diary*, October 12, 1852.
4 Laura Comer *Diary*, July n.d., 1872, Laura Beecher Comer Papers, UNC.
5 Catherine Van Rensselaer *Diary*, November 12, 1873.
6 Clara Alexander to Mama, May 14, 1877.
7 Maria Bayard *Diary*, n.d., n.p. (1814). William Bayard Collection, NYPL.
8 Emma Clements, *A Glimpse of Europe*, July 7, 1881.

9 S. Abbott Lawrence *Diary*, June 5, 1851, Appelton Papers, Baker Library, Harvard University (HBL). Her first name is unknown.
10 Louise Jewett to Girls, August 22, 1886.
11 Clara Mitchell *Diary*, July 27, 1889.
12 Mary Cadwalader Jones, *European Travel for Women* (New York: Macmillan, 1900), 135.
13 Mrs. Watt Hairston to Sister, November 25, 1888, Hairston and Wilson Papers, UNC.
14 Mabel Bragdon *Diary*, October 14, 1906.
15 Mary Jane Blair *Diary*, May 26, 1866.
16 Eliza Smith, *Reminiscence*, n.p.
17 Mamie Parsons to Family, May 1, 1895. Most likely these women smuggled the cigarettes for the men they traveled with.
18 Nina Pape *Diary*, September 6, 1867.
19 Virginia McCormick *Diary*, August 1, 1910, Virginia Taylor McCormick Papers, CWM.
20 Jane Anthony Eames, *Budget of Letters or Things Which I Saw Abroad* (Boston: William D. Ticknor and Co., 1847), 11.
21 Lucy Dudley, *Letters to Ruth* (New York: F.H. Gilson, 1896), 66, 76.
22 Henry Morford, *Morford's Short-Trip Guide to Europe* (New York: Sheldon and Company, 1872), 37.
23 Cadwalader Jones, *European Travel For Women*, 25.
24 Maria Bayard *Diary*, 13-14.
25 Sarah Cleveland *Diary*, October 3, 1844.
26 Isabella Faber *Diary*, April 30, 1838, Isabella Bowen Faber Diaries, SCHS.
27 Bullard, *Sights and Scenes in Europe*, 87-89.
28 Emily Severance *Diary*, August 4, 1867.
29 Judith Rives *Diary*, September 14, 1831.
30 Nina Pape *Diary*, September 6, 1867.
31 Ellen Prentis to Precious Loves, May 20, 1890.
32 Alma Schmidt to Father, August 1, 1914.
33 Grace Hutchins, "Letters of Travels Around the World," March 3, 1899. Grace Hutchins Papers, University of Oregon, Eugene, OR (UO).
34 Isabel Rogers *Diary*, August 19, 1892; Eliza De Rosset *Diary*, 61 (1865), Diaries of Eliza Jane Lord De Rosset, UNC.
35 Harriet Rich *Diary*, August 3, 1888. In the nineteenth century it was more common to say one talked another language rather than one spoke it.
36 Mary Watson Gay *Diary*, 52; Ann Marie Green *Diary*, 279; Mary Jane Blair *Diary*, July 5, 1866; Mary Fraser *Diary*, August 22, 1844.
37 Catherine Van Rensselaer *Diary*, July 8, 1870.

38 Ruth Church *Diary*, 113-114.
39 Mary Pierce *Diary*, 20.
40 Florence Scofield *Diary*, July 26, 1877.
41 Martha Griffis *Diary*, 52-53.
42 Sarah Elliott to Mother, December 23, 1886.
43 Marian Nichols *Diary*, November 20, 1893.
44 Sara Howell to Dear Fanny, July 16, 1886, Francis A. Dickins Papers, UNC.
45 Mary Ashhurst to Dear Child, October 16, 1865, Lewis Richard Ashhurst Papers, HSP.
46 Mary Jane Blair *Diary*, July 5, 1866.
47 Caroline Farrar *Diary*, 79.
48 Frances Stevens *Diary*, October 28, 1868.
49 E. Thompson *Diary*, 165-66.
50 Vehicles similar to diligences were called stage coaches in Great Britain and in the United States.
51 Eliza Cox, *Paris Life*, 54.
52 Caroline Townsend *Diary*, November 10, 1865, NYHS.
53 Mary Jane Blair *Diary*, July 26, 1866.
54 Eliza Rodman to Dear Aunt, October 21, 1817.
55 S. Abbott Lawrence *Diary*, April 28, 1851.
56 Alicia Middleton *Diary*, 38, 63, 65-67.
57 Isabella Faber *Diary*, March 15, 1838.
58 Margaret Gardiner, *Letters From A Young Girl's Diary* (New Haven: Tuttle, Morehouse and Taylor Co., 1927), March 2, 1841.
59 E. Thompson *Diary*, June 15, 21, 1848.
60 A. Abbott Lawrence *Diary*, June 7, 1851.
61 Bettie Kimberly to Sis, April 16, 1859, John Kimberly Papers, UNC.
62 Ann Marie Green *Diary*, Vol. II, 119-120.
63 Mrs. E.P. Thompson *Diary*, 201, Mrs. E.P. Thompson Diaries, MDHS.
64 Ellen Perry *Diary*, April 11, 1852.
65 Anonymous *Diary*, November 29, 1866, Anne Blakiston Day Papers, HSP.
66 Constance Harrison *Diary*, April 10, 1893.
67 Sarah Tuckerman *Diary*, January 29, 1837.
68 Kate Jones *Diary*, 100.
69 Caroline Farrar *Diary*, 200 (December 26, 1861).
70 Karl Baedeker, *Italy, Handbook For Travellers* (Coblenz: Karl Baedeker, 1867), xiv, xxi.
71 N. Robinson, "The Comforts and Discomforts of Travel," (*Frank Leslie's Popular Monthly*, Vol. XIV, No. 2), n.p.
72 Elizabeth Gilman *Diary*, July 25, 1889, Gilman Collection, JHU.

73 *Ibid.*, March 30, 1889.
74 Ella Cabot *Diary*, May 28, 1895.
75 Hannah Gould *Diary*, July 28, 1901.
76 Withey, *Grand Tours and Cook's Tours*, 96.
77 Elizabeth Eppes *Diary*, November 23, 1854, Eppes Family Papers, VHS.
78 Lucy Dudley, *Letters to Ruth*, 12.
79 Levenstein, *Seductive Journey*, 130-132.
80 Colin Jones, *Paris: The Biography of a City* (New York: Penguin), 284.
81 Withey, *Grand Tours and Cook's Tours*, 96-97.
82 *Ibid.*, 198.
83 John L. Stoddard, *Stoddard's Lectures* (Boston: Balch Brother, 1897) Vol. One, 135.
84 Mary and Frances Gaston *Diary*, August 25, 1901.
85 Marion Burgess *Diary*, August 1, 1882.
86 Amy Richter, *Home on the Rails: Women, the Railroad, and the Rise of Public Domesticity* (Chapel Hill: University of North Carolina Press, 2005), 49-74.
87 Lucy Dudley, *Letters to Ruth*, 58, 73.
88 Mamie Haven to Ida, December 31, 1877, Solomon G. Haven Papers, UM.
89 Helen Gould *Diary*, 8.
90 Henrietta Frank *Diary*, October 2, 1903.
91 Sarah Ogden *Diary*, September 4, 1908, Sarah and Edward Ogden Diaries, UM.
92 Thomas Knox, *How to Travel* (New York: Charles Dillingham, 1881), 121.
93 Catherine Van Rensselaer *Diary*, July 22, 1870.
94 Mary Jane Blair to Dear Friend, June 17, 1866.
95 N.A., *A Satchel Guide for the Vacation Tourist in Europe* (New York: Hurd and Houghton, 1873), xxvii.
96 Lucy Chamberlain to L.C., September, n.d., 1870, Lucy Chamberlain Papers, HSL.
97 Agnes Kummer *Diary*, March 4, 1863, Agnes Kummer Papers, CWM.
98 Elizabeth Nichols to Arthur, July 19, 1878.
99 Amy Aldis *Diary*, July 6, 1872. Sarah Merry Bradley Gamble Papers.
100 Abbie Farwell *Diary*, August 25, 1899, Abbie Farwell Brown Papers, HSL.
101 Mary Olney *Diary*, February 6, 1897, Mary McClean Olney Papers, UCB.
102 Mary Pierce *Diary*, September 20, 1872.
103 Mrs. T.T. Marsh *Diary*, December 22, 1872, Mrs. T.T. Marsh Papers, NEAS.

104 Catherine Van Rensselaer *Diary*, December 15, 1873.
105 Laura Thomas *Diary*, September 3, 1870.
106 Mrs. T.T. Marsh *Diary*, October 28, November 4, 1872.
107 Florence Alimnae *Diary*, July 10, 1896.
108 Katherine Johnson *Diary*, Vol. II, 41.
109 Mamie Parsons *Diary*, August 18, September 22, 1889.
110 Mary and Frances Gaston *Diary*, July 19, 1894.
111 Louise Kellner *Diary* (1889), 11-12.
112 Mary Pierce *Diary*, August 1, 1872.
113 Mary Sterling *Diary*, July 25, 1872, Mary Emma Betts Sterling Papers, WRHS.
114 Jenny Tracy to Papa, April 24, 1892, Biglow Family Papers, NYPL.
115 Jane Adgar *Diary*, December 20, 1902, USC.
116 Grace Taplin to Grandma, July 27, 1905.
117 Henrietta Frank *Diary* (1907), 40.
118 Elizabeth Ogden to Loulee, May 31, 1901.
119 Willie Allen to Ruth, July 2, 30, 1910, George Washington Allen Papers, UNC.
120 Dolly Whaley to Father, January 1, 1910, Mary Lee Settle Papers, UVA.
121 Wilhemina Mathews *Diary*, May 15, 19, 1906, Louis Skidmore Papers, LOC.
122 Quoted in LeClerq (ed.), *Elizabeth Sinkler Coxe's Tales*, 52.
123 Sarah Ogden *Diary*, July 13, 1908.
124 Patrice Higonnet, *Paris: Capital of the World* (Cambridge: Harvard University Press, 2002), 191.
125 Isabelle Perkinson to Mother, April 16, 1909, Isabelle Perkinson Williamson Papers, DU.
126 Mabel Bragdon *Diary*, October 14, 1906.
127 Mary McLean *Diary*, May 29, 1895, Mary McLean European Travel Diaries, NYHS.
128 Mary and Francis Gaston *Diary*, August 15, 1894.
129 Anonymous *Diary*, May 15, 1872, Paulina Wright Davis Papers.
130 Elizabeth Nichols to Arthur, October 17, 1891.
131 Harriet Curtis to Mummer, May 31, 1899, Curtis Family Papers.
132 Ann Marie Green *Diary*, p; 33; Margaret Preston, *The Life and Letters of Margaret Junkin Preston* (Boston: Houghton Mifflin, 1903), 311.
133 A. N. Wilson, *London: A History* (New York: The Modern Library, 2004), 108.
134 Alistair Horne, *Seven Ages of Paris*, (New York: Vintage Books, 2004), 289.
135 Stoddard, *Lectures*, Vol. One, 136-37.

136 David Birmingham, *Switzerland: A Village History* (Athens, Ohio: Swallow Press, 1999), 163.
137 Constance Harrison to Burton, May 1, 1891.
138 Morris Phillips, *Abroad and at Home* (New York: The Art Press, 1891), 51, 126.
139 Karl Baedeker, *Great Britain, Wales and Scotland* (Leipsic: Karl Baedeker, 1887), xxiiii.
140 Sarah Newberry *Diary*, 36-37.
141 Helen Brooks to Lizzy, June 1, 1882, Helen Laurence Brooks Papers, HSL.
142 Alicia Middleton *Diary*, 65-66.
143 Anonymous *Diary*, March 3, 1836, PEM.
144 Caroline White *Diary*, June 30, 1855.
145 Mary Sterling *Diary*, August 21, 1872.
146 Eliza Pool to Lilly, August 8, 1901, Willa G. Briggs Collection, NCDAH.
147 Mary and Frances Gaston *Diary*, August 25, 1901.
148 Laura Rutherford *Diary*, August 21, 1902, Laura T. Rutherford Diaries, UVA.
149 Jenny Tracy to Papa, April 24, 1892.
150 Caroline Farrar *Diary*, 283.
151 Clara Ritchie to Mama, September 15, 1889.
152 E.M. Middleton to Harriet Middleton, October 12, 1895.
153 Urbino, *An American Woman in Europe*, 13. Most hotels did not exclude women. These are the only reports of a hotel refusing to accommodate them or refusing to serve them in the dining room I found.
154 Clara Reed *Diary*, July 10, October 10, 1890, Miscellaneous Manuscripts, Smith College, Northampton MA (SC).
155 Mamie Parsons *Diary*, August 18, 1889.
156 Clara Alexander *Diary*, 176.
157 Marian Burgess *Diary*, September 3, 1882.
158 Ethel Dummer to Frank, May 27, 1910.
159 Urbino, *An American Woman in Europe*, 13.
160 Anonymous *Diary*, MDHS.
161 Eleanor Middleton *Diary*, April 6, 1895.
162 Martha Ann Tilton *Diary*, 28-29, John W. Williams Papers, LOC.
163 Laura Morgan to Mother, July 23, 1911, Morgan-Howes Family Papers, HSL.
164 Frances Curtis to Aunt Iz, July 3, 1896, Curtis Family Papers.
165 Mary Millis *Memoir*, 113.
166 Ann Marie Green *Diary*, 209.
167 Florence Alimnae to Mama, July 26, 1896.

168 Grace Taplin to Mother, July 15, 1905.
169 Maria L'Hommedieu Fahys, *Two Years Abroad*, 6-7 (October 28, 1887).
170 Mamie Parsons to Family, March 2,1895.
171 Ellen Perry *Diary*, June 13, 1852.
172 Louise Kellner *Diary*, 32 (1900).
173 Laura Thomas *Diary*, January 16, 24, 1871.
174 Isabelle Perkinson to Mother, February 20, 1910.
175 Eleanor Joy *Diary*, January 1, 1885, Eleanor Joy Papers, CU.
176 Mamie Parson to Family, September 6, 1889; Mamie Parsons *Diary*, April 30, 1901, February 21, 1893.
177 Judith Rives *Diary*, October 4, 1829.
178 Isabelle Busbee *Diary*, July 6, 7, 1906; Madge Preston *Diary*, 40.
179 Susie Silver *Diary*, August 9, 1867, William Silver Letters, PEM.
180 Mary and Frances Gaston *Diary*, July 21, 1894; Clara Mitchell *Diary*, June 28, 1888.
181 Mary and Fraces Gaston *Diary*, July 23, 1894; Constance Harrison to Burton, March 26, April 6, 1893; Eliza Marshall *Diary*, July 12, 30, 1891, Joseph W.W. Marshall Papers, DU.
182 Mrs. E.P. Thompson *Diary*, 137.
183 Eliza Marshall *Diary*, August 6, 1891. Cellini's masterpiece, the *Saliera*, was stolen from the Kunsthistorisches Museum in Vienna in 2003 and recovered in 2006.
184 Constance Harrison to Burton, March 26, April 6, 1893.
185 Phoebe Pember to Georgie, July 20, 1895; Phoebe Pember to Sister, June 5, 1896. Phoebe Yates Pember Letters, UNC.
186 Susie Silver *Diary*, August 9, 1867; Ann Marie Green *Diary*, 35-36.
187 Kate Jones *Diary*,152; Laura Johnson to Torquay, February 8, 1870.
188 Sarah Smythe to Lou, May n.d., 1867, Sarah Annie Smythe and Susan Dunlap Smythe Papers, South Carolina Library, Charleston, SC (SCL).
189 Clara Mitchell *Diary*, October 7, 1888.
190 Clara Ritchie *Diary*, September 9, November 3, 10, 1889.
191 Caroline Farrar *Diary*, 169.
192 Clara Ritchie to Dear Ones At Home, December 1, 1889.
193 Anonymous *Diary*, November 29, 1866, Anne Blakiston Day Papers.
194 Ann Marie Green *Diary*, 210.
195 Isabelle Perkinson to Mother, November 29, 1909.
196 Ellen Prentis to Loren and Children, July 18, 1890.
197 Mariana Starke, *Information and Directions For Travellers on the Continent* (Paris: A. and W. Galignani, 1826), 337.
198 Phillips, *Abroad and at Home*, 54.
199 Mary Chafee *Diary*, October 23, 1880, Zachariah Chafee Papers, RIHS.

200 Mary Watson Gay *Diary*, Part I, 52.
201 Laura Thomas *Diary*, October 15, 1870.
202 Mary Bradbury to Jack, September 14, 1886.
203 Jennie Reizestein *Diary*, 27, MDHS.
204 Eleanor Rutledge to Harriett Middleton, March 1, 1895, Cheves-Middleton Papers, SCHS.
205 Susan Smythe to Mother, September 13, 1868, Sarah Annie Smythe and Susan Dunlap Smythe Letters, SCL.
206 Isabelle Perkinson to Mother, April 23, 1909.
207 Gena Trumbull *Diary*, August 6, 7, 1909, Tremen Family Papers, CNU.
208 Edith Stedman *Diary*, October 30, November 5, 15, 27, December 25, 1912, Edith Stedman Papers, HSL.
209 Lucy Dudley, *Letters to Ruth*, 28.
210 Eliza Marshall to Mother, August 31, 1891.
211 Cornelia Upton *Diary*, July, n.d., 1887, Cornelia A. Upton Papers, SC.
212 Jonathan Conlin, *Tales of Two Cities: Paris, London, and the Birth of the Modern City* (Berkeley: Counterpoint, 2013), 96, 102.
213 Starke, *Information and Directions*, 337; Jones, *European Travel For Women*, 155.
214 Alicia Middleton *Diary*, 48, 57.
215 Levenstein, *Seductive Journey*, 109.
216 Caroline Farrar *Diary*, 64.
217 Laura Thomas *Diary*, December 5, 1870.
218 Ann Marie Green *Diary*, 165.
219 Jones, *European Travel for Women*, 13.
220 Frances Stevens to Husband, August 16, 1868.
221 Clara Ritchie to Mama, August 18, 1889.
222 Laura Thomas *Diary*, September 29, 1870.
223 Peter Ackroyd, *London: The Biography* (New York: Anchor Books, 2003), 320.
224 Helen Culbertson to Mamma, May 29, 1888, Matthew Simpson Culbertson Papers, UCB.
225 Gena Trumbull *Diary*, September 3, 1910.
226 Morford, *Morford's Short-Trip Guide*, 35.
227 *A Satchel Guide for the Vacation Tourist in Europe* (New York: Hurd and Houghton, 1873), xiii.
228 James R. Osgood, *Osgood's Complete Pocket-Guide to Europe* (Boston: James R. Osgood and Company, 1883), xiii.
229 Thomas Knox, *How To Travel*, 6, 14.
230 Quoted in Maxtone-Graham, *The Only Way to Cross*, 2.
231 Ann Marie Green *Diary*, 129.
232 Louise Jewett to Sophia, October 9, 1886.

233 Frances Curtis to Mother, February 12, 1897.
234 Martha Griffis *Diary*, 109.
235 Catherine Van Rensselaer *Diary*, July 29, 1870, December 7, 1869.
236 Duncan Crow, *The Victorian Woman* (New York: Stein and Day, 1972), 119.
237 Drew Gilpin Faust, *Mothers of Invention: Women of the Slaveholding South in the American Civil War* (New York: Vintage Books, 1996), 223.
238 Eliza Lamar *Diary*, July 24, 1866. Woodbridge Collection in Miscellaneous Papers, GHS.
239 Mary Jane Blair to Dearest Ones At Home, May 28, 1866.
240 Idella Plimpton *Diary*, October 17, 1869.
241 Isabelle Perkinson to Mother, August 1, September 6, 1909.
242 Frances Stevens to Husband, October 28, 1868.
243 Mary Elizabeth Gittings *Diary*, December 4, 1885.
244 Eliza Cox, *Paris Life*, 9.
245 Ann Marie Green *Diary*, Vol. III, 132.
246 Mamie Parsons to Family, July 25, 1889.
247 *Ibid.*, October 2, 1889.
248 Clara Reed *Diary*, July 28, September 15, August n. d., 1890.
249 Ellen Hammond to Jennie, April 14, 1883, Mary Gardiner Marshall Papers, HSL
250 Isabelle Perkinson to Mother, April 1, 1909. Isabelle reported the travails of a fellow passenger more fashion conscious than she was.
251 Clara Reed *Diary*, August 17, 1890.
252 Eliza Lamar *Diary*, July 24, 1866.
253 Mary Sterling *Diary*, August 21, 1872.
254 Elizabeth Adams to Loulie, January 19, 24, (1897?).
255 Phoebe Pember to n.a., September 28, 1896.
256 Mamie Parsons *Diary*, July 25, 1889.
257 Catherine Van Rensselaer *Diary*, November 12, 1869, July 4, 1870.
258 Sarah Cleveland *Diary*, July 31, 1844.
259 Mary Bates Letters, May 30, June 10, 1891, Parker Family HSL.
260 Laura Thomas *Diary*, January 7, 1871.
261 Bettie Amis to Julia, September 26, 1871.
262 *Ibid.*, July 19, 1871.
263 Catherine Pritchard *Diary* (typescript), July 23, 1829.
264 Nina Halsey *Diary*, Vol. II, August 20, 1895, Nina Halsey Papers, UVA.
265 Marion Nichols *Diary*, 23 (1893).
266 Eliza Cox, *Paris Life*, 34.
267 Mary Ronalds *Diary*, December 14, 1836, NYPL.
268 Gert to Mamie, April 11, 1901, Parsons Family Papers.

269   Mary Jane Blair to Dear Ones At Home, June 24, 1866.
270   Jane Cowl *Diary*, n.d., n.p. (1907), Jane Cowl Papers, NYPL.
271   Cornelia Upton *Diary*, July, n.d., 1887.
272   Clara Alexander *Diary*, 213.
273   Alicia Middleton *Diary*, 31.
274   Caroline Farrar *Diary*, 160.
275   Sarah Smythe to Sister, December 3, 1867.
276   Eliza Howell to Ed, May 13, 1906, Asher-Atkinson-Howell Papers, RU.
277   Isabella Curtis to Elly, March 11, 1897, Curtis Family Papers.
278   Wilhemina Mathews *Diary*, April 27, 1908.
279   Sara Elliott to Mother, December 23, 1886.
280   Cadwalader Jones, *European Travel for Women*, 21.
281   Mabel Root *Diary*, July 3, 1908.
282   *Ibid.*, 23-24.
283   Mary Millis *Memoir*, 96.
284   Clements, *A Glimpse of Europe*, July 23, 1881.
285   Mrs. Hunt's *Diary*, January 16, 1882, Hunt Family Papers, CHM.
286   Frances Stevens to Husband, July 26, August 23, September 20, November 23, 1868.
287   Constance Harrison to Burton, July 8, 1891, to Hetty, May 16, 1891.
288   Elizabeth Nichols to Arthur, May 23, 1900.
289   Gena Trumbull *Diary*, July 2, 1908.
290   Mabel Root *Diary*, June 26, 1908.
291   Laura Thomas *Diary*, February 27, 1871.
292   Nina Halsey *Diary*, Vol. I, June 28, 1895.
293   Alicia Middleton *Diary*, 71.
294   Kate Jones *Diary*, 13, 109.
295   Gena Trumbull *Diary*, July 1, November 20, 1909.
296   M.E. Winslow *Diary*, n. p., n. d. (1869).
297   Laura Thomas *Diary*, August 27, 1870.
298   Sarah Cleveland *Diary*, August 7, 1844.
299   Herbert Warren Wind, "Profiles: The House of Baedeker," *The New Yorker,* (September 22, 1975), 42-89.
300   Mary Gay *Diary*, Part II, 9.
301   Constance Harrison to Burton, May 14, 1893.
302   Henrietta Frank *Diary*, July 6, 1907.
303   *Harper's Handbook for Travellers* (New York: Harper and Brothers, 1882), x.
304   Mary and Frances Gaston *Diary*, July 21, 1894.
305   Mary Hartt to Push, n.d. (1894).
306   Ann Marie Green *Diary*, 253.

270 Notes

307 Laura Thomas *Diary*, November 30, December 16, 17, 1870.
308 Florence Scofield *Diary*, August 8-9, 1877.
309 Isabelle Busbee *Diary*, July 8, 1906.
310 Isabel Rogers *Diary*, August 19, 1892.
311 Alicia Middleton *Diary*, 72.
312 Kate Jones *Diary*, 26, 37, 46.
313 Ellen Perry *Diary*, October 14, 15, 1852.
314 Frances Stevens to Husband, August 2, 19, November 23, 1868.
315 Laura Johnson to Anne, January 5, 1870.
316 Helen Gould *Diary*, 52.
317 Anna Maria Fahnestock to Son, September 13, 1861, Fahnestock-Wolff Papers, HSP.
318 Mrs. S. Horstmann, *Account Book of Travelling Expenses*, Coles-Lippincott-Horstmann Collection, HSP.
319 Catherine Brooks to Julia, October 21, 1867, Catherine Brooks Papers, NYHS.
320 Catherine Van Rensselaer *Diary*, November 13, 17, 1873.
321 Mary and Frances Gaston *Diary*, July n.d., 1901.
322 Caroline Corson to Dear Friend, February 28, 1890, Charles Curtis Papers, CNU.
323 Mabel Root *Diary*, July 1, 1908. Both of these arrangements are discussed in greater detail in Chapter VI.
324 Withey, *Grand Tours and Cook's Tours*, 135-158.
325 Constance Harrison *Diary*, May 14, 1893.
326 Laura Libbey *Diary*, Vol. II, 364.
327 Sarah Shurtleff *Diary*, 35 (1898).
328 Laura Rutherford *Diary*, July 17, 25, 1909.
329 Henrietta Frank *Diary*, August 25, 1903.
330 Flier in Grace Taplin Papers.
331 Flier in Mary Giles *Diary* (1889), DU.
332 Flier in Emma Traxel Papers.
333 Willie Allen to Mother, July 13, 1899; to Ruth, July 30, 1910.
334 Mary Fraser to Mama, July 26, 1844.
335 Susie Silver *Diary*, September 8, 1867.
336 Mary and Frances Gaston *Diary*, August 20, 1901.
337 Elizabeth Nichols to Arthur, April 17, 1900.
338 Isabella Curtis to Ollena, February 5, 1897.
339 Eliza Marshall to Mother, July 12, July 30, 1891.
340 Quoted in Levenstein, *Seductive Journey*, 186.
341 Mary Hartt to Rollin, n.d. (1893).
342 Clara Werner to Dearest, October 23, 1908, Frank Hawley Ward Family Papers, UR.

343 Gena Trumbull *Diary*, July 26, 1908.
344 Caroline Farrar *Diary*, 26-27.
345 *Autobiography of George Bliss* Vol. II, n.p. George Bliss Papers, NYHS. Much of the autobiography was written by his wife Anais Bliss.
346 Catherine Van Rensselaer *Diary*, August 7, 25, 1869.
347 Mrs. Steedman *Diary*, June 24, 27, 1877, Charles Steedman Papers, DU.
348 Eliza Marshall to Mother, November 1, 1891.
349 Annie Speer to Mama, March, n.d., 1907.
350 Susan C. Minor *Diary*, September 4, 1892, Minor Family Papers.
351 Bessie Horstmann *Diary*, March 8-June 20, 1869.
352 Kate Jones *Diary*, 37.
353 Mary Hartt to Mother, n.d. (1894).
354 June Spencer to Mother, July 13, 1884, Cornelia Phillips Spencer Papers, UNC.
355 Berlin, the beneficiary of Prussian efficiency, enjoyed clean water and the use of disinfectants that kept it free of the disease. Charles Emmerson, *1913: In Search of the World Before the Great War* (New York: Public Affairs, 2013), 64.
356 Harriet Blanchard *Diary*, September 9, October 2, 1892.
357 Maria Bayard *Diary*, October, n.d.,1814.
358 Mary Ronalds *Diary*, January 16, 1836.
359 Bessie Horstmann *Diary*, September 8, 1873.
360 Elizabeth Ogden *Diary*, January 19, 1897.
361 American Consul to F.B. Noyes, May 22, June 6, 1914, Mary E. Flavelle Papers.

Chapter IV: My Dreams Were All of London, Paris, Rome: Itineraries of a Grand Tour

1 Ann Marie Green *Diary*, 1 (1877).
2 Daniel Kilbride, *Being American in Europe, 1750-1860* (Baltimore: Johns Hopkins University Press, 2013), 48.
3 Shirley Foster, *American Women Travellers to Europe in the Nineteenth and Early Twentieth Centuries* (Staffordshire, England: Keele University Press, 1994), 6.
4 Catherine Brooks to Mother, March 19, 1868.
5 Ruth Church *Diary*, 93.
6 Quoted in Kilbride, *Being American*, 140.
7 Sarah Endicott to Folks, August 15, 1847, Endicott Family Papers, NEAS.

8   Caroline White *Diary*, April 30, 1855; Hariette Kidder *Diary*, 248; Annie Adams *Diary*, n.d. (1859); Susan Minor *Diary*, September 28, 1892.
9   Hannah Gould to Dearest Pass, n.d.
10 Kilbride, *Being American*, 54.
11 The British abolished the slave trade in 1807.
12 Mrs. E.P. Thompson *Diary*, 6.
13 Sally Ledger, *The New Woman: Fiction and Feminism at the Fin de Siècle* (Manchester: Manchester University Press, 1997), 152.
14 Stoddard, *Lectures*, Vol. Nine, 229.
15 Jennie Reizenstein *Diary*, 85, MDHS.
16 Mrs. E.P. Thompson *Diary*, 112, 114.
17 Wilson, *London*, 99-107.
18 Ackroyd, *London: The Biography*, 567.
19 *Ibid.*, 516.
20 *Ibid.*, 515-516.
21 Stoddard, *Lectures*, Volume Nine, 283-84.
22 Sarah Tuckerman to Mother, n.d.
23 Sarah Cleveland *Diary*, May 31, June 7, 1844.
24 Agnes Kummer *Diary*, March 5, 8, 1863.
25 Frances and Mary Gaston *Diary*, September 7, 23, 1894.
26 Martha Ann Tilton *Diary*, 1.
27 Adelaide Werner *Diary*, June 20, 1906.
28 Caroline White *Diary*, May 3, 1855.
29 Louise Jewett to Girls, August 22, 1886.
30 Mary Kent Stone *Diary*, August 24-25, 1826, Kent Family Papers, CU. She was there well before Karl Marx became the cemetery's most famous resident.
31 Sarah Ogden *Diary*, July 15, 1908.
32 Julia Haylander *Diary*, 23.
33 Anonymous *Diary*, October 8, 1858, MDHS.
34 Ann Marie Green *Diary*, 80.
35 Agnes Kummer *Diary*, March 4, 1863.
36 Mary Hartt to Grandmother, n.d. (1894).
37 Catherine Van Rensselaer *Diary*, November 23, 1869.
38 E-mail from Elliott Farar, Office of Art and Archives, United States Capitol, January 13, 2013.
39 Hariette Kidder *Diary*, 254.
40 Clara Ritchie to Dear Ones at Home, August 25, 1889.
41 Louise B. Robinson, *A Bundle of Letters From Over the Sea* (Boston: J.G. Cupples, 1890), 46.
42 Quoted in Kathleen Barry, *Susan B. Anthony: A Biography of a Singular Feminist* (New York: Ballantine Books, 1988), 278.

43 Lockwood, *Passionate Pilgrims*, 190.
44 Ellen Coolidge *Diary*, July 19, 1838, Ellen Wayles Randolph Coolidge Diaries, MAHS. Ellen was Thomas Jefferson's granddaughter.
45 Bullard, *Sights and Scenes in Europe*, 41.
46 Louise Chandler Moulton, *Random Rambles* (Boston: Roberts Brothers, 1881), 16.
47 Frances Morse *Diary*, May 7, 10, 1878, Harriett Morse Papers, HSL.
48 Ester Lindsay *Diary*, n.d., n.p, Lindsay Family Papers, HSL.
49 Conant, *A Girl of the Eighties*, 257.
50 Constance Harrison to Burton, May 20-21, July 13, 1894.
51 Laura Rutherford *Diary*, 105.
52 Mary McMaster to n.a., August 3, 1905.
53 Isabelle Perkinson *Diary*, June 5, 1909.
54 Edith Stedman *Diary*, 27.
55 Gardiner, *Leaves from a Young Girl's Diary*, July 3, 1841.
56 Elizabeth Porter Gould *Diary*, n.d. (1894), Elizabeth Porter Gould Papers, BPL.
57 Elizabeth Adams *Diary*, July 7, 1901.
58 Harriet Bradbury to Lily, September 14, 1886.
59 Edith Stedman *Diary*, December 24, 1912.
60 Anna Wilcox *Diary*, 87, Anna B. Wilcox Papers, RU.
61 Lucy Baxter *Diary*, July 1, 1907, James M. Baxter Papers, USC.
62 Elizabeth Grinnell *Diary*, September 17, 1904, RIHS.
63 Clements, *A Glimpse of Europe*, July 1, 1881; quoted in Lockwood, *Passionate Pilgrims*, 333.
64 Elizabeth Adams *Diary*, July 30, 1893.
65 Sallie Wilber to Will, August (n.d.), 1892.
66 Mary Hartt to Mother, June 25, 1894.
67 Caroline Farrar *Diary*, 25.
68 Lucy Dudley, *Letters to Ruth*, 27.
69 Sophia Boardman *Diary*, June 21, 1865, UM.
70 Kilbride, *Being American*, 52.
71 M.E. Winslow *Diary*, 10.
72 Kelley, *Learning to Stand and Speak*, 180.
73 Helen Brooks to Lizzy, May 18, 1882.
74 Lockwood, *Passionate Pilgrims*, 338.
75 Martha Ann Tilton *Diary*, 9,12.
76 Eliza Marshall to Mother, July 12, 1891.
77 Kate Logan to My Little Girls, July 20, 1890.
78 Mary Pierce *Diary*, June 3, 1872.
79 Lockwood, *Passionate Pilgrims*, 346.
80 Fannie Smith, *Chronicles*, July, n.d., 1882.

81 Catherine Brooks to Ma, May 24, 1867.
82 Mary Jane Blair to Dear Ones at Home, May 28, 1866.
83 Octavia Jones *Diary*, 76, 135, Calvin Jones Papers, UNC.
84 Levenstein, *Seductive Journey*, 5.
85 M.B. Ford, "American Society in Paris," *Cosmopolitan*, 15 (May 1893), 72-79.
86 Maria Bayard *Diary*, 8-9,11,13.
87 Jones, *Paris*, 262.
88 Maria Bayard *Diary*, n.p., 9-10.
89 Abigail De Hart Mayo, *An American Lady in Paris, 1828-1829* (Boston: Houghton Mifflin, 1927), 14.
90 Kilbride, *Being American*, 61.
91 Susan Dunn, *Sister Revolutions: French Lightning, American Light* (New York: Faber and Faber, 1999), 19.
92 Alicia Middleton *Diary*, 27.
93 Eliza Cox *Diary*, 7-8, 36, February 12, May 6, 1825.
94 Judith Rives *Diary*, October 10, 1829.
95 Quoted in Levenstein, *Seductive Journey*, 56.
96 Quoted in *Ibid*.
97 Sarah Cleveland *Diary*, May 31, June 9-20, 1844.
98 Ann Page *Diary*, May 18, 1837, HSP.
99 Sarah Tuckerman *Diary*, January 29, 1837.
100 Judith Rives *Diary*, September 2, 1831.
100 Annie Fields *Diary*, October 12, 1859.
102 Jones, *Paris*, 299.
103 Horne, *Seven Ages of Paris*, 233-235.
104 Jones, *Paris*, 301.
105 McCullough, *The Greater Journey*, 296-298.
106 Mary Woodbury *Diary*, July 28, 29, 1870.
107 Catherine Van Rensselaer *Diary*, July 15, 19-22, August 8, 16, 19, 29, September 4, 1870.
108 Grace Bigelow *Diary*, September 3, 1870.
109 Barnes and Fairbank (eds.), *Julia Newberry's Diary*, 92, 99.
110 Laura Johnson *Diary*, September 13, 1870.
111 Horne, *Seven Ages of Paris*, 252.
112 *Ibid.*, 99, 266-275.
113 Laura Thomas *Diary*, August 13, September 3, 1870, March 21, 24, 25, June 9, 1871.
114 Bettie Amis to Julie, August 6, 1871.
115 Anne Bradley *Diary*, n.d. (August 1872).
116 Horne, *Seven Ages of Paris*, 275-276.
117 Grace Bigelow *Diary*, December 13, 1871.

118 Katherine Johnson *Diary*, 24.
119 Hirsler, "At Home in Paris," 62.
120 Horne, *Seven Ages of Paris*, 240.
121 *Ibid.*, 230.
122 Emmerson, *1913,* 50.
123 Angelica Van Buren *Diary*, 27-31.
124 Kate Jones *Diary*, 35.
125 Caroline Poor *Diary*, October 29, 1857.
126 Laura Johnson to Anne, November 29, 1869.
127 Clara Alexander *Diary*, 118, 129.
128 Mamie Haven to Mother, February 27, 1878.
129 Jones, *Paris*, 332-333.
130 Jill Jonnes, *Eiffel's Tower* (New York, Penguin Books, 2009), 144, 121.
134. It is unlikely that this comparison occurred to anyone else!
131 Jonnes, *Eiffel's Tower*, 121-134.
132 Lucy Dudley, *Letters to Ruth*, 101.
133 Clara Ritchie to Mama, September 9, 1889.
134 Napoleon failed to relocate Trajan's Column in Paris, but did force a treaty that gave him one hundred of the most famous works in the Papal and Capitoline collections. See Sturgis, *When in Rome*, 212.
135 Laura Comer *Diary*, August 6, 1872; Wilhemina Mathews *Diary*, April 27, 1908; Mabel Bragdon *Diary*, October 20, 1906. Harvey Levenstein's contention that in the early-nineteenth century art appreciation "was man's rightful domain" is questionable. The limited extant letters and diaries of women visiting Europe at that time reveal their keen appreciation of art; abundant sources for subsequent decades conclusively establish this was the case. Levenstein, *Seductive Journey*, 61. Few women commented on Leonardo's *Mona Lisa*, now the museum's most famous holding. Americans there from 1911 to 1913 did not see it as it was stolen and missing for two years.
136 Constance Harrison to Burton, June 6, 1891.
137 Helen Culbertson to Mama, May 29, 1888.
138 Mary Pierce *Diary*, September 23, 1873. *Venus of Urbino*, the most famous of Titian's Venuses, is in the Uffizi. There is not one in the Louvre. Mary may have seen Titian's *Pastoral Concert* there.
139 Mary Hartt to Rollin, July 10, 1894.
140 Clara Ritchie to Mama, September 1, 1889.
141 Henrietta Frank *Diary*, September 29, 1907.
142 According to Jonathan Conlin, the can-can "began life as France's 'national dance' around 1830 only to become a byword for 'Gay Paree' at its most tacky sixty years later." In the early years men did the kicking. Conlin, *Tales of Two Cities*, 137-138, 161-163.

276   Notes

143 Nina Halsey *Diary*, Vol. III, n.d. (1895).
144 Emma Witmer *Diary*, September 13, n.y.
145 Abbey Farwell, "Bachelor Girls in Paris," November 5, 1899.
146 Mary Mclean *Diary*, June 23, 1895.
147 Willie Adams to Beff, July 27, 1902.
148 Elizabeth Ijams *Diary*, April 11, 1898, Elizabeth Ijams Papers, UVA.
149 Edith Parsons to Mamie, September 11, 1912, Parsons Family Papers.
150 Sarah Elliott to Mother, December 6, 1886.
151 Isabelle Perkinson to Muzzie, April 23, 1909.
152 Eliza Smith, *Reminiscence*, n.d., n.p.
153 Caroline Kirkland, *Holidays Abroad or Europe from the West* (New York: Baker and Scribner, 1849), 123.
154 McCullough, *The Greater Journey*, 334.
155 Rosalind Williams, *Dream Worlds: Mass Consumption in Late-Nineteenth-Century France*, (Berkeley: University of California Press, 1982), 1-2.
156 Michael B. Miller, *The Bon Marche: Bourgeois Culture and the Department Store, 1869-1920* (Princeton: Princeton University Press, 1981), 3-5.
157 Charles Fulton, *Europe Viewed Through American Spectacles* (Philadelphia: Lippincott, 1874), 153.
158 Elizabeth Nichols *Diary*, February 14, 1997.
159 Willie Allen to Home Folks, September 1, 1895.
160 Hebe Dorsey, *The Belle Epoque in the Paris Herald* (New York: Thames and Hudson, 1986), 25.
161 Blanche McManus, *The American Woman Abroad* (New York: Dodd, Meade, 1911), 251.
162 Dulles, *Americans Abroad*, 75.
163 Ledger, *The New Woman*, 155.
164 Eliza Homans *Diary*, February 26, 1875, MAHS.
165 Elizabeth De Peyster *Diary*, April 30, May 20, June 3, June 8, 1874, NYHS.
166 Marie J. Pitman, *European Breezes*, (Boston: Lee and Shepard, 1882), 276.
167 Isabel Rogers *Diary*, August 19, 1892.
168 Mrs. Warren Tufts, quoted in Levenstein, *Seductive Journey*, 190-191.
169 Willie Adams to Hattie, August 25, 1895, August 25, 1896.
170 Kate Field quoted in Schriber, *Telling Travels*, 193.
171 Caroline Townsend *Diary*, November 17, 21, 23, 24, 28, 29, 30, December 3, 6, 9, 1865.
172 Caroline Farrar *Diary*, August 22, 1861.
173 Elizabeth Adams *Diary*, July 7, 1897.
174 Marion Nichols *Diary*, November 24, 1891.

175 Mamie Parsons *Diary*, November 6, 1889, May 17, 1893.
176 McCullough, *The Greater Journey*, 252.
177 Elizabeth De Peyster *Diary*, May 9, 13, 20, 23, 1874.
178 Mrs. Hunt *Diary*, April 9, 13, 17, 24, 1882.
179 Laura Thomas *Diary*, November 16, 1870.
180 Mary Hutton to Miss Jo, June 30, 1910, Atkinson Family Papers, RU.
181 Catherine Van Rensselaer *Diary*, November 25, 1873.
182 Quoted in Charles Capper and Christina Giorcelli (eds.), *Margaret Fuller: Transatlantic Crossings in a Revolutionary Age* (Madison: University of Wisconsin Press, 2008), 168. Fuller was only off by two decades.
183 E. Thompson *Diary*, April 27, May 15, 16, June 15, 1848.
184 Kate Jones *Diary*, 117.
185 Louisa Smythe, *Recollections of Louisa McCord Smythe* (typescript), 37, SCHS.
186 Bettie Kimberly to Sissie, April 21, 1859.
187 Hattie Trowbridge *Diary*, April 13, 26, 27, 30, May 1, 3, 1859, Hattie Trowbridge Papers, NYHS.
188 Harvey Levenstein claims that the number of Americans traveling to Europe actually went up during the war years; his statistics indicate that 2,000 more Americans, most of them from the North, made a Grand Tour in 1864 than had in 1860. Although my sample of over three hundred women who traveled to Europe between 1814 and 1914 is too small to be conclusive, it suggests that, to the contrary, the number of American women going abroad fell through the war years. Foster Rhea Dulles and, more recently, Daniel Kilbride concur with this interpretation. See Levenstein, *Seductive Journey*, 103; Dulles, *Americans Abroad*, 102; Kilbride, *Being American*, 7.
189 Anna Maria Fahnestock to Dear Son, September 13, October 4, 1861, to Dear Children, December 8, 16, 19, 1861.
190 Caroline Farrar *Diary*, 64, 160, 188.
191 Frances Duer *Diary*, January 9, 1864, Duer Family Papers, CU.
192 *Ibid.*, December 24, 1869. Frances Duer recalled the Ogdens' deaths while traveling in Europe in 1869.
193 Quoted in McCullough, *The Greater Journey*, 236-237.
194 Annie Fields to Dear Folks, April 9, 1868.
195 Emily Severance *Diary*, August 4, 1867.
196 Catherine Van Rensselaer *Diary*, September 21, 1870.
197 Christopher Duggan, *The Force of Destiny: A History of Italy Since 1796*, (New York: Houghton Mifflin, 2008), 348.
198 Helen Brooks to Lizzie, May 29, 1898.
199 Clara Mitchell *Diary*, June 30, 1888.
200 Eleanor Middleton to Harriet Middleton, February 22, 1896.

201 James H.S. McGregor, *Rome From the Ground Up* (Cambridge: Harvard University Press, 2005), 1.
202 Duggan, *The Force of Destiny*, 301-302.
203 Robert Hughes, *Rome: A Cultural, Visual, and Personal History* (New York: Alfred A. Knopf, 2011), 373.
204 Isabella Bowen Faber *Diary*, April 20, 1838; Mary Gibson *Diary*, July 19, 1909, UNC; Charlotte Horlbeck *Diary*, n.d, n.p. (1857); Idela Plimpton to Mother, January 11, 1870; Hattie Trowbridge *Diary*, March 20, 1859; Hannah Gould *Diary*, 24.
205 Charlotte Horlbeck *Diary*, n.d., n.p. (1857).
206 Caroline Farrar *Diary*, 200.
207 James L. Machor (ed.), *Readers in History: Nineteenth-Century American Literature and the Contexts of Response*, (Baltimore: Johns Hopkins University Press, 1993), 105-128.
208 Mary Hartt to Mama, August 8, 1894.
209 June Spencer to Mother, July 21,1884, notes for publication,161.
210 William Vance, *America's Rome: Vol. II: Catholic and Contemporary Rome* (New Haven: Yale University Press, 1989), xvi.
211 Jenny Franchot, *Roads to Rome: The Antebellum Protestant Encounter with Catholicism* (Berkeley: University of California Press, 1994), 17.
212 Sturgis, *When in Rome*, 228-229.
213 Angelica Van Buren *Diary*, Part II, 19.
214 Louise Kellner *Diary*, November 19, 1889.
215 Laura Thomas *Diary*, January 17, 1871.
216 Clara Ritchie to Mama and Papa, n.d. (March, 1889). In the twentieth century the ritual claimed to assure a return was changed from drinking the water to tossing a coin in the fountain.
217 Laura Libbey *Diary*, 33-34.
218 Constance Harrison to Burton, April 24, 1893.
219 David Watkin, *The Roman Forum* (Cambridge: Harvard University Press, 2009), 193. There are ruins of several forums in Rome; when the word is used without designation, it refers to the Roman Forum.
220 Laura Thomas *Diary*, January 17, 1871.
221 Idella Plimpton to Mother, January 11, 1870. The proper spelling is Catiline.
222 Ann Marie Green *Diary*, 250.
223 *Ibid.*, 249. Colosseum and Coliseum are both acceptable English spellings.
224 Anonymous Diary, June 20, 1867, DU.
225 Anne Bense *Diary* (1888), 137, Bense Family Diaries, NYPL.
226 Nina Halsey *Diary*, July 26, 1895. There is no evidence that Christians were killed in the Coliseum although they were in other arenas.

227 Lucy Dudley, *Letters to Ruth*, 83.
228 Constance Harrison to Burton, May 2, 1893.
229 Marion Burgess *Diary*, August 7, 1882.
230 Mary Elizabeth Gittings, February 2 (probably March 2), 1885. The statue has been replaced by a copy and is now inside the Capitoline Museum.
231 Willie Allen to Ruth, August 12, 1900. U.S. President William McKinley was killed by an anarchist the following year; both heads of state were victims of an outbreak of anarchy at the turn of the century.
232 Eleanor Middleton to Harriet Middleton, March 1, 1896.
233 Kate Jones *Diary*, 109.
234 Constance Harrison to Burton, May 2, 1891.
235 Alice to All of You, March 9, 1889, Alice Draper Carter Papers, HSL.
236 Mrs. Alfred Thompson *Diary*, n.d., n.p. (1882), NYHS.
237 Isabella Faber *Diary*, April 20, 1838.
238 Clara Ritchie to Mama, April 6, 1890.
239 Caroline Corson to Dear Friend, December 10, 1889.
240 Catherine Van Rensselaer *Diary*, January 11, 1870.
241 Mary Ronalds *Diary*, January 1, 1836.
242 Constance Harrison to Burton, May 2, 1893.
243 Marion Burgess *Diary*, August 8, 1882. Robert Hughes writes of Guido Reni: "There can be few painters in history whose careers show such a spectacular rise to the heights of reputation, followed by such a plunge to the depths." Hughes, *Rome*, 259.
244 Margaret Thomson to Father, June 29, 1912.
245 Sarah Newberry *Diary*, 224.
246 Mary Olney *Diary*, January 13, 1897.
247 Eliza Marshall to Fanny Beattie, July 17, 1892.
248 Mary Elizabeth Gittings *Diary*, February 2 (March 2), 1885.
249 Grace Bigelow *Diary*, March 3, 1873.
250 Constance Harrison to Burton, April 29, 1893.
251 Laura Thomas *Diary*, January 17, 1871.
252 Harriet Blanchard *Diary*, February 7, 1867.
253 *Ibid.*, February 23, 1867.
254 Caroline Farrar *Diary*, 268, 281.
255 Hattie Trowbridge *Diary*, March 8, 1859.
256 Dolly Whaley to Father, February 2, 1911.
257 Idella Plimpton to Mother, January 11, 1870.
258 Caroline Farrar *Diary*, 241.
259 Euphemia Olcott *Diary*, December 25, 1902, NYPL.
260 Willie Adams to Mother, August 4, 1895.
261 Lucy Baxter to Mamie, August 15, 1907.

262 Mamie Parsons *Diary*, February 10, 1895.
263 Grace Moore *Diary*, 12, Grace Roberts Moore Letters and Diaries, UCB.
264 Catherine Van Rensselaer *Diary*, January 5-6, 1869.
265 *Ibid.*, May 29, 1869.
266 Mary Pierce *Diary*, March 14, 1873.
267 Mrs. Beckley to Mamie, August 15, 1907, Sylvester Beckley Papers, USC.
268 Isabelle Perkinson *Diary*, February 7, 1910.
269 Bettie Kimberly to Sis, April 16, 1859.
270 Trowbridge, *Travels in Europe and the East*, 21.
271 Laura Johnson *Diary*, March 13, 1870.
272 Isabelle Perkinson *Diary*, February 11, 1910.
273 Ann Page *Diary*, May 18, 1837.
274 Mary Ashhurst *Diary*, January 26, 1865.
275 Anne Bense *Diary* (1888), 16-17.
276 Ruth Church *Diary*, 107.
277 Emily Severance *Diary*, August 7, 1867.
278 Mrs. Beckley to Anne, August 5, 1907. A dubious claim, but one Booker T. Washington also made when he visited Sicily.
279 Michael Levey, *Florence: A Portrait* (London: Pimlico, 1996), 456.
280 Ellen Cabot *Diary*, June 1, 1885.
281 Hattie Trowbridge *Diary*, April 4, 8, 1859.
282 Laura Johnson *Diary*, March 23, 1870.
283 Stoddard, *Lectures,* Vol. Eight, 14. A copy of the *David* was placed in front of the Palazzo Vecchio in 1910.
284 Jennie McGraw to Lettie, October 12 [1878?], McGraw Family Papers, CNU.
285 *Ibid,*. April 18, 1871.
286 Constance Harrison to Burton, May 8, 1891.
287 Susan L. Roberson, *Antebellum American Women Writers and the Road* (New York and London: Routledge, 2011), 137.
288 Mary Pierce *Diary*, Vol. II, January 12, 1873.
289 Eleanor Joy *Diary*, July 3, 1885.
290 Eleanor Middleton to Harriett Middleton, May 8, 1896.
291 John Julius Norwich, *Paradise of Cities: Venice in the 19th Century* (New York: Doubleday, 2003).
292 Martha Ann Tilton *Diary*, 30.
293 Caroline Farrar *Diary*, 191-193.
294 Catherine Van Rensselaer *Diary*, June 11, 1870.
295 Harriett Kimball to Mother, February 27, 1870, Kimball Papers, CHM.
296 Dolly Whaley to Father, March 9, 1911.

297 Mary Ronalds *Diary*, December 1, 8, 10, 1836.
298 Ruth Church *Diary*, 143-44. The Palio is still held twice a year in July and August.
299 Isabelle Perkinson to Mama, November 29, 1909.
300 Elizabeth Gilman *Diary*, April 12, 1889.
301 Anonymous *Diary*, May 25, 26, 1872, Pauline Wright Davis Papers.
302 Miss T.T. Marsh *Diary*, October 28, 1872.
303 Constance Harrison *Diary*, May 21, 1893.
304 Frances and Mary Gaston *Diary*, July 21, 1894.
305 Nina Halsey *Diary*, July 19, 1895.
306 Sarah Tuckerman *Diary*, January 29, 1837.
307 Mary Gittings *Diary*, February 2 (March 2), 1885.
308 Cadwalader Jones, *European Travel for Women*, 175.
309 Mary Jane Blair to Dear Ones at Home, June 24, 1866, to Dear Ones, One and All, July 5, 1866.
310 *Ibid.*, to My Dearest and Best Friends, October 6, 1866.
311 Mamie Parsons to Family, June 22, 1889.
312 Emmerson, *1913*, 67.
313 Jennie Reizenstein *Diary*, 7, 27, 47.
314 Elizabeth Gould to Dear Sister, September 10, 1913, Gould Family Papers, UNC.
315 Mary Hartt to Ours at Home, August 21 (1894?).
316 Catherine Van Rensselaer *Diary*, June 28, 1869.
317 Judith Rives *Diary*, September 10, 1831.
318 Laura Johnson to Anne, June 12, 1870.
319 Clara Alexander *Diary*, July 16, 1877.
320 Catherine Van Rensselaer *Diary*, July 7, 1869.
321 Julia Severance *Diary*, August 27, 1886.
322 Levenstein, *Seductive Journey*, 144.
323 Henrietta Frank *Diary*, June 27, 1899, September 22, 23, 1903, 93-94, 1907.
324 *Ibid.*, August 23, 1910.
325 Mary Fraser to Mama, July 26, 1844.
326 Harriet Johnston to Ellen, December 10, 1854, Harriet Lane Johnston Papers, HSP. Harriet was the niece of James Buchanan and served as his First Lady.
327 Mary Few to Mary, July 2, 1842, William Few Collection, GDAH.
328 Sarah Cleveland *Diary*, November 12, 1844.
329 E. Thompson *Diary*, April 29, 1848.
330 Elizabeth Gilman *Diary*, November 16, 1890.
331 Horowitz, *Wagner Nights*, 34, 2-4.
332 Jackson Lears, *No Place of Grace: Antimodernism and the Transforma-*

tion of American Culture, (Chicago: University of Chicago Press, 1982), 225-228.
333 Marian Nichols *Diary*, September 16, 1891.
334 Constance Harrison *Diary*, June 6, 1894, Constance Harrison to Hetty, July 13, 1894.
335 Hattie Trowbridge *Diary*, May 19, 1859.
336 Laura Rutherford *Diary*, 68-69 (September 1, 1902).
337 Mary Boit *Diary*, November 15, 1896, February 20, April 20, 1897, Hugh Cabot Collection, HSL.
338 Mamie Parsons *Diary*, August 18, 1889.
339 *Ibid*. to Family, June 18, 1889.
340 *Ibid*.
341 Kate Jones *Diary*, 43.
342 Frances and Mary Gaston *Diary*, May 11, 15, 1894.
343 Mamie Parsons *Diary*, August 16, 1900.
344 Anna Rew to Father, April 23, 1903, Henry Rew Papers, CHM.
345 Nina Pape *Diary*, August 1, 1897.
346 Abbie Farwell, "In the Land of Storks and Beer: Experiences of the Bachelor Girls in Kaiser William's Country," October 8, 1899.
347 Gena Trumbull *Diary*, August 6-7, 1909.
348 Caroline Farrar *Diary*, 180.
349 Grace Tapin to Farrand, July 30, 1905.
350 Clara Ritchie to Mama, January 26, 1890.
351 Edith Rosenshine, *Anecdotes of Our European Trip*, 10.
352 Stoddard, *Lectures*, Vol. Five, 253.
353 Ellen Perry *Diary*, October 22, 23, 1852, March 2, 1853.
354 Allen, *Travels in Europe*, 495.
355 Ellen Moulton, *Incomplete Account of a Trip to Spain*, n.p., n.d. (1883), Ellen Louise Moulton Papers, NEAS.
356 Mary Elizabeth Gittings *Diary*, November 23, 28, 29, 1885.
357 Constance Harrison to Fairfax, March 24, 1893.
358 Jane Adgar *Diary*, December 25, 1902.
359 Mrs. Alfred Thompson *Diary*, n.p., n.d. (1882).
360 Dulles, *Americans Abroad*, 4.
361 Bushman, *Refinement in America*, xix.
362 Fanny Hall, *Rambles in Europe*, 104-105.
363 Kate Jones *Diary*, 49.
364 Bettie Kimberly to Sis, August, 1859.
365 Alberta Taylor to Aunt Anna, July 9, 22, 1911, Edwards Family Papers, VHS.
366 Caroline Farrar *Diary*, September 2, 1861.
367 Elizabeth Nichols to Arthur, October 29, 1891.

368 Mary Gibson *Diary*, July 18, 1909.
369 McManus, *The American Woman Abroad*, 211-212.
370 Phoebe Pember to n.a., November 16, 1897; Mary Hutton to Miss Jo, June 30, 1910; Mary Boit *Diary*, 27.
371 Mrs. Beckley *Diary*, June 26, 1907; Mary Frazer to Sister, June 22, 1844; Laura Thomas *Diary*, August 24, 1870; Frances Duer *Diary*, June 15, 1895, McLaren Diaries, NYHS.
372 Mary Elizabeth Gittings *Diary*, October 3, 1885.
373 Mamie Parsons *Diary*, July 25, 1889.
374 Ann Eliza Rodman to Maria Hoffman, October 21, 1817.
375 Laura Thomas *Diary*, October 31, 1870.
376 Sarah Newberry *Diary*, 168.
377 Laura Thomas *Diary*, November 3, 13, 1870.
378 Helen Gould *Diary*, 24, 44.
379 Elizabeth Cady Stanton, *Eighty Years and More: Reminiscences, 1815-1897* (repr. New York: Schocken Books, 1973), 405.
380 Helen White to Dear Parents, September 30, 1877; Catherine Brooks to Ma, March 19, 1868; Laura Thomas *Diary*, October 31, 1870; Frances Arnold to Dad, May 13, 1897, Frances Arnold Papers, BMC; Ann Marie Green *Diary*, 76.
381 Sarah Elliott to Mother, July 7, 1887.
382 Helen Gould *Diary*, 24.
383 Phoebe Pember to n.a., November 16, 1897; Anonymous *Diary* (1851) Telfair Papers, GHS; Mary Hutton to Miss Jo, June 30, 1910; Mary Boit *Diary*, 27; Clara Ritchie to Dear Mama, September 1, 1889.
384 June Spencer, notes, 171.
385 Gena Trumbull *Diary*, August 14, 1909.
386 Mabel Root *Diary*, 6; Elizabeth Gould to Children, March, n.d., 1914; Emma Traxel *Diary*, August 14, 1905.
387 Frances Stevens to Dear Husband, August 16, 1869.
388 Hannah Gould *Diary*, July 6, 1901.
389 Marion Burgess *Diary*, July 11, 1882; Caroline White *Diary*, June 6, 1882.
390 Anais Bliss to Florence, December 18, 1889, in George Bliss, *Autobiography*, 339.
391 Caroline Corson to My Dear Friend, December 10, 1889; Kate Jones *Diary*, 91.
392 Frances Stevens to Alf, August, n.d., 1868.
393 Mary Few to Fannie, March 27, 1822.
394 Kate Jones *Diary*, 148; Annie Adams Fields to Louisa, October 28, 1859; Martha Griffis *Diary*, 44; Nina Halsey *Diary*, July 19, 1895; Idella Plimpton *Diary*, July 22, 1869.

395 Martha Griffis *Diary*, 56.
396 Ann Marie Green *Diary*, 279.
397 Anne Pluymert Heroy *Diary*, October 22, 1912, RU.
398 Ellen Perry *Diary*, March 2, 1852.
399 June Spencer, notes, October 17, 1884.

Chapter V: In the Land of Tell: Outdoor Adventures on a Grand Tour

1 Sarah Cleveland *Diary*, July 30, 31, August 14, September 2, 1844.
2 Orvar Lofgren, *On Holiday: A History of Vacationing* (Berkeley: University of California Press, 1999), 33-34.
3 Stoddard, *Lectures*, Vol. One, 124.
4 Cogan, *All-American Girl*, 29, 34.
5 Quoted in *Ibid.*, 43.
6 Farnham, *The Education of the Southern Belle*, 126.
7 Sally, *Life at Saint Mary's*,15.
8 Sheila Rothman, *Woman's Proper Place: A History of Changing Ideals and Practices, 1870 to the Present* (New York, Basic Books, 1978), 29.
9 *Ibid.*, 29-36.
10 Middleton, *Victorian Lady Travellers*, 7.
11 Emily Noyes Vanderpoel, *Chronicles of a Pioneer School From 1792 to 1833* (Cambridge: Cambridge University Press, 1903), 109.
12 Maria Degen, *Diary of a Grand Tour of Europe and the Middle East, 1850-1852* (Alexandria: Alexandria Street Press, 2002), 62.
13 Daniel Kilbride suggests many Americans first cultivated an appreciation of the sublime, which "developed the witness's appreciation for nature's majesty and the genius of creation" in their own country by romanticizing such sights as Niagara Falls. Kilbride, *Being American*, 93.
14 Cordozzo, *Diary of Emma Cullum Cordozzo*, 105.
15 George Prentiss (ed.), *The Life and Letters of Elizabeth Prentiss* (Echo Library reprint, 2008),182.
16 Frances Arnold to Frank, August 1, 1901.
17 Eliza P. Gurney, *Letters and Diaries of Eliza P. Gurney* (Philadelphia, 1884), 102.
18 Chamouni is also spelled Chamonix.
19 Preston, *The Life and Letters of Margaret Jutkins Preston*, 299.
20 Prentiss (ed.), *The Life and Letters*, 182.
21 Abbie Farwell, "Bachelor Girls in the Alps," October 22, 1899.
22 Stoddard, *Lectures*, Vol. One, 181. Mer de Glace is much smaller today and no longer a major tourist venue.

23 Laura Thomas *Diary*, January 7, 1871.
24 Anne Bense *Diary*, n.d. (1887), 32.
25 Cordozzo, *Letters of Emma Cullum Cordozzo*, 87.
26 Clara Mitchell *Diary*, June 29, 1888.
27 Grace Hutchins *Diary*, March 11, 1899.
28 Mary Gaston to Mary, August 12, 1901.
29 Catherine Brooks to Dear Ma, May 24, 1867.
30 Mary Bates *Letters*, June 10, July 19, August 2, 1891, Mary Bates Papers, HSL.
31 Caroline White *Diary*, August 3, 1855.
32 Fanny Hall, *Rambles in Europe*, 79.
33 Gardiner, *Letters From a Young Girl's Diary*, March 12, 1841.
34 Idella Plimpton *Diary*, September 12, 1869.
35 Pease and Pease (eds.), *The Roman Years of a South Carolina Woman*, 15. The French name, *chaise d' porteur* was sometimes used.
36 Sarah Cleveland *Diary*, July 30, 1844.
37 Ann F. Page *Diary*, May 2, 1837.
38 Harriet Blanchard *Diary*, January 14, 1867, Anne Blakiston Day Papers.
39 Mary Pierce *Diary*, February 24, 1873.
40 Dolly Whaley to Father, January 17, 1910.
41 Anne Bense *Diary*, August 17, 1886.
42 Louisa Smythe *Recollections*, 35.
43 Sara Newberry *Diary*, 204.
44 Clements, *A Glimpse of Europe*, July 9, 1881.
45 Susie Silver *Diary*, May 26, 1861.
46 Judith Rives *Diary*, August 2, 4, 16, 1831.
47 Alicia Middleton *Diary*, 67.
48 Kate Jones *Diary*, 135.
49 Susie Silver to Mama and Papa, July 7, 1867.
50 Amy Aldis *Diary*, June 12, 1872.
51 Mary Jane Blair to Father, Sister and Cousin, July 13, 1866.
52 Florence Alimnae *Diary*, July 24, 1896.
53 Anna De Yoe *Diary*, January 1,19, 1903, Willard De Yoe Papers, RU.
54 Degen, *Diary of a Grand Tour*, 62-63.
55 Mary Pierce *Diary*, August 21, 1872.
56 Laura Thomas *Diary*, May 31, 1870.
57 Sarah Cleveland *Diary*, September 4, 1844.
58 John Kimberly to Annie, February 5, 1859, John Kimberly Papers.
59 Caroline Farrar *Diary*, 115.
60 Amy Aldis *Diary*, July 31, 1872.
61 Ellie Pierson *Diary*, June 25, July 27, 1885, PEM.
62 Anne Bense *Diary*, August 17, 19, 20, September 3, 10, 1886.

63 Gena Trumbull *Diary*, July 2, 7, 27, August 2, 17, 23, 1909.
64 Birmingham, *Switzerland*, xi.
65 Judith Rives *Diary*, 189.
66 Mary Fraser to Sister, August 15, 1844.
67 Judith Rives *Diary*, August 4, 1831.
68 S. Abbott Lawrence *Diary*, April 25, 1851.
69 Gardiner, *Leaves from a Young Girl's Diary*, March 12, 1841.
70 Idella Plimpton to Mother, March 14, 1870.
71 Dolly Whaley to Father, January 17, 1911.
72 Kate Jones *Diary*, 134.
73 Eve Kingsland *Diary*, May 30, 1891.
74 Eugenie Homer *Diary*, March 4, 1879.
75 Anne Bense *Diary*, January 4, 1886.
76 Caroline Farrar *Diary*, 292, 300.
77 Elizabeth Ogden Adams *Diary*, May 17, 1894.
78 Maria Bayard *Diary*, n.d., n.p.
79 Caroline Farrar *Diary*, 140.
80 Abby Quincy *Diary*, 3, 188.
81 Jennie McGraw to Douglas Boardman, June 2, 12, July 5, August 4, 11, 18, 1878, Douglas Boardman Papers, CU.
82 Mary Woodbury *Diary*, August 14, 20, 24, 30, 1870.
83 Newspaper clipping in Isabella Curtis to Madam, May 6, 1907.
84 Elizabeth Adams to Loulie, December 7, 1893.
85 Ellie Pierson *Diary*, June 23, July 8, 14, 28, 1885.
86 Isabelle Perkinson to Mother, June 29, 1909.
87 Mary Whitney to Edward, July 17, 1897, Mary Whitney Papers, VC.
88 Jane Cowl *Diary*, n.d., (1907).
89 Elizabeth Nichols to Arthur, August 19, 1878, Elizabeth Nichols *Diary*, June 3, July 9, 1894, February 9, 24, March 21, 1900. In 1878 Elizabeth had two daughters, Rose and Marian, and a son, Sydney. Sydney died shortly after her return; a third daughter, Margaret, was born a few years later.
90 Eleanor Joy *Diary*, August 1, 1885.

Chapter VI: Wondering at Myself for Being Here: A Grand Tour Alone and Together

1 Elisabeth Griffith, *In Her Own Right*, 35-50.
2 *Ibid.*, 203-204.
3 *Report of the Women's Rights Convention, Held at Seneca Falls, N.Y., July 19th and 20th, 1848* (Rochester, 1848); Vivian Gornick, *The Solitude of*

Self: Thinking About Elizabeth Cady Stanton (New York: Farrar, Straus and Giroux, 2005), 3-9.
4 Arthur M. Eastman (ed.), *The Norton Anthology of Poetry* (New York: W.W. Norton, 1970), "Daffodils," 557; "Song," 653.
5 Marshall, *The Peabody Sisters*, 165.
6 Schriber, *Telling Travels*, xix.
7 Mamie Haven to Nettie, February 12, 1878.
8 Eliza Lamar *Diary,* July 1-October 4, 1866.
9 Sarah Newberry *Diary*, 52-53.
10 Caroline White *Diary*, May 5, June 25, October 3, 4, November 1, 1855, May 29, 1878, September 20, 21, June 6, 16, 1882. In 1855 Kiel was ruled by Denmark although not considered part of it; since 1864 it has been part of Germany.
11 Mamie Parsons to Mother, May 14, 25, 1901.
12 Georgette Chamberlain *Diary*, July 30, August 28, September 8, 1880.
13 Bliss, *Autobiography of George Bliss*, Vol. II, 277, 283.
14 Annie Spalding to Mama, Sunday, January [n.d.] 1907, Speer Family Papers, GDAH.
15 Henrietta Frank *Diary*, July 1905, 1, 54, September n.d., 1899.
16 Isabelle Perkinson to Mother, June 19, 1909.
17 Judith Rives *Diary,* July 14, 1831.
18 Althea Harper *Diary*, May 24, June 1, 1901.
19 Carrie Harris to Mother, June 19, July 9, October 9, 1891, Carrie M. Harris Papers, MHC.
20 Annie Spalding to Mama, n.d.,1907.
21 Mary Pierce *Diary*, March 15, 1872.
22 Mary Sterling *Diary*, July 24, 26, 1872.
23 Madame Adam, "Those American Girls in Europe," *North American Review*, No. 151 (October, 1890), 400.
24 Mildred Cox Howes *Diary*, April 9, 16, 19, 1902, Mildred Cox Howes Papers, MAHS.
25 Bessie Horstmann *Diary*, May 30, August 1, 1869.
26 Isabella Curtis to Madam, January 27, 1907.
27 Charlotte Horlbeck *Diary*, n.d.
28 Helen Gould *Diary*, 92.
29 Maria Bayard *Diary*, n.d., n. p.
30 Sarah Elliott to Mother, November 27, December 6, 1886.
31 Martha Griffis *Diary*, 81, 84, 89, 102.
32 Frances Stevens to Dear Daughter, August 13, 1868.
33 Bessie Horstmann *Diary*, June 1, 1869.
34 Adelaide Werner *Diary*, June 22, 1906.
35 Susie Silver to Mama, August 12, 16, 1867.

36 Mary Bradbury to Jack, September 14, 1886; Harriet Bradbury to Lily, September 14, 1886.
37 Mary and Frances Gaston *Diary*, May 8, 1894.
38 Mary Boit *Diary*, December 2, 1896, April 24, 1898.
39 Hamilton (ed.), *Ladies on the Loose*, xii.
40 Trafton, *American Girl Abroad*, 29, 221.
41 Blanche E. Wheeler, *Mary C. Wheeler: Leader in Art and Education* (Boston: Marshall Jones Co. 1934), 147.
42 Mary L. Ninde, *We Two Alone in Europe* (Chicago: A.C. McClurg, 1889), 7-8, 108, 162-164.
43 Elino, "Edith and I in Paris" (*The Ladies Home Journal*, 1900), 5.
44 Abbie Farwell, "Bachelor Girls in Scotland," St. Louis *Globe-Dispatch*, July 30, 1999.
45 Josephine Tyler, *Waymaker or Sola in Europe*, (Chicago: Brentano Brothers, 1885), 1.
46 Frances Stevens to Dear Husband, August 2, 1868.
47 Eleanor Middleton to Harriet, April 22, 1895.
48 Edith Parsons to Mamie, May 20, 1912.
49 Helen Brooks to Lizzy, October 6, 1882, letter fragment, n. d., 1898.
50 Caroline Corson to Dear Friend, September 19, 1892.
51 Bettie Kimberly to Husband, February 18, 25, April 2, 1860; Bettie Kimberly to Sis, February 13, 1860.
52 Frances Stevens to Eugene, July 16, 1868, to Husband, August 2, 23, 30, September 20, 1868.
53 Ethel Dummer to Frank, November 12, 20, 1909, May 27, 31, June 9, 1910.
54 Clements, *A Glimpse of Europe*, July 21, September 21, 25, 26, 1881.
55 Margaret Edsell *Diary*, November 5, 8, 15, December 24, 25, 1898.
56 Laura Winthrop Johnson *Diary*, November 29, 1869-February 17, 1870.
57 Mrs. T.T. Marsh *Diary*, November 19, 1872.
58 Elizabeth Gould to Olive, n.d., Mother to Dear Children, March 5, 1914.
59 Clara Ritchie to Mama, August 12, 18, September 1, 15, 24, 29, November 3, 10, December 10, 1889, February 16, 1890.
60 Constance Harrison to Burton, April 18, 24, May 14, 1893, to Hetty, May 16, 1893.
61 Martha Griffis *Diary*, 37, 46.
62 Henrietta Frank *Diary* (1905), 12, 35, 85.
63 Mamie Parsons to Family, June 18, 1889, to Mama, August 31, September 6, 1889.
64 Phoebe Pember to Georgie, June 20, September 11, November 20, 1895, June 20, 1896, to n.a., September 26, 1896.

65 Charlotte Crawford *Diary*, 24, Charlotte Crawford Papers, CNU; Mabel Root *Diary*, July 1, 7, 10, September 3, 11, 17, 1908.
66 Laura Thomas *Diary*, August 12, 14, 18, September 5, October 26, November 3, 1870, February 2, 3, March 24, April 26, May 1, 5, 18, June 9, 1871, March 21, 1871.
67 Mary Raoul Millis *Memoir* (typescript), 96, 105-110, 116-117, 122-129.
68 Caroline Corson to Friend, February 28, 1890.
69 Nina Halsey *Diary*, July 10, 19, 1895, and undated entries.
70 Mrs. D.A. Tufts *Diary*, June 24, 1907, NYPL.
71 Willie Adams to Mother, June 18, August 7, 1896, to Hattie, August 25, 1896, to Beff, June 16, 1899, June 26, July 17, 1902, to Bryce, June 15, 1902. Most likely "Old Pat" was a black man known to Willie's family. It was the kind of demeaning nickname commonly given elderly black men. Willie may have been simply mentioning the two most famous French royals, but if she thought Marie Antoinette was the queen of Louis XIV rather than Louis XVI, she was as ignorant of French history as those she criticized.
72 Maria Bayard *Diary*, October 17, 1814.
73 Mary Few to Mother, November 22, 1821.
74 Annie Winsor Diary, August 23, 1885.
75 Mamie Parsons to Family, July 6, 1889.
76 Anna De Yoe *Diary*, 9, December 20, 1902, March 16, 1903.
77 Herma Clark to Mrs. Blair, July n.d., 1907.
78 Abby Quincy *Diary*, December 16, 30, 1887, BPL.
79 Isabelle Perkinson to Mother, June 19, 29, November 3, 1909.
80 Charlotte Crawford *Diary*, 99-102.
81 Constance Harrison *Diary*, June 18, 1894.
82 Eleanor Middleton to Harriet Middleton, July 14, 23, October 12, 1895.
83 Mary Pierce *Diary*, April 9, October 6, 7, 1873.
84 Katherine Johnson *Diary*, 4, 6, 12, 16-17.
85 Elizabeth Nichols to Arthur, September 11, 17, 1878.
86 Abby Choate *Diary*, August 19, 21, 1891, PEM.
87 Emma Trexel *Diary*, August 14, 1905, CNU.
88 Sarah Elliott to Mother, July 7, 1887.
89 Clara Reed *Diary*, September 8, 1890.
90 Schaller, *Deliver Us From Evil*, 75.
91 Eugenie Homer to Mother and Father, January 12, October 1, 1879, to Mother, February 8, March 25, April 6, July 18, August 12, September 23, October 23, 1879, to Father, January 19, September 9, 1879.
92 Laura Comer *Diary*, June 16, July 19, 26, 28, August 1, 6, 13, 15, 25, 29, September 3, 6, 17, 18, 22, October 18, 1872.
93 Elizabeth Porter Gould *Diary*, n.d. (1894).

94 Carol U. Sisler, *Enterprising Families: Ithaca, New York* (Ithaca: Enterprise Publishing, 1986), 70-71.
95 Jennie McGraw letters, May 2, 1878-June 9, 1879, Douglas Boardman Papers, CNU.
96 June Spencer to Mama, June 19, 29, July 8, August 5, 23, notes, 179, 187.
97 Phoebe Pember to n.a., September 26, 1896.

Chapter VII: How I Wish I Was Safely Out of This: The *Titanic*, the Great War and a New Grand Tour

1 Geoffrey Blainey, *A Short History of the 20th Century* (Chicago: Ivan R. Dee, 2005), 5.
2 Philipp Blom, *The Vertigo Years: Europe, 1900-1914* (New York: Perseus Books Group, 2008), 5-11.
3 *Ibid.*, 27.
4 *Ibid.*, 3.
5 *Ibid.*, 2-3, 398.
6 Margaret Curtis to Aunts, April 13, 1912.
7 Wade, *The Titanic*, 35.
8 Steven Biel, *A Cultural History of the Titanic Disaster*, (New York, W.W. Norton, 1997), 100-106.
9 Quoted in *Ibid.*, 29.
10 *Ibid.*, 37. From its unveiling in 1931 to 1966 the statue stood on the present location of the Kennedy Center in Washington DC. It was moved to Channel Park in SW Washington to make way for that building.
11 Wade, *The Titanic*, 316.
12 Harriet Curtis to My Dear, April 17, 1912, to My Dear Little Pet, April 21, 1912.
13 Nancy Cott, *The Grounding of Modern Feminism* (New Haven: Yale University Press, 1987), 143.
14 Hannah Gould to Daddy, September n.d., 1911.
15 Elizabeth Gould *Diary*, September 10, 1913.
16 See Eric Larson, *Dead Wake: The Last Crossing of the Lusitania* (New York: Crown Publishers, 2015).
17 Sarah Bolton *Diary*, August 4, 1914, Sarah Bolton Journals, HSL.
18 James Srodes, *On Dupont Circle: Franklin and Eleanor Roosevelt and the Progressives Who Shaped Our World* (Berkeley: Counterpoint, 2012), 66.
19 Francis Carolan to Hatta, August 14, 15, 19, 1914, Francis J. Carolan Papers, CHM. Hatta was George Pullman's daughter.
20 Alma Peterson to Mother, July 28, September 6, 1914, to Father, August 1, 1914.

21 Schallar, *Deliver Us From Evil*, 116-125. When Nancy's grandchildren questioned why she insisted on keeping all of her luggage, she acknowledged that in retrospect it appeared silly, but "it seemed very important to me at the time."
22 Dulles, *Americans Abroad*, 150-152.
23 Mary A. Colles *Diary*, August-September, 1914, Wick-Blachly-Colles Papers, NYPL.
24 Ruth Pike, *My Trip Abroad, 1914* (Alexandria: Alexandria Street Press, 1992).
25 Horne, *Seven Ages of Paris*, 322.
26 Levenstein, *Seductive Journey*, 247-250.
27 Henrietta Szold to Eva, October 27, 1909, to Chester Teller. n.d., to Dr. and Mrs. Magnes, January 3, 1910. Henrietta Szold Papers, NYPL. Szold was forty-nine and already a prominent Jewish activist when she made this trip. On her return she founded Hadassah, an organization dedicated to improving the health of Jewish women in Palestine.
28 Quoted in Levenstein, *Seductive Journey*, 236.
29 Hamilton (ed.), *Ladies on the Loose*, xi.
30 Anderson, *Women and the Politics of Travel*, 14.
31 Louise Jewett to My Dear Ones, September 17, 1893.

Epilogue: Laying Up Stores of Knowledge and Experience: After a Grand Tour

1 Eliza Smith, *Reminiscence*, n.p.
2 Kirkland, *Holidays Abroad*, 218.
3 Annie Fields to Mother, March 3, 1860.
4 Lucy Chase to Brother and Sister, May 3, 1870, Chase Family Papers, NEAS.
5 June Spencer to Mother, August 23, 1884.
6 Ella Cabot *Diary*, Vol. II, November 15, 1885.
7 Clara Ritchie to Mama and Papa, February n.d.,1890, to Mama, April 13, 1890; Martha Maltby to Mrs. Ritchie, n.d, Clara Belle Ritchie Family Papers.
8 Frances Arnold to Dr. Ward, August 25, 1901.
9 Delia Austrian *Diary*, May 31, 1902.
10 Sara Day, *Coded Letters, Concealed Love: The Larger Lives of Harriet Freeman and Edward Everett Hale* (Washington, DC: New Academia Publishing, 2013), 337. These comments are presented in chronological order and represent most of the decades studied here.

Bibliography

PRIMARY SOURCES

Books

Adams, Hannah. *A Memoir of Miss Hannah Adams: Written By Herself with Additional Notices by a Friend.* Boston: Grey and Bowen. 1832.

Barnes, Margaret Ayer and Janet Ayer Fairbank (eds.). *Julia Newberry's Diary.* New York: W.W. Norton & Co. 1932.

Bullard, Mrs. A.T.J. *Sights and Scenes in Europe: A Series of Letters from England, France, Germany, Switzerland and Italy in 1850.* St. Louis: Chambers and Knapp, 1852.

Conant, Mary Pike. *A Girl of the Eighties at College and at Home.* Boston: Houghton Mifflin, 1931.

Cordozzo, Emma Cullum. *Letters of Emma Cullum Cordozzo, 1842-1918.* Meadville, PA.

Deese, Helen R. (ed.). *Daughter of Boston: The Extraordinary Diary of a Nineteenth-Century Woman.* Boston: Beacon Press, 2005.

Degen, Maria Kittredge Whitney. *Diary of a Grand Tour of Europe and the Middle East, 1850-1852.* Alexandria: Alexandria Street Press, 2002.

De Vert, Madame Octavia Walton. *Souvenirs of Travel.* New York: S.H. Goetzel and Co., 1857.

Dudley, Lucy. *Letters to Ruth.* New York: F.H. Gilson, 1896.

Eames, Jane Anthony. *Budget of Letters or Things Which I Saw Abroad.* Boston: William D. Ticknor and Co., 1847.

Fulton, Charles. *Europe Viewed Through American Spectacles.* Philadelphia: Lippincott, 1874.

Gardiner, Margaret. *Letters From A Young Girl's Diary.* New Haven: Tuttle, Morehouse and Taylor Co., 1927.

Gurney, Eliza P. *Letters and Diaries of Eliza P. Gurney.* Philadelphia: Lippincott, 1884.

Hall, Fanny W. *Rambles in Europe: Or, A Tour Through France, Italy, Switzerland, Great Britain, and Ireland, in 1836*. New York: E. French, 1839.
Hall, Mrs. Herman J. *Two Travelers in Europe*. Springfield, MA: Hampden Publishing Co., 1898.
Harpers Handbook for Travellers. New York: Harper and Brothers, 1882.
Higginson, Thomas Wentworth. "Books and Reading" in *The Woman's Book*. New York: Charles Scribner's Sons, 1894.
Jones, Mary Cadwalader. *European Travel for Women*. New York: McMillan, 1900.
Kirkland, Caroline. *Holidays Abroad or Europe from the West*. New York: Baker and Scribner, 1849.
Knox, Thomas. *How To Travel*. New York: Charles T. Dillingham, 1881.
LeClerq, Anne Sinkler Whaley (ed.). *Elizabeth Sinkler Coxe's Tales from the Grand Tour, 1890-1910*. Columbia: University of South Carolina Press, 2006.
Mayo, Abigail De Hart. *An American Lady in Paris, 1828-1829*. Boston: Houghton Mifflin, 1927.
McManus, Blanche. *The American Woman Abroad*. New York: Dodd, Meade, 1911.
Morford, Henry. *Morford's Short-Trip Guide to Europe*. New York: Sheldon and Company, 1872.
Moulton, Louise Chandler. *Random Rambles*. Boston: Roberts Brothers, 1881.
Ninde, Mary L. *We Two Alone in Europe*. Chicago: A.C. McClurg, 1889.
Osgood, James R. *Osgood's Complete Pocket-Guide to Europe*. Boston: James R. Osgood and Company, 1883.
Pease, William H. and Jane H. Pease (eds.). *The Roman Years of a South Carolina Artist: Caroline Carson's Letters Home, 1872-1892*. Columbia: University of South Carolina Press, 2003.
Phillips, Morris. *Abroad and at Home*. New York: The Art Press, 1891.
Pike, Ruth. *My Trip Abroad, 1914*. Alexandria: Alexandria Street Press, 1992.
Pitman, Marie J. *European Breezes*. Boston: Lee and Shepard, 1882.
Prentiss, George. (ed.). *The Life and Letters of Elizabeth Prentiss*. Echo Library (reprint), 2008.
Preston, Margaret. *The Life and Letters of Margaret Junkin Preston*. Boston: Houghton Mifflin, 1903.
Robinson, Louise B. *A Bundle of Letters From Over the Sea*. Boston: J.G. Cupples, 1890.
Satchel Guide for the Vacation Tourist in Europe. New York: Hurd and Houghton, 1873.
Stark, Mariana. *Information and Directions For Travellers on the Continent*. Paris: A. and W. Galignani, 1826.

Stephens, Louisa. *Golden Adventure: A Diary of Long Ago*. Pasadena: San Pasqual Books, 1941.
Trafton, Adeline. *American Girl Abroad*. Boston: Lee and Shepard, 1872.
Trowbridge, Harriet. *Travels in Europe and the East*. New Haven: Tuttle, Morehouse & Taylor, 1879.
Tyler, Josephine. *Waymaker or Sola in Europe*. Chicago: Brentano Brothers, 1885.
Urbino, Lavina. *An American Woman in Europe: The Journal of Two Years and a Half Sojourn in Germany, Switzerland, France, and Italy*. Boston: Lee and Shepard, 1869.
Vanderpoel, Emily Noyes. *Chronicles of a Pioneer School From 1792 to 1833*. Cambridge: Cambridge University Press, 1903.

Periodicals and Brochures

Adam, Madame. "Those American Girls in Europe." *North American Review*, No. 151. October, 1890.
Elino, "Edith and I in Paris." *The Ladies Home Journal*, January, 1900.
Robinson, N. "The Comforts and Discomforts of Travel," *Frank Leslie's Popular Monthly*, Vol. XIV, No. 2.
Tomes, Robert, "The Americans on Their Travels." *Harpers New Monthly Magazine*, June 1865.

Manuscripts

Boston Public Library (BPL)
Castilian Club Papers (Susan Hale)
Elizabeth Porter Gould Diary
Abby A. Quincy Diary

Bryn Mawr College (BMC)
Arnold Papers (Augusta Arnold) (Frances Arnold)
Grace De Laguna Papers
Helen Clements Kirk Papers (Emma Clements)
Grace Taplin Papers

Chicago History Museum (CHM)
Francis J. Carolan Papers (Hatta Carolan)
Herma Clark Papers
Crane-Lillie Family Papers (Frances Crane)
Mary Flavelle Papers
Greenbaum Sisters Papers (Henrietta Frank)

Hunt Family Papers (Mrs. Hunt)
Hyde Park Travel Club Papers
Kimball Family Papers (Hariett Kimball)
Laflin Family Papers (Josephine Laflin)
Henry Rew Papers (Anna Rew)

College of William & Mary (CWM)
Mabel Bragdon Papers
Agnes Kummer Papers
Virginia Taylor McCormick Papers

Columbia University (CU)
Julia Sands Bryant Diaries
John W. Burgess Papers (Ruth Burgess)
Duer Family Papers (Frances Duer)
Eleanor Joy Diary
Kent Family Papers (Mary Kent Stone)
Maria L'Hommedieu Fahys Papers
Winslow Papers (M.E. Winslow)

Cornell University (CNU)
Douglas Boardman Papers (Jennie McGraw)
Charlotte Crawford Papers
Charles Curtis Papers (Frances Curtis)
Gould Family Papers (Elizabeth Berry) (Hannah Gould)
Emma Hopkins Papers
Mcelheny Family Papers (Jennie McGraw)
McGraw Family Papers (Jennie McGraw)
Mabel Virginia Root Papers
Tremen Family Papers (Gena Trumbull)
Emma J. Trexel Diary
Helen Macgill White Papers

Duke University (DU)
Anonymous Diary
Frances Yates Aglionby Papers (Jeanette Aglionby)
Georgette A. Chamberlain Papers
Coleman Family Papers (Isabel Coleman)
Mary DeSaussure Fraser Papers
Mary Zilpha Giles Diary
Robert Hargadine Papers (Annie Hargadine)
Charles Hartt Papers (Mary Hartt)

John Knight Papers (Frances Beall Knight)
Joseph W.W. Marshall Papers (Eliza Marshall)
Alfred Landon Rives Papers (Judith Rives)
Charles Steedman Papers (Mrs. Steedman)
Mary Evelyn Stiles Papers
Amelia Van Vleek Papers
Aaron Wilbur Papers (Sallie Wilbur)
Isabelle Perkinson Williamson Papers

Georgia Department of Archives and History (GDAH)
William Few Collection (Mary Few)
Mary Raoul Millis Memoir (typescript)
Fannie R.K. Smith Papers
Speer Family Papers (Annie Spalding)

Georgia Historical Society (GHS)
Anderson Family Papers (Nina Pape)
Telfair Family Papers (Anonymous)
Woodbridge Collection (Eliza Lamar)

Harvard University – Baker Library (HBL)
Diaries of S. Abbott Lawrence (Miss Lawrence)

Harvard University – Gutman Library (HGL)
Emma Willard School Catalogues, 1829, 1830, 1840, 1850.
Troy Female Seminary Catalogue, 1850.
Vermont Academy Catalogue, 1881

Harvard University – Schlesinger Library (HSL)
Elizabeth Agassiz Papers
Mary Bates Papers
Sarah Bolton Journals
Louise Bosworth Papers
Helen Lawrence Brooks Papers
Abbie Farwell Brown Papers
Elizabeth Rogers Cabot Diaries
Hugh Cabot Family Papers (Mary Anderson Boit) (Elizabeth Cabot)
Alice Draper Carter Diary
Lucy Chamberlain Diary
Cornelia Van Auken Chapin Papers
Anna W. Chase Papers
Curtis Family Papers (Frances Curtis) (Isabella Curtis) (Harriet Curtis) (Margaret Curtis)

Ethel Dummer Papers
Margaret Harding Tileston Edsall Papers
Emily Eliot Diary
Emerson-Nichols Family Papers (Elizabeth Nichols) (Rose Nichols) (Marian Nichols) (Margaret Nichols)
Sarah Bradley Gamble Papers
Eva Kingsland Papers
Elizabeth Fisher Homer Nichols Papers
Lindsay Family Papers (Catherine Lindsay) (Ester Lindsay)
Mary Gardiner Marshall Papers (Ellen Hammond) (Julia Brannam)
Minnie Millette Papers
Morgan-Howes Family Papers (Laura Morgan)
Morse Papers (Frances Morse)
Nichols-Shurtleff Papers (Sarah Shurtleff)
Parker Family Papers (Harriet Parker) (Mary Bates)
Poor Family Papers (Mary Pierce) (Mary Poor)
Smythe-Story Papers (Nancy Story)
Edith Stedman Papers
Margaret Thomson Papers
Annie Ware Winsor Allen Papers
Women's Rest Tour Association Papers

Historical Society of Pennsylvania (HSP)
Lewis Ashurst Papers (Mary Ashurst)
Humphrey Atherton Papers (Emily Atherton)
Biddle Family Papers (Julia Rush) (Pauline Biddle) (Anne McKennan Biddle)
Coles-Lippincott-Horstmann Collection (anonymous) (Bessie Horstmann)
Cox Family Papers (Eliza Cox)
Anne Blakiston Day Papers
Fahnestock-Wolff Papers (Anna Marie Fahnestock)
Anna Hazen Howell Papers
Harriet Lane Johnston Papers
Louise Kellner Journals
Ann Page Journal
Hattie Trowbridge Diary

Johns Hopkins University (JHU)
Gilman Collection (Elizabeth Gilman)
Marge Preston Diaries
Harry Reid Papers (Mary Elizabeth Gittings)

Library of Congress (LOC)
Henry Allen Papers (Dora Allen)
George Becker Papers (Sarah Tuckerman)
Burton Harrison Papers (Constance Harrison)
Louis Skidmore Papers (Wilhemina Mathews)
John W. Williams Papers (Martha Ann Tilton Williams)

Maryland Historical Society (MDHS)
Anonymous Diary
Gilman Papers (Elizabeth Gilman)
Jennie Reizestein Diary
Eliza Thomas Diary
Mrs. E.P. Thompson Diaries

Massachusetts Historical Society (MAHS)
Annie Adams Fields Papers
Elizabeth Ogden Adams Papers
Ellen Wayles Randolph Coolidge Diaries
Gardner Family Papers (Eliza Gardner)
Sarah Guild Diary
Herter Family Papers (Mary Pratt Herter)
Elizabeth Homans Diary
Mildred Cox Howes Papers
Lamson Family Papers (Mary Lamson)
Jacob M. Manning Papers (Anna Manning)
C.M. Sedgwick Diary
E. Thompson Diary

Missouri Historical Society (MHS)
Malcolm MacBeth Papers (Clara Mitchell)

Mount Holyoke College (MHC)
Carrie Harris Papers
Louise Jewett Papers
Idella C. Plimpton Papers

New England Antiquarian Society (NEAS)
Chase Family Papers (Lucy Chase)
Endicott Family Papers (Sarah Endicott)
Marsh Diary (Mrs. T.T. Marsh)
Ellen Louise Moulton Papers

James Monroe Scofield Papers (Florence Scofield)
Caroline Barrett White Papers

New York Public Library (NYPL)
William Bayard Collection (Maria Bayard)
Bense Family Diaries (Anne Bense) (Isabella Bense)
Bigelow Family Papers (Grace Bigelow) (Jenny Bigelow Tracy)
Anne Bradley Diary
Cleveland-Perkins Family Papers (Sarah Cleveland) (Abbie Perkins)
Jane Cowl Diary
Laura Winthrop Johnson Papers
Laura Libbey Diary
Euphemia Olcott Diary
Mary Lorillard Ronalds Diary
Henrietta Szold Diary
Mrs. D.A. Tufts Papers
Wick-Blachly Colles Papers (Mary Colles)
Miriam Shomer Zunser Papers

New York Historical Society (NYHS)
George Bliss Papers (Mrs. George Bliss)
Catherine Brooks Papers
Delafield Family Papers (Emily Delafield)
Elizabeth De Peyster Diary
Erving-King Papers (Catherine Van Rensselaer)
Gallatin Papers (Frances Stevens)
Gould Family Papers (Helen Gould)
Harper, Lathrop, Colgate Papers (Althea Harper)
Katherine Johnson Papers
MacLaren Diaries (Frances Duer)
Mary McLean European Travel Diaries
Parsons Family Papers (Edith Parsons) (Gert Parsons) (Mamie Parsons) (Rachel Parsons)
Caroline Poor Papers
Robinson Papers (Eliza Smith)
Mrs. Alfred Thompson Diary
Caroline Townsend Diary
Helen M. Turner Papers
Tunis Van Benschoten Papers (Lizzie Van Benschoten)

Newberry Library (NL)
Alma Schmidt Peterson Papers (Clara Schmidt) (Alma Peterson)

North Carolina Department of Archives and History (NCDAH)
Willa Briggs Collection (Eliza Pool)
Aaron Burtis Hunter Collection (Sarah Hunter)
Thomas Merritt Pittman Collection (Eliza Pittman)
Gertrude Weil Papers

Oregon Historical Society (OHS)
Ruth Church Papers

Peabody Essex Museum (PEM)
Anonymous Diary
Anna Northend Benjamin Diary
Abby P. Choate Diaries
Susan March Emerson Diary
Samuel and Eliza Endicott Collection
Pierson Family Papers (Ellie Pierson Perry)
William Silver Letters (Susie Silver)

Rhode Island Historical Society (RIHS)
Sophia Harris Babbit Diary
Amos Barstow Papers (Grace Barstow)
Mariam Burgess Diary
Zachariah Chafee Papers (Mary Chafee)
Elizabeth Grinall Diary
Jeanie Lippitt Weeden Diary

Rochester Public Library (RPL)
Isabel Rogers Diary

Rutgers University (RU)
Atkinson Family Papers (Mary Atkinson)
Francis Eugene Butler Papers (Julia Colt Butler)
Willard De Yoe Papers (Anna De Yoe)
Freeman Family Papers (Ginevra Freeman)
Gaston Family Papers (Frances Gaston) (Mary Gaston)
William E. Griffis Papers (Martha Griffis)
Anne Pluymert Heroy Diary
Asher Atkinson Howell Papers (Eliza Howell)
Daniel Kidder Papers (Harriette Kidder)
Neilson Family Papers (Mary Woodbury)
Anna Miller Place Papers

Adelaide Werner Papers
Anna Wilcox Papers

Smith College (SC)
Miscellaneous Manuscripts (Clara Reed)
Cornelia Upton Papers

South Carolina Historical Society (SCHS)
Charleston Female Seminary Papers
Cheves-Middleton Papers (E.M.)
Isabella Faber Travel Diaries
Charlotte Horlbeck Travel Journal
Middleton-Blake Papers (Mary Middleton)
Smythe-Stoney Papers (Louise McCord Smythe) (Sarah Smythe) (Nancy Smythe)

South Carolina Library (SCL)
Mary Montcrieff Allen Papers
Miscellaneous Manuscripts (Jane Adger)
Sarah Annie Smythe and Susan Dunlap Smythe Papers

University of California at Berkeley (UCB)
Matthew Simpson Culbertson Papers (Helen Culbertson Kip)
Hitchcock Family Papers (M.T. Fall)
Mary Robertson Bradbury Howard Papers
Mary Mclean Olney Diary
Grace Roberts Moore Diary and Letters
Rosenshine Papers (Edith Rosenshine)

University of Chicago (UC)
Austrian Family Papers (Delia Austrian).

University of Michigan (UM)
Sarah Boardman Diary
Fenno-Hoffman Papers (Anne Eliza Rodman)
Solomon G. Haven Family Papers (Mamie Haven)
Miscellaneous Collections (Judith Page Rives)
Sarah and Edward Ogden Diaries

University of North Carolina at Chapel Hill (UNC)
George Washington Allen Papers (Willie Allen)
Isabelle Busbee Papers

Laura Beecher Comer Papers
Eliza Jane Lord De Rosset Diaries
Charles Dewey Papers (Julia Ann Haylander)
Francis A. Dickins Papers (Sara Howell)
Sarah Barnwell Elliott Letters
Mary Gibson Diary
Gould Family Papers (Elizabeth Gould)
Hairston and Wilson Papers (Mrs. Watt Hairston)
Hunt Family Papers (Mrs. Hunt)
Harriett Kimball Papers
John Kimberly Papers (Bettie Kimberly)
Anne Catherine Boykin Jones Papers
Calvin Jones Papers (Octavia Jones)
Catherine McAlpin Wray Pritchard Papers
McBee Family Papers (Mrs. Vardry McBee)
Phoebe Pember Letters
Cornelia Phillips Spencer Papers (June Spencer)

University of Oregon (UO)
Grace Hutchins Papers

University of Pennsylvania (UP)
Emma Repplier Witmer Diary

University of Rochester (UR)
Caroline Weld Farrar Diary
Markham Family Papers (Linda Markham)
Frank Hawley Ward Family Papers (Clara Werner)

University of South Carolina (USC)
Jane Adgar Papers
James Baxter Papers (Lucy Baxter)
Sylvester Beckley Papers (Mrs. Beckley)
Fitz William and Mary Jane Macfre McMaster Papers
Alicia Middleton Papers
Angelica Van Buren Papers

University of Virginia (UVA)
Charlotte Berkeley Cole Letters
Coleman, Twiggs, McEwen & Houston Papers (Hetty Kennedy)
Nina Withers Halsey Diary
Elizabeth Ijams Papers

Minor Family Papers (Susan Minor)
Laura T. Rutherford Diaries
Mary Lee Settle Papers (Dolly Whaley)
Laura Thomas Papers

Vassar College (VC)
Paulina Wright Davis Papers (Anonymous)
Mary Watson Gay Papers
Mary Whitney Papers

Virginia Historical Society (VHS)
Edwards Family (Alberta Taylor)
Eppes Family (Elizabeth Welsh Eppes)
Mary Evelyn Stiles Diary

Wellesley College (WC)
Alimnae Papers (Florence Alimnae)

Western Reserve Historical Society (WRHS)
J. Park Alexander Family Papers (Clara Alexander)
Mary Jane Blair Papers
Ann Marie Green Papers
Adella Prentiss Hughes Family Papers
Sarah Newberry Diary
Clara Belle Ritchie Family Papers
Severance Family Papers (Julia Severance) (Emily Severance) (Helen Millikin Nash)
Mary Sterling Papers
Belle Whitney Journal

SECONDARY SOURCES

Books
Ackroyd, Peter. *London: The Biography*. New York: Anchor Books, 2000.
Adler, Kathleen. Erica Hirshler and Barbara Weinburg. *Americans in Paris, 1860-1900*. London: National Gallery of Art, 2006.
Anderson, Monica. *Women and the Politics of Travel, 1860-1914*. Madison, NJ: Fairleigh Dickinson University Press, 2004.
Aron, Cindy S. *Working at Play: A History of Vacations in the United States*. New York: Oxford University Press, 1999.
Baker, Paul. *The Fortunate Pilgrims: Americans in Italy, 1800-1860*. Cambridge: Harvard University Press, 1964.

Barry, Kathleen. *Susan B. Anthony: A Biography of a Singular Feminist*. New York: Ballantine Books, 1988.

Berkin, Carol. *Wondrous Beauty: Betsy Bonaparte, the Belle of Baltimore Who Married Napoleon's Brother*. New York: Knopf, 2014.

Bernard, Paul. *Rush to the Alps: The Evolution of Vacationing in Switzerland*. New York: Columbia University Press, 1978.

Biel, Steven. *Down With the Old Canoe: A Cultural History of the Titanic Disaster*. New York: Norton, 1997.

Birmingham, David. *Switzerland: A Village History*. Athens, Ohio: Swallow Press, 1999.

Blom, Philipp. *The Vertigo Years: Europe, 1900-1914*. New York: Basic Books, 2008.

Bushman, Richard. *Refinement in America: Persons, Houses, Cities*. New York: Knopf, 1992.

Buzard, James. *The Beaten Track: European Tourism, Literature and the Ways of Culture, 1800-1918*. Oxford: Clarendon Press, 1993.

Caesar, Terry. *Forgiving the Boundaries: Home as Abroad in American Travel Writing*. Athens: University of Georgia Press, 1995.

Capper, Charles and Christina Giorcelli (eds.). *Margaret Fuller: Transatlantic Crossings in a Revolutionary Age*. Madison: University of Wisconsin Press, 2008.

Chew, William L. III (ed.). *National Stereotypes in Perspective: Americans in France, Frenchmen in America*. Amsterdam: Rodoopi, 2001.

Cocks, Catherine. *Doing the Town: The Rise of Urban Tourism in the United States, 1850-1915*. Berkeley: University of California Press, 2010.

Cogan, Frances B. *All-American Girl: The Ideal of Real Womanhood in Mid-Nineteenth-Century America*. Athens: University of Georgia Press, 1989.

Conlin, Jonathan. *Tales of Two Cities: Paris, London, and the Birth of the Modern City*. Berkeley: Counterpoint, 2013.

Cott, Nancy (ed.). *No Small Courage: A History of Women in the United States*, New York: Oxford University Press, 2000.

Cott, Nancy. *The Grounding of Modern Feminism*. New Haven: Yale University Press, 1987.

Crow, Duncan. *The Victorian Woman*. New York: Stein and Day, 1972.

Davidson, Cathy N. (ed.). *Reading in America*. Baltimore: Johns Hopkins Press, 1989.

Day, Sara. *Coded Letters, Concealed Love: The Larger Lives of Harriet Freeman and Edward Everett Hale*. Washington DC: New Academia Publishing, 2013.

De Botton, Alain. *The Art of Travel*. New York: Vintage International, 2002.

Deiss, Joseph Jay. *The Roman Years of Margaret Fuller*. New York: Thomas Crowell Company, 1969.

Dizikes, John. *Opera in America*. New Haven: Yale University Press, 1993.
Dorsey, Hebe. *The Belle Epoque in the Paris Herald*. London: Thames and Hudson, 1986.
Druett, Joan. *Hen Frigates: Wives of Merchant Captains Under Sail*. New York: Simon and Schuster, 1998.
Duggen, Christopher. *The Force of Destiny: A History of Italy Since 1796*. New York: Houghton Mifflin, 2007.
Dulles, Foster Rhea. *Americans Abroad: Two Centuries of European Travel*. Ann Arbor: University of Michigan Press, 1964.
Dunn, Susan. *Sister Revolutions: French Lightning, American Light*. New York: Faber and Faber, 1999.
Farnham, Christie Anne. *The Education of the Southern Belle*. New York: New York University Press, 1994.
Faragher, John Mack and Florence Howe (eds.). *Women and Higher Education in American History*. New York: W.W. Norton and Company, 1988.
Faust, Drew Gilpin. *Mothers of Invention: Women of the Slaveholding South in the American Civil War*. New York: Vintage Books, 1996.
Foster, Shirley. *American Women Travellers to Europe in the Nineteenth and Early-Twentieth Centuries*. Staffordshire: Keele University, 1994.
Fox, Stephen. *Transatlantic: Samuel Cunard, Isambard Brunel, and the Great Atlantic Steamships*. New York: Harper Collins, 2003.
Franchot, Jenny. *Roads to Rome: The Antebellum Protestant Encounter with Catholicism*. Berkeley: University of California Press, 1994.
Gemme, Paola. *Domesticating Foreign Struggles: The Italian Risorgimento and Antebellum American Identity*. Athens: The University of Georgia Press, 2005.
Gilmour, David. *The Pursuit of Italy: A History of a Land, Its Regions, and Their People*. New York: Farrar, Straus and Giroux, 2011.
Gornick, Vivian. *The Solitude of Self: Thinking About Elizabeth Cady Stanton*. New York: Farrar, Straus and Giroux, 2005.
Griffith, Elisabeth. *In Her Own Right: The Life of Elizabeth Cady Stanton*. New York: Oxford University Press, 1984.
Hamilton, Leo (ed.). *Ladies on the Loose: Women Travelers in the 18th and 19th Centuries*. New York: Dodd, Mead and Co., 1981.
Hedrick, Joan D. *Harriet Beecher Stowe: A Life*. New York: Oxford University Press, 1994.
Hibbert, Christopher. *Rome: The Biography of a City*. New York: Penguin Books, 1985.
Higonnet, Patrice. *Paris: Capital of the World*. Cambridge: Harvard University Press, 2002.
Horne, Alistair. *Seven Ages of Paris*. New York: Vintage Books, 2004.
Horowitz, Joseph. *Wagner Nights: An American History*. Berkeley: University of California Press, 1994.

Jones, Colin. *Paris: The Biography of a City*. New York: Penguin Book, 2004.
Jones, Howard Mumford. *American and French Culture, 1750-1848*. Chapel Hill: University of North Carolina Press, 1927.
Jonnes, Jill. *Eiffel's Tower*. New York: Penguin Books, 2009.
Kelley, Mary. *Learning to Stand and Speak: Women, Education, and Public Life in America's Republic*. Chapel Hill: University of North Carolina Press, 2006.
Kelley, Mary. *Private Woman, Public Stage: Literary Domesticity in Nineteenth-Century America*. New York: Oxford University Press, 1984.
Kilbride, Daniel, *Being American in Europe, 1750-1860*. Baltimore: Johns Hopkins University Press, 2013.
Kroeger, Brooke. *Nellie Bly*. New York: Random House, 1994.
Larson, Erik. *Dead Wake: The Last Crossing of the Lusitania*. New York: Crown Publishers, 2015.
Lears, Jackson. *No Place of Grace: The Transformation of American Culture, 1880-1920*. Chicago: University of Chicago Press, 1981.
Ledger, Sally. *The New Woman: Fiction and Feminism at the Fin de Siècle*. Manchester: Manchester University Press, 1997.
Leed, Eric J. *The Mind of the Traveler: From Gilgamesh to Global Tourism*. New York: Basic Books, 1991.
Levenstein, Harvey. *Seductive Journey: American Tourists in France from Jefferson to the Jazz Age*. Chicago: University of Chicago Press, 1998.
Levey, Michael. *Florence: A Portrait*. London: Pimlico, 1996.
Lockwood, Allison. *Passionate Pilgrims: The American Traveler in Great Britain, 1800-1914*, New Brunswick, NJ: Cornwell Books, 1980.
Lofgren, Orvar. *On Holiday: A History of Vacationing*. Berkeley: University of California Press, 1999.
Lueck, Beth. *American Writers and the Picturesque Tour: The Search for National Identity, 1790-1860*. London: Routledge, 1997.
Lueck, Beth, Brigitte Bailey and Lucinda Damon-Bach (eds.). *Translantic Women: Nineteenth-Century American Women Writers and Great Britain, 1790-1860*. Lebanon: University of New Hampshire Press, 2012.
MacCannell, Dean. *The Tourist: A New Theory of the Leisure Class*. Berkeley: University of California Press, 1999.
McCullough, David. *The Greater Journey: Americans in Paris*. New York: Simon and Schuster, 2011.
Machor, James L. (ed.). *Readers in History: Nineteenth-Century American Literature and the Contexts of Response*. Baltimore: Johns Hopkins University Press, 1993.
McInnis, Maurice D. with Angela Mack (eds.). *In Pursuit of Refinement: Charlestonians Abroad, 1740-1860*. Columbia: University of South Carolina Press, 1999.

Marks, Patricia. *Bicycles, Bangs, and Bloomers: The New Woman in the Popular Press*. Lexington: University of Kentucky Press, 1990.
Marshall, Megan. *The Peabody Sisters: Three Women Who Ignited American Romanticism*. Boston: Houghton Mifflin, 2005.
Maxtone-Graham, John. *The Only Way to Cross*. New York: Barnes and Noble, 1972.
Middleton, Dorothy. *Victorian Lady Travelers*. Chicago: Academy Chicago Publishers, 1965.
Miller, Michael B. *The Bon Marche: Bourgeois Culture and the Department Store, 1869-1920*. Princeton: Princeton University Press, 1981.
Mills, Sarah. *Discourses of Difference: An Analysis of Women's Travel Writing and Colonialism*. London: Routledge. 1991.
Morgan, David and Sally M. Promey (eds.). *The Visual Culture of American Religions*. Berkeley: University of California Press, 2001.
Mulvey, Christopher. *Anglo-American Landscapes: A Study of Nineteenth-Century Anglo-American Travel Literature*. Cambridge: Cambridge University Press, 2009.
Mulvey, Christopher. *Transatlantic Manners: Social Patterns in Nineteenth-Century Anglo-American Travel Literature*. Cambridge: Cambridge University Press, 1990.
Norwich, John Julius. *Paradise of Cities: Venice in the 19th Century*. New York: Doubleday, 2003.
Rahv, Philip. *Discovery of Europe: The Story of American Experience in the Old World*. Boston: Houghton Mifflin, 1947.
Richter, Amy. *Home on the Rails: Women, the Railroad, and the Rise of Public Domesticity*. Chapel Hill: University of North Carolina Press, 2005.
Roberson, Susan L. *Antebellum American Women Writers and the Road*: New York and London: Routledge, 2011.
Robinson, Jane (ed.). *Unsuitable for Ladies: An Anthology of Women Travellers*. New York: Oxford University Press, 1994.
Rogers, Daniel T. *Atlantic Crossings: Social Politics in a Progressive Age*. Cambridge: Harvard University Press, 1998.
Rothman, Sheila M. *Woman's Proper Place: A History of Changing Ideals and Practices, 1870 to the Present*. New York: Basic Books, 1978.
Ryan, Mary P. *Women in Public: Between Banners and Ballots, 1826-1880*. Baltimore: Johns Hopkins University Press, 1990.
Sally, Katherine (ed.). *Life at Saint Mary's*. Chapel Hill: University of North Carolina Press, 1942.
Schriber, Mary Suzanne (ed.). *Telling Travels: Selected Writings by Nineteenth-Century American Women Abroad*. DeKalb: Northern Illinois University Press, 1995.
Sears, John. *Sacred Places: American Tourist Attractions in the Nineteenth Century*. Amherst: University of Massachusetts Press, 1999.

Stebbins, Theodore E. Jr. (ed.). *The Lure of Italy: American Artists and The Italian Experience, 1760-1914*. Boston: Museum of Fine Arts, 1992.
Stout, Cushing. *The American Image of the Old World*. New York: Harper, 1963.
Stowe, Steven. *Intimacy and Power in the Old South: Ritual in the Lives of the Planters*. Baltimore: Johns Hopkins University Press, 1987.
Stowe, William. *Going Abroad: European Travel in Nineteenth-Century American Culture*. Princeton: Princeton University Press, 1994.
Stuart, Amanda Mackenzie. *Consuelo and Alva Vanderbilt*. New York: Harper, 2005.
Sturgis, Matthew. *When in Rome: 2000 Years of Roman Sightseeing*. London: Francis Lincoln Limited, 2011.
Vance, William. *America's Rome*, Vols. I and II. New Haven: Yale University Press, 1989.
Wade, Wyn Craig. *The Titanic: End of A Dream*. New York: Penguin Books, 1979.
Ware, Susan (ed.). *Modern American Women: A Documentary History*. New York: McGraw-Hill Company, 1997.
Watkin, David. *The Roman Forum*. Cambridge: Harvard University Press, 2009.
Wheeler, Blanche. *Mary C. Wheeler: Leader in Art and Education*. Boston: Marshall Jones Co., 1932.
Williams, Rosalind. *Dream Worlds: Mass Consumption in Late-Nineteenth-Century France*. Berkeley: University of California Press, 1982.
Wilson, A.N. *London: A History*. New York: Modern Library, 2006.
Withey, Lynne. *Grand Tours and Cook's Tours: A History of Leisure Travel, 1750-1915*. New York: William Morrow and Company, 1997.
Woodward, C. Vann. *The Old World's New World*. Oxford: Oxford University Press, 1991.
Woodward, C. Vann and Elisabeth Muhlenfeld (eds.). *The Private Mary Chesnut: The Unpublished Civil War Diaries*. New York: Oxford University Press, 1984.
Ziff, Lazar. *Return Passages: Great American Travel Writing, 1780-1910*. Berkeley: University of California Press, 1982.

Articles

Dupont, Brandon, Alka Gandhi and Thomas J. Weiss. "The American Invasion of Europe: The Long Term Rise in Overseas Travel, 1820-2000," *National Bureau of Economic Research Working Paper* (May, 2008).
Gassman, Richard. "The First American Tourist Guidebooks," *Book History*, Vol. 8, 2005.

Kelley, Mary. "Reading Women/Women Reading: The Making of Learned Women in Antebellum America," *The Journal of American History* (September, 1996).

Kerber, Linda K. "Separate Spheres, Female Worlds, Woman's Place: The Rhetoric of Women's History." *Journal of American History* (June, 1988).

Kilbride, Daniel. "Travel, Ritual and National Identity: Planters on the European Tour, 1820-1860. *Journal of Southern History* (August, 2003).

Liebersohn, Harry. "Recent Works on Travel Writing, "*The Journal of Modern History* (September, 1996).

Schriber, Mary Suzanne. "Julia Ward Howe and the Travel Book." *The New England Quarterly* (June, 1989).

Schwager, Sally. "Educating Women in America," *Signs* (Winter 1987).

Wind, Herbert Warren. "Profiles: The House of Baedeker." *The New Yorker* (September 22, 1975).

Name Index

(Pre-eighteenth century names and those mentioned in passing are not included)

Abbott, Miss 70, 261n9
Adams, Elizabeth 113
Adams, Elizabeth 103, 127-28, 144, 195
Adams, Hannah 16
Adams, Henry 231
Adams, John 30
Adgar, Jane 86, 172
Aglionby, Jeanette 42-43
Aldis, Amy 83, 190
Alexander, Clara 62, 70-71, 91, 106, 137, 166
Alimnae, Florence 84, 92, 188
Allen, Harriet 171
Allen, Willie 86, 113, 140, 142-43, 156, 159-60, 220-21, 289n71
Amis, Bettie 105, 135
Anderson, Monica 241
Andrews, Mrs. 7
Arnold, Augusta 182, 243
Ashhurst, Mary 75, 161
Austrian, Delia 243

Baedeker, Karl 109
Barrett, Robert S. 219
Bates, Mary 103, 184, 193
Baxter, Lucy 127, 160
Bayard, Maria 4, 70, 72, 117, 119, 122, 129-30, 193-94, 207, 221, 246n4
Beckley, Mrs. 160
Beecher, Catherine 13
Bense, Anne 155-56, 161, 183. 187, 190-91,193
Berkin, Carol 4
Biddle, Pauline 66
Bigelow, Grace 134, 136, 158
Bird, Isabella 181
Birmingham, David 192
Bisland, Elizabeth 26
Bismarck, Otto von 133
Blackwell, Elizabeth 180
Blainey, Geoffrey 231
Blair, Mary Jane 40-41,43, 56, 61, 71, 75-76, 82, 101, 106, 129, 164, 188
Blanchard, Harriet 117, 159, 186
Bliss, Anais 115, 205, 271n345
Blom, Philipp 231
Bly, Nelie 26
Boardman, Sophia 128
Boit, Mary 168, 208-09
Bolton, Sarah 224-25
Bonaparte, Betsy Patterson 4-5
Bonaparte, Napoleon 77, 129-30, 132, 138, 246n4, 275n134

312 Index

Bonaparte, Napoleon III 132, 134
Boykin, Mary (Chesnut) 15, 21
Bradbury, Harriet 127
Bradbury, Mary 43, 96, 20
Bradley, Annie 135
Bradley, Sarah 188
Bragdon, Mabel 51, 71, 87
Bright, Florence 113
Brooks, Catherine 111, 129, 184
Brooks, Helen 89, 128, 210
Bulfinch, Charles 30
Bullard, Mrs. A.T. 41, 73, 126
Bulwer-Lytton, Edward 183
Burgess, Marion 41, 81, 91, 156, 158
Burns, Robert 128
Busbee, Isabelle 46, 65-66, 110
Bushman Richard 3, 172
Butler, Julia 47
Byron, George Gordon Lord 182

Cabot Elizabeth 27
Cabot Ella 63, 80, 161, 243
Carolan, Hatta 235, 290n19
Carson, Caroline Petigru 15, 186, 248-49n15
Carter, Alice 157
Chafee, Mary 96
Chamberlain, Frank 205
Chamberlain, Georgette 50, 62, 205
Chamberlain, Lucy 83
Channing, William Ellery 18
Chapin, Cornelia 64
Chase, Lucy 243
Church, Ruth 48, 69, 74-75, 161, 163, 176, 260n2
Clark, Herma 42, 52, 54, 58, 61-62, 222
Clements, Emma 61, 70, 107, 187-88, 212
Clements, Frank 187-88
Cleveland, Sarah 38, 52, 59, 73, 103, 109, 123, 131-32, 167, 179, 186, 189-90

Cogan, Frances 180
Coleman, Isabel 51
Coleridge, Samuel Taylor 182
Colles, Harriet 236-37
Colles, Mary 236-37
Comer, Laura 70, 225-26
Conant, Charlotte 126
Conlin, Jonathan 275-76n142
Cook, Thomas 112
Coolidge, Ellen 125-26, 273n44
Cooper, James Fenimore 30
Cordozzo, Emma 27, 183
Corson, Caroline 112, 157, 210-11, 219
Cott, Nancy 233
Cowl, Jane 106, 195
Cox, Eliza 37, 76, 102, 105, 131
Cox, Mildred 206
Coxe, Elizabeth Sinkler 15
Crawford, Charlotte 66, 112, 217, 222-23
Crow, Duncan 101
Culbertson, Helen 99, 139
Culler, Lucy 128
Curtis, Frances 92, 100
Curtis, Harriet 87, 195, 233
Curtis, Isabella 106, 114
Curtis, Margaret 195, 232
Cushing, Caroline 131

Davis, John 152
Davis, Miss 48, 87, 163, 255-56n92
Degen, Maria 181, 189
De Peyster, Elizabeth 143, 146
De Yoe, Anna 221
Dickinson, Emily 16
Dorsey, Hebe 142
Douglass, Frederick 55, 199
Dudley, Lucy 72, 80, 82, 97, 128, 138, 156
Duer, Frances 150
Duggan, Christopher 152

Dulles, Foster Rhea 8, 142, 172, 277n188
Dummer, Ethel 55, 91, 212
Dummer, Frank 212

Eames, Jane 72
Edward VII 52, 120, 126, 233
Eliot, Emily 33
Elliott, Sarah 51, 75, 106, 141, 175, 207, 224
Emelie 26-27
Emerson, Ralph Waldo 18, 200
Emerson, Susan Marsh 29, 57, 59, 64
Emmerson, Charles 136, 165
Endicott, Sarah 121
Eppes, Elizabeth 80

Faber, Isabella 73, 77, 157
Fahnestock, Anna 111, 114
Fahys, Maria 92-93
Farnham, Charlotte 19
Farnham, Christie Anne 12, 20
Farrar, Caroline 61, 75, 79, 90, 95, 98, 106, 114-15, 128, 144,149-50, 152, 159, 162-63, 170, 174, 190, 193-94
Farwell, Abbie (Brown) 140, 170, 182, 209-10
Faust, Drew Gilpin 101
Few, Mary 167, 176, 221
Field, Kate 144
Fields, Annie 57, 132, 150, 243
Flavelle, Mary 54, 117
Foster, Shirley 120
Fox, Stephen 33, 36, 49, 54, 65
Franchot, Jenny 153
Frank, Henrietta 29, 47, 57, 62, 82, 86, 109, 113, 166-67, 205, 216
Frank, Henry 166-67, 216
Franz Joseph I 170
Fraser, Mary 41, 113, 167, 192

Freeman, Ethel 243
Freeman, Ginevra 52
Fuller, Margaret 16-17, 19, 21, 35, 14
Fulton, Charles 142

Gardner, Eliza 29, 43, 45, 59, 77, 185, 193
Gardner, Julia 185
Gardner, Margaret 77, 127,185, 193
Garibaldi, Giuseppe 73, 147
Gaston, Frances 44, 85, 87, 90, 110, 112, 114, 123, 184 254n64
Gaston, Mary 85, 110, 123, 163-64, 169, 184, 254n64
Gautier, Homophile 136
Gay, Mary 41, 52, 96, 109
Gaze, Henry 113
George III 119
Germey, Eliza 182
Gibson, Charles Dana 180
Gibson, Mary 174
Gilman, Charlotte Perkins 180
Gilman, Elizabeth 80, 163,168
Gittings, Mary Elizabeth 102, 156, 158, 164, 171, 174
Gould, Elizabeth 214-15, 233-34
Gould, Elizabeth Porter 127, 166, 226-27
Gould, Hannah 54, 58. 65, 80, 121, 176, 233
Gould, Helen 6, 45, 64, 82, 111, 207,110, 247n14
Gould, Jay 6, 207 247n14
Green, Ann Marie 78, 88, 92, 95, 98, 100, 102, 119, 124, 155, 175, 177
Griffis, Martha 41, 43, 52, 75, 100, 176-77, 207, 216
Griffis, Willie 207-08
Grinnan, Cornelia 120
Grinnell, Elizabeth 127
Guild, Sarah 52

Hairston, Mrs. 71
Hale, Susan 49
Hall, Fanny 27, 29, 173, 185
Halsey, Nina 105,108, 139-40, 156, 164, 219-20
Hamilton, Agnes 16
Hamilton, Leo 209, 241
Hammond, Ellen 102
Harding, Margaret (Tileston) 13, 213
Harding, Mary 213
Harper, Althea 52, 60, 206
Harris, Caroline 206
Harris, David 206
Harrison, Constance 23, 56, 78, 89,94,108-109, 112, 126, 139, 154, 156-159, 162-163, 168, 172, 215, 223
Hartt, Mary 54, 110, 114, 117, 124. 139, 152-53, 166
Haussmann, Georges-Eugene 87, 132, 137
Haven, Mamie 82, 137, 201
Hawthorne, Nathaniel 21, 154
Haylander, Julia 45, 124, 139
Healey, Caroline (Dall) 17, 19, 23-24
Heroy, Anne 177
Higginson, Thomas Wentworth 19
Homans, Elizabeth 143
Homer, Eugenie 58, 62, 193, 224-25
Horlbeck, Charlotte 39, 152, 207
Horne, Alistar 132, 134-35
Horowitz, Joseph 24
Horstmann, Bessie 48, 62-63, 116-17, 206-08, 259n207
Horstmann, Elizabeth 111, 116
Horstmann, Mamie 62-63, 116-17, 259n207
Horstmann, Sallie 116
Horstmann, Sigmund 116
Howe, Julia Ward 25

Howell, Eliza 106
Howell, Sara 75, 106
Hughes, Adella 42, 73
Hughes, Robert 279n243
Hunt, Mrs. 107, 146
Hunter, Sarah 54, 57
Hutchins, Grace 74, 184

Ijams, Elizabeth 140

Jaher, Frederic 26
James, Henry 3, 22, 142
Jefferson, Thomas 30
Jerome, Jennie (Churchill) 4
Jewett, Louise 60-61, 71, 123, 206, 241
Johnson, Bessie 213-14
Johnson, Katherine 22, 84 136, 223
Johnson, Laura 111, 134, 137, 161, 166, 213-14
Johnson, Nancy 224, 235-36, 291n21
Johnson, Oliver 213-14.
Johnston, Harriet 167, 281n326
Jones, Anne Catherine (Kate) 53, 56, 61, 79. 98, 109, 111, 117, 137, 148, 156, 169, 173, 188, 257n150
Jones, Colin 130, 132-33
Jones, Mary 208
Jones, Mary Cadwalader 72, 98, 107, 164
Jones, Octavia 129
Joy, Eleanor 93, 162, 196

Kelley, Mary 12, 20, 22, 24, 128
Kellner, Louise 42, 49, 51, 57, 85, 93, 153
Kemble, Fanny 20
Kennedy, Hetty 60
Kerber, Linda 1, 24, 245n2
Kidder, Harriette 125
Kilbride, Daniel 120, 131, 277n188, 284n13

Kimball, Harriett 163
Kimberly, Bettie 78, 148, 161, 173, 190, 211
Kimberly, John 211
Kirkland, Caroline 59, 141, 243
Knox, Thomas 99
Kummer, Agnes 83, 123-24

Lacy, Bessie 11-12, 241
Lamar, Eliza 101, 103, 202-03
Lamar, Janie 101,202-03
Lawrence, Miss 77, 192-93
Ledger, Sally 121, 143
Ledoux, Katherine 100
Levenstein, Harvey 2, 41, 47, 129, 239, 275n135, 277n188
Libbey, Laura 29, 112, 154
Lindsay, Ester 126
Lockwood, Allison 125
Lofgren, Orvar 180
Logan, Kate 129

McCormick, Virginia 71
McGill, Helen 64
McGraw, Jenny 162, 194-95, 227-228
McGregor, H.S. 151-52
McLean, Mary 87, 140
McManus, Blanche 2, 142, 174
McMaster, Mary Jane 57, 66, 126
Maltby, Martha 99, 153, 215, 243
Marsh, Mrs. 84, 163, 214
Marshall, Eliza 94, 97, 114-15, 128, 158
Mathews, Wilhemina 86, 106
Maxtone-Graham, John 39, 59
Mayo, Abigail 130
Mazzini, Giuseppe 147
Metternich, Prince 147
Middleton, Alicia 47, 77, 38, 89, 98, 106, 108-111, 188
Middleton, Dorothy 181

Middleton, Eleanor 57, 90, 92, 151, 156, 162, 210, 223
Miller, Michael 141-42
Millis, Mary 67, 92, 107, 218-19
Minor, Susan 49
Mitchell, Clara 1-2, 64, 71, 95, 151, 184, 241 245n3
Mitchell, S. Weir 180
Morford, Henry 99
Morris, John 49, 85
Morris, Lydia 49, 85
Morse, Frances 126
Mott, Lucretia 199
Moulton, Ellen 171
Moulton, Louise 126
Murray, John I 109
Murray, John III 109

Neilson, James (Jamie) 64
Newberry, John 204
Newberry, Julia 29, 134
Newberry, Sarah 38, 42, 89, 158,175, 187, 204
Nichols, Elizabeth 27, 47, 83, 87, 108, 114, 142, 174, 193, 196, 224, 286n89
Nichols, Margaret 196, 286n89
Nichols, Marian 63, 75, 105, 144, 168, 196, 286n89
Nichols, Rose 63, 105, 286n89
Ninde, Mary 209

Offenbach, Jacques 136
Ogden, Eliza 117, 181, 193
Ogden, Sarah 60, 82, 86
Ogden, Mr. and Mrs. Edward 150
Olcott, Euphemia 159
Olney, Mary 83, 158

Page, Ann 132, 161, 186
Pankhurst, Emmeline 126
Pape, Nina 46, 52, 56, 60, 62, 71, 73, 170, 254n63

Index

Parsons, Charlie 204-05
Parsons, Edith 140-41, 210
Parsons, Gert 106
Parsons, Mamie 50,57, 71, 84, 91, 93-94, 102-03, 144, 160, 164-65, 169, 174, 216, 221
Parsons, Rachel 204-05
Peabody, Eliza 17-18
Peabody, Elizabeth 17-19, 21, 200-01
Peabody, Mary (Mann) 18-19
Peabody, Sophia (Hawthorne) 18-19, 21, 23.154. 162
Peirce, Mary 49
Pember, Phoebe 95, 103, 216-17
Perkins, Abbie 51
Perkinson, Isabelle 87, 93, 95-96, 101, 126-27, 141, 160-61, 163, 195, 205, 222
Perry, Ellen 70, 93, 111, 171, 177
Peterson, Alma 4, 66, 73, 235
Phillips, Morris 89, 96
Pierce, Gus 83, 206
Pierce, Mary 75, 83. 85, 129, 139, 160, 162, 186, 189, 206, 223
Pierson, Ellie 190, 195
Pike, Ruth 237-38
Pius IX, Pope 147, 159
Plimpton, Idella 55, 101,154-55, 159. 193
Pool, Eliza 90
Poor, Caroline 60-61, 137
Prentiss, Elizabeth 181-82
Preston, Madge 29, 40, 44,45, 88
Preston, Margaret 182
Pritchard, Catherine 37
Pullman, George 82
Putnam, Caroline 55
Putnam, Mary 133

Quincy, Abby 194, 222

Rankin, Elizabeth White Nims 15, 23, 249n17
Reed, Clara 91,102, 224
Reizenstein, Jennie 96, 12
Rew, Mary 169-70
Rich, Harriet 62, 74
Richter, Amy 82
Ritchie, Clara 49, 56, 90, 95, 98-99, 125, 138-39, 153-54, 157, 171, 173, 215-16, 243
Rives, Judith 37, 58, 73, 94, 131-32, 166, 188, 192, 205
Rives, William Cabell 205
Roberts, Grace 160
Robinson, Louise 125
Rodgers, Daniel 30
Rodman, Anne Eliza 34, 38, 77, 174
Rogers, Isabel 43-44, 110
Ronalds, Mary 105, 117, 157-58, 163
Root, Mabel 47, 55, 66, 107-08, 112, 217
Rosenshine, Edith 33, 171
Rush, Julia 50, 61
Rutherford, Laura 90, 113, 126, 168
Rutledge, Eleanor 96

Schiller, Friedrich 181
Schmidt, Clara 66 -67
Schriber, Mary Suzanne 8, 35, 39, 201
Schroeder, Henrietta 114
Scofield, Florence 35, 75, 110
Scott, Sir Walter 14, 18, 30, 128
Sears, John 7
Severance, Emily 49-50, 69, 73, 150, 161
Severance, Julia 166
Shelley, Percy Bysshe 182
Shurtleff, Sarah 113
Sicherman, Barbara 16
Silver, Susie 113, 18
Smith, Amy 129

Smith, Eliza 33, 36-37, 43, 47, 63, 71, 141, 243
Smith, Fannie 42, 129
Smythe, Louise 148, 187
Smythe, Sarah 95, 106
Smythe, Susan 96
Spalding, Annie 115, 205-06
Spencer, Cordelia 228
Spencer, June 117, 153, 175, 177, 228-29, 243
Stael, Madame de 18
Stanton, Elizabeth Cady 24, 125, 175, 199-200, 202, 229
Stanton, Henry 199
Starke, Mariana 96, 98, 109
Stedman, Edith 97, 127
Steedman, Mrs. 115
Sterling, Fred 206
Sterling, Mary 86, 90, 103, 206
Stevens, Elizabeth 86
Stevens, Frances 76, 98, 101, 107, 111, 176, 208, 210-12
Stevens, Josy 211
Stevens, Louisa 43
Stoddard, John 81, 88, 122-23, 162, 171, 179
Stone, Lucy 21, 245n2
Stone, Mary Kent 124
Stoney, Nancy 60
Stowe, Harriet Beecher 13, 225
Szold, Henrietta 239-40, 291n27

Taplin, Grace 65, 86, 92, 170-71
Taylor, Alberta 173
Thomas, Bettie 57, 93, 96, 109-10, 159, 189, 217
Thomas, Laura 57, 84, 93, 96, 98-99, 103-05, 108,-10, 135, 146, 153-54, 162, 174-75, 183, 189, 217
Thomas, M. Cary 24-25
Thompson, E.P. 57, 76-78, 94, 148, 157, 167, 172

Thomson, Margaret 87, 158
Thoreau, Henry David 200
Thornwell, Emily 180
Tilton, Martha Ann 92, 123, 128, 162
Tocqueville, Alexis de 1, 33, 38, 172
Townsend, Caroline 56, 76, 144
Tracy, Jenny 86, 90
Trafton, Adeline 71, 99, 20
Trexel, Emma 52. 57, 224
Trowbridge, Harriet 44, 149, 159, 161, 168
Trumbull, Gena 96, 99, 108-09, 114, 170, 175,192
Trumbull, John 15
Tuckerman, Sarah 38, 79, 132, 164
Tufts, Mrs. D.A. 220
Tussaud, Madame Marie 124
Tyler, Josephine 210

Upton, Cornelia 97, 106
Urbino, Lavina 48, 90-91

Van Benschoten, Lizzie 53-54, 61
Van Buren, Angelica 57, 136-37, 153
Van Rensselaer, Catherine 40, 70,74,82, 84, 100, 103, 112, 115,125, 133-34, 147, 151, 157, 160, 163, 166, 175-76
Van Rensselaer, Eleanor 40, 70, 160
Van Rensselaer, Mrs. 70, 115
Vanderbilt, Consuelo (Duchess of Marlborough) 4
Veblen, Thorstein 142
Verdi, Giuseppe 167
Victor Emanuel I 148, 15
Victoria I 119-20, 125-26, 231

Wagner, Richard 24, 167-69
Walworth, Ellen 8
Ware, Annie 61-62, 193
Washington, George 30

Webster, Noah 30
Werner, Adelaide 50-51, 123, 208, 123
Werner, Clara 114
Whaley, Dolly 86, 159,163, 187
Wheeler, Mary 209
White, Caroline 45, 59-60, 89-90, 123, 184, 204, 245n2
White, Frank 204
Whitney, Mary 195
Wilbur, Sallie 51,128
Wilcox, Anna 127
Wilhelm I 164
Wilhelm II 165
Willard, Emma 12, 131
Williams, Rosalind 141
Wilson, A.N. 122-23
Winslow, M.E. 40,49, 58, 109, 128
Winsor, Annie 221
Witmer, Emma 63, 140, 260n210
Wollstonecraft, Mary 3
Woodbury, Mary 64, 133, 195
Worth, Charles Frederick 146
Wren, Christopher 122

www.ingramcontent.com/pod-product-compliance
Lightning Source LLC
Chambersburg PA
CBHW021802220426
43662CB00006B/156